PORTRAIT OF AN ARTIST

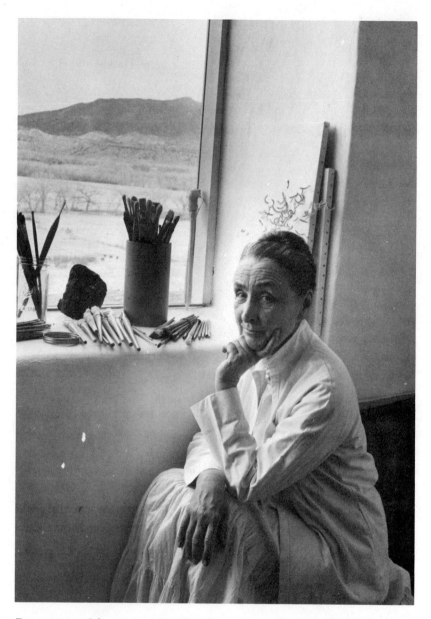

*Frontispiece: Silver print of O'Keeffe in her studio at Abiquiu c. 1953.
© 1981. Laura Gilpin Collection, Amon Carter Museum, Ft. Worth, TX.*

PORTRAIT
of an
ARTIST

❖

A Biography of Georgia O'Keeffe

❖

Laurie Lisle

University of New Mexico
Albuquerque

Library of Congress Cataloging in Publication Data

Lisle, Laurie.
    Portrait of an artist.

    Bibliography: p.
    Includes index.
    1. O'Keeffe, Georgia, 1887–   . 2. Painters—
United States—Biography.   I. Title.
ND237.O5L57 1986   759.13 [B]   86-16061
ISBN 0-8263-0907-0

Design: Barbara Jellow

Contents

Foreword and Acknowledgments

The idea for this book had its genesis in 1970 when I went to a retrospective of Georgia O'Keeffe's paintings at the Whitney Museum of American Art in New York. There, four floors above the cacophony of Madison Avenue, her images of skulls floating in spacious, serene desert skies as well as blossoms of mysterious depths and brilliant hues spoke strongly to me of another world, bigger and more beautiful than the one around me.

The Whitney had purchased its first O'Keeffe in 1932, almost a decade after the artist had come to prominence with the first generation of American modernists, yet I was only vaguely aware that she had been married to the great photographer Alfred Stieglitz, and that in old age she lived on a remote New Mexican ranch. My curiosity was aroused: Who was the little-known creator of these powerful paintings?

When I tried to find out, I was astonished to discover that no book existed to answer my questions. I continued searching and in 1976 visited the Beinecke Rare Book and Manuscript Library at Yale University. I pored over letters that O'Keeffe had written as a young woman to her friend Anita Pollitzer and in middle age to New Mexicans Mabel Dodge Luhan and Dorothy Brett. As I read her words, written in an upright calligraphic script composed of distinctive curlicues and wavy flourishes, their intensity seemed to vibrate off the paper and transmit a vigorous jolt the way her paintings did. I realized with growing excitement that her story was not only that of a gifted artist, but also of a forceful American woman with extraordinary qualities of intellect and character—and it was a story that I wanted to tell.

I learned, however, that she had a reputation for being exceedingly reticent. Her desert ranch blends in with the surrounding ocher earth tones, much as her brushstrokes are concealed in the smooth surface of her canvases. Over the years she had rebuffed even the efforts of loyal, fond friends like Anita Pollitzer to write about her. I approached her warily and my contact with her was brief; she took her accustomed position and chose not to participate in my project. But she did say to me, "You are welcome to what you find."

With the backing of a publisher, I set out on an odyssey that took me to twenty-four states, dozens of libraries and museums, and resulted in scores of interviews with O'Keeffe's schoolmates, family, and friends. In her isolated corner of New Mexico I hiked up mesas she had climbed many times to view the majestic valley she called her own. I parked my car on the road she had painted, where it provides an overview of the muddy pink Chama River greening her dramatic dry landscape. I even danced to Latin music with her Spanish-American neighbors in a gym that was O'Keeffe's gift to the village of Abiquiu.

My portrait of the artist—the evolution of a Wisconsin farmer's daughter nicknamed Georgie into the matriarch of modern art known as O'Keeffe—was written with the hope that others might be moved by the example of her courageous, independent, and successful life. Writing this book has been an engrossing, exciting experience, for despite her elusiveness, Georgia O'Keeffe has given us great gifts not only in her paintings but also in the very way she lived her life.

❖

It would have been impossible to have written this book without the generosity of other people. My interest in biography began in childhood, when I voraciously read the pumpkin-colored "famous people" books for beginning readers, so my first thanks go to my mother, Adeline Congdon, who kept me abundantly supplied with them. I am also indebted to my agent, Sarah Jane Freymann, for her instinctive belief in the book when it was only an idea. My deep appreciation goes to my editor, Sherry Huber, for the many ways she helped bring the book into being, especially for her steady encouragement and enthusiasm as the manuscript took shape. My special thanks go to Albert Litewka for his sensitive readings and reactions to the earliest drafts.

More than a hundred people who crossed O'Keeffe's path in life graciously and freely shared their memories and insights with me. I would like to mention them all, but their numbers preclude that. Moreover, some of the most significant and discerning contributors have asked me not to reveal their names, so my private thanks to them must suffice. Each person's recollections have helped make the story of Georgia O'Keeffe more complete, and to each one, named and unnamed, I give my heartfelt thanks.

Among those whom I am pleased to be able to thank publicly, a few stand out vividly. Susan Wilson of Virginia, who went to boarding school with O'Keeffe, displayed an extraordinary memory the afternoon we spoke. Although she was a semi-invalid, she touchingly confessed an urge to hitch a ride with me out West in order to see her girlfriend once again. In north Texas, I remember with affection Emma Jean Smith, who taught with O'Keeffe at West Texas State Normal College, as well as the charming Mattie Mack, one of O'Keeffe's former students.

In San Francisco I interviewed Blanche Matthias, born the same year as O'Keeffe and her friend since the early twenties. Mrs. Matthias's mind was as perceptive as ever, but as she sat sightless in a pink bathrobe and dark glasses she was tragically no longer able to see the panoramic view from her Nob Hill apartment.

Among my numerous interviews in New Mexico, the most memorable was with Dorothy Brett. Brett's observant brown eyes were clouded by age, but her clipped British words remained warm and humorous as she remembered, then did not remember. When I reminded her that O'Keeffe was almost ninety (at the time), Brett—four years older than her friend—exclaimed: "Ninety! Oh, how *horrible* for her. . . . It's very unnecessary the way people die, isn't it?" Brett was to die a few weeks afterwards.

In New York I had the privilege of meeting Herbert J. Seligmann, one of Stieglitz's close friends, who knew O'Keeffe since 1918. I took great pleasure in talking with members of the Stieglitz family, notably

x   *Foreword and Acknowledgments*

Flora Straus. I also had several delightful visits with Dorothy Norman in a room decorated with pretty seashells, delicate feathers, and extraordinary roses in her home in East Hampton, New York.

I also wish to acknowledge the dozens of librarians and researchers in archives and museums throughout the country who have been of immense help. Among them were Cam McRae at the Historical Society of Sun Prairie; Paul Hensly at the Colonial Williamsburg Foundation; Claire Kuehn at the Panhandle–Plains Historical Museum in Canyon, Texas; Orlando Romero at the New Mexico State Library (Southwest Room) in Santa Fe; Ellen Dunlap of the Humanities Research Center at the University of Texas in Austin, Texas; and Donald Gallup of the Beinecke Rare Book and Manuscript Library at Yale Univesity in New Haven, Connecticut. Other people were very helpful at the State Historical Society of Wisconsin in Madison; the National Gallery of Art and Library of Congress in Washington, D.C.; the Art Institute of Chicago and the Newberry Library in Chicago; the Center for Creative Photography in Tucson, Arizona; the Alderman Library at the University of Virginia in Charlottesville; and the Museum of Modern Art, the Whitney Museum, the Metropolitan Museum of Art, and the New York Public Library, all in New York City.

LAURIE LISLE

June 1986, Sharon, Connecticut

1 ❖ Sun Prairie

Late in the autumn of 1887, the *Sun Prairie Countryman*, a rural Wisconsin newspaper, briefly noted that a baby girl had arrived two days before on Tuesday, November 15, in the farmhouse of Ida and Francis O'Keeffe. The birth, assisted by a country doctor in the O'Keeffe home, was the second for the young couple. The twenty-three-year-old Ida named her infant Georgia Totto for her patrician Hungarian grandfather, George Totto. Georgia, it appeared, would have Ida's dark hair, and her round face was pure Irish, like her father's. The variegated pigment of her eyes suggested the mingled bloodlines of brown-eyed maternal forebears and blue-eyed paternal ones.

Georgia was born into a rapidly industrializing world. The country's longest suspension bridge, linking Brooklyn to Manhattan, had recently opened, and the Eiffel Tower in Paris was still under construction, due to be completed in two years. The American government in Washington, under the reformist leadership of President Grover Cleveland, was attempting to exert some control over capitalist monopolies and to bring order to the grim, oppressive factories where immigrant laborers often erupted into violence and strikes. But in the western part of the country, the last great Indian war was still to be fought against federal troops.

Little of this turmoil affected the pastoral life on the Sun Prairie farm, however. It remained like farm life everywhere, suspended in a timeless ritual governed by the rhythms of nature. The newborn baby was kept indoors during the long, dark, icy northern winter. When the snow finally melted, the sunlight became warm, and the prairie was touched by the bright green of spring, Georgia was carried outside for the first time. She was placed on a handmade patchwork quilt spread on the new grass and propped up by pillows. Those very first moments of seeing in the brilliant sunlight became indelibly etched in her memory: She precisely remembered the quilt's patterns of flowers on black and tiny red stars as well as the startling blond looks of her mother's friend.

Yet another perception during those minutes in the pool of yellow sunshine was not so pleasant. Georgia, less than a year old, was acutely aware that two other children playing on the patterned quilt were getting all the admiration. One of them was her older brother, Francis Jr., two years old, the firstborn child with dark Totto eyes, who was adorable in his mama's eyes. When he was born, weighing a plump ten and a half pounds, it had been heralded as a grand event by the *Countryman*. As Georgia crawled around the cotton quilt, she felt a sharp sting of neglect. "Why doesn't anyone think *I'm* beautiful?" she recalled wondering many years later. She squirmed off the quilt, she remembered, and was impatiently thrust back onto it.

❖

Georgia's was a uniquely American heritage—three of her grandparents were immigrants, and the fourth was descended from one of the earliest colonists in the New World. Her O'Keeffe grandparents had settled in Sun Prairie first during the initial large wave of immigration to America. Pierce O'Keeffe and his wife, Catherine Mary, and other family members left for the American frontier when their family wool business in Ireland faltered. They arrived in Milwaukee through the chain of Great Lakes, then traveled directly west by oxcart for about eighty miles inland to the young settlement of Sun Prairie in the southern part of the state. In July 1848 Pierce O'Keeffe bought his first acres along the Koshkonong Creek from the federal government for less than a dollar an acre. As he turned virgin forest into rolling farmland, his wife, Kate, gave birth to four sons: Boniface, Peter, Francis, and Bernard.

The O'Keeffes began to homestead just two months after Wisconsin ceased being a territory and entered the union as a state. Meanwhile, the last of the Winnebago Indians were being driven westward as the arriving farmers cut down the thick forests, plowed the hunting trails under, and decimated the deer. More and more land was being laid out in neatly numbered lots, and roads increasingly followed the straight lines of the surveyor's measure. At the same time, railroads were inching into the newly settled regions to transport the wheat harvests and the iron ore to other parts of the country.

About ten years after the O'Keeffes had settled in Sun Prairie in 1848, George Victor Totto and his wife bought land next to the O'Keeffe farm. Whereas the Irish family had emigrated to Wisconsin because of a business failure in the old country, George Totto had fled to America because of his belief in liberty. A count from Budapest, he had fought in a doomed Hungarian uprising against Austrian rule as an aide-de-camp to the revolutionary hero Lajos Kossuth. Family legend has it that Totto was ransomed from jail with the family jewels. In any case, he escaped to America and wound up in Sauk City, Wisconsin, later known as Prairie de Sac, where another Hungarian political refugee of a flamboyant stripe had bought land.

Totto's wife, Isabel, prided herself on her heritage as well. One of her granddaughters later uncovered many European coats of arms designed for both grandparents' families. Her roots, as deep as any in America, could be traced to a Dutchman who arrived in New York in 1637. Two hundred years later, one of his descendants, Charles Wyckoff, fathered Isabel and her younger sister Jane. Wyckoff, a hotelkeeper in the East, apparently had business troubles, and, after his wife died, he moved with his teen-age daughters and a new wife to Sauk City to try his luck at running a hotel on the frontier. Wyckoff hadn't been in Wisconsin long when a cholera epidemic broke out. Although he made plans to move his family out, a day before their departure he came down with the disease and died shortly afterwards.

It was in Sauk City that the exiled George Totto and the orphaned Isabel Wyckoff met and fell in love. In the twenty-five-year-old Isabel's eyes, the pedigreed Hungarian patriot ten years her senior was a cut above the other marriage prospects on the frontier. Formal photographs show that Totto was a thin-lipped, rather homely man with a light brown beard and that Isabel with her long, raw-boned face, could never have been called pretty. The poise and good breeding of the tall, dark-haired girl with the eastern education appealed to the European, and in May 1855 the two were married.

A year after the wedding their first child, Alletta, was born. Her birth was followed in rapid succession by those of Josephine, Charles, Ida, Leonore, and George. Meanwhile, the Tottos had moved to Sun Prairie, where the 1870 census revealed that their farm was larger and more abundant than the neighboring O'Keeffe property. But farming in the harsh midwestern climate proved too difficult for George and Isabel. In the 1870s Totto gave up and returned to Hungary, supposedly to claim his share of the family fortune. Totto may have visited his family in Wisconsin again, but he eventually died in his homeland, still worshiped, in absentia, by his daughters. Left to fend for themselves, Isabel and her six sons and daughters moved to nearby Madison in the early 1880s. The town had been a high-brow university town for more than forty years, and she must have imagined that it held better prospects for her children.

❖

Georgia's father, Francis Calixtus O'Keeffe, was around thirty when he began to drive his mother's buggy the twelve miles to Madison to court the fourth Totto child, Ida Ten Eyck, a poised, brown-eyed teen-ager. Frank had known Ida all his life as the little girl on the neighboring farm. Now Ida had grown tall like her mother and developed a more handsome version of her mother's dark looks. Frank was a wiry, good-natured farmer with fair Irish skin and curly hair. His schooling had stopped in adolescence when his father died and he had to help his mother and brothers run the farm. Then in October 1883, the brother closest in age, Peter, died of tuberculosis. It is likely that his brother's death startled Frank into the realization that his life was rapidly passing, because about this time he proposed to Ida.

Ida's family favored the match, partly because Frank wanted to buy the Totto pastures in Sun Prairie. But Ida's two older sisters weren't married, and she had little inclination to wed and return to her childhood home of Sun Prairie, a simple farm community of a few hundred people without even a library. Ida was a serious girl who kept a diary, loved books, and dreamed of becoming a doctor. It was also commonplace at the time to avoid marriage to someone with tuberculosis in the family in the mistaken belief that the highly infectious disease was hereditary. Ida, however, was young, obedient, and fond of Frank, so she reluctantly accepted his proposal. A few weeks after she turned twenty, they were married. The Sun Prairie newspaper carried the announcement:

> Wedded—At the residence of the bride's mother, in the city of Madison, on Tuesday, Feb. 19, 1884, by the Rev. J. B. Pratt, Mr. Francis O'Keeffe of Sun Prairie to Miss Ida Totto, of Madison. The contracting parties in the nuptial affair above chronicled are well and favorably known hereabouts, and the best wishes of the community are extended to Frank and his charming bride.

The Tottos considered themselves to be a notch above the O'Keeffes because of their lineage and cultivation, and the wedding was entirely a Totto affair. Although Frank was a Roman Catholic, the Tottos' Episcopal clergyman officiated. And even though either of Frank's two brothers could have signed the marriage certificate, an older brother and sister of Ida's were the witnesses. Thoughout their marriage Frank would appear to be in Ida's shadow, even though he was eleven years older than she. People often echoed Ida's early doubts and wondered why a woman who carried herself like an aristocrat had married a humble Irishman.

❖

After the wedding, Ida had no more time to pen her thoughts in her diary. Within six months she was pregnant, and for the next eight years she was either pregnant or nursing an infant. Interestingly, only the births of the first two, Francis and Georgia, were entered into the public record. A few weeks before Georgia's second birthday a sister was born, named Ida Ten Eyck for their mother. Sixteen months later another sister arrived: Anita Natalie, with a tiny round face and large dark eyes. And when Anita was only sixteen months old a brother, Alexius Wyckoff, was born.

Ida, as a mother, above all enjoyed spending evenings and Sunday afternoons reading to her little children. In her enthusiasm for books, Mama seemed to make them come alive, Georgia recalled many times afterwards, and she adored listening to the warm, glowing tones of her mother's beautiful, well-bred voice. Since the stories were picked for the benefit of her eldest, Francis, the first ones that Georgia heard were boys' books such as James Fenimore Cooper's *Leatherstocking Tales* about pioneer days and cowboy-and-Indian adventures in the state of Texas and the New Mexico territory.

Reading aloud was one of the ways that Ida showed her interest in the mental development of her offspring—the daughters as well as the sons. Education for women was a family tradition: Her own mother had been educated in the East, her sisters had become schoolteachers, and she had joined a group of Sun Prairie women with intellectual and charitable interests who gave themselves the lofty name of The King's Daughters. Furthermore, Ida took great interest in the curriculum of the nearby schoolhouse, and the schoolteacher usually boarded with the O'Keeffes. Ida quietly had high expectations for her daughters. "Our mother had a very good opinion of herself, and she wanted all of us to be the same way," Georgia told a younger sister later. When in time Mama tried to provide the girls with private schools and special lessons, she was motivated, in part, by her own disappointment at having ended her schooling too soon as well as by her desire that her daughters be able to care for themselves. Since all of Ida's daughters but one became professional women, her influence on them is evident. What's more, since they also had an extremely low birthrate—only producing two children among the five of them—it's likely that they also sensed her dissatisfaction with domesticity.

In fact, Ida seemed to spend more time cultivating her children's minds than cuddling them in an affectionate, maternal way. That kind of mothering apparently was taken over by others in the large household, particularly by Ida's aunt, Jane Varney. Aunt Jenny, as she was known, had been a teen-aged bride when she went to California during the Gold Rush in a covered wagon. But she soon was widowed and returned to Wisconsin on a sailing ship via Cape Horn to help care for the children of her sister Isabel. When her niece, Ida, gave birth to her first child, Aunt Jenny moved to the O'Keeffe household and oversaw it with a stern eye for the rest of her life. The presence of the small, alert woman (some said a busybody) in the family freed Ida to continue to pursue her quest for self-education, and gave her the chance to visit her mother and friends in Madison frequently and even to go to the opera in Milwaukee on occasion.

❖

By the time Georgia was a four-and-a-half-year-old solemn brown-haired girl—remembered by one of her teachers as a "little, dark-skinned, wide-eyed, spritelike child"—she had four brothers and sisters to compete with in the struggle for the grown-ups' attention. She believed that her good-looking older brother was her mother's favorite, and that her affectionate little sister, Ida, was the other family pet. Whether or not those perceptions were true, Georgia adapted her early behavior to them and remained convinced of them all her life. But because of the numbers of grandmothers, aunts, and uncles in the extended family, Georgia apparently got all the attention she needed, which was probably less than that required by the ordinary child in any case. "I was not a favorite child, but I didn't mind at all," she insisted many years later.

Until the death of Grandmother Totto—when Georgia, her eldest granddaughter, was six—the girl used to visit the Totto household on the edge of Madison's Lake Monona, where her maiden aunts and bachelor uncles lived. Georgia probably knew best her Grandmother O'Keeffe, who lived on the adjoining farm until the age of eighty-five, when Georgia was almost ten. Both her grandmothers—the deserted Grandmother Totto and the widowed Grandmother O'Keeffe—were strong matriarchs who had kept their large families together after the loss of their men. In Sun Prairie Kate O'Keeffe was highly respected for her sharp intelligence and deeply loved for her sweet nature, according to her lengthy obituaries. The two women, along with Georgia's mother, were part of that tradition of capable frontier women: They sewed the family clothes, preserved the food, decorated the home, nursed the sick, taught the young, and, in general, nourished life in all its forms. In time, Georgia herself would be called the expression of these women's creative spirit.

Born agile and alert with pretty hands, Georgia was a quiet child, who, one imagines, walked long before she talked while always intently observing everything around her. Her earliest years were spent stoically tagging along behind her brother, who was a year and a half older. Soon it was evident that she had advantages in her rivalry with him. He had weak eyes and her keen sight didn't miss a thing. She was also naturally athletic and before long she was outrunning and out-climbing him. Georgia thought about it carefully and came to the conclusion that she was better than her brother—even if their mother preferred him.

Not close to her brother and believing herself to be too grown-up to play with her baby sisters, Georgia began to play apart from the other children at a very young age. A teacher who boarded with the O'Keeffes on school days and sometimes stayed over on weekends to help Aunt Jenny with the children when their mother visited Madison recalled that self-reliant Georgia required little care. "I had more to do with the younger children—Ida, my favorite, and Anita, sweet and cute, and Alexius, never in sight." In time Georgia discovered that not being the focus of the adults' attention had its advantages. She learned that she could easily elude her great-aunt's discipline and stealthily do the forbidden things that interested her while, at the same time, appearing obedient.

Later Georgia remembered being happy keeping to herself. Under the apple trees she invented an imaginary household with a park of clipped grass, trees of tall weeds, a shingle boat in a dishpan lake, and doll people for whom she stitched little clothes, as she vividly recalled in her book, *Georgia O'Keeffe*. The little girl directed her miniature-doll family to behave according to her childish rules and whims, creating a make-believe world within the confines of her actual one. It provided her with hours of fantasy as well as with the growth of a comfortable, centered place that would always be within her. This early behavior also set the pattern for relationships throughout her life. She often seemed to recoil instinctively from others and never needed anyone to entertain her. "I've never been bored," she once stated flatly when she was elderly.

As the solitary hours nurtured her imagination, they also strengthened her natural inclination to have things her own way. She wanted to be distinct, only wearing white stockings, for instance, when her little sisters were not wearing theirs. "From the time I was a little girl, if my sisters wore their hair braided, I wouldn't wear mine braided," Georgia recalled. "If they wore ribbons, I wouldn't. I'd think they'd look better without it too."

Although unadorned clothes or atypical friends embarrassed Georgia's sisters and brothers, she was merely kidded and her ways were tolerated. Mama and Papa pursued their separate interests and seemed to be unusually permissive about their children's behavior, as if they had no doubt about their underlying talent and motivation. For example, after Georgia's younger sister, Ida, ran away from school because she disliked the teacher, she was tutored at home. Although perhaps Georgia carried the family tendency to individuality the fur-thest, her brothers and sisters all became irrepressible individualists as well.

It was a family in which the prevailing emotional climate appeared to be that of kindness and mildness. By virtue of being the oldest daughter, Georgia had a room of her own in the farmhouse's Victorian tower (built by her father) with large windows facing north and west. Jessie Flint, one of Georgia's playmates who spent many nights with her in the tower room, remembered that her friend was so content with her family life that she had no desire at all to visit Jessie in the village.

❖

When Georgia was grown, she recalled with pride that her father's land stretched over a great distance in the best farm country in Wis-consin. It was three and a half miles southeast of the village of Sun Prairie, so the mailman delivered the mail on horseback to the outlying farms. By the time Georgia was a toddler, her father owned four hundred and forty acres, according to an 1890 plat map, and, by the time she was a teen-ager, he owned a great deal more. In order to provide for his rapidly growing household, he planted a wide variety of crops, ran a dairy, and traded livestock. In fact, he traveled to the Dakotas to trade a herd of horses for some "fat cattle" a few months after his first child was born, according to the *Countryman*. His neigh-bors had known him all his life and respected him as a fine farmer and dairyman as well as an affectionate family man who kept any wanderlust well in check.

As Georgia became old enough to wander beyond the wide lawn around the white colonial-style O'Keeffe farmhouse, she began to discover the wonders of her father's farm. Georgia and the other children liked to play Handy Andy Over and other children's games among the milk cans and cream separators of the creamery. Its dank air, cooled by huge chunks of ice cut by creamery patrons from a nearby lake in winter, was a refuge from the midsummer heat. Georgia's father was also intrigued by the latest inventions, and he hired a man to mow his corn-fields with one of the newly invented harvesters the September that Georgia was eight.

The rotation of the seasons, each with its dramatic changes, forced open all of the perceptive child's senses, and they absorbed the marvel of it all. She learned that metal stuck to her fingers in the bitter cold and that flower petals felt velvety soft. She tested the sweet spring grasses, listened to the high notes of the songbirds, and carefully observed the profusion of brilliantly colored wildflowers that appeared when the meadows thawed each year. She remembered the squares of dark, rich, moist earth where a plow had turned the soil, the patterns that were created when neat rows of green seedlings began to sprout, and the wide wheat fields that gilded the land in midsummer. In the fall, the maples and oaks around the farmhouse flared red and orange, then the harvested fields darkened to autumn browns and the heavy horsedrawn hay wagons ambled toward the barn before the snow silently shrouded everything once again.

The country days of her childhood, beginning with daybreak and ending when darkness fell, left Georgia with a profound feeling for the companionship of nature and an acute sensitivity to its moods. At mealtimes she used to hear serious talk by her father and his farmhands about the life-or-death power of the weather. She learned to accept even the brutality of the melodrama around her, which she came to understand as the underside of life force. Like other farm children, she found out about conception and birth at a young age, particularly since her mother went through childbrith at home five more times after Georgia was born. As a result, she grew up unashamed of her sensuality, even though she came of age in the Victorian era.

Georgia gravitated to her laughing Papa, who kept his pockets full of sweets and played Irish melodies on his fiddle. As a child, she thought him handsome, and she appropriated many of his tastes and habits, always saying that she liked him more than her aloof mother. She preferred his love of the land, for instance, to her mother's world of learning. Even after she had achieved great success among New York sophisticates, she continued to fancy that she was more like her farmer father than her cultured mother. When Georgia returned to Wisconsin in her fifties to receive an honorary degree, during the ceremony one of her old Sun Prairie schoolteachers fell into the academic procession beside her and remarked that she strongly resembled her father. "She seemed very pleased and smiled with both eyes and mouth," recalled the teacher, "and then she *did* look like him."

Papa was a lapsed Catholic, but his bachelor brother, Uncle Bernard, used to pick up Georgia in his horse and buggy and take her to Mass at the stone Sacred Hearts of Jesus and Mary Church in the village. She developed a childhood crush on the Catholic church, warming to parishioners—many of them immigrants, who continued to arrive in large numbers—who crowded into the pews and spoke with the same soft brogue as her grandmother O'Keeffe. She also liked the pools of colored light created by the high, narrow, arched stained-glass windows, the pictures of saints, the pungent puffs of incense, the somber music, and the priests' colorful robes. Years later Georgia speculated that she might have overcome her intellectual reservations and converted to catholicism if the church had gotten a firmer grip on her in childhood. However, all but the youngest O'Keeffe children were baptized in their mother's Grace Episcopal Church in Madison, and most Sundays the children were taken to the simple Congregational services at the church nearest the farm.

❖

Two months before her fifth birthday, Georgia started school in the little one-room Town Hall schoolhouse, where her parents had gone, with two dozen or so other children from the neighboring farms. Although she was a year younger than the other first graders, she was bright, curious, and clever—and her education had already begun. Her imagination had been limbered by the children's classics her mother read aloud. Also, it is possible that one of Georgia's schoolteacher aunts or a school-mistress who boarded with the O'Keeffes had already started her reading or writing. At any rate, her first day of school was undoubtedly not a fearful prospect. Only a quarter of a mile down her long driveway, past the high hedge, across the dirt road, and surrounded by her father's land, the white clapboard schoolhouse was a familiar place. She would attend it for nine years, until she was thirteen.

Her second-grade teacher recalled that Georgia excelled in the school yard, beating most of the boys in the running and jumping games. In the classroom, she was remembered as a well-behaved schoolgirl who dutifully did her lessons with ordinary ability. Since she later insisted that she had always hated school, preferring to run wild on the farm to sitting in a schoolroom, she must have been trying hard to please her mother through her obedience. Georgia later said that she was the type of self-disciplined child who liked to save the raisin in the cookie for the last because it was the best.

When she was in the second grade, she was extremely inquisitive, and her incessant questions sometimes perplexed her young teacher. "When two big clouds bump together, is *that* thunder?" she once inquired. "If Lake Monona rose up, way up, and spilled all over, how many people would be drowned?" she asked another time. She was often dissatisfied by the inexperienced teacher's replies and indicated that she thought her teacher was a bit dumb. When an answer was particularly unsatisfactory, she used to reply evenly, "Well, I'll just ask Aunt Lola—she knows everything."

Her mother's younger sister, Leonore, a soft-spoken schoolteacher nicknamed Lola, used to spend holidays on the Sun Prairie farm. Georgia enjoyed Aunt Lola's attention, particularly at the age of seven, when her mother's attention was, once again, absorbed by the birth of a new baby, Catherine Blanche. At the end of August, in 1897, when Aunt Lola returned by train to her teaching job in Milwaukee, she took Georgia, who was nine and a half then, along for a visit. Perhaps the trip was an attempt to compensate for the fact that Papa was planning to take her older brother to Chicago in September. In any case, it was most likely Georgia's first journey outside of Madison. A few months later, when her beloved Grandmother O'Keeffe died of cancer, the loss was probably eased by the increasing closeness to youthful Aunt Lola. For Georgia it was a time of passage from her pretend dollhouse world to the actual world beyond the farm.

❖

As long as Georgia was preoccupied with her dollhouse, she did not give the grown-ups any evidence of an artistic gift. They doted on what they considered to be the real talent for drawing demonstrated by the more forthcoming little Ida. Without the adults' knowledge, however, Georgia had closely observed the illustrations in her cloth Mother Goose, in her mother's books, and in her schoolbooks. She had also struggled to draw a man with a black lead pencil on a brown paper bag and to copy pictures of exotic places out of her geography book.

Both of her grandmothers dabbled in art and painted pictures of flowers and fruit in flat, naive folk styles. Two of Grandmother O'Keeffe's precisely done paintings hung in the farmhouse—one was of two plums and the other of a moss rose. It was assumed that Georgia and her younger sisters would also learn the ladylike art of painting. Since the country schoolteacher had little time to teach more than the three R's, the girls' mother arranged for private art lessons when Georgia was close to twelve. That winter the three oldest O'Keeffe girls spent evenings copying cubes, squares, and spheres from a standard drawing book.

The next year Ida decided that her daughters were ready for painting lessons from an amateur painter, Sarah Mann, who lived in Sun Prairie. The elm-shaded village—a cluster of tobacco warehouses, blacksmith shops, brick stores, and a high school—was home to about nine hundred people. Georgia must have realized that art was something very special, for her and her sisters to be driven the seven miles round-trip in the buggy every Saturday afternoon. Mrs. Mann allowed them to choose illustrations to copy in watercolor, and Georgia picked subjects typical for a young girl, such as an Arabian horse and a red rose. She was being given training in realism at an age when a child quite naturally obeys rules. Shortly, however, she began to wrestle on her own with such puzzling problems as how to depict the brightness of sunshine and moonlight on the snow. Those initial experiences with colored pigment, in a medium with which she would eventually amaze the New York avant-garde, were exceedingly pleasant for her.

At this time, Georgia's right-handed facility with a paintbrush and a pencil became immeditely apparent, the family remembers. She progressed rapidly, executing at around the age of twelve a startingly accurate sketch of Aunt Jenny. She cared strongly about how her pictures looked, disliking the interference when her teacher touched them up or when her mother elaborately framed them. Her mother was trying to be encouraging, perhaps imagining that her oldest daughter would, at the least, become an accomplished young lady or even an art teacher. It was unheard of for a young girl to take her training one step further and become an artist.

Her mother did not know, however, that the desire to be an artist was exactly what Georgia was experiencing. One day when she was twelve, Georgia asked her friend Lena, the daughter of the O'Keeffes' washerwoman, what she wanted to be when she grew up. Lena replied that she didn't know. "Well, I'm going to be an artist," Georgia blurted out. She was surprised at the sureness of her own words, and she stood silently for a few moments, contemplating their barely perceived meaning.

In retrospect, Georgia never precisely put her finger on what prompted her at such an untried age to declare her intent to be an artist. No great women artists were mentioned in her school books, she didn't know any professional artists, and she cared little for the few paintings she had seen. But, as she observed in her book, a small illustration of a comely Grecian maiden in one of her mother's books had inspired her to create something as lovely herself. "I think my feeling wasn't as articulate as that, but I believe that picture started something moving in me that kept on going and has had to do with the everlasting urge that makes me keep on painting," she wrote.

What's more, she had lived with the annoying, but not painful, label of being the black sheep in the family, always being teased about her "crazy notions." As she matured, she discovered that no one minded at all when she gave her imagination free rein in colors and shapes. "I decided that the only thing I could do that was nobody else's business was to paint," she liked to say in adulthood. "I could do as I chose because no one would care."

Painting had begun to fill the same need for privacy and freedom that her dollhouse once satisfied. When she told the grownups that she was going to be an artist when she grew up, they humored what they regarded as a childish ambition by inquiring what kind of artist. Since Georgia didn't know that there were different kinds of artists, the only answer she could come up with, recalling the dark, formal portraits of her great-grandparents Wyckoff, was "a portrait painter." When one of the adults remarked that sometimes she would have to paint ugly faces, Georgia became extremely irritated and emphatically denied it. To be an artist, in her evolving concept of the term, meant that she could do as she wished.

Even though the United States Senate had rejected an attempt to grant women the right to vote the year Georgia was born, she did not grow up feeling limited by her sex. From a young age she understood that it was both possible and a fine thing to become a professional woman as well as a mother. Higher education had been available to women in nearby Madison since two years before her birth, when the Univeristy of Wisconsin began to take female students. As she grew up, it is likely that her educated female relatives told her about the World Columbian Exposition, which opened in Chicago, only a day's journey away, the year she started school, and which the feminist Susan B. Anthony attended. The fair contained a Woman's Building that displayed women's handicrafts as well as a large feminist mural on the theme of the modern woman—"plucking the fruit of Knowledge and Science"—painted by the American artist Mary Cassatt.

Also, self-assurance came to Georgia rather easily. One day she and her older brother quarreled about the gender of God. Georgia stated that God was a woman, and, when Francis scorned the idea, she went to their mother for support. When Mama's answer disappointed her, Georgia stubbornly refused to change her mind. She calmly restated her conviction to both her brother and her mother that God *was* a woman. One can only suppose that it was the existence of the strong matriarchs in her family and her growing confidence in herself that made her so insistent. At any rate, throughout her life she was unashamed of her womanhood and refused to accept the traditional role assigned to her gender.

❖

Meanwhile, the O'Keeffes had become increasingly visible and prominent in their small farm community. By the end of 1897, the weekly *Sun Prairie Countryman* began to round up the local news into a column fondly dubbed "O.K. Neighborhood." Its social notices were sprinkled with news of Mama's teas, her trips to Madison, and the many visitors to the O'Keeffe farmhouse. On Saturday nights, the O'Keeffe kids were likely to show up at the nearby Town Hall community center to hear the South Sun Prairie String Band or to see such entertainment as magic shows by local talent. Even at that time little Georgia O'Keeffe stood out: Once the editor published the news that she was sick and, another time, announced that she had celebrated her ninth birthday.

As Georgia reached adolescence, however, the size of her extended family sharply declined. After Grandmother Totto's death, most of the Totto aunts and uncles scattered. Then after Grandmother O'Keeffe's death in October 1897, tuberculosis began to drain the life from Papa's only surviving brother, Bernard, who was still bachelor. (His oldest brother, Boniface, had succumbed to the disease the year after Georgia's birth.) As the months passed, Bernard became weaker, until finally he moved into his brother's farmhouse, where his sister-in-law, Ida, was able to nurse him. By summer his condition had become so critical that he deeded the land he had inherited from his mother to Frank and Ida "for one dollar and love and affection bestowed." He only had the strength to scribble a small "X" on the papers, and a month later he died.

Tuberculosis had stalked the four O'Keeffe brothers for thirteen years and had finally killed three of them. The winter after Bernard's death, which was more bitterly cold than usual, Frank became obsessed with the belief that consumption would strike him down as well. In February 1899, five days after his wife gave birth to another child, Claudia Ruth, the temperature dropped to thirty-four degrees below zero, and high winds made the cold far worse. Without any snow cover, the frost had gone four and half feet deep, and the well water and food stored in the cellars were freezing.

Frank's dreams of escaping the tyranny of farming and the merciless weather were revived by the brutal winter. There was also an element of necessity to such dreams. A story has been told that the O'Keeffes were prohibited from operating their dairy because of the danger of contaminating the milk with tuberculosis. It was also at this time that American farmers were caught in a pinch between declining farm prices and rising machinery costs. Agrarian parties had formed to press the government in Washington to ease the farmers' plight, but when their candidate lost a national election in 1896, their defeat was signaled.

Escape was now a possibility because, after Bernard's death, the O'Keeffes had become so land rich that they leased part of the farm to another farmer. Much of their acreage, bought by Pierce O'Keeffe fifty years before for a few cents an acre, was now fine farmland worth up to seventy-five dollars an acre. It had been augmented by the hundreds of Totto acres that Frank had bought from his mother-in-law six years after his marriage, so that the farm stretched several miles in one direction and was said to be as large as six hundred acres.

At this time there was a man in Madison—Chandler Chapman—who had a business selling Virginia land to midwesterners. It's probable that the O'Keeffes saw a booklet published by businessmen in Williamsburg, Virginia, who were attempting to attract commerce to their historic but sleepy town. The booklet boasted that winters in the old colonial capital were mild and that the climate was healthy. "Come, investigate, see for yourselves, be convinced," it urged. "It is the garden spot of Virginia."

Ida had always been restless on the farm, so she was interested in the idea of a move. In her eyes, lovely Williamsburg was a cultured college community, the home of the long-established College of William and Mary. By then Ida was close to forty, Frank was approaching fifty, and they had no relatives left in Sun Prairie. A new century was beginning. The couple pledged to sell the Wisconsin farm and to begin a new life in Virginia.

❖

In the fall of 1901, a few months before Georgia turned fourteen, her mother entered her in an exclusive convent boarding school on the outskirts of Madison instead of the Sun Prairie high school. That year, Sacred Heart Academy, located in an old stone estate, enrolled seventy-eight "young ladies" from as far away as California and Canada. Georgia already had repeated the eighth grade (she had started school a year early) because her mother thought she was still too young to leave home. Nevertheless, Sacred Heart represented an abrupt change from her lenient household routine, her freedom to roam over the farm, the easy schoolhouse lessons, the privacy of her own bedroom, and the security of a community in which she knew everyone. The Dominican nuns reserved the right to restrict visitors to Saturday afternoons, to inspect the pupils' own books, and to read their personal mail. Although Protestants like Georgia were excused from taking religious instruction, each girl was required to drape a black-silk lace-edged veil over her head for daily chapel and to dress entirely in funereal black on Sundays.

The school catalog emphasized that since the eye "is the most open and ready road to the mind, it should make drawing . . . as necessary as reading or writing." Georgia's parents paid the extra twenty dollars (on top of an eighty-dollar annual tuition fee) so that their daughter could receive art instruction in the top-floor art studio overlooking woods and one of Madison's lakes, Lake Wingra. On her first day in the studio, the pupils were given charcoal and instructed to draw a baby's hand from a white plaster cast. Georgia worked hard at her drawing and finally was satisfied. When the nun saw it, however, she scolded her for making it too tiny and too black. Since Georgia had always been treated gently at home, the unexpected criticism mortified her to the verge of tears. Consequently, she began to make her marks on paper larger and lighter to please the exacting Sister Angelique. Her strategy was successful. At the end of the school year, the nun exhibited her drawings, chose one of them—a duck hunter aiming his rifle—to be published in the catalog, and awarded her a gold pin "for improvement in illustration and drawing."

Surprisingly, Georgia did not win one of the prestigious gold medals in art, but achieved more recognition in other areas. Enrolled in the most rigorous academic program, she won the school prize in ancient history with a grade of ninety-two, and all her other grades were good (algebra, ninety; physiography and English, both eighty-five). And despite her discomfort with the strict rules, she adjusted effortlessly in the eyes of school officials—conducting herself with such ladylike manners that the nuns awarded her a gold medal for her excellent "deportment."

It is probable that she tolerated the rules and regulations instead of rebelling for several reasons. First of all, young people at the turn of the century were expected to be well behaved, particularly someone like the eldest daughter of the dignified Ida Totto. In addition, Georgia was eager to have access to the advantages of Sacred Heart, such as the classical music concerts and the intellectually exciting classes. In fact, in years to come, Georgia lavishly praised the nuns' teaching, wryly adding that her stay with them was the only time she learned any new ideas in school.

The next fall, in 1902, Georgia was taken out of Sacred Heart, and two of her younger sisters, Ida and Anita, were entered instead. Although the reason for her withdrawal is not clear, at the time it was not unusual to send a child to a private academy for only a year if tuition money was limited. Meanwhile, the children's parents, along with Aunt Jenny, Alexius, Catherine, and the baby, Claudia, left for Virginia to get settled before the older children would join them at the end of the school year.

Georgia and her brother Francis were sent to live with Aunt Lola, now a beloved teacher in Madison, a city of almost twenty thousand situated on an isthmus between two lakes and dominated by a mammoth white marble state capitol building on one hill and the gold dome of the state university on another. Aunt Lola lived in the unpretentious two-story Totto family house on Spaight Street, a quiet residential street that wound around the pine-studded edge of Lake Monona. It was the first time Georgia had lived in a city, but from Aunt Lola's windows she had a fine view of the choppy turquoise-blue lake and the dark-green hills on the opposite shore.

She was enrolled in Madison High School, a large Victorian edifice, with hundreds of other students. In her second year of high school, her grades were all B's in civics, biology, geography, algebra, and English—only a little less outstanding than the year before. She recalled little about art lessons aside from a memory of the day she passed the art classroom where the spinsterish teacher in a big flowery hat was speaking. Standing in the doorway, Georgia was fascinated as the bright-eyed woman held up a jack-in-the-pulpit plant in order to let the students examine the unusual shapes and subtle shades of its interior. Although Georgia had seen masses of the wild flower in the marshy places on her father's farm, she had never studied one in an art class before. It was the first time, she claimed in her book, that it occurred to her to paint a living thing rather than to copy pictures or draw from plaster casts. The memory stayed with her, and a quarter of a century later she painted a powerful series of oils based on that very flower.

❖

When classes ended in the spring of 1903, the four eldest O'Keeffe children left Wisconsin by train to join the rest of the family in Virginia. Georgia, by then fifteen and a half, was fortunate to have spent her childhood in the farmhouse where she was born. When her parents sold the family home, she had already left home to get an education. (The farmhouse survived another seventy years until a Christmas candle ignited a disastrous fire.) When she headed for Virginia, she was an independent, self-confident, successful teenager who was ready to leave all vestiges of childhood behind. Since she had not been uprooted too soon or too suddenly, she would have a deep, strong sense of herself for the rest of her life.

The most extraordinary thing about her childhood was that it was so ordinary. Perhaps because it had been neither bruising nor blissful, she was able to shrug it off emotionally and allow it to recede as a pleasant memory. She developed into a person who never looked backward with the kind of acute nostalgia painter Marc Chagall felt for the Russian village where he was born in the same year as she. After she left Wisconsin, she returned only rarely to visit, despite an invitation extended by another Wisconsinite a generation older, Frank Lloyd Wright, to join his Taliesin artists' colony in Spring Green, and despite the wistful pleas of the people of Sun Prairie, who wanted to be thought of as more than a footnote in her history.

Yet the images, ambience, and ethics of Sun Prairie had fully formed her. From time to time she spoke of herself as emerging from the soil of the American heartland like a growing plant, and she would always be uneasy in cities. She was also marked by the midwestern strain of Old World Catholicism and became celebrated for her lifelong habit of wearing devout convent-school black. Most important, she drew heavily on her observations in the natural paradise of her early farm life for much of her iconography as a artist. Another strong influence was the Middle West's democratic egalitarianism, which profoundly affected her as an artist. When she wondered at a critical point if she really had the "right" to paint as she wished, she decided that yes, freedom of artistic expression was her birthright as much as freedom of speech.

In later years, Georgia realized that the most dominant and wholesome aspect of her makeup emerged from her middle western background. "The barn is a very healthy part of me," she wrote several decades later to a collector about her painting of a red Wisconsin barn. ". . . It is my childhood—I seem to be one of the few people I know of to have no complaints against my first twelve years—." Believing that the prairies were the "normal" part of the country, she found it impossible to talk about America to those who did not know them. Once she half-joked that the East was too European, the South too tropical, the West Coast too Asian, and the Southwest merely a "playground." When she moved to New York and her rural roots appeared remarkable to the urbanites, she never lost her belief in their normalcy and her feeling of blessedness at having been born a farmer's daughter in the American Midwest.

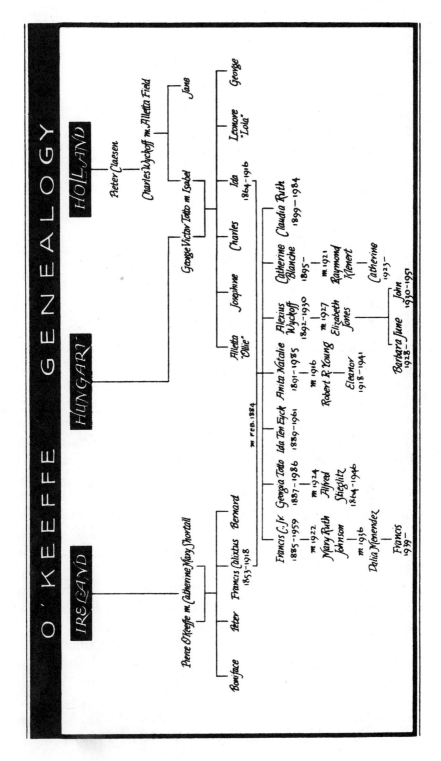

2 ❖ School

The Williamsburg the O'Keeffes found on their arrival was a sluggish town of five hundred white and Negro families in which time seemed to have stood still for more than a hundred years. Unpaved Duke of Gloucester Street was lined with elegant eighteenth-century houses whose exquisite proportions were half-hidden by crumbling red-brick facades, sagging verandas, and a riotous growth of flowering bushes and trees. The soft, sultry air was pungent with the fragrance of the fecund gardens that bloomed most of the year behind box hedges. The oysterman broke the dawn slumber by walking the lanes and shouting out the day's price for James River oysters. Besides the historic college, Williamsburg housed an inn, a few shops with erratic business hours, a pier from which peanuts and watermelons were shipped, and a lunatic asylum.

In March 1903 Ida and Francis O'Keeffe sold the Wisconsin farm for twelve thousand dollars, and the next month they bought a rambling, white Williamsburg homestead on nine and a half acres for thirty-five hundred dollars. "Wheatlands," as the house was called, was larger than the Sun Prairie farmhouse, and, with its breezy porches, carved columns, and dark shutters, it was far more gracious as well. Yet most of its eighteen rooms remained half-empty after the O'Keeffes moved in since the family brought little furniture and few valuables, other than some jewelry, a music box, and Papa's fiddle, from the Midwest.

At the time, it was unusual for strangers to settle in Williamsburg, and the "odd" Yankee ways of the O'Keeffes stood out. For one thing, neighbors noted, they didn't have black servants like the rest of white Williamsburg. For another, few of them ever went to church, and, even worse, the name O'Keeffe sounded suspiciously papist in the pious Protestant town. The seven children were a loosely disciplined, irrepressible, uninhibited breed who didn't quarrel much but who didn't show any southern-style clannishness either. In the summer, the family liked to rent an appallingly rough vacant house on the river at Yorktown in order to swim and sail. Like other midwesterners, the O'Keeffes valued education as a means of getting ahead, while the southerners relied on a fixed system of family pedigree, according to which newcomers were placed firmly near the bottom. Matters weren't helped when gossips decided that it wasn't old money with which Francis O'Keeffe had bought land and opened a grocery store. A seemingly coarse man who lacked education and didn't hesitate to work with his hands, Mr. O'Keeffe was clearly not a Virginia gentleman— and at least one little Williamsburg girl was terrified of him.

Townspeople were puzzled by the match of Francis and what they called his "very fine-looking" wife, who combed her heavy, dark hair straight back from her handsome face. Because of her erect carriage, her gentlewomanly manners, her cultivated tastes, and the way she articulated her words, people were sure that Ida was "a lady" and invited her to their teas. After she showed one of Georgia's friends some jewelry that came from the titled Tottos, neighbors were fascinated by false rumors that she was a White Russian and had royal blood.

They also thought that the two eldest O'Keeffe children, Francis Jr. and Georgia, had their mother's aristocratic quality but that the younger ones did not. Georgia was considered the most interesting of the rather plain, dark-haired O'Keeffe sisters, particularly since she had a gift for accurately sketching people's likenesses. Because of her artistic talent, they tended to overlook her aberrant behavior, such as her habit of taking long solitary walks at dawn in the countryside.

In Virginia, Georgia's behavior underlined the differences between her and her mother. Ida pressed her oldest teen-age daughter to act in a more conventional way, so as to conform to the mores of Williamsburg. But Ida's Wisconsin-bred daughter was not a social creature like her mother and was nonchalantly unconcerned with the views of the conservative Virginia ladies. Around her mother she said very little, trying to appear obedient to her authority and not to come into conflict with her. Open resistance wasn't worth it, she reasoned, because she now lived away from home most of the time.

❖

The first fall in Virginia, Ida enrolled her son Francis in the College of William and Mary, hired a tutor for the younger children, and sent Georgia to an excellent small girl's boarding school two hundred miles away. Chatham Episcopal Institute was a white clapboard mansion on a wooded hill overlooking the little courthouse town of Chatham, Virginia. In contrast to southern finishing schools that emphasized the social graces, Chatham was a school where Episcopalian ministers and middle-class families sent their daughters for a modern education.

Life at the school was simple and Spartan: Baths were a weekly ritual, outhouses were communal, meals consisting of such dishes as black-eyed peas were served at long tables, and little wood stoves heated the bedrooms. On Sundays the boarders walked down the hill to church in line behind a chaperone; they wore navy uniforms and school caps or, in warm weather, white piqué dresses with white hats. From time to time there were all-girl dances at which some pupils donned feminine gowns and others danced as 'boys" in the more masculine navy uniform.

Georgia's arrival in evening study hall a few days later than the others was vividly recalled by a classmate, Christine McRae, thirty years later:

> The most unusual thing about her was the absolute plainness of her attire. She wore a tan coat suit, short, severe, and loose, into this room filled with girls with small waists and tight-fitting dresses bedecked in ruffles and bows. Pompadours and ribbons vied with each other in size and elaborateness, but Georgia's hair was drawn smoothly back from her broad, prominent forehead, and she had no bow on her head at all, only one at the bottom of her pigtail to keep it from unplaiting. Nearly every girl in that study hall planned just how she was going to dress Georgia up, but her plans came to naught, for this strongminded girl knew what suited her and would not be changed though she approved of other girls dressing in frills and furbelows.

Georgia, almost sixteen, may or may not have known how well her tailored, midwestern, corsetless style complemented her boyish looks. Although her widely spaced eyes were "pretty," Christine remembered, "her features were plain—not ugly, for each one was good, but large and unusual-looking. She would have made strikingly handsome boy." Christine also marveled at her long-fingered "slender, smooth, capable" hands. She went on to observe that the newcomer's skin was dark, her brown hair was straight, "while the shape of her head and the set of it on her shoulders was perfect."

It was immediately apparent that Georgia, having been away from home for two years, was self-possessed and knew how to handle herself well. During the first recess, she walked up to a cluster of unknown girls and began to talk to them in an easy, friendly way. "I started out not having any friends at all, but I didn't pay any attention to it," she recalled many years later. The others sensed the new girl's distinct personality—"her exuberance and her enthusiasm," in the words of Christine. "Everyone in the group could feel it, and two of us remarked as she left us on the grip of her fine strong hands." Afterwards, when Georgia heard that Alice Beretta, a schoolmate from Texas, hated her, on a dare she coolly campaigned to get the girl to like her. Keeping the younger girls at arm's length, she saved her warmth and wit for her classmates. In her self-assurance, Georgia believed she had the right to boss others around. "When so few people think at all, isn't it all right for me to think for them and get them to do what I want?" she asked Christine.

Georgia was lucky to have an intelligent and sensitive art teacher during her two years at Chatham—Elizabeth May Willis. Also Chatham's principal, Mrs. Willis—a tall, fair-minded widow who was paralyzed on one side of her face—had graduated from Syracuse University and, before her marriage, had directed the art department of a large midwestern university. Georgia's talent immediately caught her eye. Yet, as Georgia surmised after she had been a teacher herself, she was something of a problem pupil. Sometimes she worked intensely, and, other times, she refused to work for days and instead pestered the other girls in the studio, pulling their hair ribbons or indulging in other antics. When the others complained to Mrs. Willis that she didn't make Georgia work, the principal was known to reply calmly, "When the spirit moves Georgia, she can do more in a day than you can do in a week." To her immense credit, Mrs. Willis allowed Georgia the freedom to work at her own pace, encouraging her, for instance, to return to the studio after dinner when the others went to study hall.

At the same time, Georgia was intently studying the piano at Chatham and did well enough to perform a Grieg piece, the *Peer Gynt* suite, at a school recital in December 1904. For the rest of her life she cared deeply for music, claiming that she could have become a musician as easily as a painter and that she didn't know which she valued most—her ears or her eyes. "Singing has always seemed to me the most perfect means of expression," she was to say in 1922. "It is so spontaneous. And after singing, I think the violin. Since I cannot sing, I paint."

But by the age of sixteen, after five years of private art lessons, Georgia had far greater artistic than musical facility. With art skills that overshadowed those of others her age, she knew precisely how to blend her colors and exactly how wet to make her large water-color brush. She astonished her classmates by penciling the precise set of one girl's chin and the tilt of another's nose, then casually crumpling up the sketch and tossing it into the wood stove. Before long, she was acknowledged the queen of the art studio. Christine remembered:

> Her easel always stood in the center of the floor and was
> the high spot of interest. Here she would stand for hours,
> perfectly silent, working on something that seemed to us
> already finished, adding colors that our ordinary eyes
> could never see and serenely undisturbed by our incessant
> chatter as to how she got that purple, or the red, or the
> green. Presently, though, she would drop to earth, look
> around, and if Mrs. Willis was gone, spin on her heels,
> run up to somebody, give her a hug and get the whole
> studio in an uproar. Then she would quiet down and by
> the time Mrs. Willis returned would be working away in-
> tently.

The girls chose her to be art editor of the school's first yearbook, a handsome fawn-suede volume with gold lettering, in which her class-mates rhymed: "O is for O'Keeffe, an artist divine;/Her paintings are perfect and her drawings are fine." Susan Young, a friend who liked to paint china, said that besides accepting her as an artist, they all fully expected her to become famous.

Elizabeth May Willis was an important influence in getting Georgia to focus on art. She marveled aloud to others about the girl's gift and, at the end of Georgia's senior year, gave her a special diploma in art as well as the art prize for a watercolor of red and yellow corn. After graduation, Mrs. Willis's strong personal interest in her talented pupil continued. When Georgia began to exhibit, the headmistress proudly published in the alummae news that she was "making a name for herself as an artist in New York City." It seemed to some of her classmates that Georgia, who rarely looked back, was reluctant to acknowledge her debt to her old teacher. But when a dinner was held in Mrs. Willis's honor in New York in the 1930s, Georgia went and was touched to learn that the principal had traveled to the city on earlier occasions to see her shows. Having Georgia as a pupil had clearly remained the highlight of her career. It was only natural therefore that when she died a decade later, her obituary in the *New York Times* ran the subhead: "Had Georgia O'Keeffe as a Student."

Although Georgia was considered "different" at Chatham, she was used to being teased by her siblings about her nonconformity, so she knew how to handle it—even when her unadorned clothes once caused her to be mistaken for a maid, much to the hilarity of the other girls. Whereas the southern girls tended to be effusive and flirtatious, Georgia remained reserved and calmly indifferent to boys. Her classmates described her in the yearbook as "A girl who doesn't give a cent for men—and boys still less." Futhermore, she was the only girl from the North at Chatham that year and spoke with a flat midwestern inflection instead of a lilting southern drawl. But this didn't bother her either; she was certain that hers was the correct way to speak.

In actuality, the Chatham girls liked Georgia and admired her artistic skill as well as the flair with which she stitched her clothes, especially a skirt with such smooth seams that it was reversible. Affectionately nicknamed "Georgie," she played on the basketball team, joined the German Club, and was made treasurer of the tennis team. In the fall of her second year at Chatham, she was initiated, along with an elite handful, into the school chapter of the social sorority Kappa Delta.

Although Georgia tried to restore peace when her sorority sisters made catty remarks about one another, she was far from a model pupil. She had an impulsive streak, was often bored by school routine, and tried to liven things up through such pranks as pinning a bow to the back of a teacher's shirtwaist. Like the other girls, she fried biscuits illegally on one of the small bedroom stoves—but she was the only one to pull up onions from the school vegetable garden, place them on the biscuits, and eat them raw. After teaching her friends how to play poker, she kept a poker game going. For the yearbook, she drew a number of wickedly humorous caricatures of teachers. She also received many demerits for infractions of such rules as getting out of bed after the 10:00 P.M. lights-out bell, and often spent Saturdays "writing them off" by copying some platitude over and over. But usually she made sure that her mischief escaped notice, since she preferred to hide her less-than-perfect behavior behind a facade Christine described as "serene" and "poised."

She was lackadaisical about studying for her diploma—which required passing subjects like art, history, mythology, physiology, and French—but she succeeded in getting one in June 1905 at the normal high school graduation age of seventeen. However, it was a close call since she had to take the spelling test a half dozen times before she finally passed it. (Spelling was to be her *bête noire* all her life.) Chosen to give the graduating class's prophecy, she predicted rosy futures for the other six graduates. Much to the amusement of the assembled girls and their parents, however, she imagined that in twenty years she would still be attempting to pass spelling, even after her hair had become gray and her eyes dulled from the monotony of the effort.

Afterwards, Georgia presented some of her watercolors to classmates as graduation gifts; she gave a nosegay of pansies painted in soft pink and lavender hues to Susan Young, for example. Then she tore up the rest so that her student work wouldn't be around to embarrass her when she became famous, she told her friends. The graduates, in their high-necked white dresses, also planted a tree and lit a bonfire before departing for their homes throughout the South.

❖

Both Georgia's art teacher and her mother wanted her to continue to develop her artistic talent. Even though females had been admitted to most American art schools since the turn of the century, it was still considered "advanced" to send a daughter to such a school before World War I. Puritanism retained a tight grip on the country. After all, at art schools students drew nude models, albeit in separate male and female "life" classes, and their behavior was unsupervised by the school administrators. But if Ida had doubts about the propriety of art school for her eldest daughter, it's certain that Mrs. Willis was able to dispel them convincingly because she had gone to art school herself. What's more, Ida herself continued to be eager for Georgia to become accomplished.

So in September 1905, Georgia was packed off to the huge school of the Art Institute of Chicago, one of America's largest, most active art museums. Her destination was undoubtedly decided by the fact that the art school was within walking distance of the Indiana Avenue apartment of her mother's older brother and sister. It was arranged that Georgia would live with Charles W. Totto, who was in the credit business, and Alletta (or "Ollie" for short) Totto, who was a stenographer.

Aunt Ollie, close to fifty at the time, was a strongly opinionated woman with heavy-lidded eyes and a long face. She had been a headstrong girl who loved galloping on her horse, her long hair flying, over the Totto's Sun Prairie farm. She was the oldest child in her family, and when her father returned to Hungary, she found work as a schoolteacher to help support her mother and younger brothers and sisters. After her stint as a stenographer in Chicago, she ran a shoe store in Madison and then became the only female proofreader among hundreds of newspapermen on the Milwaukee *Sentinel* for many years. Living until she was almost one hundred and two, Ollie was recalled by a great-niece as "very small, independent, autocratic in bearing, brilliant, strong-willed and with piercing blue eyes." Her favorite niece was Georgia, who was named for her revered father. (Ollie's own middle name was Georgiana.) In time Georgia evidently adopted many of the qualities of the aunt who helped her make her way in the world.

The gigantic Italian-Renaissance Art Institute, whose steps are flanked by bronze lions, was one of Chicago's major monuments, but it was no place to nourish a fresh, original, indigenous American talent. Proud of its European collection, it exhibited the work of Millet, Courbet, and Rosa Bonheur the winter Georgia was there, as well as its collection of Dutch masters. It encouraged its art-school instructors to study in Paris, the sacrosanct art capital. It also adopted the harsh, judgmental, competitive French teaching system. Aspiring artists gathered around a professor, who ranked their work by number according to merit each month so "the students have this opportunity to compare their work with others, and to see what qualities their master values most highly." Those with the highest numbers won the right to pick the best seats for the next drawing pose and were rapidly promoted. Those with consistently low numbers were grouped glumly in the back of the studios and were eventually drummed out in shame.

Three days before classes began, Georgia registered along with nine hundred other students, paid her fee, and was given a locker for her smock, charcoal, easel, and drawing board. She was assigned to an elementary drawing class taught by Matilda Vanderpoel, an advanced student and daughter of one of the school's instructors. Miss Vanderpoel's students set up their easels in the museum's vast main gallery—where huge columns and larger-than-life classical statues dwarfed them—to sketch armless torsos balanced on pedestals. In her book, Georgia recalled that there was a young man in this class who used to examine her delicate drawings and who managed to convince her of their inferiority compared to his bold dark ones.

Quickly realizing that she could no longer afford the indulgence of moodiness in the classroom, Georgia began to apply herself seriously to learning how to succeed at the art student game. When the first month's work was judged at the end of October, Georgia was surprised to learn that she had ranked fourth out of forty-four pupils—and ahead of the young man. Students were assigned to their proper level after the first month, and Georgia was promptly elevated to an intermediate class. With the new instructor, she again competed well: She ranked fifth in her class in December, seventh in January, and first in February.

Meanwhile, she also registered for anatomy, as preparation for an advanced life class. One day a very attractive male model with a dark moustache who was nude except for a skimpy loincloth stepped out from behind a curtain and stood before the students. While the instructor pointed out the anatomical parts of the man's body, giving them long Latin names, Georgia blushed hotly at the model's artificial nakedness, she recalled in her book. After class, she agonized over her embarrassment and dreaded the next class. She didn't know what to do because anatomy was a hurdle one had to clear on the route to becoming an artist. When the class met again, however, she found herself following the others into the classroom. Although she managed to get used to such experiences and was advanced to a life class in March, she never developed an interest in painting the human body.

On the other hand, she liked the weekly lectures on composition by John Vanderpoel, a little Dutch-born hunchback and well-known authority on human anatomy, who lucidly illustrated the importance of line with black and white crayons on sheets of tan paper. His meticulous drawings—if not his interest in the human form—made a lasting impression on her. She later praised him as a fine teacher and bought his textbook, *The Human Form*. When, as supervisor of her life class, he judged the twenty-nine women in May, he ranked Georgia's drawings first and gave her several honorable mentions as well. A year later, a recommendation from the art school concluded that Georgia's "record is exceptionally high."

❖

After classes ended in June, Georgia left large drab Chicago and headed for home in the South. She roamed the Virginia countryside, lovely and lush with such sights as the huge, waxy, white magnolia flowers blooming against dark, glossy leaves. Her pleasure was short-lived, however. Although her father had believed that he was moving his family to a healthier climate, malaria, smallpox, and other diseases flourished in Williamsburg's muggy air, and that summer Georgia came down with the dreaded typhoid fever.

Her temperature ran high and she was delirious for a while. Typhoid deaths had occurred in Williamsburg that spring and summer, and her family's fears for her life were grave. Finally, by the end of September 1906, she was out of danger. She had survived, but the high fever had caused her long straight hair to fall out, and she had to wear a little lace cap to conceal her baldness. The illness also left her with dreamy memories of events around that time, and these drifted back to her when she read Goethe's *Faust* several years later. During the many weeks she spent in bed trying to regain the strength to walk, her hair slowly began to grow back in little curls.

Too weak to return to art school that fall, Georgia watched her older brother leave for New York and young Ida and Anita for Chatham. Besides her parents and Aunt Jenny, the household contained the three youngest children—Alexius, Catherine, and Claudia—as well as several college boys, called "table boarders," who took meals at the O'Keeffe house. Claudia, an eight-year-old tomboy, was the leader of the neighborhood kids. The children used to flock to the welcoming O'Keeffe home to play in their vast, empty attic, ride their swaybacked horse, romp with their amiable mongrel, play tennis on their handmade court, roughhouse with Claudia's father, and, as Georgia got better, go on excursions with her oldest sister. "Georgia was great fun with the children—she was like her father that way," recalled John Henderson, the seven-year-old doctor's son who lived next door that year with his little towheaded sisters. "She would gather up all the kids in the neighborhood for an afternoon walk. You always saw her with a line of children behind her." She led the children into the woods—where she told them how to pick chickpeas and boil them so they tasted like chestnuts—until the day one of them threw a handful of cockleburs at her. "The burs were all in her hair, her gorgeous black hair that made her look like a gypsy with curls," recalled Carra Winder, and Georgia became so angry she refused to take the youngsters on any more walks.

Nevertheless, Georgia seemed to enjoy the children and their frank, fresh qualities more than the company of the other teen-agers in town who lived at home. Still an outsider, she was more serious and sophisticated than most of the Williamsburg girls, particularly after her year in Chicago. That winter the girls performed a frothy operetta, *Cinderella in Flowerland*, which Georgia probably thought was ridiculous. But in their eyes she looked very little like a southern belle since her illness had sharpened her strong features and left her skin sallow and her hair short at a time before females bobbed their hair. Nevertheless, in May she accepted an invitation to a spring dance hosted by a young woman named Jetta Thorpe, whose home was decorated with May flowers for the occasion. Georgia must have realized that she had been extremely lucky: In August 1907 one of the girls who had danced at Jetta's party came down with typhoid fever and died of it.

As Georgia regained her strength, she painted a little at an easel set up in the yard, asked some of the children to pose for her, and made plans to return to art school. She tried to barter German lessons in exchange for teaching a small girl to paint until she became impatient with the child's lack of talent. She apparently did not wish to return to the Art Institute of Chicago, whose spring 1907 letter of recommendation read in part: "Miss O'Keeffe is a young lady of attractive personality, and I feel that she will be very successful as a teacher of drawing." Since her father was planning to put the big white house up for sale because of business setbacks, the statement suggests that she was preparing for a teaching job in order to earn a living. At any rate, she now planned to go to the Art Students League in New York, where Elizabeth May Willis had gone.

❖

In September, Georgia boarded a train for the twelve-hour journey north to New York. In 1907 Manhattan was a teeming, treeless city centered in an area that extended from Washington Square to the Metropolitan Museum of Art, near where Eighty-sixth Street now runs. Along Fifth Avenue, shops catering to the wealthy—jewelers, milliners, dressmakers, and art dealers—occupied more and more of the stately brownstone residences. The last of the old horse-drawn omnibuses were being replaced by trolleys, and underground subways and modern elevated lines were being built. The air of the great metropolis crackled with excitement along the densely crowded sidewalks lined with hotels, saloons, bookstalls, concert halls, and art galleries.

Through the Art Students League on West Fifty-seventh Street, Georgia rented a room in a nearby rooming house for a few dollars a week. At once she was thrown into a milieu of high-spirited art students who played such pranks as stealing and eating the fruit used for still lifes. The young artists also liked to bring hurdy-gurdy street musicians into the League, push back the furniture, and dance to the cranked-out folk tunes. School life at the League was capped during a festive week in May when a group called the Fakirs used to lampoon the revered paintings of the great masters.

Georgia had arrived in New York after a brush with death, followed by a convalescent year in a troubled household in a town where she was something of a misfit. It was unusual for a girl not yet twenty to have so much freedom, particularly one who had never lived alone or been to New York City before. But times were changing, and, as the twentieth century got under way, women's skirts now cleared the ground by six inches. The atmosphere was exhilarating to Georgia, and she was remembered that winter as someone who smiled a lot, with a captivating dimpled grin and a nonchalant kind of Irish gaiety. The other aspiring artists were fascinated by her expressive intelligent features and her slim boyish grace, and long afterwards she was referred to as a beauty. For her part, Georgia recalled that they all wanted to run their fingers through her curious, cropped, soft, curly tresses that flattered the line of her shapely head. "Everyone called her Patsy," remembered Lila Wheelock, a sculpture student at the League that winter. "Patsy—because her name was O'Keeffe."

Despite her diffidence at Chatham at the idea of beaux, Georgia was eagerly courted by the young men who enrolled in the League in greater numbers and at an older age than the young women. One of them was George Dannenberg, a good-looking artist of twenty-five who had arrived from San Francisco on a scholarship and enrolled in the same still-life class as Georgia. George, who later had a reputation as something of a ladies' man, loved to dance and escorted Georgia to some of the school parties. She went to the Valentine's Day costume party as a charmingly boyish Peter Pan and was remembered as an enchanting dancer. At the Leap Year dance, when the men donned long gowns and feathery hats and the women wore white shirts and tailored jackets, Georgia was photographed sitting cross-legged on the floor with a crooked bow tie under her chin, looking directly into the camera, a glint of amusement in her eye. Besides their interest in art and dancing, Georgia and young Dannenberg shared a love of the outdoors—and, apparently, they were very close. Many years later, Dannenberg spoke of her emotionally, glowing as he recalled her.

In the afternoons Georgia took William Merritt Chase's portrait and still-life class. A successful painter in his own right, Chase was a member of the artistic elite who presided over a fashionable salon. He was eager to establish art as an honorable profession in America and, considering himself a representative of American art, he dressed elegantly in pale spats, chamois gloves, silk scarves, and, often, in a white suit with a red carnation in his lapel. Although in retrospect his realism seems superficial and his style derivative, he painted with technical virtuosity and stylish élan.

Chase was famous as a teacher of art. In his efforts to make American art less provincial, he taught the best European methods in perspective, foreshortening, highlighting, and shadowing. His specialty was the flashy brushstroke so popular in Paris, which was executed with a brush loaded with rich pigment. Georgia remembered how he praised his friend, society portraitist John Singer Sargent, for delineating a gold watch chain with a single swift stroke of his brush. As he painted before his pupils' admiring eyes, he used his strong, witty personality to provoke the class into painting with individuality and boldness, and into making spirited, interesting canvases. Chase's great pride, enjoyment, and enthusiasm in being an American artist was infectious. Whenever he entered the League for the weekly critique, Georgia remembered, "a rustle seemed to flow from the ground floor to the top that 'Chase has arrived!'"

Close to sixty when Georgia took his class, Chase was still an awesome, whiskered, dashing masculine figure, albeit more portly and fatherly than in his younger years. He demanded that his pupils execute a new painting every day, one on top of the other, until the canvas became too thick with paint to continue. "There was something fresh and energetic and fierce and exacting about him that made him fun," Georgia later wrote in her book, and she worked hard to emulate his sensuous delight in textures. Afterwards, she said she believed that she had learned a great deal from him about the use of painting materials.

The portrait students often used to ask striking Patsy O'Keeffe to pose for them. One of them, Eugene Speicher, was a big, genial, well-liked class monitor. Georgia had refused to take the time to sit for him because it would have meant cutting one of her daily classes. One morning he blocked her way to the women's life class, teasing her with the warning that she couldn't pass until she agreed to pose. "It doesn't matter what you do," he taunted in words she never forgot. "I'm going to be a great painter, and you will probably end up teaching painting in some girls' school." When Georgia finally got to class, she found the model repulsive. She recalled Eugene's very handsome features and decided that instead of propping up her drawing board and setting to work, she would return to pose for him.

His finished portrait shows an unsmiling girl with pale skin and wavy dark hair looking directly at the viewer. She wore a simple white blouse, with a small black bow at her throat, instead of one of the high-necked blouses with puffed sleeves that were stylish at the time. The oil of popular Patsy O'Keeffe won Eugene Speicher a fifty-dollar prize and his first formal recognition as a portraitist. The next year it was published in the League catalog as an example of superb student work, and it hangs today in an oval frame in the Members' Room.

Georgia had many decisions to make that year, the first time she lived without supervision. She bought a notebook and began to list why she should do one thing in a column titled "Yes," or why she should not in one headed "No." "The essential question was always if you want to do *this*, can you do *that*?" she explained later. Under "Yes" went the reasons that she must repress her impulsiveness and exercise her will power for the sake of long-term goals. One of the decisions she had to make was whether or not she should pose. Students could earn a dollar for a four-hour pose in the portrait class, and Georgia needed the money. She could have allowed herself to be flattered by the astonishing discovery that she had a "prize-winning" face. But her drive to be a painter was stronger than any wish to be a likable model for others, so she decided in midwinter to refuse to model anymore.

The winter Georgia was at the League, students heard many stories about some controversial drawings by French sculptor Auguste Rodin on display in a little gallery run by photographer Alfred Stieglitz. The drawings' deceptively simple pencil lines and suggestive patches of watercolor seemed to be deliberately awkward, as if the sculptor had done them with his eyes shut. If they were working drawings, why did Stieglitz show them except as a devil's advocate? If they were not working drawings, what was the great sculptor up to? "One instructor told us that he didn't know whether Rodin was fooling Stieglitz and America too by sending over such a ridiculous group of drawings to be shown here," Georgia recalled, "or maybe Stieglitz knew what he was about and had his tongue in his cheek trying to see what nonsense he could put over on the American public."

Most of the instructors at the League were academicians who taught neoclassic figure painting, such as the conservative Kenyon Cox, who was revolted by the Rodins. Chase, who had been shocked by the themes of urban ugliness being portrayed in a group of new paintings by Robert Henri and others, complained to Stieglitz that if his students saw the Rodins, they would question everything they had been taught. When Stieglitz replied that that's what they were supposed to do, Chase angrily banged his high silk hat down so hard that he crushed it and stormed out of the gallery, vowing never to return.

On a snowy January afternoon when Georgia was posing for Eugene Speicher, a classmate dropped by and proposed that they all go see the notorious Rodins. The group of students headed down Fifth Avenue toward the gallery—in an attic of an old brownstone mansion—where the drawings were on exhibit. When they arrived, they crowded into the tiny elevator, which was slowly raised by a tall West Indian who pulled on a rope. The students got out, and there they found Alfred Stieglitz. He was coming out of a darkroom with a dripping photographic negative in his hand, his bushy black hair looking electrified and his gray moustache bristling, and his dark eyes behind pince-nez spectacles shot them an irritated look.

Alfred Stieglitz had studied photographic chemistry in Berlin in the 1880s and had achieved many technical triumphs with the camera. He was the first to successfully take a photograph in the rain, during a snowstorm, and at night, for example. The pioneer photographer had gone home to America to work in the photoengraving business, but before long he was embarked on a battle to make the "craft" of photography accepted as a tool of artistic expression. After being expelled from a group of more conventional photographers at the turn of the century, he had opened the gallery at 291 Fifth Avenue to exhibit the photographs he chose. But the Rodins marked the start of his showing avant-garde drawings and paintings that his friends, such as Edward Steichen, shipped to him from Europe. Nothing of the kind had been shown in America before, and the exhibit threatened to upset the country's staid ideas about art.

After the students who were with Georgia had told Stieglitz that they had come to see the Rodins, they deliberately baited him with a provocative question in order to unleash one of his famous, impassioned speeches, which would animate his wiry frame until he shook with furious energy. "I very well remember the fantastic violence of Stieglitz's defense when the students with me began talking with him about the drawings," Georgia later said. "I had never heard anything like it, so I went into the farthest corner and waited for the storm to be over. It was too noisy. I was tired. There was nothing to sit on, so I stood."

Georgia was intimidated by Stieglitz and unimpressed by the Rodins. Her mind was absorbed by her work in the Chase class, and at the end of the year she was well rewarded. Over the heads of older students at the League, she won the top still-life prize of a hundred dollars for a shadowy oil of a dead rabbit with brownish fur lying limply beside a gleaming copper pot adroitly rendered in Chase's style. As a result, she was one of a handful of students invited to attend the League summer school at Lake George, New York.

❖

When Georgia returned home to Williamsburg at the end of the summer of 1908, it was soon apparent to her that her family's problems had worsened. At one time her father had believed the town bankers when they predicted that their backwater was on the brink of an economic renaissance. Instead, Williamsburg had sunk deeper into a slump and it was impossible for Francis O'Keeffe, a Yankee outsider, to keep a business going. About the time of Georgia's graduation from Chatham, his grocery and feed trade had folded. A year later a real estate partnership dissolved. Plans he made for renting a pier on the James River came to nothing. His scheme for operating a profitable creamery never got off the ground. Before long he began to subdivide and build on the nine acres around the family home.

Finally, just before Georgia left for New York, it was announced in the local newspaper that O'Keeffe and a partner had begun to manufacture hollow concrete blocks from cement they had bought cheaply when plans to pave a nearby road were abandoned. Unfortunately, the block was an unpopular building material in traditionally red-brick Williamsburg. So O'Keeffe, in an attempt to recover his investment, began to build himself a house out of the block next to the lovely white house. The structure he painstakingly raised had asymmetrical windows, haphazardly placed doors and gables, and a two-story concrete porch. Years later, a Virginia farmer reflected the sentiments of shabby but genteel Williamsburg when he damned the O'Keeffe cement house for being nothing more than a prison.

As Francis O'Keeffe's dreams repeatedly exceeded his means of implementing them, the family nest egg disappeared and debts piled up. O'Keeffe became a silent and morose man, and Georgia was undoubtedly acutely pained for him. She quickly realized that he could not afford to send her back to the Art Students League for another winter. Things were so bad that he couldn't even come up with the tuition money to send her sisters Ida and Anita back to boarding school, even though they hadn't graduated yet. Following the usual pattern of deferring girls' education in favor of the boys', the O'Keeffes sent only sixteen-year-old Alexius back to private school—the academy of the College of William and Mary.

In later years, Georgia offered proud rationales for why she did not return to the Art Students League. She said that she rejected the use of realism for its own sake ("If one could only reproduce nature, and always with less beauty than the original, why paint at all?" she asked rhetorically) as well as the idea of mimicking the styles of others ("Rather than spend my life on imitations, I would not paint at all," she said). But although her reasons have a grain of truth to them, they also have the intellectualized, carefully articulated ring of hindsight.

It's extremely doubtful that Georgia rejected her academic art school training at that time, before she had found a better way of her own. Although she was never to emulate Professor Chase's bravura brushstroke technique during her career, she always praised the way he had taught his students to experiment, to express themselves freely with an individualistic style (albeit within limits), but, above all, to paint. "Seek to keep up courage," he liked to exhort the young artists, "even if you seem to be conceited."

At worst, Georgia may have felt vague stirrings of discontent during the winter in New York. She was independent-minded, and her prize rabbit-and-pot painting did not mean as much to her as certain other recent efforts undertaken to please herself. And although European Impressionism was the vogue among League students, she didn't see shattered prisms of light everywhere the way they did. Neither was she attracted to portrait painting, the social realism of the Henri group, or even to the fifty-eight Rodins. "They made no sense," she remembered. "They were very beautiful but really just a lot of little scribbles to me."

But although the Rodins did not fit in with anything Georgia was being taught, she had been interested enough to return to Stieglitz's "291" gallery in April to see a Matisse exhibition of equally abstracted forms. She wasn't ready to break artistic conventions herself, but an idea had taken root in her mind as she groped for self-expression. In time she would realize that an artist didn't always have to obey the rules and that, indeed, rules often had to be broken. Eight years later, in fact, she painted a series of nudes in reddish watercolors with a sparseness of line that startlingly echoed the Rodins. And thirty years later, when she saw a few of the Rodins again, she enjoyed them more than anything that Stieglitz had owned.

Nevertheless it's likely that Georgia was simply unable to return to New York because of her family crisis rather than for any other reason. Sixteen years later a League classmate was to write: "O'Keeffe will not admit to personal tragedies, although her face tells a story. . . . She only tells you that she had to give up the thing she had loved best, painting, in order to fit into the narrow hemmed-in existence which circumstances made for her. Painting remained her passion, but it was all or nothing. Since she could not devote herself to it, she never touched a brush, [and] could not bear the smell of paint or turpentine because of the emotions they aroused."

Georgia had first articulated her desire to become an artist when she was twelve, but now she was twenty and had to make her way in the world. It was extremely difficult for a woman to be a serious artist around the turn of the century—you were regarded as a "freak," according to sculptor Louise Nevelson. Furthermore, a female had to choose between art and marriage, and, perhaps, after her social whirl at the League, Georgia's will to forfeit marriage wavered. At any rate, how could she be an artist without the means of going to art school? Whatever the combination of reasons, around this time Georgia abandoned her adolescent ambition to be a painter. Adjusting rapidly to reality, perhaps to spare her father, she left Williamsburg two days before her twenty-first birthday to look for a job. The next few years were among the most difficult and wavering in her life as she struggled to survive in the world by herself. "If you were a young person, you had to find your own way the best you could," she once remarked, dismissing the subject.

When she left Williamsburg in November 1908, she headed to Chicago to live with her Totto relatives. There she found freelance work in the young advertising industry, mainly drawing lace and embroidery for dress advertisements. Since most of the ads were for daily newspapers, the illustrators who sketched rapidly enough to meet their deadlines were in demand. Georgia, who had learned to do a painting a day in Professor Chase's class, competed well and, afterwards, attributed her ability to paint quickly to her high-pressure career in commercial art. Apparently, she also came up with some good advertising ideas. Her sister Catherine, who visited Chicago at the time to recover from malaria, claimed that her sister created the bonneted Dutch girl chasing dirt with an upraised broom—an image still used today to sell cleanser.

Despite her skill, Georgia was learning the horror of meaningless work and seemed deeply unhappy, to the point where she would enter a Catholic church from time to time, to kneel silently in prayer. "There seemed no time to think of anything else, and she didn't want to think about advertising all the time," a friend explained afterwards. Georgia disliked Chicago, a crowded city of three million whose skies were often iron-gray, locked, cold, and thick with factory smoke.

Finally, after two years, she came down with the measles—which temporarily weakened her eyes, forcing her to give up detailed illustration work—and she returned to Virginia.

Upon arriving back in Williamsburg around 1910, Georgia found her parents living in the cinder-block house. Presumably her father hadn't been able to find a buyer for his eyesore, so in desperation he moved the family in after selling the big white house. Georgia also saw that her mother's health was tragically broken: She had been infected by the dreaded family tuberculosis, apparently by nursing her husband's youngest brother, and now, as family fortunes declined, the disease was activated. She rarely went downstairs now, lying night and day on the porch outside her bedroom, feverish, thin, and suffering from malaise. "We loved talking to Mrs. O'Keeffe because she was so gentle and sweet, but she would always be tired," said a Williamsburg girl who remembered that her dark eyes looked very large. At that time, when there were few drugs to treat consumption, tubercular patients felt constantly exhausted, coughed blood, and eventually died. A photograph taken of Mrs. O'Keeffe in the grip of the disease shows her dark brown hair streaked with gray, the fine bones of her face protruding sharply, her expression grim. Young Ida, meanwhile, is smiling ingratiatingly at the camera, her arms wrapped around her mother, who seems to lack the strength to sit up.

Francis O'Keeffe was now more deathly afraid than ever of the tuberculosis that had killed his three brothers, and his wife was bitterly disappointed by his business failures. Their unlikely marriage, which had functioned for the sake of the children for some time, was gravely strained. (The only time little Claudia remembered seeing any display of emotion between her parents was one Christmas when her mother thought that her father had helped himself to too much rum-laced eggnog.)

For several summers, Ida had gone to the University of Virginia summer school in Charlottesville, located in the mountainous part of the state. Apparently, her mother imagined that the college town, called "the Athens of the South," had advantages that the smaller, coastal Williamsburg lacked. For one thing, it had a sanatorium, and it was away from the damp, depressing concrete house where the rainwater trickled down the hollow inside walls. Furthermore, during the eight years that the O'Keeffes had lived in standoffish Williamsburg, they were never completely accepted. Beginning in 1909 Mrs.

O'Keeffe rallied enough to leave her dungeonlike home and to rent a house near the university in Charlottesville, where, with the help of her daughters, she began to take in student boarders.

Back in Williamsburg, Georgia found herself without any money, without much education, and with few prospects. At twenty-three, an age when many young women got married, she was still corresponding with one of her beaux whom she had met at the Art Students League three years before. He had hinted in his letters that he was about to take her abroad to Paris with him, at a time when this was the ambition of young American artists. Georgia later speculated that if the young man had come to Williamsburg and proposed to her, she would have married him. But when he sailed for Europe in early 1911 without visiting her in Virginia, her hope that anything would come of the romance faded.

Shortly after the young man's departure, her old Chatham mentor lent her a hand. Elizabeth May Willis had been pleased when Georgia returned to art school after her bout with typhoid, and now she was distressed to learn that her former pupil had given up art. In the spring of 1911, Mrs. Willis took a leave of absence for a few weeks and she asked Georgia to teach art in her place. Georgia readily agreed. In Chatham she renewed her boarding school friendship with Susan Young, who was engaged to marry. Probably inspired by the fashionable ones she had sketched in Chicago, Georgia stitched her friend a lacy white shirtwaist as a wedding gift, and quietly apologized for not being able to afford to buy her a present.

Ida and Francis O'Keeffe had gambled on a better life for their family in Virginia, but they had lost drastically and life became an agonizing downhill slide until the family fractured into two households. Although Georgia rarely, if ever, spoke about the family's misfortunes, it's clear that they affected her deeply. As she was thrown back on her own strength to make her way alone, her serious side emerged. The trauma also gave her a sharp eye for opportunities, a strain of toughness, and an edge of aggressiveness. "Georgia O'Keeffe has had her feet scorched in the laval effusiveness of terrible experience," wrote the artist Marsden Hartley in 1921 in his exaggerated style. Her work reflected a realistic understanding of the ability of life to silence "the spirit of adventure," he added. But Georgia's spirit had been shaped in Sun Prairie, so she saw the family troubles as temporary, and she was soon to escape them.

3 ❖ Search

Around 1912 Francis O'Keeffe left the house in Williamsburg, moved to Charlottesville, and opened a creamery. The family was reunited. Now all five O'Keeffe girls lived at home with their parents while their brothers were elsewhere, presumably working. When June came to the red-clay, emerald-green rolling farms of central Virginia, Ida and Anita enrolled once again in the summer school of the University of Virginia. The university had been conceived by Thomas Jefferson as an ideal academic community for young men. A classical Greek rotunda with soaring white columns, topped by an eagle, dominated a leafy sloping lawn, and the ivy-covered brick houses for the professors, linked by graceful colonnades, lined the rectangular green. Each summer the prestigious university lifted its ban on female students and instructed more than a thousand teachers-in-training for the Virginia public schools.

That summer Anita signed up for courses in southern literature, music, and drawing. Drawing was taught by a professor from the North, who, Anita quickly decided, had unusual ideas about art. She told her talented sister Georgia, who had given up art, that she was sure she would be interested. The middle child of seven siblings, Anita was a canny twenty-one-year-old to whom Georgia had learned to listen. So she went to the class with her, although in a highly skeptical frame of mind.

The sisters walked to the classroom, which was at the far end of the shady lawn, overlooking five ridges of soft lavender-hued hills, each more purple than the next, fading into the distance. The course was Drawing I, designed for elementary school teachers, and the instructor who had interested Anita was a funny little man who talked in clipped New England tones. He was Alon Bement, a rotund bachelor of thirty-seven, who was assistant professor of fine arts at Columbia University Teachers College in New York. Affected and effete, he was known as a performer who liked to make elegant gestures with his hands before a class. In a fabric design class, he used to make dramatic gyrations as he draped fabric over his shoulder and arm, then swirled around like a toreador. One of his associates at Columbia, Arthur Young, found him vain, foolish, and "curiously uninteresting."

But Bement was an associate of Arthur Wesley Dow, head of the fine arts department at Teachers College, and Dow's way of teaching art was quietly revolutionary. Unlike the instruction at most art schools, it had little to do with copying nature or the styles of the masters. Dow had devised exercises that enabled non-artists, even those who couldn't draw, to master the principles of design. "It was a freeing device so that you didn't have to draw feet, elbows or ankles," explained Young. Dow's exercises included dividing a square, working within a circle and enclosing a drawing with a rectangle, then balancing the composition by adding or eliminating elements and changing the placement of masses.

As Bement encouraged his pupils to create pleasing and inventive patterns of their own, Georgia, startled, listened intently. In most cases, the Dow method resulted in dull student work ("Mondrian muffled," in the words of Young) and it was abandoned after Dow's death in 1922, but for Georgia it suddenly provided intellectual underpinnings for art. Leafing through Dow's textbooks, *Composition* and *The Theory and Practice of Teaching Art*, she absorbed lessons on the aesthetics underlying paintings—in actuality, the principles of abstraction. The Dow method was a step beyond the realism that seemed purposeless to Georgia. It was also comprehensive. Dow's idea was very simple, Georgia later said, but it could be used to make every aesthtic decision. It also provided an alphabet, so to speak, that could be arranged and rearranged, resulting in a great deal of individualism. "It seemed equipment to go to work with," Georgia recalled. "Art could be a thing of your own."

The next morning, Georgia returned to the university and en-rolled in Bement's most advanced class, Drawing IV, which met late each weekday afternoon in what remained of the six-week summer session. Bement was immediately impressed by the new student. She caught on quickly and was far more skilled and original than any of the others, and he gave her a nearly perfect final grade of ninety-five. He learned that she had spent two years in art school and had worked professionally as an illustrator. He was so taken by the young woman, in fact, that he asked her to be one of his teaching assistants the next summer. Although Georgia's sisters made fun of Bement's exaggerated and effeminate mannerisms, she was willing to let him take her under his wing, and she readily agreed.

In the meantime, Bement offered to help her get a winter teaching position even though she lacked both a degree and, except for the few weeks she had taught at Chatham, teaching experience. After Georgia had written friends that she was looking for a schoolteaching job, her boarding school friend from Texas, Alice Beretta, wired her that the job of drawing supervisor in Amarillo had suddenly opened up. Georgia jumped at the opportunity. She had been excited as a child by the Wild West adventures she heard, and, undoubtedly, she was eager to get far away from the tedious chores and limited life of the family boardinghouse.

She soon landed the position, apparently after Bement or some-one else exaggerated her credentials. On August 15, 1912, the *Amarillo Daily News* proudly announced that the year's "drawing work will be under the supervision of Miss Georgia O'Keeffe, who has the highest degree known to her profession." Right after summer school ended in early August, Georgia, just shy of twenty-five, packed her warmest woolens in a truck and bought a train ticket that would get her to Amarillo, Texas, for a teacher's meeting on August 31.

❖

The locomotive chugged slowly toward the Texas Panhandle, an arid plateau shouldering its way up between Oklahoma on the east and New Mexico on the west. It had been buffalo and Comanche territory before cattlemen moved in and a few hardy squatters built shelters on the bald prairie. Railroads followed and, at the convergence of two of the lines, cattle drives terminated and the town of Amarillo sprang up. It was still cattle country when Georgia arrived in 1912, since no oil or gas had yet been pumped. A rough and rowdy frontier boom town with a population of fifteen thousand, Amarillo was inhabited by a mixture of merchants, lawyers, hotel proprietors, whores, barbers, and aging cowboys. More saloons than churches thrived in Amarillo, and, the autumn of Georgia's arrival, after the Grand Opera House had hosted a cattleman's convention, it featured a naughty girlie musical called *Miss Behave*.

Georgia was acutely aware of her lack of qualifications for her position, so she stayed aloof from the other teachers. Instead of rooming at one of the boardinghouses with her colleagues, she boarded by herself at the small, modest, wooden Magnolia Hotel on busy Polk Street where lilac bushes struggled to grow on either side of the steps. Since the other teachers thought she was unsociable as well as odd-looking in her plainly tailored outfits, her social life came to center around the lively life at the hotel. The Magnolia's dining room was popular with the ravenous cowboys fresh from the cattle drives whose lips were blistered by the sun and eyes were bloodshot from the wind. Georgia watched with amazement as they wolfed down two or three complete dinners in one sitting. Hard drinkers, old-timers, loose women, and card sharks also frequented the hotel, and she heard vivid talk about outlaws, cattle rustlers, and violent frontier justice. Perhaps some of it reminded her of stories she had heard about the Wisconsin frontier when Indians used to peek in the windows of log cabins.

After she had been in town only two weeks, she had a tale of her own to tell. On a Saturday night, September 14, she was playing dominoes in the hotel's back room with other guests when three shots rang out. She rushed to the door with the others and saw a black-bearded rancher approaching, a derby pulled down over his eyes and a sawed-off shotgun in his hand. As he passed the hotel, one of the women in the doorway called, "What's the trouble?" "Nothing," the man replied evenly. "I've got him." Across the street lay the body of his victim, who, onlookers later learned, had run off with his wife. The gunman, a wealthy cotton rancher named Beal Sneed, had already knocked off the dead man's father, a prominent banker, for insulting him. The nickel newspapers ran headlines about the scandal until the end of the trial, when the gunman was acquitted after ten minutes of deliberation. His lawyers let out cowboy yelps at the news of the courtroom victory.

In addition to following the shoot-outs, newspaper headlines warned of deadly twisters, dust storms, and prairie fires on the wide plains around Amarillo that were vaster than the Wisconsin prairie. While the shoot-'em-up antics of the town amused Georgia, she was serious in her wonder at the flat brown land with the kaleidoscopic sunrises and sunsets that played over it. When she walked to where the wood sidewalks ended at the edge of town, it was as if she were standing on top of the world and seeing the sky for the first time. Day after day its blueness arched above her, with only an occasional white billowy thunderhead racing across it. She could see so far that she was able to detect the approaching weather. She could also spot cattle drives a few days away—first by a puff of brown on the pale blue horizon, and then by sparks of cowboy campfires twinkling like tiny stars in the inky nights.

The wind beat constantly, sometimes gusting wildly, and drove everything before it that was not nailed down: tumbleweeds, shingles, buggies, and, above all, great clouds of dust. It also carried the mournful lowing of the cattle that were separated from their calves and penned near the railroad station for shipment to big city stockyards. Georgia later observed that the sparsely populated land contained the same raw power and sudden terrifying violence as the sea, and she noted at dusk that a mirage effect sometimes made it ripple like surf. The unleashed forces of nature seemed to meet, and free, some similar emotional energy in Georgia, and, instead of intimidating her, their wildness and unpredicatability made her euphoric and repeatedly she enthusiastically described them as "beautiful." For the rest of her life she would speak of the plains as her spiritual home. "That was my country—terrible winds and a wonderful emptiness," she later said.

As "supervisor of drawing and penmanship," Georgia was responsible for the art education of hundreds of pupils in Amarillo's half-dozen schools. Determined to succeed in her new profession, which promised to be more gratifying than commercial art, she knuckled down to learn the job. It was a challenge for many reasons, among them the fact that much of what she had learned during the brief weeks in Alon Bement's class was useless in Texas. One exercise he taught, for example, called for children to arrange maple leaves into seven-inch squares—but most of the pitifully few trees in Amarillo were scraggly locusts with leaves too small to use. Georgia's pupils, too poor to buy fruits and flowers to bring to class, were able to find little more than ragweed and round pebbles to draw. Georgia enjoyed the children, particularly the naturally gifted Mexican ones, and sympathetically tried to invent solutions to her problem. "I'd get them to draw a square and put a door in it somewhere—anything to start them thinking about how to divide a space," she remembered.

Despite such difficulties and her teaching inexperience, Georgia soon went to the defense of Dow's ideas. In his writings, Dow had praised the freedom and freshness of children's designs, and he maintained that they should draw objects from their everyday lives so they wouldn't be inhibited. Georgia, herself, fiercely opposed the old-fashioned teaching technique of "copying," and she told her pupils not to buy an expensive drawing book full of exotic objects that had been recommended by the educators. In the spring of 1913, however, the Texas legislature passed a law requiring the use of textbooks chosen by the state commission. When Georgia returned to Amarillo the following fall, the school superintendent ordered her to buy the drawing books. Law or no law, Georgia had taken a principled stand and she stubbornly refused to obey. A tense, lengthy struggle between Georgia O'Keeffe and the state of Texas ensued—but when the school year ended, the books had not been bought.

Upon Georgia's return to Charlottesville in the spring of 1913, she found in the century-old campus, apple and peach orchards, meadows full of thoroughbreds, and the decorum of Virginia life a sharp contrast to Texas. Although she received a job offer in another state at several hundred dollars more a year, she declined it, preferring to continue to go back and forth between her Virginia life and the one in Texas. In the West she had found a wild, desolate land that called out to her strongly and, in one sense or another, she would always feel its pull.

❖

For four summers, from 1913 through 1916, Georgia returned to Charlottesville to teach drawing at the university. The campus was a ten-minute walk from the solid red-brick house that the O'Keeffes had rented on hilly Wertland Street. Few of the people in the middle-class neighborhood, made up largely of professors and old families, got to know the midwesterners well, partly because newcomers weren't easily accepted and partly because the family members tended to keep to themselves as they grappled with illness and poverty. Mrs. O'Keeffe, who had made most of the social overtures in Williamsburg, was now an invalid. Nevertheless, the O'Keeffes maintained a respectable facade, and neighbors came to think of them as different and independent, but also pleasant and fine people.

The first summer Georgia spent as one of Alon Bement's teaching assistants, she taught two intermediate classes for high school art teachers. One of her students was her sister Anita. Georgia sensed that her younger sister was very gifted and later remarked that she would have painted circles around her oldest sister if she had not been afraid to free her imagination on paper. But although Georgia gave Anita A's, she couldn't give her the kind of boldness she needed. The experience later made Georgia realize that besides talent, an artist needed to have the daring—"nerve," she called it—to paint well. But Nita (as Anita was called), with her large brown eyes and the type of conventional round-faced prettiness that cast her in the role of family beauty, was an assertive middle child with a strong instinct for survival, and she chose a traditional path. She was the first of the O'Keeffe sisters to marry—in 1916—and the young university student she chose eventually became a millionaire businessman.

When she wasn't teaching, Georgia enthusiastically took long walking and camping trips through the mountainous countryside with her sisters and university friends. An anecdote survives from an August day in 1913 when Georgia, two sisters, and two boarders set out by foot for Monticello, Thomas Jefferson's mansion, three miles outside of Charlottesville. Two of the O'Keeffe girls went ahead to get some ice cream from their father's creamery, then met the others at the foot of the streetcar line. After Georgia had divided up the ice cream and they had started up the mountainside, they heard horse's hooves and turned to see a horse-drawn runabout coming around a bend. "A nice-looking young man plainly showed his astonishment at what he saw— five girls, each carrying a saucer of ice cream," recalled Iantha Bond, one of the boarders. "Someone waved a hand. He removed his hat with a bow and was gone."

At the university, Bement acted as Georgia's mentor, talking her work over with her in a tactful manner and, at first, encouraging her to follow her instincts. She was painting pictures in her small basement studio of the hollyhocks in her backyard as well as what she recollected from her excursions; for example, she did a watercolor bordering on abstraction in shades of blue of the night sky framed by the tent opening. Called *Tent Door at Night*, the painting's strong curves and verticals suggest much later mature work. But, more important, Bement was a conduit to the heady new ideas about art that were infiltrating New York. Through him she discovered two books that were important to her development. He told her that one had important ideas (Wassily Kandinsky's *On the Spiritual in Art*, translated into English in 1914), while the other had important pictures (Jerome Eddy's *Cubists and Post-Impressionism*, in which she saw her first abstraction, of leaf forms, by the American painter Arthur Dove).

Bement had often urged his talented assistant to study directly with Arthur Dow in New York at Columbia Teachers College. By the summer of 1914, Georgia decided to find a way to do it. Although the plains of Texas thrilled her, she found herself, after two winters there, locked in a battle with the authorities over teaching methods. If she left her postion to go to college in New York, she would not have to capitulate to the Texas textbook law. What's more, she undoubtedly had fond memories of the winter of 1907–1908 when she had been a well-liked, prize-winning pupil at the Art Students League.

Planning carefully, Georgia persuaded the couple who boarded with her family to remain for the winter—everyone, she pleaded earnestly with them, deserved the chance for an education. At the time it was typical for a young woman to have to snatch educational opportunities from domestic duties or when enough tuition and travel money could be borrowed or saved from meager wages. Georgia was successful in her campaign for freedom, and at the end of the summer she resigned her job in Amarillo and, now almost twenty-seven years old, headed for New York City.

❖

Compared to the time when Georgia had studied in New York seven years earlier, the city was now in ferment over many new ideas and it was evident that the safe old Victorian conventions were gone forever. Pretty, plump Mabel Dodge, for one, was hosting "evenings" in her white parlor, where current issues such as socialism, free love, and Freudianism were hotly discussed. Greenwich Village had emerged as a bohemia in which Eugene O'Neill was writing bold new plays, intellectuals—like Max Eastman who edited *The Masses*—published radical little magazines, feminists like Ida Rauh and Neith Boyce agitated for birth control and the vote for women, and artists who had studied in Europe experimented with the new theories of abstract art.

Old assumptions about art had been vigorously shaken the previous winter of 1913 when hundreds of avant-garde European and American paintings had been exhibited at the New York Armory—pictures that only Alfred Stieglitz had dared to show in previous years. Perhaps the greatest furor was created by Marcel Duchamp's *Nude Descending a Staircase*, a cubist abstraction of a body in motion, which was ridiculed in the newspapers as "shingles descending a staircase." If Georgia's old professors at the League had been irritated when Stieglitz showed the Rodins, they were outraged by the Armory show. Kenyon Cox attacked it as the work of a group of "savages." And William Merritt Chase, who had not been invited to exhibit, did not know what to make of it.

But Arthur Dow, a reserved Bostonian who had studied with Gauguin and other postimpressionists in Brittany at the time of Georgia's birth, had a much greater understanding of the new and tolerance for experimentation than her old League instructors. "Art is decadent when designers and painters lack inventive power and merely imitate nature or the creations of others," Dow had written. "Then comes realism, conventionality, and the death of art." His tastes had turned him away from the naturalism of Europe taught by the academicians. Gentle, slender, soft-spoken, Dow was a great admirer of the order, tranquillity, and reverence for nature to be seen in the flattened forms of the Japanese prints he ardently admired and privately collected.

Since Georgia hadn't studied in Paris and been drilled in its European ideas and techniques, she was more open to Dow's influence than others. But his views also seemed in accord with her natural tendency. She preferred the organic wholeness of Oriental forms to shattered cubist shapes, liking the work of such Europeans as Henri Rousseau, who respected the integrity of natural forms. Dow's influence on O'Keeffe was profound and long-lasting. "The artistic mind is always trying to find new ways of expressing a beautiful idea," Dow had written, believing that the creation of beauty was the purpose of art. In her ninetieth year, Georgia was to say: "Filling a space in a beautiful way—that is what art means to me."

By the time Georgia got to Teachers College in 1914, smiling

"Patsy" of the Art Students League had become a serious woman whom people called "Pat." Much older than her classmates and far more mature, she said little and what she did say was forthright, thoughtful, and intelligent. She seemed ravenously curious about new paintings and ideas. "There was something insatiable about her—as direct as an arrow and hugely independent," observed a classmate named Anita Pollitzer. Since she had very little money, she doled out her dollars carefully. She slept in a small, ascetic four-dollar-a-week room that was bare of any personal touches except for a pot of blazing geraniums visible outside the window on the fire escape.

Her Kandinsky book had equated color waves with sound vibrations, and Dow had written that the curve of a line or the repetition of a motif could create an elevated emotional reaction exactly the way music did. One day at Teachers College, Georgia passed a classroom where Bement was teaching and heard music coming from a Victrola. The pupils were making rapid charcoal sketches to the sound of a low-tone, somber rhythmic record, and then to one with higher, faster notes. Fascinated, Georgia sat down and began to draw too, and made an abstraction of floating curves, squares, and lines. Music was her second love and this seemed a way to integrate it with art. Later, she was to carry this fusion further and paint fantastical abstractions based on her rhapsodic feelings about music.

Since she only had enough money to study for one winter, Georgia was careful about how she spent her time. A dance craze had hit New York and a number of restaurants were converting themselves into cabarets so customers could do the Castle walk (popularized by Vernon and Irene Castle) and other new dance steps. Although Georgia loved to dance, she refrained from joining the current mania because if she went dancing at night, she discovered, she was too depleted to paint well the next day. Painting was clearly her first priority now. Color was becoming a rich idiom for her and she went "color mad" that winter, she later confessed. "Her colors were always the brightest, her palette the cleanest, her brushes the best—although to accomplish this she would do without much else," Anita Pollitzer said.

Georgia's grades at Teachers College reveal her growing focus on painting. She did well in creative courses, but, although she was a fine arts education major in a B.S. program, she did surprisingly poorly in the teacher-education requirements. She got a low C in principles of teaching, for example, and received a D in English, probably as a result of her ineffectual struggle to spell correctly. Since she had done well in non-art courses in high school, her undistinguished grades at Teachers College suggest that she was neglecting courses that seemed boring or irrelevant to her, and are proof of the distance she had traveled since her obedient schoolgirl days. In a job recommendation written in July 1915, Professor Dow hedged about her teaching credentials but not about her ability as an artist. Since she had not taken his senior teaching methods course, he would only say that he had heard excellent reports about her teaching. He went on to praise her cleverness, originality in design and handicrafts, and her excellence in drawing and oil painting. "Miss O'Keeffe is an exceptional person in many ways," he wrote. "She is one of the most talented people in art that we have ever had."

She got an A from redheaded Professor Charles Martin, who allowed her and two other students of outstanding ability to sit behind a screen and draw still lifes of their choice while the less advanced pupils drew plaster casts in the main part of the classroom. One of the three students was Dorothy True, a curvaceous girl from Maine, and the other was Anita Pollitzer, the twenty-year-old daughter of a prosperous Jewish cotton broker in Charleston, South Carolina. Anita was the kind of girl who rushed enthusiastically from one thing to the next, forgetting about the smudges of paint in her brown hair, usually carrying a pile of sketch pads, sheet music, and political periodicals under her arm. When she saw the Picassos at 291, for instance, she appeared "radiant, a hundred per cent alive, intelligent, unafraid of her own emotions," Alfred Stieglitz remembered.

Despite their age and temperamental differences, Georgia and Anita were drawn to one another. Anita, the youngest daughter in her family, treated Georgia like an adored older sister. Georgia responded affectionately, and eventually trusted Anita with some of her deepest feelings, expressed in letters after the school year was over. When they first met, they shared an eagerness for life, a love of music, excitement about the new ideas in art, and enthusiasm for the suffragette movement. Georgia, who had seen front-page stories in Amarillo newspapers about the massive suffragette march in Washington, D.C., the day before Woodrow Wilson's inauguration in early 1913, learned that Anita was a member of the militant National Woman's Party. Anita described the drive to win the vote to her friend, and Georgia joined the NWP and kept up her membership in it for three decades.

Sometimes the friends took the long trolley ride from Morningside Heights at 120th Street to Mr. Stieglitz's gallery on lower Fifth Avenue at Thirty-first Street, where the first Picassos and Cézannes in America had been displayed. Thousands of people a year were drawn there, to hear Stieglitz's rambling monologues on a wide range of subjects, delivered in his low, rich, resonant voice in words that could be mischievous, bitter, or exuberant. Someone who grasped personality by intuition, he was once compared to "a Japanese teacher who produced illuminations by jolts, contradictions and rudeness," in the words of one writer. Stieglitz exalted in defending the spirit of the artist in the face of repressions from society—for which he had been called an "arch satanist." But he was able to transmit courage to younger listeners, several of whom could always be seen perched on packing crates, the odd chair, or, most often, just standing around him. At mealtimes he used to lead whatever followers were around across the street to the dining room of the fashionable Holland House, to continue their arguments there. He always picked up the check, which was ultimately paid by his wealthy wife of twenty-two years, the former Emmeline Obermeyer, heiress of a brewery fortune.

At the time, intellectuals were talking excitedly about creating a new American culture, free at last of European domination. Stieglitz, accordingly, was trying to nourish an indigenous art by encouraging and exhibiting the paintings and photographs of promising young Americans. He deeply believed that American society needed its own artists, and he wanted the country to support these artists by buying their works. He was fighting against great odds—even the Armory show had tended to inhibit the expression of anything genuinely American because of its overwhelmingly European slant. Georgia, of course, had been in Amarillo and had missed the exhibit, so she got her exposure to European painting in smaller doses.

That winter she went with some friends to a show of Braque and Picasso drawings at which Mr. Stieglitz presided. He began to ask her friends some probing, personal questions. The great photographer's deep-set eyes "were like two powerful lenses," wrote Mabel Dodge, "and when he turned them upon one they burned through to the core." Georgia, who rarely shared her deepest feelings, particularly with strangers, was alarmed and kept her distance. Nevertheless, Stieglitz's "laboratory" of ideas, as he liked to call it, continued to exert its magnetic effect. "I didn't understand some of the things he showed, but it was a new wave, I knew that," she remembered. "It showed you how you could make up your mind about what to paint."

After this visit, Georgia went to Stieglitz's show of pictures by the American watercolorist, John Marin. Dispirited, Stieglitz told her, an unknown and penniless young woman on the fringe of the art world, that the money he had made for Marin to live on for a year had been squandered by the artist on the purchase of an island in Maine. Georgia, looking at the Marins, thought that the succinct splatters of color were strange but also quite wonderful. But the question uppermost on her mind was whether Marin was able to make a living by painting such pictures. She asked Stieglitz if a particular blue crayon abstraction had sold, and when he nodded yes, she realized with a start that perhaps one *could* make a living by painting as one wished. Georgia later wrote Anita that she returned to 291 one last time at the end of the season when the walls were bare, just to soak up the ambience.

❖

In June 1915, Georgia had only a few weeks remaining between the end of the spring semester at Columbia Teachers College and the beginning of summer school at the University of Virginia. After the stimulating winter in New York, she was restless and discontent with her work. The placid patterns and balanced harmonies of Dow's tidy exercises could not contain the strong feelings that sometimes welled up within her—emotions that matched the excesses of the Texas plains. Dow, a low-key man, shunned violent colors and strong contrasts, even preferring muted black and off-white to pure white or black. "I was liking such snorting things," Georgia complained in a letter to Anita, and "his [pictures] seemed so disgustingly tame to me." But Dow did not submit his highly gifted students to rigid exercises, and his ideas, which had drawn her back to art three years before, would allow her to go on beyond him and his disciples.

Georgia also felt increasingly impatient with Alon Bement's timid suggestions about painting. Bement was considered a designer by his peers, not a painter, and his advice was geared to teachers of art, not artists. The uselessness of his advice, however, forced Georgia to seach for her own way, which turned out to be an advantage, she later acknowledged. "I had a teacher who was very good because he didn't know anything," is the way she later put it. Rebelliously, she began to tell her classes at the University of Virginia to ignore his advice about painting. Although Bement never felt she recognized her debt to him afterwards, she continued to refer to him fondly, if somewhat condescendingly, in letters.

Furthermore, after her winter in New York, Bement's suggestions about what to read and see were no longer necessary because she had begun to forge her own tenuous links to the avant-garde. She subscribed to the radical Greenwich Village newspaper, *The Masses*, as well as to Stieglitz's beautifully printed quarterly, *Camera Work*, which had been published for a few hundred sophisticated subscribers since 1903. Besides fine reproductions of modern art, the latter contained provocative articles such as homages to Picasso and Matisse by Gertrude Stein. Georgia was so enthusiastic that she sent for back issues. She also sent for the new satirical magazine, *291*, which liked to lampoon conventional art galleries and their visitors. Georgia even decided that Anita Pollitzer could give her more valuable feedback than Bement, and that summer she began sending her friend watercolors rolled up in tubes.

She now talked excitedly about modern art in her classes. One of her students, Margaret Davis, had only seen traditional art previously. She found Miss O'Keeffe a fascinating, surprising teacher of "verve, confidence and charm" who told her eighteen students how to relate personally, directly, and even joyfully to the new art. "Even my very short exposure to her teaching has afforded me great freedom emotionally and psychologically in my response to art," Margaret recalled many years later. "I do feel that much of the joy that I've experienced in the world of art has been strongly laced with that one summer session of 1915 with Miss O'Keeffe as teacher."

Georgia was also enjoying herself immensely outside the classroom. She took long walking trips throgh the soft, verdant Virginia countryside with Arthur Macmahon, a good-looking, gentle New York intellectual from Columbia University who was teaching government at the university summer school. Arthur was struck by the drawing teacher's extraordinary sensitivity to the beauty of nature, a response that involved all her senses. She liked to rub a leaf between her fingers to feel its velvety texture or, in a daring action for that era, thrust her unstockinged feet into streams to feel the pulsations of the water.

Arthur described his liberal political theories to her and recommended that she read feminist books. (One of them, *Women As World Builders* by Floyd Dell, urged women to abandon conventional roles in order to develop their talents and become better comrades to men.) In turn, Georgia told the young professor—surely the kind of person who would have encouraged her in her ambition to be an artist—about art, and raved about him to Anita. A few weeks before the end of summer school, probably with the idea of a gift for Arthur in mind, she arranged her hair into a modified pompadour, slipped on a handsome striped shirtwaist and a white skirt, and was photographed in a Charlottesville photo studio.

After summer school ended and Arthur returned to New York, Georgia had to find a job for fall. She toyed with the idea of getting work in New York, but realized that her energy would be absorbed by earning money in the expensive city and, perhaps, also by people. She applied for the postion of drawing supervisor for the schools of Wilmington, Delaware. Then a job at a teachers college for women in South Carolina was offered, but even though it was a job on the college level and represented a career advancement, she was hesitant about accepting it. What made her consider it was the fact that the job required she teach only four classes a week, so she anticipated that there would be many free hours for painting. "I had gotten a lot of new ideas and was crazy to get off in a corner and try them out," she said.

While making up her mind, she took long walks at dawn, read, painted, and stitched some underwear. Again, as with the decision about whether or not to model at the Art Students League, she saw the issue as a conflict between nourishing her social or artistic selves and heeding her immediate or far-off desires. In a pattern that was to persist all her life, she kept her options open and told friends that she didn't know what she would do until she did it. Finally, just four days before the women's college opened in September, Georgia wired her acceptance with a heavy heart.

❖

Columbia, an old Confederate city in the heart of South Carolina cotton country, still bore the scars of General Sherman's cannonballs in the side of its elegant state capitol. Two miles outside of Columbia by streetcar was Columbia College, which specialized in training South

Carolina girls to become music teachers. When Georgia arrived in the fall of 1915, the brick college looked forlorn. It had recently been rebuilt after a disastrous fire and it stood among piles of rubble on a treeless hill. And with the First World War raging in Europe, causing the bottom to fall out of the cotton market, many families could no longer afford to pay their daughters' tuition, and the college was deeply in debt. Only about one hundred and fifty girls and a handful of teachers were on campus that year. The faculty members had been released from their contracts—and most had left— because there was no money to pay them. Undoubtedly the college had offered Georgia a position at a salary even lower than its meager standard because she lacked a degree.

The milieu of southern femininity in which Georgia exiled herself was excruciating to her at first. Many of her colleagues at the pious Methodist college were silly and vacuous, she thought, and she wondered if she had the strength to remain aloof from their lassitude and to keep herself from stagnating. Characteristically, she seemed most interested in the young faculty chidren. She delighted four-year-old Cecelia Ariail with a sketch of her doll, and then pleased her father, gregarious Latin professor James Ariail, from Chicago, by giving him a large portrait of his dark-haired daughter. It was little Cecelia who innocently pointed out how Miss O'Keeffe differed from the others. One evening, when Georgia had combed her hair into a severe bun and put on a plain black dress with a square white bodice, the child exclaimed that the art teacher looked like "a little man." Long accustomed to such comments in the South, Georgia was more amused than embarrassed.

Soon she turned to nature for pleasure, and her spirits began to revive. When her teaching duties ended in midafternoon, she liked to go for long walks in the piny woods around the college in the foothills of the Appalachians, collecting large flaming bunches of chrysanthemums and other fall flowers with which she filled her dormitory room. In her letters, she marveled at the gloriously warm southern autumn, and she continued to wear her white summer dresses into November.

Her mood was also buoyed up be a lifeline of letters from friends in New York. Arthur Macmahon, back teaching at Columbia University, was sending her tender letters. Anita Pollitzer, now a senior at Columbia Teachers College and sensing her loneliness, wrote her almost daily in her changeable, messy, childlike scrawl about professors, concerts, books, and her frequent, spellbinding visits to Stieglitz's gallery. Georgia wrote Anita often in return, and also continued to send watercolors, about which she knew Anita would be perceptive, encouraging, and sometimes rhapsodic.

Gradually, Georgia became absorbed in her art. She claimed a small studio next to the larger art classroom where she could work undisturbed between classes and meetings. As she had accurately predicted, there was plenty of time. "Hibernating in South Carolina is an experience that I would not advise anyone to miss," she wrote a few months later. "The place is of so little consequence—except for the outdoors—that one has a chance to give one's mind, time, and attention to anything one wishes." With few people around to talk to, she began to grapple with such philosophical questions as the meaning of art and why one painted. She had mastered the artist's tools, she realized, but wondered to what purpose. Meanwhile, she struggled tenaciously, persistently painting the same picture over and over, determined to break the impasse, driving herself to paint every day and feeling guilty when she didn't.

She also wrestled with the question of whether to paint for herself or for others, and, if the latter, for whom? She thought it would be wonderful to impress Alfred Stieglitz, still a remote giant of a figure to whom she had only spoken a few words in the seven years she had known about his gallery. Even though his volatile personality and searching questions had alarmed her, she knew that he was the only person in New York who was interested in the art of Americans working in a modern idiom. She wrote Anita:

> I believe I would rather have Stieglitz like something—
> anything I had done—than anyone else I know of—I
> have always felt that—If I ever make anything that satis
> fies me even ever so little—I am going to show it to him
> to find out if it is any good. Don't you often wish you
> could make something he would like?

Then she declared to her friend with bravado, "I don't see why we ever think of what others think of what we do—no matter who they are—isn't it enough just to express yourself?"

One day in the middle of October, Georgia went into her studio, shut the door, and turned the key. She was still dissatisfied with her work, and she didn't know why. She hung her most recent drawings and watercolors on the walls. Then she analyzed them with ruthless detachment: She noted which ones were painted to please one professor, and those to please another; she noticed which well-known artists had influenced other pictures. She sat, looked, and thought. Then an idea dawned on her. There were abstract shapes in her mind, integral to her imagination, unlike anything she had been taught. "This thing that is our own is so close to you, often you never realize it's there," she later explained. "I visualize things very clearly. I could think of a whole string of things I'd like to put down but I'd never thought of doing it because I'd never seen anything like it." Although she didn't know exactly how she would express these "things," it suddenly seemed very simple. She made up her mind: This was what she would paint.

To Georgia, recalling her breakthrough seven years later, art still represented the kind of freedom of expression that it had when she was a teen-ager:

> I grew up pretty much as everybody else grows up and one day seven years ago found myself saying to myself—I can't live where I want to—I can't go where I want to—I can't do what I want to—I can't even say what I want to—. School and things that painters have taught me even keep me from painting as I want to. I decided I was a very stupid fool not to at least paint as I wanted to and say what I wanted to when I painted as that seemed to be the only thing I could do that didn't concern anybody but myself—that was nobody's business but my own.

Georgia put all her work away ("I feel disgusted with it all and am glad I'm disgusted," she wrote to Anita) in order to rid her mind completely of the influence of others. She also put away her watercolor box, feeling a distaste for the distraction of color. She decided to work only in black and white until she had exhausted all their possibilities. Toward the end of her twenty-seventh year she started all over again, in the simplest way, with charcoal. "It was like learning to walk," she remembered.

Every night she spread rough student sketch paper on her bedroom floor and crawled around it, rubbing it with charcoal, until her body ached and the charcoal crumbled into powder beneath her fingers.

Her right hand became so sore that it was painful for her to hold a pen to write a letter, she complained to Anita, but she would attempt to relax by trying to coax music from a borrowed violin. During those weeks her emotions, heightened by loving letters from Arthur, see-sawed between euphoria and despair. Sometimes she wondered whether the abstract shapes that leapt into her mind's eye meant that she was crazy—not an illogical thought since both creativity and insanity have been linked to the ability to perceive reality differently. But now that she was expressing images that were hers alone, she often worked in an excited, elated state of pure pleasure, totally in tune with herself—and, she declared to Anita, at those times she didn't care if she *was* a lunatic. Those weeks were a high point in her life, a state of grace, which she would always try to re-create. "I was alone and singularly free, working into my own, unknown—no one to satisfy but myself," she recalled.

Others who later looked at those abstractions saw a violent clash of explosive emotions, fueled by erotic energy, which threatened to tear the artist apart. Sharp edges grated against soft forms. Undulating shapes leapt up like flames reaching for oxygen. One of the drawings, later labeled *Number Nine*, showed volcanolike fissures erupting with fire and steam that she visualized during one of the frequent, severe headaches with which she was afflicted at the time.

She had the clear insight that she was revealing a female sensibility. "The thing seems to express in a way what I wanted it to but—it also seems rather effeminate—it is essentially a woman's feeling—[it] satisfies me in a way," she confided to Anita. A few years later, however, when male art critics began to belabor this point, she tended to reject irritably as exaggerations their rhetoric on the subject.

Georgia wondered if her heightened feelings meant that she was falling in love. When Arthur wrote in November to say that he was coming down to visit for Thanksgiving, she was ecstatic. During his four-day holiday she felt great happiness, and the two made plans to spend the summer together with his family in the North Carolina mountains.

After Macmahon had returned to New York, however, Georgia felt disoriented, depressed, and estranged from her work. Partly because of the struggle to reimmerse herself in her drawings, she resisted the temptation to go to New York for Christmas. She stayed at the empty college over the holidays even though she ended up working only once—from early one evening straight through the night to daybreak. As the months went by, she seemed to back away from the romance, trying to divert her intensified feelings into art. The feminists of the day viewed love as as obstacle to women's creativity. "The woman who finds her work will find her love—and I do not doubt cherish it bravely," Floyd Dell had written. "But the woman who sets her love alone above everything else I would gently dismiss . . . as belonging to the courtesan type." Painting was still her paramount priority. She pledged to keep her head clear and conserve her energy for art, and she vowed not to get carried away by infatuation again.

❖

On the first day of 1916, Anita Pollitzer received an unregistered roll of charcoal drawings in the mail from South Carolina. Georgia had told her not to show them around Teachers College, so Anita took the tube into a classroom and locked the door behind her. She spread the drawings out on the floor and stared at their unusual shapes, deeply affected by the emotions they expressed. "I was struck by their aliveness," she recalled later. "They were different. Here were charcoals—on the same kind of paper that all art students were using, and through no trick, no superiority of tools, these drawings were saying something that had not yet been said."

After spending an hour with them, Anita rolled them up again, put the tube under her arm, and left for a Saturday matinee of *Peter Pan*. Late in the afternoon, the theater emptied, she found herself walking with the roll of drawings through the dark, chilly, rainy city streets to Stieglitz's gallery, where, she felt strongly, her friend's powerfully uttered black-and-white feelings belonged. It was a brave impulse. Many art students were terrified to ask Mr. Stieglitz even a simple question because he was famous for answering impatiently. Also, Georgia was extremely sensitive about who saw her pictures. She had admitted to Anita in the fall: "I always have a curious sort of feeling about some of my things—I hate to show them—I am perfectly inconsistent about it—I am afraid people won't understand—and I hope they won't—and am afraid they will. Then too they will probably be all mussed up." But Georgia had also made it clear in letters that it was Stieglitz's approval, above all, that she wanted.

When Anita got to 291, she discovered that the rickety elevator was broken so she walked up the four flights of stairs to the little attic gallery. Stieglitz was alone, Anita recalled, "weary and discouraged" after a long day of Saturday visitors. Anita politely asked him if he would like to see what she had under her arm. Recognizing her as a frequent visitor and always curious, Stieglitz nodded yes and led her behind a gray curtain to a semi-private room in back. She unrolled the charcoals and spread them out on the floor in the dim yellow light. Stieglitz looked at each sheet of paper closely, saying nothing. Then he looked through them again. Finally he looked up and smiled at Anita. Legend has it—and the story has been told and retold—that he dramatically declared, "At last, a woman on paper!", but Anita's earliest recollection of the moment, in the letter she immediately wrote to Georgia, omits this famous remark. Still, it is likely that Stieglitz thought something of the sort for he evidently was astounded by the strong female sensitivity he perceived in the lines of the drawings.

Stieglitz had admired and exhibited women who were first-rate photographers, like Anne Brigman and Gertrude Kasebier. The first female nonphotographer he had exhibited was artist Pamela Colman Smith in 1907, and he had shown the work of two other women, Marion Beckett and Katharine N. Rhoades, in 1915. He though that the female experience was spiritually distinct from that of the male, and that it left women more "advanced" and freer of society's inhibitions than American men. Stieglitz was fascinated by the rarely expressed female viewpoint, and his expectations of finding it had been raised by the outburst of feminism. Looking at Georgia's drawings, he thought that perhaps this was the exceptional woman who was big enough to dare reveal herself on paper. Clearly she was unique. He told Anita to tell her friend that the drawings were the "purest, finest, sincerest things that have entered 291 in a long while." Then he added that he wouldn't mind showing them sometime.

Upon her return to her room with the charcoals, Anita excitedly wrote to Georgia, confessing what she had done. Georgia immediately wrote back, thanking her. Although Anita had ignored her instructions not to show the drawings to anyone, the younger woman had correctly sensed, and acted on, her friend's deeper need for encouragement from Stieglitz. It's also probable that Georgia, who knew that being sponsored by Stieglitz could mean survival for a young artist, had actually wanted Anita to act as a go-between—and years later she admitted that she would not have risked incurring devastating criticism by taking her work there herself. Her answer to Anita's confession went, in part:

> I had just about decided it wasn't any use to keep on amusing myself ruining perfectly good paper trying to express myself . . . there are things we want to say—but saying them is pretty nervy—What reason have I for getting the notion that I want to say something and must say it.—
>
> Of course, marks on paper are free—free speech—press—pictures all go together I suppose—but I was just feeling rather downcast about it—and it is so nice to feel that I said something to you and to Stieglitz. I wonder what I said—I wonder if any of you got what I tried to say—Isn't it damnable that I can't talk to you. If Stieglitz says any more about them—ask him why he liked them.
>
> Anyway, Anita—it makes me want to keep on—and I had almost decided it was a fool's game.

Next, Georgia impulsively wrote Stieglitz and asked him bluntly what he liked about her drawings. Stieglitz briefly replied that he would have to tell her in person. On February 1, Georgia answered him in a rambling letter, describing her solitude, her urge to express herself on paper, and, again and again, her desire to talk with him.

> Mr. Stieglitz—
> I like what you write me—Maybe I don't get exactly your meaning—but I like mine—like you liked your interpretation of my drawings.
>
> It was such a surpise to me that you saw them—I am so glad they surprised you—that they gave you joy. I am glad I could give you once what 291 has given to me many times—
>
> You can't imagine how it all astonishes me.
>
> I have just been trying to express myself—I just have to say things you know—Words and I—are not good friends at all except with some people—when I'm close to them

and can feel as well as hear their response—I have to say
it someway— . . .

I can't tell you how sorry I am that I can't talk to you—
What I've been thinking surprises me so—has been such
fun—at times has hurt too—that it would be great to tell
you. . .

After she sealed the letter, she scribbled on the back of the envelope:

I put this in the envelope—stretched—and laughed. It's
so funny that I should just write you because I want to. I
wonder if many people do,—You see—I would go in and
talk to you if I could—and I hate to be outdone by a
little thing like distance.

In South Carolina the warm February sun was incubating an early
spring, and Georgia was increasingly restless. "Some of the fields are
green—very very green—almost unbelievably green against the dark
of the pine woods—and it's warm—the air feels warm and soft—and
lovely—," she wrote Stieglitz. Instead of introspection, she now wanted
reaction, particularly from Stieglitz, the advocate of everything new,
bold, and authentic in art, in order to get a sense of the value of her
first efforts at genuinely expressing herself. At one point, when she
was offered a tempting job in Texas that began in the summer, she
despaired of getting to New York for another year.

But then the Texas educators asked her to take Professor Dow's
teaching-methods course first—reason enough, Georgia decided, to
leave immediately for New York. Only a month into the second semester at Columbia College, she resigned and left the college without
an art teacher for the remainder of the spring term. She also left
behind a reputation for being spirited and ambitious. Although fond
of the college president, an elderly soft-spoken Methodist clergyman
who three months later resigned because of the stress of the job,
Georgia was not going to let anything keep her in the backwater of
South Carolina any longer. It's unlikely that any excuse she gave for
going to New York was well recieved because she didn't list Columbia
College among her credentials in her next job.

❖

In the first week of March, Georgia arrived in New York and

enrolled in Dow's class a few weeks late. Because she had little money, Anita's uncle, dermatologist Dr. Sigmund Pollitzer, offered her the large, sunny, front spare bedroom on the top floor of his brownstone at 51 East Sixtieth Street, off Park Avenue. (Anita lived elsewhere.) Georgia kept her own hours, eating her meals in the college cafeteria and never spending an evening with the family during the entire three months of her stay. The Pollitzers accepted her aloofness from their family life because they sensed that she was a very private person and, somehow, extraordinary.

Georgia was closest to their nineteen-year-old daughter, Aline, who was overwhelmed by her charcoal drawings and fascinated by her looks: "incredible" eyes, beautiful hands, and "a wide, sensitive mouth— and a slow, marvelous thing happened to it when she smiled," Aline recalled many years later. Her distinctive looks were set off by her habit of wearing black clothes at a time when other young women never wore black.

Coincidentally, that semester Aline was taking political science at Barnard College with Georgia's beau, Arthur Macmahon. During their talks, Georgia confided to Aline that Arthur wanted to marry her, but she did not want to marry him. Her reluctance didn't surprise Aline, who thought that they were a peculiar match. Professor Mac-mahon was several years Georgia's junior and very "straight, prim and proper" while Georgia appeared totally indifferent to what others thought of her. Not particularly interested in politics or social issues, Georgia had become more absorbed in art than ever. Arthur, who could only share her passion on an intellectural level, said afterwards that he had been forced to recognized that she was committed to art on her own terms. Their relationship never developed fully, and soon they would part.

The news Georgia received from home during this time was deeply disturbing. Her mother's tuberculosis had worsened, making it increasingly impossible to maintain the boardinghouse. Meals were no longer provided, and they tried to attract boarders by offering the rock-bottom rate of a dollar a week. The O'Keeffe brothers had long since departed. Georgia's father, whose Charlottesville creamery had been short-lived (he only paid a head-of-household tax in town through 1913), tried the trucking business and went wherever he could find work. Twenty-one-year-old Catherine was studing nursing in Wisconsin. Besides the aging Aunt Jenny, only Ida, who was twenty-six and an art teacher, Claudia, who was still in high school, and Anita remained at home. Then in late April, Anita, at twenty-five, married Robert R. Young, a nineteen-year-old Texan studying at the University of Virginia. Five days later, the O'Keeffe family was finally splintered forever when Mama died at the age of fifty-two.

The story of her death, as told by Ethel Holsinger, who was a neighbor on Wertland Street, is tragic. On May 2 the landlady went to the O'Keeffe house and demanded the overdue rent. The girls told her that they had no money to give her, but she refused to budge from the doorstep, insisting that their mother come to the front door. As Mrs. O'Keeffe got slowly out of bed and began to inch her way down the hallway, she was seized by a lung hemorrhage, collapsed, and died. In the following days, people were shocked to find the family's kitchen cupboards almost bare. If there was a funeral in Charlottesville, Georgia did not return for it. Her mother's body was buried by her brothers and sisters in the Totto family plot of the Grace Episcopal Church cemetery in Madison.

Meanwhile, in early April Stieglitz had begun to exhibit at 291 Marsden Hartley's vibrant Berlin abstractions of red flags and military insignias. Georgia had gone to see the show, which remained on the walls until the end of May, and Stieglitz had lent her one of Hartley's dark Maine paintings. Exactly three weeks older than her mother, Stieglitz now had a white moustache and unconventionally long, graying hair. Georgia had probably taken her charcoals back to him, for he was incessantly talking about them. They continued to suggest to him the emergence of a wonderful new kind of woman. Once he took the young writer Herbert J. Seligmann to marvel over them in his apartment on upper Fifth Avenue, where he often slept in a small room crammed with paintings and photographs, apart from his wife and eighteen-year-old daughter, Kitty. Finally, after Marsden Hartley's show was dismantled and most art critics had left New York for the summer, he decided to hang ten of the O'Keeffe charcoals along with abstractions of two young male friends. Oddly, he failed to inform Georgia of his plan.

One day she was eating in the college cafeteria when a girl stopped by her table and inquired if she was "Virginia O'Keeffe." Georgia replied no, and the girl explained that someone named Virgina O'Keeffe was having a show at 291. Georgia realized with alarm that the show was hers—that Stieglitz had cavalierly exhibited her intensely personal drawings without asking her, telling her, or even getting her name right. The young artist felt acutely exposed to the uncomprehending eyes of strangers for the first time. "For me the drawings were private and the idea of their being hung on the wall for the public to look at was just too much," she recalled in her book. If they were to be exhibited, she also reasoned, they should at least generate some needed money or some useful reaction.

Georgia headed angrily for 291, but when she arrived, she learned that Stieglitz was away on jury duty. She lingered long enough to note that her drawings were hung in the larger room, whereas those of the two men were in the smaller ones. Light from a skylight, filtered by a panel suspended from the ceiling, bathed her carefully spaced charcoals on walls covered with sage-green velour. A square platform stood in the middle of the room holding a large gleaming brass bowl of artfully arranged dried flowers.

A few days later she returned and marched up to Stieglitz. "What right do you have to show these drawings?" she asked, and then she demanded that he take them down. Looking surprised, but with his determined chin firmly set, Stieglitz peered through his glasses at the slender young woman, who was wearing a severe black frock with a prim white collar. Her drawings were so wonderful, he started to say, that he simply *had* to show them. It was marvelous, he continued, that she had opened herself like a flower. It was remarkable, especially for an American woman. He asked where one image had come from, and she replied that it came to her when she had a headache. He asked about another, and she started to explain, then stopped. "Do you think I'm an idiot?" she snapped. "Intellectually, you don't know what you've done," he replied. "In reality you do." Stieglitz kept talking while Georgia remained silent. When he finally paused for breath, she asked him what he was going to do with the drawings when the exhibit was over. He replied that he would take care of them and asked her to send him more. The two lunched together.

Stieglitz had predicted that the drawings would cause a sensation, and he was right. Word spread among the cognoscenti that there was something to see at 291, and the curious streamed in. Some people, horrified that drawings by an unknown female schoolteacher had been hung on the same walls that had displayed Picassos and Cézannes, ridiculed them. Her "woman's feeling," as Georgia put it, caused women to experience a shock of recognition, and prompted Mabel Dodge to bring psychoanalysts to see the work. "But, Stieglitz," complained scandalized art critic Willard H. Wright, a brilliant battler for the new art, "all these pictures say is 'I want to have a baby.'" "That's fine," Stieglitz retorted, "a woman had painted a picture telling you that she wants to have a baby." Many people, shocked by the naive sexuality, questioned whether what they saw was really art, whereas others said it was. "Such a scuffling about for draperies there never was," wrote critic Henry McBride wryly several years later. "Even many advanced art lovers felt a distinct moral shiver. And, incidentally, it was one of the first great triumphs for abstract art, since everybody got it."

Stieglitz enjoyed being in the middle of another uproar. He believed that art was the expression of deep feeling, even sexual feeling, and argued that erotic energy should be expressed in America so as to shake the country free of its repressive Puritan heritage and to liberate its artists. He hotly defended Georgia's drawings and tried to protect the young artist from the viewers' whispers. "Never since the tower of Babel has there been such general chaos of utterance and confusion as prevails in the art world today," was the way he dismissed the talk—and then he extended the show into July.

By then Georgia had left New York to teach summer school for the last time at the University of Virginia. The weeks in Charlottesville were difficult for her. It was the first time she had been back since her mother's death. She seemed depressed and drained, and had to rest in bed between classes. But the events of the past few weeks in New York had been an immense affirmation of her as an artist. An underlying optimism steadied her and was reinforced as she received letters Stieglitz as well as nine photographs he had taken of the show. Then in August she left Virginia, after the family house had been evacuated, and headed west for her new position in Texas.

4 ❖ Canyon

Georgia had yearned for the big spaces of north Texas since she had left Amarillo more than two years before. Now, in September 1916, she arrived to take a well-paying job twenty miles south of Amarillo at a young, expanding two-year teachers' college. The huge, splendid, modern yellow-brick home of West Texas State Normal College dominated the little town of Canyon, a conservative county seat of twenty-five hundred people. The town—a cluster of churches, filling stations, blacksmith shops, banks, dry-goods stores, flour and feed mills—was a small speck on the immense prairie, a human settlement linked to others by iron railroad tracks that looked like fragile threads in the vastness. Town life was a peculiar mixture of strict propriety and casual brutality, as if civilization could not be taken for granted in the tiny community encircled by the untamed land. Clubbing wild rabbits to death was a Sunday family sport, and, a few weeks after Georgia's arrival, early settler Charles Goodnight hosted a buffalo kill. He hired Indians to hunt down the prey with bows and arrows before the eyes of hundreds of spectators, who afterwards feasted on buffalo steaks.

The new college building had just been dedicated the previous spring, and chairs were yet to arrive, so one of Georgia's first tasks was to round up wooden boxes for her students to sit on. Since she was the only teacher in the art department, she could, to her delight, choose which books, prints, and other art materials to order from the

East—and she promptly sent for Dow's textbooks. Many of her new Texas students, particularly the boys, earned the money they needed to go to college and they were eager for an education. Georgia liked them tremendously, even appreciating the mediocre pupils, who, she observed, worked harder than the more facile ones.

That fall Georgia taught two morning classes in design to younger students and afternoon classes in costuming and interior decoration to home economics majors. She enjoyed trying to open her students' eyes to the beauty of the harsh plains around them, and attempting to convince them of the importance of art in their hard lives. The point was not to teach them to paint pictures, she later explained, but to show them a way of seeing. "When I taught art, I taught it as the thing everyone has to use," she said. She told them that there was art in the line of a jacket and in the shape of a collar as well as in the way one addressed a letter, combed one's hair, or placed a window in a house. Every decision should be affected by the same consideration: what was aesthetically sound or, to put it simply, what looked good.

It was soon evident that the new art teacher from the East could fire up her students with enthusiastic classroom talk that ranged far beyond the lesson plan. One teen-ager, Mattie Swayne, first heard about Russian literature from Miss O'Keeffe, and eventually became an instructor of English. "She introduced a number of ideas that were new to me—ideas from an intellectural world that was part of her common knowledge," Mattie recalled. Georgia also tried to arouse the Texas youngsters' curiosity about such exotic objects as the African carvings that Stieglitz had exhibited in 1914. She did not condescend to her students, assigning them some of the most advanced books on the theory of art at the time, such as Clive Bell's *Art* and Willard H. Wright's *The Creative Will*. The students, in turn, greatly appreciated her exciting teaching and retained fond memories of her all their lives. "She was a good teacher," remembered Mattie. "There was a strength to her teaching—she knew what she thought and she expressed it."

But the adults in Canyon were less sure what to make of her. The only teacher from the East at West Texas State, Georgia was immediately typecast as a bohemian by the staid community. For one thing, in costume class she preached the importance of straight lines in women's dress rather than the customary corseted curves, and she herself always wore loose garments in either black or white, sometimes with a dark green smock. "I'll never forget the sight of her hurrying up to the stage where the faculty met for chapel in her flowing, robelike gown," recalled Mattie. Georgia also tromped around in heavy, flat walking shoes and usually just combed her dark hair straight back, caring little for conventional styles. Once, when another teacher, Emma Jean McClesky, asked why she wore her hair so simply, Georgia snapped, "Because I feel like it!" and thereby brusquely ended the questioning. But she also told Emma Jean another time that she lined her plain woolen skirts with pure silk. Once, when Georgia posed for a faculty photograph on a flag-decked stage, she wore her habitual black dress with a white collar—but with a large flower flamboyantly pinned to the bodice.

Townspeople thought that Miss O'Keeffe had queer, even laughable, ideas about decoration. When she first arrived in Canyon, she quickly moved out of a rooming house because she couldn't bear to look at the sentimental pink-rose bedroom wallpaper. After renting rooms in various homes for a while, she asked the West Texas State physics professor to rent her the upstairs bedroom—which had a large window facing east—in his new home. Douglas Shirley and his wife, Willina, protested that they hadn't planned to rent the room and couldn't afford to decorate it, and only agreed after Georgia had convinced them that she didn't need much furniture or want curtains that would obstruct her view of the sunrise. When she later asked the Shirleys if she could paint the room's wood trim black (they said no), the story spread around town that the interior-decoration teacher wanted to paint her entire bedroom black.

Georgia managed to violate those customs of Canyon that got in her way, and, unlike the years when she was a schoolgirl, she didn't seem to care who noticed. Her first November in Canyon, she accepted an invitation from a faculty wife to a ladies' tea, where "time was spent in fancy work and pleasant games were engaged in," noted the social column of the Canyon newspaper. Georgia must have thought that it was an inane waste of time, because no one remembered her attending another. She also raised eyebrows in the pious small town by not going to church or teaching Sunday school in one of the six Protestant churches as virtually all the other teachers did. Instead, she liked to spend her Sundays taking long walks on the prairie (in the days before hiking had become an accepted pastime).

According to convention in Canyon, unmarried males and females did not spend time alone together. Consequently, Miss O'Keeffe earned a "reputation" after allowing the Yale-educated local prosecuting attorney to call on her in her room and then, after her landlady had objected, for letting him take her driving on the prairie, which was so empty of trees and fences that one could drive straight away from town in any direction. But Georgia seemed to have been innocent of any "misbehavior." As the two sat in the moonlight in his parked car, she tried to talk to him about art—and she was startled into hysterical laughter when he tried to put his arm around her, according to a letter she wrote to Anita Pollitzer.

Furthermore, professors were not supposed to socialize with their students. When Georgia volunteered to take charge of costumes and scenery for two short Drama Club plays, she got to know the club's president, twenty-one-year-old Ted Reid, a tall, lanky football player with a big smile. Despite the town taboo, Ted used to drive her out into the country in his older brother's automobile. She would sketch and they would watch the sunset until the play of orange and pink light dimmed; then they would return by the light of the town.

Georgia was so indifferent to the small-town censors, in fact, that she later remembered her years in Canyon as among the freest in her life. For one thing, she had found in the Shirleys open-minded landlords who respected her privacy. People didn't dare criticize her to her face because of her reputation for outspokenness and sarcasm. On walks after dinner with other women teachers, for instance, she delighted in mimicking other professors and various personalities in town. Only through her excitement in teaching modern art did she reach out to the town establishment. In January 1917, she gave a short talk on cubism before the Faculty Circle, and was pleased when it aroused so much curiosity that the question period cut into the time allotted for the music teacher's talk on Wagner.

Since she made little effort to be part of the social network, townspeople got the impression that she didn't need others to make her life interesting. But during this time she had the companionship of seventeen-and-a-half-year-old Claudia, her youngest sister. Before her death, their mother had asked Georgia to be responsible for "Claudie," probably realizing that Georgia was most able to do it. Upon arriving in Canyon, therefore, she enrolled her shy, dark-haired little sister in West Texas State, bought her a train ticket, and made plans to share her room at the Shirleys with her.

Increasingly, the only person's opinion that Georgia really cared about was that of the famous czar of 291, Alfred Stieglitz. His belief in her potential answered her deep need for validation as an artist. From time to time she rolled up a batch of drawings and watercolors that the year before would have gone to Anita Pollitzer, affixed the necessary stamps, and addressed them to him in New York. Stieglitz, a prolific letterwriter (he once penned twenty-nine letters to various people in a twenty-four-hour period), wrote her often in his characteristic voices—at times challenging, lofty, encouraging, provoking, or inspiring.

His steady stream of approving letters also helped her to ignore the small-town mores in Canyon, and to keep in touch with what was going on in New York intellectual circles and round out her reading. It was Stieglitz who suggested that she read Goethe's *Faust* that winter, and she also read Nietzsche, Ibsen, the works of feminists, art critics, and a great deal of fiction. In her letters to the overpowering older man, she undoubtedly revealed more about herself than she would have in conversation. The young artist described, in her strong upright longhand, what she was seeing and feeling in Texas, using astoundingly lucid phrases. She also employed her inventive spelling and minimal punctuation, mostly consisting of long wavy dashes, which were curiously charming. In their use of black ink and white paper, as well as the flash and vigor of their pen strokes, Stieglitz and the young O'Keeffe wrote letters that looked strikingly alike.

❖

Around Canyon the universe seemed divided into two planes—endless prairie and infinite sky with little in between but scattered windmills and the pounding wind. Cumulus raw-white western clouds, which continually boiled into new shapes, appeared sharply etched against the luminescent sky. Georgia loved it all as much as she had remembered. She liked to rise before dawn to watch the morning train arrive in Canyon, roaring, throbbing, whistling, and steaming through the sunrise. She walked great distances over the flat tableland, acquiring a reputation for outwalking any man in the county, and returning to town with her face scorched by the strong sun, chilled to the bone by the gale winds, and with her clothes caked with brown dust. At sundown she liked to walk beyond the last house toward the west to watch the fiery sun drop below the long, dark, level line of the land. Meanwhile, she marveled at how wonderful it was that a woman was able to walk alone without fear at night in the emptiness.

She often made excursions to Palo Duro canyon, a lonely crevice that sliced the earth a thousand feet deep in places, about twenty miles due east across the open space. Sometimes she chaperoned a group of students, but usually she and her sister Claudia set out for the canyon on Saturday mornings. Indians had once found shelter in the canyon, but by 1916 it was primarily a place where cattle found refuge from the winds, which were able to blow snow and rain right over the top of it. Georgia used to hike down the treacherous cattle paths or descend by clinging to roots in order to get a better look at the golden sandstone formations, the veins of white gypsum, and the orange mudstone above the green wetness on the canyon floor. There a little creek tumbled into a waterfall and watered large junipers and cedars as well as wild grapes and plums. Once she let out a loud whoop and, when the faculty couple with her called out to see if she was all right, shouted back, "I can't help it—it's all so beautiful!" As late-afternoon shadows fell across the canyon, sometimes she saw "a long line of cattle like black lace against the sunset sky" high up on the plain, she wrote poetically in her book. Then it was time to climb out of the crack in the earth and drive westward toward home into the blazing sky.

Although Stieglitz had once advised Georgia to stay with black and white, she was slowly returning to color. It had begun the previous June when she started using blue again, painting blue watercolor forms hovering over and anchored by bold blue slashes. This use of color was accelerated in Texas, particularly after she had stayed overnight with friends in Amarillo one time and returned to Canyon early the next morning. She rode up front in the horse-drawn taxi with the driver because the other passenger was an unruly drunk. That morning an extraordinary sunrise broke over the sky. "The light would begin to appear and then it would disappear and there would be a kind of halo effect, and then it would appear again," is the way she later described a Texas daybreak. "The light would come and go for a quite a while before it finally came." The sunrise that particular morning affected Georgia so intensely that when she got to Canyon she felt compelled to use a wider range of colors to paint it. In time, she explored yellow again, then green and red, until, once again, she was using the whole rainbow of hues in her color box.

The previous fall she had purged herself of academic techniques in the search for her own style. Now in Texas she had found a series of wonderful subjects. She painted on days when she didn't teach and between classes on other days—continually, prolifically, spontaneously, urgently, with growing excitement and sureness. As she invented a way to express her intense feelings, she reduced her pictures to a few simple, straightforward shapes and colors, much like the uncluttered landscape itself, and much the way her Mexican pupils in Amarillo had painted—and her own style began to emerge.

Most of the time she worked in watercolor because she lacked the long uninterrupted hours required for oil. But watercolor, it turned out, was ideal for her subject, the western sky, since she could let colors flow into one another. The medium had the pale translucence and watery thinness that caught the ephemeral glow of a sunrise or sunset—and those washes were later aptly called "colored light." They were rapidly done in bold brushstrokes, and sometimes the thin inexpensive paper they were done on was saturated with water to make it ripple. She painted many versions of an idea, adjusting to the changing light and trying to get closer to its essence. Georgia's semi-solitude in the big country—and her realization that Stieglitz might exhibit the pictures in the spring—spurred her to a great outburst of creativity. At least fifty watercolors have been recorded as coming from that fifteen-month period.

Georgia often arrived at the boardinghouse where she ate her meals fresh from a walk, a roll of paintings under her arm, and flushed with excitement. One evening after the other teachers had asked to see her pictures, she unrolled one of a great radiant oval of liquid light, then asked them to guess what it was. Mary Hudspeth, the mathematics and Spanish teacher who owned the boardinghouse, ventured that it was a watermelon. When Georgia explained that it was the light of the town against the black night sky, everyone burst into laughter.

Another time, she showed a picture to Douglas Shirley, explaining that it was the canyon. Perhaps it was her Palo Duro oil of a lavalike flow bubbling through an inferno of hot oranges and searing yellows, or maybe it was her drawing with curved, boiling, and sawtoothed forms of terrifying climbs. "It doesn't look like the canyon to me," Shirley stated firmly. When Georgia replied that it was the way she *felt* about the canyon, Shirley joked, "Well, you must have had a stomachache when you painted it!"

Her daring forms and unusual colors—once she did a painting of snow that was fuchsia-colored—startled those who assumed that art was supposed to be something "pretty for the parlor." Once in a while Georgia tried to explain that if you wanted a replica of nature, such as snow that was white, then you should take a photograph. But most of the time she didn't bother. No one in Canyon was really interested in abstract art or in why Georgia painted as she did, and she ignored their little jokes. After all, she had Alfred Stieglitz's distant applause. When she later became the focus of attention in New York, she looked back on her privacy in Canyon with nostalgia. "It was all so far away— there was quiet and an untouched feel to the country and I could work as I pleased," she said.

❖

On April 3, 1917, Stieglitz opened Georgia's first solo show. Since there was no catalog, the record is incomplete as to what was exhibited. But judging from photographs taken of the show, it was primarily composed of Texas watercolors as well as some charcoals and oils and a lone piece of Plasticine sculpture—a sensitively molded phallic form. It was not a commonplace occurrence for an avant-garde woman painter to have her own show—the last time Stieglitz had presented one was the second show for Pamela Colman Smith eight years before. What's more, Georgia's charcoals had created a considerable stir the previous year, and now the critics took notice again.

On May 4 the *Christian Science Monitor* published a review by Henry Tyrrell that dwelt on Georgia's "female" message:

> The recent work . . . of Miss Georgia O'Keeffe of Can-yon, Texas . . . has to speak for itself as it is not num-bered, catalogued, labeled, lettered or identified in any way—in fact, it is not even signed. The interesting but little-known personality of the artist . . . is perhaps the only real key, and even that would not open all the chambers of the haunted palace which is a gifted wom-an's heart. . . . [She] has found expression in delicately veiled symbolism for "what every woman knows," but

what women heretofore kept to themselves . . . the loneliness and privation which her emotional nature must
have suffered put their impress on everything she does.
Her strange art affects people variously and some not at
all . . . artists especially wonder at its technical resourcefulness for dealing with what hitherto has been deemed
the inexpressible—in visual form, at least. . . . Now perhaps for the first time in art's history, the style is the
woman.

The show included some of Georgia's all-blue watercolors and
one, called simply *Blue Lines*, struck many as extraordinary. She had
painted it with a delicate Japanese brush, influenced by Asian calligraphy. She first drew its two vertical lines of varying width in charcoal,
worrying that she didn't have the fluency to do it with a brush. Then
she progressed to black watercolor, until, finally, blue seemed right.
Freudians interpreted the two forms as the conflicting forces of the
psyche, an art historian saw them as the poles of Eastern and Western
philosophies, and others, including Stieglitz, viewed them as the di-
chotomy of male and female sensibilities. Stieglitz felt that the wash
was so wonderful, in fact, that he had hung it over his table behind
the gray curtain at 291 during the winter. His marriage had been
unhappy for many years, and he was searching for a more satisfying
kind of relationship with a woman, and the blue lines seemed to point
the way. The male and female pair, wrote Tyrrell, "grow straight out
of the earth like two graceful saplings, side by side, straight and slender,
though their fluid lines undulate in unconscious rhythmic sympathy."

The spring 1917 issue of Stieglitz's *Camera Work* indicated that
the next edition might contain a portfolio of Georgia O'Keeffe's work.
Even though the number of discerning art lovers who still subscribed
had dwindled from a few hundred to a few dozen, publication would
have been a prestigious event for the young artist. But the spring issue
turned out to be the last—and an occasion when Georgia had a stroke
of bad luck with timing. The world was in crisis: Three days after her
exhibition had opened at 291, the United States declared war on
Germany and entered World War I.

The outbreak of hostilities between his native land and Germany,
where he had studied as a youth, deeply depressed Stieglitz. Friends
remarked that he seemed to have aged suddenly and lost his old fire.
He put his photographic equipment away, fearing that his creativity

was dead. After constant exhibitions at 291, publishing *Camera Work*, and single-handedly defending modern art during much of the past decade, he was exhausted. (Over the thirteen years that the gallery had been in existence about a hundred thousand people had trooped into the little rooms.) Prohibition had cut into his wife's brewery dividends, so family finances were uncertain. He had broken with his helper Marius de Zayas, who set up his own modern art gallery, and he knew that 291 was no longer the only center of avant-garde art in Manhattan. For years his landlord had threatened to tear down the old mansion that housed 291. Finally, that spring, Stieglitz gave up. He decided not to renew his lease and to close the gallery at the end of June. "Well, I'm through," he remarked at the O'Keeffe show, "but I've given the world a woman.'

Georgia was aware from his letters that Stieglitz's mood was black and that her show would be his last. It had seemed impossible to her to travel the two thousand miles from Canyon to New York to see the show. Her classes didn't end until the day it closed, and she had agreed to teach summer school in Canyon, which began a mere three weeks after the term ended. When classes recessed in mid-May, however, she suddenly felt the urge to go. Perhaps Stieglitz had sent her reviews or told her that she had sold her first painting, the one of a train moving through the dawn, reportedly for four hundred dollars. It was clear that she also wanted to see Stieglitz. A longtime acquaintance of Stieglitz's, the journalist Hutchins Hapgood, was to write a few years later:

> For many years I felt every now and then, every few weeks or months, a need to see him again—not to say anything to him, for conversation with Stieglitz is extremely difficult, as he talks nearly all the time—not even to get any thoughts or ideas from him, for I had my own, and in definite thoughts and ideas he was not rich—but to feel his life, his living being, see where it was carrying him; and in that way, to feel again the freshness, the value of life again.

In the isolation of Texas, Georgia must have felt a similar but stronger urge. Five days after her last class had ended, she impulsively decided to leave. Since it was Sunday, she had to go to the home of the bank president and persuade him to open the bank and allow her to withdraw her savings. That done, she packed a bag and simply left.

In New York Georgia found that the city's pace was quicker and more purposeful than it had been the year before. The nation was beginning to gear up for battle, and colorful flags of the Allies flapped along Fifth Avenue, Broadway actors and actresses spoke to crowded Liberty loan rallies on Wall Street and in Times Square, and the harbor was becoming filled with camouflaged warships. Georgia, who probably stayed with friends, soon headed for 291. Stieglitz was there, talking to rapt listeners in the gallery, amid rows of paintings stacked against the bare walls. He felt the quiet presence of someone behind him, turned, and was astonished to see Georgia O'Keeffe.

For many years afterwards, Stieglitz liked to marvel at the way the young artist had abruptly reappeared in his life from far-off Texas. Her trip to New York was spontaneous, intuitive, and sure—just like her paintings. In Stieglitz's eyes, Georgia was an unusual American girl, untainted by studies in Europe, who painted with a direct, clear, strong—even fierce—force. What appealed to him even more was that she had her whole creative life ahead of her whereas his, he thought, had ended. The young woman differed sharply from his wife, Emmy, who was now in her midforties, fearful, proper, and conventional—and had disliked Georgia's show.

Although he had photographed her show before dismantling it, Stieglitz insisted on rehanging it for Georgia to see. He also introduced her to several artists and showed her the work of others, such as John Marin and the talented young photographer whom he had exhibited, Paul Strand, whose photographic close-ups seemed more abstract than realistic. Then Georgia, along with Strand, Stieglitz, and an inventor friend, spent May 30, Decoration Day, at the Coney Island amusement park at the edge of the sea. On their return to Manhattan as they sat on the top of an open trolley car, Stieglitz protectively wrapped his heavy black loden cape around Georgia's shoulders.

Stieglitz only photographed people who aroused strong feelings in him and he soon asked Georgia to model for him. As an artist he was interested in Georgia's large, unusual features. He though her prominent nose and firm chin formed an exquisite profile, and he was fascinated by what he called her enigmatic Mona Lisa smile. He posed the entwined fingers of her handsome hands in front of her drawing of a curled fetus-form, then photographed them against the bodice of her long-sleeved black dress with white lapels. As the photographer examined this woman who did not easily express herself in words, the camera recorded the circles under her eyes and the untamed hairs under her heavy brows. It also caught the beginning of an amused, dimpled smile playing around the corners of her beautiful mouth and a straightforward, casual, soft, and interested look in her eyes.

❖

After a few whirlwind days in New York, Georgia departed for Texas again and her first summer in the Southwest. In July a chautauqua stopped in Canyon and filled the warm evening air with the sounds of Scottish bagpipes, Italian ballads, and a female Hungarian quartet. When the sky blackened at night, Georgia liked to sit outside for hours and watch the sudden shimmers and furious bursts of heat lightning as well as the lights of automobiles. "A glow in the sky would come from below the horizon, the lights would dim as the car went down in a hollow only to brighten again as it came up, waxing and waning until finally the headlights came into view," she recalled.

Georgia and Claudia liked to walk out beyond the town in the long, lingering sundowns. Claudia used to toss glass bottles into the air and shatter as many as possible with her shotgun, causing slivers of light to explode into the sky and the gun's roar to vibrate in the vastness around them. Georgia, meanwhile, watched the brightening of the evening star—an exciting beacon to her—as the blue around it deepened in the dusk. When she first attempted to paint the star, she made it small, the way it actually was, but that didn't express her expansive feelings about it. Next, she left the star as a dot of white paper, encircled it with a yellow halo, then rings of hot reds and cooler colors beyond, until its intensity filled the paper the way her feelings filled her.

The sisters had a month free between the end of summer school and the start of the autumn semester, so they planned a vacation in the Colorado Rockies. When they tried to buy their tickets to Denver, however, they discovered that floods had washed out railroad bridges along the direct northwest route. Georgia refused to abandon the plan since she had wanted to go to Colorado for some time, so they bought tickets around the flooded area, which happened to be west via Albuquerque, New Mexico. It was then that Georgia got her first glimpse of the bald pink hills dotted with scraggly green piñon trees at the foot of the Sangre de Cristo Mountains in northern New Mexico. Georgia painted what she saw along the way—for example, the bell of a little wooden mountain church in Ward, Colorado.

On the way back from Colorado, the sisters stopped for a few days in Santa Fe. One of the oldest towns in America, Santa Fe was also an artist's colony with a museum of fine arts that was just about to open formally. They walked around the streets, which were filled with Indians and Mexicans in colorful dress, and lined with earth-colored adobe houses that were tinted golden by the late afternoon sun. Everything was drenched in the brilliant light of the high, dry desert air. "I loved it immediately," Georgia recalled later. "From then on I was always on my way back." Her journey back was roundabout, however, and would take her twelve years.

Back in Canyon, the war fever was high. Citizens were exhorted to fly the stars and stripes and to drape red, white, and blue bunting around their homes. The administrators of West Texas State urged the teachers to drill military companies on campus, to organize Red Cross units, and teach food preservation. The 1917 yearbook was full of sentimental verses praising the young men who had left the campus for the battlefield. The college authorities encouraged them to volunteer by granting them graduation certificates even if they enlisted before final examinations. Fanned by the college community, the patriotic frenzy eventually drove a third of the students to war—and only five male students remained to graduate with their class in the spring of 1918.

Georgia's views on the war had been shaped by neutral and pacifist viewpoints she had heard in the East. She was also instinctively repelled by mass hysteria, particularly since it had induced her younger brother, the dashing twenty-five-year-old Alexius, to enlist in July. She tried to ignore the war and to continue to just teach art, and she managed to bring an art exhibit to the campus in the fall of 1918. But in the classroom she tended to link art to everyday issues, and outside it she was too outspoken to hide her irritation with what she considered irrational rhetoric. "What does patriotism have to do with seeing a thing as green when it is green and red when it is red?" she once asked a colleague. She successfully discouraged Ted Reid from enlisting until after he had graduated in spring 1918, a delay that also enabled him to get into the service branch he preferred and become a pilot. One day during a chapel lecture when she thought a history professor was distorting Nietzsche for propaganda purposes, she suddenly stood up and demanded to know if he had actually read the philosopher. The man's reply has been forgotten, but not the deeply shocking incident. Another time she further angered the local patriots by trying—and failing—to have a shopkeeper stop selling Christmas cards that urged the annihilation of Germany.

There was little room for nonconformity in Canyon during the war. The strenuous teaching schedule was beginning to tire Georgia. In November she had hit the milestone of her thirtieth birthday. In December her sister left Canyon to student-teach in the tiny town of Spur, Texas, and Georgia was more alone than ever. For three months she lost the desire to paint—her longest dry spell since she had returned to art four years before. She even doubted that Stieglitz would be able to arrange an exhibition of the work that had poured out of her during the previous summer—the best work of her life she thought. "The war makes me feel as if I'm dangling in the air—can't get my feet on the ground," she complained to Anna Barringer, a medical school professor's daughter who had taught with her at the University of Virginia. "Everything seems so uncertain that it seems almost impossible to feel anything definite or think anything definite."

In January the thermometer dropped way below zero and high winds drove the chill factor even lower. Because of the war, it was difficult to get enough heating coal. Georgia began to stuff paper in the front of her dresses to try to protect herself from the icy blast of the wind when she walked from her rented room to the classroom building. Nevertheless, after Christmas she caught influenza and canceled her classes. A few weeks later on February 14, 1918, the Canyon newspaper printed two conflicting announcements. One reported that Miss O'Keeffe had been ill for two weeks, and the other, in another section of the paper, noted that the art teacher had spent the previous Sunday in Amarillo. The two stories suggested that the West Texas State administrators had been told the art teacher was too sick to teach but that, in actuality, she was well enough to visit Amarillo.

The dissembling, or error, was probably the last straw for the college, which had barely tolerated Georgia's unconventionality. Whatever the actual facts, the next edition of the Randall County *News*, dated February 21, announced that Miss O'Keeffe had been granted a leave of absence due to illness. A national influenza epidemic had left a great many deaths in its wake, and undoubtedly Georgia was sincerely worried about the effect on her health of the same type of bitter cold that had driven her family from Wisconsin. The rumor spread, nevertheless, that the art teacher had been forced out of her position because of her antiwar sentiment. There must have been some truth to this, for afterwards Georgia acknowledged that teaching in Texas during the war had been all but impossible.

Georgia left north Texas for a farm in the southern part of the state that belonged to a tall, dark-haired girlfriend, Leah Harris, who taught food canning in Amarillo. The farm was in Waring, Texas, in a hilly, warm, green region watered by the Guadalupe River, where pecan trees grew, birds sang, and roses bloomed all winter. It was a welcome change for Georgia, and she began to get some much-needed rest before the time came for teaching summer school again in Canyon, where she had painted prodigiously the year before.

During the winter of 1918, Stieglitz, for his part, felt penniless, purposeless, and very much alone. Sitting in the tiny room that had been a part of 291, he grandiosely compared himself to Napoleon on his retreat from Moscow. When Georgia wrote him that she was ill and had left her job, he urged her to visit New York. His devoted niece, Elizabeth Stieglitz, wrote Georgia long letters on his behalf, offering her the loan of her New York studio, which Stieglitz had been using as a darkroom. By April his feelings for Georgia were so intense that he moved his personal possessions out of the bedroom he shared with his wife and began to sleep in his study. The way he put it was that Georgia had become the living spirit of 291, and fighting for her was the same as keeping its spark alive. It seemed that the more Georgia hesitated about taking a trip to the East, the more Stieglitz became obsessed by its necessity. He anxiously fretted that she might have tuberculosis, that she wasn't painting, but he was indecisive about how to "rescue" her from the alien West. Finally, in May, he hit on the idea of sending youthful Paul Strand to Texas to fetch her. Stieglitz gave Strand, who had been in Texas in 1915, the money for train tickets and then waited in great suspense.

In Texas, Georgia's mind had often been on Stieglitz. With great excitement, she had shown her pupils and colleagues the photographic images of her face and hands that Stieglitz had sent her. His motivating idea—that through the fulfillment of the individual artist the truth would emerge—was appealing to her. As her mentor, he was ready to devote himself to her flowering as an artist. Her ambition had been fueled by him, and she had fervently told one of her classes that she hoped a museum would exhibit her work someday. Paul Strand waited while she made up her mind. She loved Texas, but, again, her position had become untenable there. A few years later she described her decision-making process as "the vague intuitive way that I go at life—am interested—amused—like—or dislike—for no particular reason—excepting that it is inevitable at the moment." At last it was inevitable that she postpone her return to Canyon. In early June, she and Strand began the long train trip back to New York together. On June 10th, when Stieglitz's two young protégés arrived in New York at dawn, they found him anxioualy awaiting them.

5 ❖ Flowers

On seeing Stieglitz on the station platform, Georgia immediately moved
to his side, leaving twenty-six-year-old Paul Strand standing alone.
Paul had become enamored of her during their week together in Texas
and their trip back East, according to Stieglitz's young friend, Herbert
Seligmann. But during the next few weeks in New York, it was clear
that Georgia's affection was for the older man. Although disappointed
by Georgia's choice, Paul remained loyal to his mentor. To remove
himself from the uncomfortable position of onlooker, he enlisted in
the army in June and left the East.

Whereas Paul, like Georgia, was struggling to survive as an artist,
Stieglitz, at the age of fifty-four, had won recognition as a photographer, and now his energies were devoted to championing others.
Through brief encounters and lengthy letters, Georgia had grown to
know him as a profoundly fascinating, personally appealing man. There
was much about him that was contradictory. One friend observed that
his shapely head had two looks—a jagged one due to a nose with a
broken ridge, and one in which the planes of his face were smooth.
His finely chiseled mouth was as sensitive as a girl's, but his graying
hair bristled fiercely, even from his ears. Under his dour black cape,
he often wore a flamboyant red vest. And although he was a European-
educated intellectual, he liked to read the "sporting" page of the
newspaper first. (He had a passion for thoroughbred horses and used

to brag in German under his breath while reading the paper, "I can ride the wildest horse.") In 1921 this complicated man described himself simply: "I was born in Hoboken. I am an American. Photography is my passion. The search for truth is my obsession."

Stieglitz, who in his youth in the 1880s had lived in Germany with a young prostitute named Paula, always enjoyed the company of women. But his wife, Emmy, a painfully prosaic woman, neither understood nor sympathized with his drives and aspirations, and their marriage was agonizing. Before Stieglitz met Georgia, he had dreamed three vivid, violent dreams about his and his wife's terrible inability to meet each other's needs for love. He took no action to end the marriage, however, because though fearless in the realm of ideas, he tended to be timid in the personal domain.

Stieglitz seemed destined to be attracted to someone with Georgia's style. At the age of two he had become infatuated with a female relative who highlighted her white skin and dark hair by wearing black gowns, and he never forgot "the lady in black," as he called her. The day before he turned thirteen he confided to a diary (interestingly called "Mental Photography") that his favorite color was black. As a young man, he chose the black-and-white medium of photography for his artistic expression. In adulthood he continued to be fascinated by women who dressed in mysterious black. By the time he got to know Georgia, her signature was a black dress with a little touch of white at the throat so she naturally caught his attention.

In contrast to Emmy, who favored stylish, expensive Parisian gowns, Georgia disdained the parasols, high heels, corsages, and flowery hats that were fashionable at the time. Although her nunlike uniform made no concession to fashion, it had its own style, particularly because of the inexplicably perfect way she wore it. Her exotic look prompted people to refer to her at various times as Nefertiti or as a "Chinese lady." Artist Arthur Young, eight years younger than Georgia, thought that in her severe, mannish black she had absolutely no feminine appeal, a deficiency accentuated, he felt, by the fact that she rarely seemed to smile and made no effort to be ingratiating. Despite detecting melancholy in her intelligent eyes, he acknowledged that her colorless face was that of a magnetic person "one wanted to know."

Military transports were steaming down the Hudson River at this time in New York, and diners rose in restaurants when anthems of the Allies were played. Stieglitz brought Georgia to the bright little studio apartment of his niece, Elizabeth, who was living elsewhere. When Georgia had arrived in New York, she was tired and ill. Stieglitz ordered her to stay in bed, and had his brother, a well-known doctor, examine her. Stieglitz himself visited every day, and even learned how to boil eggs for her. He returned to his apartment after his wife was asleep. Within a week he was writing to Arthur Dove of Georgia's "uncommon beauty, spontaneity, clearness of mind and feeling, and the marvelous intensity with which she lived every moment." A month after her arrival, they had become lovers and Stieglitz was also living in the studio at 114 East Fifty-ninth Street, a blanket modestly hung between their sleeping quarters. His wife had found him photographing Georgia in his study and she had lost her temper, telling him to either stop seeing the young artist or to move out. In two days Stieglitz had moved all his possessions to the studio or to storerooms in the Anderson Galleries. He told his brother-in-law George Englehard to begin divorce proceedings. (Three days after giving Alfred the ultimatum, Emmy begged him to return to no avail.) As Stieglitz began to free himself from his unhappy marriage of twenty-four years, he gained courage from Georgia's indifference to convention and her willingness to act on her feelings, demonstrated by her decision to live openly with another woman's husband.

Soon Stieglitz took Georgia up to Lake George in the Adirondack Mountains, to his family's estate, one of the many grand summer homes that dotted the shore of the long, narrow lake. They were met at the Lake George train station by old Fred, the Stieglitz family's longtime servant, and driven to Oaklawn, a big turreted Victorian structure, situated in a pine grove and wrapped around by airy verandas. True to its era, it was crammed with heavy upholstered furniture, thick dark draperies, formal marble busts, and numerous paintings in ornate gilt frames. Georgia, who associated Stieglitz with the plain decor of 291, was surprised and repelled by what she later called all the "horrible atrocities jumbled together." In the large dining room, three times a day servants passed platters loaded with food to the numerous relatives and guests who visited throughout the summer.

The Stieglitz clan was a more volatile breed than the restrained O'Keeffe family. The Wisconsin family observed a casual sort of Christianity, and the Stieglitzes were nominally Jewish. The O'Keeffes had become desperately poor, whereas the Stieglitzes were accustomed to a certain amount of wealth. The O'Keeffe siblings were not very intimate with one another, but the Stieglitzes were intensely involved. Furious family fights occasionally erupted, but they were always healed because of the deep, unbreakable bonds. The free exchange of feelings at mealtimes startled Georgia at first. But, as befitted the eldest daughter of the aristocratic Ida Totto, she sat with a ramrod-straight back and maintained a courteous kind of cool dignity.

Stieglitz's widowed mother, Hedwig Werner Stieglitz, ruled her high-strung brood of children, in-laws, grandchildren, and great-grandchildren with a gentle hand. She was seventy-four the summer of 1918, small and stout, with warm, widely spaced brown eyes set in an extremely sweet, round face. She had indulged Alfred, her eldest son, since childhood and, in her eyes, he could do no wrong. He had always returned her devotion, confessing at the age of twelve that his favorite perfume was his mother's White Rose, and in adulthood passing long summers in her home and visiting her twice a week all winter in her New York town house.

Hedwig Stieglitz and her autocratic, hot-tempered husband, Edward, had been born in Germany, but the couple met, married, and raised their six children in America. After fighting in the Civil War, Edward made a tidy fortune as a wool merchant and retired at the age of forty-eight, having secured financial independence and a trust fund for each of his children. In his life of leisure, he took up painting, and, as his son Alfred would do after him, he became a patron of artists and writers, whom he generously received at Lake George.

The cultured couple wanted their children to have the finest educations available in the world, so they moved the entire family to Europe when their brilliant, imaginative firstborn, Alfred, was seventeen. Since he had a bent for mathematics, they encouraged him to study mechanical engineering, but he spent most of his time in Berlin competing in billiards, going to horse races, and taking prize-winning photographs with a black box camera. In a few years his parents and sisters returned to New York, and, finally, in 1890, Alfred was summoned home at the age of twenty-six, after the death of a sister in childbirth.

His father wanted Alfred to settle down and go into business. He put up the money for him to open a photoengraving shop with two partners. Three years later one of the partners, Joseph Obermeyer, who had also been a roommate in Berlin, urged Alfred into marrying

Emmeline, his twenty-year-old orphaned sister. After a few years, Alfred withdrew from the photoengraving business, which was not a commercial success. His income from his father combined with his wife's comfortable means allowed him to devote himself to photography and, eventually, to the defense of avant-garde art.

Once Alfred had brought Georgia to Oaklawn it became obvious to everyone that the two were passionately in love. They exchanged hot, intense glances and Georgia, surprisingly, was remembered as the more demonstrative of the two. Alfred's black depression lifted, and he became less bad-tempered. "They were gloriously, rapturously happy," recalled Flora Straus, one of Alfred's nieces. The couple mingled little with the others except at mealtimes; they spent most of their time alone together, often disappearing upstairs to their bedroom after luncheon and not reappearing until dinner and then taking a row on the lake alone together after dinner. They also liked to take day trips on a Lake George sightseeing boat, sometimes with a young niece in tow, and acted at such times like young honeymooners.

The Stieglitz family had always disliked Emmy, who, they thought, treated Alfred rather heartlessly. A great romantic, Hedwig saw that the handsome young woman whom Alfred had brought to her made him deliriously happy, and that sufficed for her. As far as she was concerned, her favorite child had fled from a cruel wife into the arms of a young artist with striking grayish-green eyes and beautiful long hands who treated her son affectionately. Her family loyalty and amiable tolerance made her greet Georgia cordially and take her under her wing. She had the aloof newcomer sit beside her at meals to ensure that she was treated with respect. She also paced the porch when the couple went rowing at dusk until her son returned safely. Her courtesy and hospitality toward her son's companion did not waver, even though some of her visitors were so offended by her acceptance of the illicit lovers that they left and never returned.

Her strategy worked. Since the rest of the family adored Hedwig, they lined up behind her and treated Georgia politely. Eventually, when Georgia unbent and allowed them to come a little closer, they genuinely warmed to her and grew to like her very much—although a few family members detected a lingering superciliousness in her attitude toward them.

Alfred's wife had made a special point of asking him not to have Georgia at the lake when their daughter Kitty was visiting, and he had agreed. Apparently he forgot his promise, and when Kitty arrived at the lake she became so upset that the lovers abruptly left for New York. Even though Kitty then insisted that her father return, it was the virtual end of their affectionate relationship.

Georgia had long stretches of free time at Lake George in which to paint. Stieglitz photographed her as she sat on top of a layer of doormat, board, and cushion at the base of a drainpipe where damp-loving flowers flourished, her high-buttoned shoes tucked beneath her and a heavy dark sweater wrapped over her white summer dress, working in watercolor. She also had uninterrupted hours to devote to the more demanding medium of oil. As she improved in her mastery of it, her compositions became larger and lighter. Stieglitz was fascinated by what he saw because, as he put it, Georgia was like Eve—the first woman who could genuinely paint what it was to be "Woman."

As autumn approached, Stieglitz couldn't bear the idea of Georgia returning to her position at West Texas State. One day he asked her what she wanted more than anything else. Georgia loved the Texas plains and she realized that her job was a good one, but teaching in Canyon during the war had ultimately stifled her development as an artist. After a summer of new work, she saw the progress she made when she had time to paint all day, every day. Although she would lose some of her cherished independence at Stieglitz's side, life with him would be an exciting personal adventure in which she would feel, see, and hear things she had never known before. Stieglitz had an extraordinary integrity that she trusted, an intimate knowledge of art that she respected, and his belief in her was enormously encouraging. For such reasons she replied that she wanted to stop teaching for a year in order to paint full-time. "All right," Stieglitz replied, "I'll manage it for you."

Stieglitz had little money, but he had many wealthy friends. He approached one patron who sometimes helped struggling artists and told him about Georgia. "Alfred, I've heard you've left your wife," the man responded. "Is this woman involved?" In Stieglitz's mind, being with Georgia was so natural that he thought that the man might just as well have asked if a cloud or the sky was involved. He sincerely denied it. He was also truly worried about their future together because his wife didn't want a divorce, and he doubted his ability to support Georgia. "I already knew I loved her," he said afterwards, "but I also knew I was an old man and I couldn't take care of a woman and a family." The man agreed to loan Alfred's protégé roughly a thousand dollars, equivalent then to five times that amount today. When Stieglitz told Georgia about the loan, she wrote West Texas State and resigned her position as head of the drawing department.

Stieglitz had good reason for his concern, knowing that when he left his wealthy wife to live with a penniless young artist, he would face a difficult economic struggle. Georgia was an unknown painter at a time when few people were buying modern art, and when they did, they usually paid two or three hundred dollars, at the most, for a painting. Georgia herself had never seriously expected to earn a living by her painting. Although Stieglitz's income from his father's estate was not large (between one and three thousand dollars a year, at various times), he had always refused on principle to take a photograph for money, even once turning down a request from President Theodore Roosevelt. Scorning American materialism, he once remarked that he would rather be a true blade of grass than a papier-mâché tree. (When, a few years later, they were in urgent need of money, Georgia was said to have persuaded him to take the picture of a wealthy woman for fifteen hundred dollars, to his regret afterward.) Stieglitz also refused to allow his photographs to be reproduced for fear that their subtle tactile quality would be lost.

He romanticized their plight as brave lovers facing an uncertain but, somehow, destined future together. "I believe in woman, not women," he liked to say. "I have had enough pain because of them to shut them out of my heart forever, yet I will believe." In their first months together, the kind of coincidences arose that make lovers feel that they are fated for one another. Years earlier his father had asked Stieglitz to help decide between a landscape and a portrait in a student contest he was judging. Stieglitz deliberated and then selected the portrait of a serious dark-haired girl; it turned out to be Georgia, painted by Eugene Speicher, in her former Art Students League days.

Despite their many differences in age and background, Alfred and Georgia were also alike in many ways. Stieglitz, who had always despised deceitfulness, admired Georgia's extreme candor and absolute genuineness. Both felt compelled to express creatively what they perceived as the truth of experience. They shared a passion for the best in everything, he demanding the finest photographic paper and she the best paints (her pictures, as a result, were to look fresh fifty years later). "O'Keeffe came along and we found we were co-workers," he explained many years later. "We believed in the same things and finally we lived together."

In the autumn they rode through the gentle, green Adirondacks back to New York City. They moved into the studio of Elizabeth Stieglitz, who was soon to marry and leave it to them completely. Shortly, Georgia's winter clothes, books, drawings, and paintings arrived from Texas in a wooden barrel. The day she unpacked, Georgia looked over her old pictures and, influenced by the thought of her new work, decided to discard them. That night when she returned with Stieglitz to the studio, they discovered an O'Keeffe picture of a hollyhock protruding from a trash can and others tumbling around the street in the brisk fall wind, she recalled in her book. She decided to allow them to nose-dive and somersault as part of the urban landscape.

❖

Georgia's boarding school friend Susan Young, by then Mrs. Walter Wilson, visited New York in October 1918, when the couple first lived in the studio. Georgia sounded delighted when Susan telephoned, and asked her to come right over for breakfast—but quickly told her to being an egg because she didn't suppose she had one. After climbing the stairs to the studio (she had already eaten breakfast), Susan was introduced to Stieglitz, who had been delayed from his appointed rounds in order to meet her. He talked on and on, puzzling the Kentucky woman as he told her how someone had committed the sacrilege of turning a book of beautiful paper he had given him into a scrapbook by pasting pictures in it.

When Stieglitz got up to go, Georgia rose to fetch his cape and hat for him. As they said good-bye, she patted him affectionately on the back and he walked jauntily out the door, swinging his cane and looking, in Susan's eyes, for all the world like an artist. "Isn't he wonderful? Isn't he just *wonderful?*" Georgia asked after closing the door. Susan nodded. She though he was attractive and nice, but she wondered to herself what her friend wanted with an old man. Susan figured that since Georgia was almost thirty-one, she must have decided that the time had come to settle down. After all, hadn't the Chatham yearbook editors published a poem that half-seriously joked that by the age of thirty a girl would marry anything in pants? "When did you get married?" Susan asked her friend. "Oh, let's not talk about that," Georgia replied, and Susan never suspected that the couple were not husband and wife.

When Stieglitz left his wife to live with Georgia, a banker he knew warned him not to destroy himself for a young woman. Stieglitz said nothing, but took him up to the studio. With two southern windows and a skylight that Georgia liked to sleep under, the studio was flooded with light, which was intensified by pale yellow walls and an orange floor. All the quivering color made it a poor place for an artist to paint in, but it had a quality of joy for both of them. In 1919 Georgia painted an oil of the studio, in which the dark little bedroom was delineated by a jubilant, magical band of pale blue, its window backlighted by the reddish glow of the city; this was telling evidence of her feelings for Stieglitz as well as her less comfortable ones for New York. In the studio, Stieglitz showed his banker friend some of their new work, in which it could be seen that he was recording with his camera the moods his model was expressing on canvas. The banker, the way Stieglitz told it, said he never dreamed that love between a man and a woman could generate such mutual inspiration.

Bewitched by O'Keeffe the artist, Stieglitz didn't want their relationship to divert her from art. In fact, he hoped that their love would inspire her to finer work. Stieglitz constantly and copiously expressed himself in letters and talk, but rarely in poetry. In 1918, however, in the first flush of their affair, he wrote a poem in which he pictured himself as a lover who did not block his beloved's creativity. The poem, which was published in a small literary magazine, began:

> The flesh is starving
> Its soul is moving starward
> Seeking its own particular star
> A man intercepts . . .

In the rest of the poem Stieglitz wrote that the man relieves the starving flesh, and the soul continues to rise in the heavens.

Actually, he was helping her move "starward" in an essential way not suggested by the poem. Stieglitz was the kind of individual who wasn't afraid to reveal himself, even in casual conversations. But although she was direct when she spoke, Georgia was very guarded about many personal things. For this reason she disliked writing letters and in conversations she tended to remain silent unless she felt she had something significant to say. People around Stieglitz often responded to him in kind, risking the expression of deep feelings and, by doing so, becoming reconciled to suppressed parts of themselves. Like the others, Georgia began to entrust her intimate feelings to Stieglitz. Acting as a kind of therapeutic catalyst, he helped her to release and translate more of her deepest intuitions and feelings into paint.

After they began to live together, Georgia remarked to a friend that every woman should have Stieglitz for a lover. As her awareness of her sexuality was heightened, she started painting marvelously original abstractions in exuberant, uninhibited rainbows of pastel colors that appeared to melodiously celebrate her happiness. In *Music—Pink and Blue I*, painted in 1919, she encircled a blue vaginal void with pulsating waves of rippling pink and white. Stieglitz comprehended that she was painting erotic iconography, and he photographed the phallic form she had sculpted some years earlier in front of the painting's cavity in a most suggestive way.

Stieglitz had been annoyed when a friend suggested that the power of his photographic portraits lay in his ability to "hypnotize" his models with his personality, so he began to search for a subject he could not appear to put under a magic spell. In their third summer together, in 1921, Stieglitz, who had always been fascinated by weather, took on the immense challenge of photographing the ever-changing clouds in the skies over Lake George. In these photographs, Stieglitz deliberately tried to create the exact equivalent of intense moments between Georgia and himself. Some of his prints of low-floating clouds, backlit by the sun, appear electrified by a powerful emotional charge. Sometimes he discovered actual female forms in their undulating edges. Georgia didn't, however. "Can you find the woman in these?" she once asked the son of the painter Arthur Dove. "I can never find the woman."

Stieglitz's talk of "equivalents," however, influenced her. After thinking it over, she decided that a painting of a flower, for instance, couldn't give anyone else *exactly* the same feeling of enjoyment she derived from the flower, so she began to search for equivalents to recreate the feeling it had given her. "I know I cannot paint a flower," she was to write in years to come, ". . . but maybe in terms of paint color I can convey to you my experience of the flower or the experience that makes the flower of significance to me at that particular time."

Although she took very few snapshots, Georgia looked at thousands of prints, and, inevitably, the techniques of photography seeped into her consciousness. Sometimes Stieglitz made a hundred prints from a negative before he developed one that satisfied him. A friend observed that he worked "like a priest in a religious ritual" in the bathroom across the hall from the studio and rinsed the negatives in the basin in the back room. For her part, Georgia frequently painted the same object over and over—often a small, intricate natural form. Her images were often painted with a sharp photographic focus, and her invisible brushstrokes produced a smooth photographic-like finish. Although Stieglitz didn't make blowups or use bizarre angles, younger cameramen around him did, and Georgia noticed. She was known to paint only a fragment of an object or to place it off-center like a cropped photo. The distortion of the lens seemed evident in other compositions in which forms were tilted or receded in unrealistic ways. Working alongside the young medium of photography gave O'Keeffe a fresh viewpoint and the license to break painterly rules.

From time to time in their early years together, she felt discouraged by Stieglitz's achievements. At other times his good intentions had a negative effect. For instance, when he gave her thick, expensive paper for watercolor painting, she found it inhibited the bold experiments she had done in Texas on cheap, thin paper she used for kindling fires in her potbellied stove. Working so closely together produced other problems as well. Occasionally, they uncomfortably shared subjects—she painted Lake George clouds after he photographed them, for example—but they also competed for them. "Once Stieglitz got ahead of me," she recalled. "He shot a door before I could paint it." Eventually she did a farmhouse window instead, a painting regarded as one of her best.

Awed by what Stieglitz had accomplished in his own field, Georgia struggled in the fall of 1922 to compose an answer to the question "Is photography art?" for a little magazine named *MSS*, which was published by some of Stieglitz's friends and for which Georgia designed a cover. She wrote that Stieglitz's photographs were "spiritually significant in that I can return to them, day after day, have done so almost daily for a period of four years and always with a feeling of wonder and excitement akin to that aroused in me by the Chinese, the Egyptians, Negro Art, Picasso, Henri Rousseau, Seurat, etcetera, even including modern plumbing or a fine precise piece of machinery." "If a Stieglitz photograph of a well-to-do Mid-Victorian parlor filled with all sorts of horrible atrocities jumbled together makes me forget that it is a photograph," she also wrote, "and creates music that is more than music when viewed right side up or upside down or sideways, it is Art to me. Possibly I feel it is Art because I am not clogged with too much knowledge. Or is it Stieglitz?"

Their professional respect for one another was a firm cornerstone of their love. When Georgia sized up their relationship in old age, she said it was "really very good" because, despite their differences, each was keenly interested in the other's work. She admired the way he continued to be innovative as he aged, and she later refused to consider old age a barrier to her own creativity. Stieglitz's work "is always a surprise to me—one feels there can be nothing more for him to do—and then away he goes—shooting way ahead just like the last time," she had written to Sherwood Anderson in earlier years. Their mutual esteem was also an important strength in their situation, when they were faced with people who disapproved of Stieglitz leaving his wife and college-age daughter to live openly with a striking woman almost twenty-five years his junior. New York was not as easygoing as Paris in the twenties, and Victorian prohibitions hung on.

❖

From the moment Georgia arrived in New York, Stieglitz began to photograph her feverishly. "I was photographed with a kind of heat and excitement and in a way wondered what it was all about," she wrote at the age of ninety, when she decided to publish some of the photographs. The couple tried to be in the studio at the times of day when the light was right, and at those times Georgia learned to expect that the large camera that stood by the wall, with its old black cloth, rickety tripod, and stained white umbrella (to reflect soft light into shadows), would be set up and posing would begin. In less than three years, Stieglitz perfected two hundred prints—the beginning of a massive, majestic portrait of Georgia that amounted to more than three hundred portraits by the time he put down his heavy cameras in 1937 at the age of seventy-three.

The great photographer felt compelled to discover with his camera the "truth" about this remote woman he loved. In his quest, each part of her body came under the close scrutiny of his lens and was immortalized: hair, earlobes, nose, lips, neck, breasts, navel, hips, labia, buttocks, fingers, legs, and toes. He focused his lens with such precision that the prints reveal that his subject wore no makeup and did not tweeze or shave a hair from her body. The down on her upper lip and belly was delicately recorded as well as the fuzz in her armpits. She didn't look into a mirror before she began to pose, and he didn't touch up the prints afterwards. What was important was that her face did not freeze before the camera but kept its naturalness. It was not important that her angular features weren't perfectly regular, but only that they were definite and expressive. Stieglitz positioned his camera so that the composition within the frame brought into taut balance the marks and features unique to the body of his beloved.

Most of the erotic poses are from the first few years of their love affair. Her lover caught Georgia among crumpled white bed sheets in a starkly sexual pose or just arisen, with her long hair tangled around her shoulders. Occasionally she posed with only her little black straw derby on her head, placed at a rakish angle like a vaudeville performer. In these sexually playful poses, more frank than coy, her serious, reflective eyes were concealed by the shadow of her hat brim while amusement danced around her mouth. One imagines that she was amused by the whimsical poses she struck for the cameraman, whose agitation while photographing, she later confessed to a friend, she sometimes found "infinitely ridiculous."

It's obvious that although Georgia's sense of the absurd was familiar to her friends, Stieglitz thought of the essential O'Keeffe as stern and even a bit tragic. Many more black than clowning moods were recorded in the photographs, particularly as the years went by. She often looked ageless or, at least, older than her years. But when a rare flicker of amusement crossed her face, it totally erased her severity. A smile wide enough to reveal her beautiful even teeth, however, was as scarce before the camera as the proverbial hen's teeth.

Once Stieglitz shot her on a windswept Lake George hill, her hands on her hips and her black cloak flung around her shoulders and buttoned up to her chin, as he crouched with his camera at her feet. He angled the lens so as to set her head against the stormy, threatening autumn sky, while she stared down her nose at the world with unafraid heavy-lidded eyes.

In the photographs, the consistent contrast between her soft, rounded body and her strong, forbidding face is startling. Her usual expression was one of utter gravity, even hauteur, and there is virtually no picture showing her with a gentle or contented look. Her mouth often turned down at the edges into a scowl whereas her heavy, un-plucked eyebrows flew up like inquisitive wings. The harshness was often accentuated by poses in which the relentless glare of the mid-summer sun revealed every nuance of her look. "I try to show life as it is, not as it should be or as I would like to have it," Stieglitz once said about his work.

One day in 1919, when she was extremely thin, he instructed her to pose on the radiator in front of a studio window that was curtained in gossamer to diffuse the daylight. First Georgia stood in her white kimono with its long, flowing, embroidered sleeves, and next she took it off and posed naked. In the photographs, her classic, chiseled profile rivets the eye; her bun of dark hair was balanced by a tuft of pubic hair; her arms were raised, reaching, revealing the bones of her chest above her heavy, drooping breasts. She look like a spirit, weighed down by womanhood, trying to take flight. Indeed, this is what Stieglitz believed that O'Keeffe, the artist, was trying to do, against great odds—what no woman had ever done before.

Many of the photographs from 1918 and 1919 suggest that Stie-glitz viewed Georgia and her art as part of the same elementary creative force. He often photographed her posing in front of one of her charcoal drawings in such a way that her pale arms or bare breasts were coun-terpoints to the charcoal forms on paper. In one composition he asked her to raise her chin, then angled his camera from below her jawline as she froze motionless against a turbulent drawing of Palo Duro can-yon. With her pointed ears and flared nostrils that acted as counter-weights, her eyes that looked dark and fierce, and her parted lips, she symbolized a forceful, proud artist—the artist-hero whom her mentor worshiped and who was so rare in America.

Stieglitz marveled when his model was able to stay absolutely still for the three- or four-minute-long exposures on glass plates, and he roared at her when her eyes blinked, her mouth twitched, or an uplifted, aching arm trembled and ruined his picture. For her part, Georgia complained that she didn't like posing for him any more than she had liked posing at the age of twenty at the Art Students League. He was not easy to pose for, recalled his niece Georgia Engelhard in a article she later wrote, because in his obsession he demanded endless patience in difficult poses without permitting a pause or uttering a sympathetic word. But apparently O'Keeffe felt obliged to turn herself periodically into a statue for the sake of her mentor, her lover, her provider. She grumbled that posing demanded iron discipline when her skin itched all over, the wind froze her motionless body, and the fierce Lake George cow flies buzzed around her head. (Later she used the memory of her own discomfort as her excuse for never painting human beings—she wanted to spare others her torture.) The difficulties, however, added a degree of anguish to her face and helped Stieglitz capture the look he was after.

As they worked to create an image, the pictures became theatrical, said one critic, Sanford Schwartz, fifty years later in *The New Yorker*:

> O'Keeffe didn't allow that much of herself to flow out, and Stieglitz never got one definitive, psychologically rounded image of her. What he did get was a performance. In these pictures, O'Keeffe is the one great actress of still photography. She can appear as a madonna or a clown, an icy romantic princess or a waif, and throughout the series the mood is never more than surface deep. Yet the photographs of her aren't superficial, and you don't question her sincerity or Stieglitz's, because she seems so lost in surface. She isn't mugging or impersonating, she's entrancing herself. She may be wearing masks, but they have been brought up from within—they are her own.

Nonetheless, Stieglitz's photographs of her affected Georgia deeply from the time he first sent some to her in Texas. When she moved to New York, they were the proof that she was the center of his life—for he had never before photographed another woman in the same compulsive way. The picture taking was much on her mind. When asked to describe herself in 1922, she wrote in her article for MSS, "I have not been in Europe. I prefer to live in a room as bare as possible. I have been much photographed."

She was fascinated by the image of the artist that Stieglitz saw when he peered at her through the lens. Stieglitz had written to Paul Strand when he first began to photograph O'Keeffe that "whenever she looks at the proofs she falls in love with herself.—Or rather her Selves—There are very many." She seemed actually to see her face for the first time: the curved forehead, strong cheekbones, firm jaw.

"You see, I'd never known what I looked like or thought about it much," she explained. "I was amazed to find my face was lean and structured. I'd always thought it was round." She later credited his photographs of her personas as being helpful to her as a painter. " know now that most people are so closely concerned with themselves that they are not aware of their own individuality," she later remarked. "I can see myself, and it has helped me to say what I want to say— in paint."

Since she came from a family of sisters who were not conventionally pretty, her beauty revealed in the poses under the little black hat must have particularly surprised her. But she did not like the playful prints as much as the serious shots that served to affirm her strongly as an artist in her own eyes. Although posing for Stieglitz did not tempt her to become a coquette, she did begin to comb her hair uncompromisingly back from her broad forehead more often.

Friends who habitually visited the couple's studio saw the daring photographs (which "registered new tones of gold, unspeakable explorations of black," wrote Stieglitz's friend Jerome Mellquist. "They were volcanic and they had a pinpoint delicacy"), and the word spread that Stieglitz was working again. Soon his friend Mitchell Kennerley, president of the Anderson Galleries, a famous art auction house that stood back-to-back to the studio on swank Park Avenue and Fifty-ninth Street, offered him two large rooms on the top floor of the stone building for a retrospective. On February 7, 1921, Stieglitz, whose friends had once said he had put away his camera equipment forever, reigned over an exhibition of a hundred and forty-five photographs. In his review for the *New York Herald*, Stieglitz's old friend and contemporary Henry McBride welcomed him back and noted the contrast between the Anderson Galleries and his old quarters at 291. There was "considerable red plush instead of the inconsiderate gray paint, but the main thing, Alfred, was there and they [his friends] were happy . . . but greater than his photographs was Alfred, and greater than Alfred was his talk—as copious, continuous and revolutionary as ever."

Forty-five, or nearly one third, of the brown-toned prints were of a young artist named Georgia O'Keeffe. Many of them were semi-nudes, and although those of her most private parts were withheld, people whispered about their existence. They also gossiped about the photographer's relationship to the young woman who was not his wife.

No man had ever recorded his poignant love for a woman so intimately before, they said, and perhaps out of curiosity as much as out of interest in art, three thousand visitors crowded into the rooms during the weeks of the show. "Stieglitz achieved the exact visual equivalent of the report of the hand . . . as it travels over the body of the beloved," critic Lewis Mumford recalled. Some compared the photographs to the joyous biblical love "poem," the Song of Solomon, and innocently asked Stieglitz to take similar photographs of their wives. One young woman standing in front of them became tearful, and when asked why, she murmured, "He loves her so." Others observed that the ecstasy of Stieglitz in love had enabled him to do his best work since his peak creative years. He later agreed that the expression of pure feeling in his photographs of Georgia was the artistic pinnacle he had sought.

Although Georgia had not exhibited much of her work for four years, when Stieglitz's retrospective caused a sensation, it brought her to the attention of the critics again. Who was the photographer's model with the haughty expression and the lovely body? They could tell that she was an artist because she posed with her unusual pictures in the background. Years later McBride wrote in the *New York Sun:* "There came to notice almost at once . . . some photographs showing every conceivable aspect of O'Keeffe that was a new effort in photography and something new in the way of introducing a budding artist." McBride continued in his humorous way, "It made a stir. Mona Lisa got but one portrait of herself worth talking about. O'Keeffe got a hundred. [The number was distorted in his memory.] It put her at once on the map. Everybody knew the name. She became what is known as a newspaper personality."

❖

After Stieglitz's show, Georgia became much more visible at a time when it was extremely difficult for any artist—but particularly a woman—to achieve recognition. In spring 1921, painter Arthur Carles asked Stieglitz to help put on a show of modern art at the Pennsylvania Academy of the Fine Arts, where Carles was an instructor. "But I don't want any goddam women in the show," the bearded Carles added. Stieglitz, who espoused the integration of "male" and "female" qualities in people and liked to show paintings by men and women together rather than separately, told him that O'Keeffe was always included in any show he was involved in. "Take it or leave it," he told Carles. "There'll be no show without her." Stieglitz was on the selection and hanging committees, and his strong will prevailed. Not only were three women included among the twenty-seven artists, but Georgia was represented by more paintings—*Red, Pink,* and *The Black Spot*— than any other artist. Later that year the leading literary journal of the twenties, *The Dial,* published an article about her by one of Stieglitz's friends as well as a reproduction of *The Black Spot,* an oil she painted in 1919. The picture's hard geometric forms that press against softly rounded ones have sometimes been interpreted as the mix of femininity and masculinity in the artist's personality.

In the summer of 1922, when she was thirty-four, Georgia began to frame some of her paintings. Stieglitz felt that the time was right for her to have an exhibition of her own, after a hiatus of almost six years, and he interceded with Mitchell Kennerley to arrange for one. Then in the fall and winter articles appeared about her in *Vanity Fair* (along with a portrait of her by Stieglitz's friend Marion Beckett), and other publications. Stieglitz wrote Henry McBride that he was going to introduce Georgia to the world, promising that his protégée's show would be something "different."

Georgia had mixed feelings about her upcoming show. Although she liked to see her pictures hung together for purposes of comparison, she recoiled at the idea of strangers viewing them. It was a reaction that had first emerged when Stieglitz unexpectedly hung her charcoal drawings in 1916 and that lasted, with varying intensity, throughout her life. She painted out of a need to express herself in the language of color—not to show, sell, or to be parted from her pictures. Painting was a private act for her, not a public one, and she liked to call showing "a necessary evil." She felt that her paintings were "intimate and beautiful, like beautiful children," Stieglitz explained to Sherwood Anderson a few years later. "The greasy, vulgar people, the thought of such people coming into contact with her work, made her feel ill."

Nevertheless, her exhibition opened at the Anderson Galleries on January 29, 1923, and lasted for two weeks. The flyer that announced it made clear who was responsible for the display of the one hundred paintings, ninety of which had never been exhibited before:

Alfred Stieglitz
Presents
One Hundred Pictures
Oils, Water-colors
Pastels, Drawings
by
Georgia O'Keeffe
American

As in her shows in the old days at 291, the paintings were untitled—only dated and numbered—but it can be assumed that the exhibit contained her best work of the past few years. In general, the new pictures were in a softer, quieter, more intimate mood than the Texas ones, and her style was more confident and mature. The many abstractions included those inspired by music, by spring, and by leaves under the water of the lake. Her palette, reviewers noticed, was overwhelmingly red and white in her paintings of such fruits and flowers as flaming red cannas and rosy red apples.

Critics who had seen the Stieglitz photographs of the alluring young artist two years before took note and, consequently, five hundred people a day saw her show, one newspaper reported. Curiosity had been aroused by reviews saying her pictures were suppressed Freudian desires on canvas, sublimations of a powerful and unusual personality. For example, Henry McBride wrote:

> Georgia O'Keeffe is probably what they will be calling a few years a B.F. [before Freud] since all her inhibitions seem to have been removed before the Freudian recommendations were preached upon this side of the Atlantic. She became free without the aid of Freud. But she had aid. There was another who took the place of Freud. . . . It is of course Alfred Stieglitz. . . . He is responsible for the O'Keeffe exhibition in the Anderson Galleries. Miss O'Keeffe says so herself, and it is reasonably sure that he is responsible for Miss O'Keeffe, the artist. . . .
>   Her progress toward freedom may be gauged from a confession of hers printed in the catalogue. She couldn't live where she wanted to, couldn't go where she wanted to, couldn't do or say what she wanted to; she decided that it was stupid not at least to say what she wanted to say. So now she says anything without fear. . . . The outstanding fact is that she is unafraid. . . . The result is

calmness. . . . In definitely unbosoming her soul she not only finds her own release but advances the cause of art in her country. . . . She is a sort of modern Margaret Fuller sneered at by Nathaniel Hawthorne for a too great tolerance of sin and finally prayed to by all the super-respectable women of the country for receipts that would keep them from the madhouse. . . . She will be besieged by all her sisters for advice—which will be a supreme danger for her. She is, after all, an artist, and owes more to art than to morality. My own advice to her . . . is, immediately after the show to get herself to a nunnery.

Although she didn't care for the talk about Freud, Georgia found McBride's witticisms hilarious. An iconoclast among critics, McBride had reviewed art since the Armory show and he applauded modern art. Tall and reserved, he was described by artist Peggy Bacon as having a "long head with flat falling cheeks recalling a well-bred hunting dog." He "speaks with a great caution and courtesy concealing a wayward twinkle in a great deal of flippant humor," Bacon went on to say. McBride habitually gave Georgia slightly mocking praise, yet she usually enjoyed his barbed humor, perhaps because it also poked fun at her fans as well. In the winter of 1923 she joked in a letter to him that she would head straight for a nunnery if she weren't sick in bed from all the excitement. It was to be a common reaction for her to be felled by exhaustion, a midwinter virus, perhaps anxiety over a show's reception, and, certainly, distaste for meeting her public.

Predictably, the show established her as an artist in her own right rather than merely a great photographer's model, and her one year of being a full-time artist in New York was to extend to thirty years. More people began to refer to her as "O'Keeffe"—a neuter, professional-sounding name that Stieglitz had used right from the start. Her paintings appealed to buyers and, in all, three thousand dollars' worth were sold, perhaps adding up to a half dozen pictures. She had developed a friendship with another midwesterner, Sherwood Anderson, a moody, talkative, heavyset man, who had begged off from writing a statement for her catalog. Anderson returned to the show five or six times—admitting that he had not taken her work seriously until then—and bought a painting.

Once her reluctance to exhibit again was overcome, Georgia was ready to show and to earn money the next year. It was decided that she and Stieglitz would have simultaneous shows in the Anderson Galleries in early 1924, Georgia taking a large room and Stieglitz using two smaller ones for his pictures of clouds. Although Georgia didn't seem particularly pleased about the arrangement, the joint show opened for two weeks in March. Once again she was presented as Stieglitz's protégée, and she was represented by fifty-one pictures. She was rediscovered that year by one of her old Art Students League classmates, Helen Appleton Read, who had become an art critic for the *Brooklyn Eagle*. Read was surprised to find that pretty "Patsy" O'Keeffe had metamorphosed into "an ascetic, almost saintly appearing, woman with a dead white skin, fine delicate features, and black hair severely drawn back from her forehead. Saintly, yes, but not nun-like, for O'Keeffe gives one the feeling that beneath her calm poise there is something that is intensely, burningly alive, and that she is not only possessed of the most delicate sensibilities but is also capable of great and violent emotions."

❖

In 1916 a critic had read into one of Georgia's charcoal drawings that she wanted to have a baby, and he was right. She had always been eager to experience life fully, and she felt that giving birth was one of life's tremendous events. Also, she had found young children to be charming—for instance, her sister's playmates in Virginia, faculty children in South Carolina, and schoolchildren in Amarillo. In Canyon she never forgot the childlike grace of her landlord's small blond daughter when she leaned over a bowl of forced yellow jonquils in the winter twilight. On a walk at that time, she confided to fellow teacher Emma Jean McClesky, "I've just *got* to have a baby—if I don't, my life just won't be complete."

Starting in 1918, the first year she lived with Stieglitz, he openly told people that Georgia wanted to have a child but that he was convinced she should not. Being a parent had been an anxiety-ridden and, finally, heartbreaking experience for him. His relationship with his daughter Kitty was deeply wounded when the girl, who was then twenty and at Smith College, learned that her father had left her mother to live with Georgia. But more fundamentally, Stieglitz was against it because as he approached sixty he had little interest in babies.

He was far more interested in nurturing talented young American artists so they could attain their full potentials.

Essentially still filling the role of her mentor, Stieglitz told Georgia that motherhood would divert her from painting. He loved her pure artistic spirit, which he thought of as "Whiteness," and he didn't want it contaminated. Feeling himself to be physically and figuratively "gray" at times, he wrote to a friend in the fall of 1923, "I have a passion for Whiteness in all its forms." He devoted himself to encouraging it in her and to keeping her on the trajectory he had set her on. During the twenties, many of his letters to mutual friends reflected either his worry that she wasn't painting or his exultation that, once again, she was turning out her "wonders."

The year they began to live together, he wrote a paean to her that depicted her as a solitary artist with her eyes steadily on her goal. It ran in part:

> The Stars are Playing in the Skies
> The Earth's Asleep—
> One Soul's Awake
> A woman
>   The Stars Beckon—
> Her Room is a Whiteness
> Whiteness Opens its Door
> She Walks into Darkness
> Alone
> With the Night—alone with the Stars
> A Mountain nearby
> Its Peak near those Stars—
> She climbs the Steep Mountain
> Alone—
> To the Top . . .
>   The Woman Walks Homeward
>   To her Little White Room
>   No longer Alone
>   She Carries Dawn
>   In Her Womb

By the summer of 1923, when she was thirty-five, Georgia seemed to have given in to Stieglitz and agreed not to have a child. That was the summer that Stieglitz's daughter, after having married Milton

Stearns of Boston, gave birth to a son and sank into a severe postpartum depression from which she never fully recovered. It was also the summer after Stieglitz had presented a hundred of O'Keeffe's paintings to the world, and Georgia felt she was on her way to becoming a successful artist. "His belief in the authority of her work and his unbounded enthusiasm are as contagious as was his cheering for Matisse in the old days," a visitor to her 1923 show had exclaimed. Her choice was brutally clear—stay with Stieglitz and be an artist or leave and, perhaps, become a mother.

Georgia remained with Stieglitz, stayed childless, and devoted the rest of her life to art. Her personality gradually took on an uncompromising edge that made many of her friends, particularly those who were mothers, believe that she would not have enjoyed the conflicts, sacrifices, and adjustments inherent in raising a child and that, indeed, it was a good thing that she did not have one. "Unlike most women, O'Keeffe does not encourage compromise," a close friend was to say a few years later. "She wants that which she takes, else she takes nothing. She never accepts a second choice." Others, however, were not so sure that she had no regrets about her decision. In old age the subject was still on her mind. She observed to a young female poet that a mother could leave a typewriter in midsentence to do something for a child, but a painter must have uninterrupted hours for preparing materials and must not be stopped in the middle of a brushstroke by a child's demand.

When it became evident to Stieglitz's wife that her marriage to Alfred was irretrievable, she began divorce proceedings, which became official on Sept. 9, 1924 after six years of resistence by Emmy and her brothers. After the divorce was final, Stieglitz began to insist that Georgia marry him. He wanted to make it possible for Georgia to inherit his estate and to maintain his hold on the younger woman. Also, at the time it was far easier for a couple to be man and wife than to "live in sin." But Georgia reasoned that they had lived together since 1918 and had already withstood all the scandal, so why bother to marry now?

Still, her sisters had scattered and she may have felt she had little family to speak of. A few years earlier, in November 1918, her father had died in a fall from a roof. In what can be taken as the final statement about his marriage, he was buried alongside his parents and brothers in the Catholic cemetery in Sun Prairie rather than beside his wife in the Episcopal graveyard in Madison. Although Georgia had not written to him in years, she was shaken when a relative notified her of his death. Then, a month later, her tall, attractive younger brother, Alexius, was sent to Wisconsin on a stretcher from the battlefield in France, his health broken by the flu and suffering from the effects of having been gassed. Her older brother, Francis, who was said to have an aristocratic manner, married in 1922 while working in New York as an architect. For some reason that Georgia didn't talk about, she barely recognized his existence. Francis eventually dropped the second "f" from his last name and moved out of the country.

Stieglitz's various arguments finally prevailed, and Georgia reluctantly agreed to get married. They waited three months. On a cold Tuesday in December 1924, on the eleventh, Georgia, just thirty-seven, and Alfred, almost sixty-one, boarded the ferry from New York to New Jersey because the divorce decree banned remarriage in New York State. Accompanying them was Stieglitz's brother-in-law George Engelhard, a lawyer, who was to act as a witness. The couple had told few people about their upcoming wedding; it was practically kept secret.

In New Jersey, they were met at the Weehawken ferry slip by the second witness—John Marin, an artist who had been close to Stieglitz for many years. Marin drove them in his new Chandler touring auto to the office of Joseph Marini, the Cliffside Park mayor and a merchant and justice of the peace. Where the marriage license application asked for the bridegroom's occupation, Stieglitz penned the word "artist." His future wife had no similar question on her part of the form, so she put nothing down. When the couple recited their vows, no wedding rings were exchanged, and, bowing to her feminist beliefs, the bride omitted the words "love, honor, and obey."

As they all drove back to the ferry, Marin, in a moment of animated talk, swerved his new auto into a grocery wagon and careened across the road into a lamppost. Bystanders gathered around, a policeman arrived, accusations were made, and license plate numbers were exchanged. Nobody was hurt, but when the hullabaloo had died down and the four of them were sitting there in stunned silence, Georgia remarked grimly that she felt as if she had lost a leg. The way the story was repeated, no one was ever quite sure whether she meant that the accident or her wedding felt like an amputation.

6 ❖ New York

On November 11, 1918, the Armistice was signed, signaling the victorious end to the First World War. New Yorkers poured into the streets singing and dancing, automobile horns blared, church bells pealed, and factory whistles screamed while ticker tape floated down from the city's tall buildings. A white-plaster arch of triumph was erected at Madison Square, and a canopy of glass beads was suspended above Fifth Avenue, which glittered brightly at night when multicolored searchlights were turned on it.

The outburst was a fitting start for the decade of the twenties. The war had unleashed technologies that spun off new peacetime pleasures. Autos jammed the city streets, radios blared jazz rhythms, and silent films in lavish movie palaces drew large crowds. The tempo of life had rapidly accelerated, particularly in New York, the hub of all the excitement.

While the nation was turning to its pleasures, the League of Nations was rejected and President Wilson decided not to run for reelection. In 1920 Republican Warren Harding was elected in his place. Four years later Calvin Coolidge was elected, and in New York, popular playboy mayor Jimmy Walker seemed to spend more time amusing New Yorkers with his quips, dandified airs, and piano playing than in keeping an eye on City Hall.

There was a dark underside to all the fun, however. The end of the war caused severe economic disruptions and violent labor strikes broke out. An anarchist bombing killed a number of people on Wall Street in 1920. Of even greater impact was the nationwide ban on liquor, which went into effect at midnight on January 15, 1920. Thereafter thousands of speakeasies began to open up in the basements of brownstones in midtown Manhattan. Bootleggers' links to the underworld were forged, and organized crime became highly profitable.

The nation's self-indulgent mood did not benefit artists, and many fled to Europe. But Georgia had no thought of doing so, and Stieglitz had made a commitment to America. In fact, Georgia's pure American spirit was one of the qualities that had drawn him to her. "There is no limitation of Europe in her," is the way the sculptor Brancusi later put it. "It is a force—a liberating free force." But whereas both of Georgia's parents were born on Wisconsin farms, Stieglitz's parents were born in Europe and had taken him back there to complete his education. Consequently, his conviction that he was truly an American was as shaky as hers was steady and strong.

The couple lived in their sunny little studio for about two years. After the rent was raised, they moved in December 1920 into rent-free quarters on the top two floors of the nearby brownstone owned by one of Alfred's younger brothers, Dr. Leopold ("Lee") Stieglitz, an internist who lived and had an office at 60 East Sixty-fifth Street. He was a great admirer of Georgia's paintings, and Stieglitz gave him three or four of them over the years. The address was right off Park Avenue, then the most fashionable street in New York, since hugh department stores had pushed the old mansions off Fifth Avenue. Stieglitz had a large red-carpeted front room on the top floor; a maid's bedroom was in back. Georgia's room was on the floor below along with the room of Lee's mother-in-law. She chose neutral pale gray for her walls, a tone that was best for thinking visually in, she had decided. They had their own telephone, and Stieglitz had a darkroom.

The couple made their own breakfast in their rooms and ate other meals out to preserve everyone's independence and privacy. They took most of their meals in places like Joe's Spaghetti Restaurant, a cheap but excellent bistro on Third Avenue at Fifty-eighth Street where they frequently dined. They stood out from the other diners in their look-alike black capes (worn only in Paris at the time) and black hats. "They were a rather solemn couple who seldom smiled and were very curiously subdued—there was very little talking," observed Arthur

Young, the young artist, who also ate there regularly. "It was almost as if they weren't happy together." Their apparent lack of conviviality pointed rather to Stieglitz's normal seriousness and Georgia's quietness rather than to a true lack of rapport. There was never much laughter around Stieglitz, and Georgia's mischievousness was more likely to surface with her lighthearted contemporaries.

Although they lived on very little money, Georgia's first few winters in New York at Stieglitz's side provided her with a lively, informal, rich education in art, music, literature, and other areas. The two artists made the rounds of exhibitions where modern art was on display, heard chamber music recitals, and tried to go to every concert conducted by Arturo Toscanini. Years later, Georgia remarked that it was Stieglitz who had taught her how to *really* listen to music.

All sorts of people continued to seek Stieglitz out. Some of the most talented artists and writers in New York those days rang their Rhinelander telephone number—from poet William Carlos Williams to sculptor Gaston Lachaise. Stieglitz also had a group of loyal disciples, like Herbert Seligmann, Waldo Frank, and Paul Rosenfeld, who shared their mentor's excitement about the discovery of their Americanism. In his rooms at his brother's, Stieglitz held forth in his magnetic, even fanatic way, holding in thrall anywhere from two to twenty listeners who might be overflowing from the chairs and onto the floor. It was a kind of one-man show, an American "salon," a continual happening. Visitors dropped in, departed, or lingered into the early morning hours. "Privacy in the ordinary sense seemed hardly to exist for Stieglitz," recalled Seligmann. "He was on call, seemingly at any hour, any day, for anyone who chose to participate in the experience he was having."

Fueled by nervous energy and a passionate interest in people and ideas, Stieglitz was characterized by a friend as a "smoldering volcano in whom fire never died out and seldom subsided." His "widely carved, crooked, talking mouth, muscular, well-exercised, argumentative, the bursting outlet for a torrential stream of thought," was constantly in motion. Stieglitz seemed to survive on six pieces of zwieback and a cup of watery cocoa for breakfast and little else until dinner. Although he frequently complained about an assortment of aches and pains, even they didn't stop him.

At first Georgia was jealous of his constant stream of visitors and endless letter writing. She naturally wanted more of her lover to herself, and their first months together had some difficult moments. But she came to realize that although she barely existed when he was with others, when they were alone together she was the calm center of his life. "And when you find this woman moving through the wordy whirlwind that ever rages round the rooms of Alfred Stieglitz, you have the effect of silence," wrote Waldo Frank somewhat melodramatically. "To see her is to be minded of some Scriptural wife tilling the soil and homing with her husband under the storms and sunbeams of Jehovah." Possibly she was able to accept the situation for the additional reason that in childhood she had learned to be content on the sidelines of her family.

Proud of the slender American woman with the steady eyes and low, purring voice, Stieglitz wanted her to meet those people she would not have met on her own. Her sharp intelligence and sound intuition enabled her to sense which of the visitors around Stieglitz were worth bothering with, and often she found someone who interested her. "When she looks at a person or a thing she senses the effluvia that radiate from them and it is by this that she gauges her loves and hates or her tolerance of them," observed Marsden Hartley in 1920. Unable to chitchat easily, she was also introduced to many people whom she didn't like and who didn't care for her.

One of those who wanted to meet her after seeing the show of Stieglitz's photographs in 1921 was Chicago art critic Blanche Matthias. However, when Stieglitz took Blanche—a beautiful, warm, perceptive, wealthy married woman—back to the rooms at Leopold's, Georgia, curled up in a big chair, greeted her icily, perhaps distrusting her rapport with Stieglitz. Nevertheless, Blanche pursued the friendship, inviting Georgia to luncheon in her room on a high floor of the Hotel Ambassador. Georgia accepted but remained remote and spoke about herself "haltingly" until, in her enthusiasm for a spectacular snowstorm that was swirling outside the hotel windows, she lost her reserve, relaxed, and began to talk more openly.

The two women, both born in the same year, both childless and from the Midwest, became lifelong friends. Blanche traveled from Chicago each year to see Georgia's annual show, liked to give her gardenias, and to take long walks together with her in Central Park. "What do you see?" Georgia asked one day when they were walking. "I see green trees against the blue sky," Blanche replied. "What do *you* see?" "I see blue sky against the green trees," Georgia responded, much to her friend's delight at Georgia's unique way of seeing. Blanche, who both Stieglitz and O'Keeffe felt was able to write about her truthfully and well, described Georgia in the *Chicago Evening Post* on March 2, 1926:

> She is like the unflickering flame of a candle, steady, serene, softly brilliant. . . . From the delicately poised head to the small stout shoes is a rhythm unbroken by any form of hampering. Delicate, sensitive, exquisitely beautiful, with the candor of a child in her unafraid eyes and the trained mind of an intuitive woman for a tool, it is no wonder that O'Keeffe disdains the ordinary trappings and lip rouge of her less favored sisters and faces the world unconcernedly "as is."

❖

After 291 had closed in 1917, Stieglitz kept alive his dream of a group of like-minded artists clustering together to help each other out, since it was difficult for an American artist to survive alone. Although his income was not large, he bought paintings and photographs from anybody whose work represented an honest creative effort during years when there was little buying. Sometimes he helped to arrange an auction or a show for his loyal friends at willing galleries. "He had faith in the painters and the writers and the plumbers and all the other fools," Georgia wrote in 1922. "He seems to be the only man I know who has a real spiritual faith in human beings."

Stieglitz wanted New York to see the work of the artists he had believed in since the days of 291. Mitchell Kennerley, who had generously given him exhibition space in 1921, 1923, and 1924, loaned him the top floor of the Anderson Galleries for a large group show in early 1925. Seven Americans (plus "X," an unknown), as the show was called, contained one hundred and fifty-nine beautifully arranged works: photographs by Stieglitz and Paul Strand, and paintings by John Marin, Arthur Dove, Charles Demuth, Marsden Hartley, and the only woman, Georgia O'Keeffe. The exhibitors' styles varied widely (Georgia's paintings were remarked on for their surprising "aggressiveness"), but they were all influenced by the abstract art movement and inspired by nature.

When the exhibition ended, Stieglitz was reluctant to return the pictures to their storage vaults, where they would not be seen. He asked his friend Kennerley, who was interested in contemporary writers and painters, if he could rent a room in the building on a permanent basis. Stieglitz wanted "his" artists to be able to exhibit regularly and for a longer time each year so that they would be able to sell enough to keep on working. He also wanted them to be independent of the commercial galleries, which catered to the public's conventional tastes and encouraged artists to paint in an "acceptable" way. For about two thousand dollars a year Kennerley agreed to rent to Stieglitz a small, narrow northwest corner room on the top floor of the Anderson Galleries, which was surrounded by shops selling jewelry, antiques, and other luxuries.

The Intimate Gallery—situated in Room 303 and soon dubbed "the Room" by the regulars—opened its doors to the public in December 1925. Stieglitz explained in a 1927 announcement:

> The Intimate Gallery is a Direct Point of Contact between Public and Artist. It is the Artist's Room. It is a Room with but One Standard. Alfred Stieglitz has volunteered his services and is its directing Spirit.

> The Intimate Gallery is not a Business nor is it a "Social" Function. The Intimate Gallery competes with no one nor with anything.

Although the roar of city traffic vibrated through its three big windows, the gallery looked like a cross between a sanctuary and an operating room. It was devoted to the worship of the creative spirit, and all else was pared away. Except for a small crystal ball on a table, there was no decoration of any kind, and whatever furniture there was was utilitarian. Georgia, who supervised the design of the room, left the black carpet and dark oak woodwork alone, but covered the high, black stamped-velour walls with white cheesecloth. Electric lights, which glittered overhead, made the walls look silvery gray.

The gallery only showed the work of a small clique, yet the intense atmosphere was similar to that of 291 when Stieglitz was introducing avant-garde art to America back in the teens. One visitor remarked that one should pay admission because an hour there was as entertaining as going to the theater. Georgia once said that being there was "like taking part in a sustained and violent love affair." Sometimes when her pictures were on the walls and she sat quietly in a corner, wrapped in her black cloth coat with her long hands folded calmly in her lap, an inquisitive look in her eyes and a small smile on her lips, visitors felt trivial and awkward in contrast to her and her pictures.

Stieglitz lorded over his "salon" six and a half days a week, from ten in the morning until six at night, sometimes pausing at lunchtime for a drugstore sandwich that he ate in the storage room. He relished seeing his artists' new work each year and everyone's reaction to it. "He also enjoyed complaining about the problems and the difficulties of the artists, even when [their problems] were most difficult," Georgia recalled after his death. "He would have denied this."

In his black cape, walking stick, and flat pancake hat, Stieglitz looked like a shepherd to his flock of artists. He told them that they were an elite group of truth seekers, superior to ordinary Americans. He passionately protected them, even to the point of refusing to lend their work to museums that had not bought their pictures. He did not take a sales commission and was convinced that their survival as artists depended on his martyrdom. In return, he expected unquestioning loyalty. "He was the leader or he didn't play," Georgia explained later. "It was his game and we all played along or left the game."

The Intimate Gallery first showed the work of John Marin, and Marin shows became the traditional way to open each season. Marin was a slight, spry, puckish Yankee, with long brown bangs framing a wrinkled face dominated by a sharp nose and mobile mouth. He had known Stieglitz since they first met in Paris in 1909. Stieglitz and others ranked Marin's watercolors—suggestive splashes of color flashed on paper with sure, strong, staccato brushstrokes, reminding some of cubism and others of Chinese calligraphy—even higher than the work of O'Keeffe. Deferring to Marin's greater experience and age (he was seventeen years her senior), Georgia once said she didn't mind if he was first because he was a man. The remark, if true, had an uncharacteristic note of false humility about it, but it may have been inspired by the fact that competition was taboo in the group, and outsiders saw little evidence of it.

Marin and O'Keeffe, who painted many of the same subjects over the years, enjoyed an easy comradeship. She liked his oblique, roguish sense of humor and respected his absolute loyalty to Stieglitz. But she was bitterly aware that he was so completely absorbed in his own painting that he failed to take notice of anyone else's work, including her own.

She was most fascinated by the painting of Arthur Dove. His early abstractions had first interested her as an art student, and she felt a close kinship with them. Although usually based on the forms of nature, his work was also influenced by musical themes, such as six collages he did in the midtwenties, much the way she had painted what Stieglitz called "color music." She discovered that Doves were the only pictures—aside from her own—that she could endure on her walls for more than a day.

To her gratification, it was a mutual artistic attraction. When Dove first saw her early drawings, he told Stieglitz, "That girl is doing without effort what all we moderns have been trying to do." The only painting he hung in the cabin of his yawl, where he lived with the painter Helen "Reds" Torr, was a small O'Keeffe—a green, black, and white abstraction that looked like a biopsy of a plant stalk.

Georgia had a cordial, but somewhat formal, friendship with Dove, a quiet man who was seven years older than she. Since she admired him as much as any artist of her generation, she was disturbed that he never sold very many of his small, subtle abstractions or had a major museum show during his lifetime. When her realistic, dramatic paintings began to sell and attract public attention, she tried to divert some of it to him and bought some of his paintings herself. But throughout the twenties Dove still had to accept illustration jobs from *Collier's* and other magazines in order to support himself. O'Keeffe's mistrust of the public's judgment was reinforced, and she came to believe that it was luck, not merit, that made people interested in a painter.

She greatly enjoyed the company of Charles Demuth, who was closer to her in age than the others and lived with his mother in the family house in Lancaster, Pennsylvania. He had an acerbic wit and an ear for gossip, which he repeated in a high voice, periodically punctured by a high-pitched giggle. A frail diabetic with a clubfoot, Demuth ate and drank forbidden foods during his visits to New York, and once suffered a diabetic attack in the gallery. Although far from handsome—he was short, his eyes crossed, his jaw protruded, and his ears flared—Demuth liked to dress like an elegant dandy.

He painted oils of industrial buildings in a precisionist style, and he also did dainty flowers and fruits in watercolors. Georgia and he joked about doing a big flower painting together—she would do the big blooms up high and he would do the little ones down low. She was pleased when he hung an O'Keeffe in his studio, and she bought at least one Demuth during his lifetime. In 1924 he dedicated a work to her, and he bequeathed his oil paintings to her at his death a decade later.

❖

Stieglitz had shown the work of the others at 291 before he met Georgia, and she was the last to be taken into his intimate circle of artists. But after her discovery by Stieglitz in 1916, a struggle of another kind began. With her intelligence, outspokenness, and sense of humor, she was able to hold her own easily as a person with the men. But because she was a young woman, not trained in Europe, and Stieglitz's beloved, she had to battle to win their acceptance as a serious painter on a par with the best of them. At that time she complained bitterly to her friend Susan Young Wilson that most women didn't have the chance to develop as people, let alone as artists.

She sensed that the men were uneasy with a woman among them, although they shared similar, modernistic approaches to art. "All the male artists I knew, of course, made it very plain that as a woman I couldn't make it—I might as well stop painting," she remembered many years later. When she realized that they didn't expect her to keep on painting, she became more determined than ever to prove them wrong—much as she had defied her older brother's attitudes about the subordinate place of females. Understanding that "the boys," as she mockingly called them, carefully watched everything she did, she also resolved to be meticulous about the way she stretched her canvases and framed them. Later, she never forgot that in the early years a great portion of the hard, boring work of the gallery—such as getting paintings out of storage and putting them away again—fell into her competent hands. Since everyone agreed that she hung shows superbly, that job was often her responsibility as well.

Even Stieglitz couldn't completely protect her from the widespread male conviction that being a woman was incompatible with being an artist. The year she had moved to the East, an art magazine published an article that declared that women can best create by giving birth. There has never been a great woman artist, the article explained, because it is impossible for a childless woman to feel as deeply or to see as clearly as a mother—and, of course, a woman painter with a child rarely has the time or concentration necessary for creating on canvas.

Stieglitz had always rejected this kind of pseudologic. Even though he believed that a female psyche was different from a male psyche—a woman felt through the womb before perceiving with her mind, as he explained it—he was convinced that the creative process was essentially the same. "Women can only create babies, say the scientists, but I say they can produce art—and Georgia O'Keeffe is the proof of it," he declared in 1923, at her first show in the twenties.

When some people resented her special postion as Stieglitz's paramour, she found it necessary to remind them that he had given her two shows before "he knew me personally," as she put it. After their marriage, when people addressed her as "Mrs. Stieglitz," she briskly corrected them with, "I am Georgia O'Keeffe." "I've had a hard time hanging on to my name, but I hang on to it with my teeth," she explained. "I like getting what I've got on my own." Once when an interviewer referred to Georgia as his "wife," Stieglitz objected on her behalf. "Don't call her my 'wife.' There was a Mrs. Stieglitz I was married to for twenty-four years," he said. "From the beginning she just felt she was Georgia O'Keeffe, and I agreed with her. She's a person in her own right."

Although she eventually became respected as an artist, Georgia always remained outside the circle of intellectual talk. On Saturday nights Stieglitz usually took a half dozen friends to the Far East Tea Garden, a moderately priced Chinese restaurant on the second floor of a building at Columbus Circle overlooking Central Park. While the men argued across the marble-topped tables, Georgia sat wordlessly, bemused and detached, amazed that they could talk so much. She had a very good mind and her schooling had given her a rudimentary exposure to various schools of thought, but most of their debates about such topics as the meaning of art were too esoteric for her direct way of thinking. She claimed that she often found herself wondering what they were talking about—even when the subject was her own work. "I would listen to them talk and I thought, my, are they dreamy," she recalled. "I felt much more prosaic but I knew I could paint as well as some of them who were sitting around talking."

Being familiar with the role of outsider, she did not let the talk undermine her self-confidence. In fact, she didn't even seem to listen or try to understand what the men were talking about. Discussions about Freudian theories abounded around this time, yet she claimed late in the decade not to know what the "ego" was. She also said she was puzzled by talk about the "plastic" quality of Cézanne's famous mountain motif, based on a craggy peak in the south of France (a quality that particularly fascinated the restless, rootless Marsden Hartley). When she finally visited Aix-en-Provence in 1953, she was amazed. "All those words piled on top of that poor little mountain seemed too much," she said. She also scorned manmade labels and refused to be defined by them. "I am not an exponent of expressionism," she told her friend Blanche Matthias. "I don't know exactly what that means, but I don't like the sound of it. I dislike cults and isms. I want to paint in terms of my own thinking and feeling."

Neither did she think much of the men's theories about being Americans, particularly since they seldom traveled west of the Hudson. "One can not be an American by going about saying that one is an American," she remarked to Blanche. "It is necessary to feel America, like America, love America and then work." She thought it was absurd that those same Americans used to regularly flee to Europe. "I seemed to be the only one I knew who didn't want to go to Paris," she recalled. "They would all sit around and talk about the great American novel and the great American poetry, but they all would have stepped right across the ocean and stayed in Paris if they could have. Not me, I had things to do in my own country."

If she had participated in the talk, Georgia, with her logical mind, probably would have contradicted Stieglitz, whose thinking was more circular and complex than hers. "He would start out in the morning saying one thing, and by noon he would be saying the exact opposite, and then in the evening he would have changed his mind again," she observed. "He thought aloud, you see." Stieglitz did not take well to disagreement. When he was rebutted, he was likely to lash out fiercely. "If they crossed him in any way, his power to destroy was as destructive as his power to build—the extremes went together," Georgia said. Since she had always preferred peace to discord, she seldom argued with him and was inclined, instead, to humor him. But though Stieglitz, an intellectual who was far better educated than she, expressed himself with overwhelming power, she learned to hold her own. "His mind was quicker than mine, of course, but when I really knew I was right I could often wear him down," she later said.

From her silence, the men concluded that she was an intuitive creature with creative instincts. Hartley, who wrote in 1936 that she didn't know one aesthetic or philosophical theory from another, got closer to the truth when he added that she was more interested in what her eyes saw than what her ears heard. He also called her a "highly developed intuitive," which neatly fit his theory that the males of the species were naturally rational and intellectual whereas females were dominated by subrational feelings.

If being part of a male milieu had its disadvantages, Georgia had little choice in the matter; there simply was no group of female artists for her to turn to. When the Nineteenth Amendment became law in 1920, women across America were allowed to vote for the first time. Their lives began to change superficially: They bobbed their hair, exchanged whalebone corsets for elastic girdles, and raised the hems of their chemises to their knees. Feminists had hoped that gaining the vote would ensure female emancipation, but few feminist beliefs were accepted by the culture at large. Instead, the movement lost its momentum, and many creative women lapsed into isolation once again.

Most other female artists worked in Europe or were unknown to Georgia, with the exception of wealthy Florine Stettheimer and a few others. Florine was sixteen years older than Georgia, and the two had virtually nothing in common. Dainty and demure, with dark bangs, a large nose, and closely spaced eyes, Florine was a maiden lady who affected bohemianism. She wore white satin trousers and went in for an ultra-feminine decor of white lace, crystal blossoms, gilt fringe, and cellophane curtains. Too shy to show her fanciful, satirical, mock-naïve paintings in public, she used to unveil each new one before a small admiring cult. Along with her older sisters—the brocaded and bejeweled Ettie, a novelist, and Carrie, the creator of an elaborate doll's house, complete with a gallery of artists' works in miniature— she liked to entertain frequently and received the likes of Marcel Duchamp, Henry McBride, as well as Stieglitz and O'Keeffe. A water-color of one of those evenings by Carl Sprinchorn, *The Three Stettheimer Sisters and Some Friends*, shows Georgia in a black turban, her arms folded across her chest, a watchful look on her face.

Georgia also came to know Dorothy Brett, an English painter who had followed D. H. Lawrence to America and who occasionally visited New York. Not the caliber of painter that O'Keeffe was, she had little to offer Georgia besides moral support. She liked to go with her to the Intimate Gallery on Sunday mornings—the only morning it was closed to the public—when Georgia liked to give herself a private show. The two women carried the O'Keeffes out of the store-room and propped them up against the walls. "It was an unbelievable orgy of color and form," Brett remembered. "The whole room blazed and quivered with color—it was shockingly beautiful."

Georgia discussed with Blanche Matthias the fact that the prog-ress of women in art was slow because they were not militant, but just quietly trying to express their female experience. "You seem to feel something about women akin to what I feel—and if what I am doing moves toward that—it is something," Georgia said to her. Through Blanche she got to know a group of younger middle western women writers who passed through New York—Zona Gale, Meridel LeSueur, and Margery Latimer. Meridel LeSueur, who was born in 1900, recalled that Georgia urged them to have confidence in "the woman experi-ence," and said that they probably would not have written without her encouragement and example.

It was rare for an American or a female to be an artist, and because Georgia was both, it was overwhelmingly women—wealthy matrons, groups of club ladies, earnest girls—who jammed her shows. As had happened when they were first shown in 1916, her pictures spoke directly to women, who instinctively felt they knew what Geor-gia was saying. Her paintings at times inspired some of her sex to self-expression, others to adulation. One young woman confessed that she fantasized about buying an O'Keeffe and building a room around it. "There were more feminine shrieks and screams in the vicinity of O'Keeffe's work this year than ever before," noted McBride in 1926. "I begin to think that in order to be quite fair to Miss O'Keeffe I must listen to what women say of her—and take notes."

Georgia did her share to advance directly the cause of women. When her old friend, Anita Pollitzer, now an officer in the National Woman's Party, asked her to address a dinner in Washington, D.C., being held to urge more women to run for political office, the artist of few words agreed. In late February 1926, she was one of several women who spoke before almost five hundred people at the Mayflower Hotel. Later, listeners remarked, according to Anita, that Georgia's speech had been the most lucid of them all. Characteristically, she had ignored the tangential issues and spoken directly to the point, saying that women must take responsibility for their lives. Believing that women should try to earn their own living and develop their abilities rather than be dependent on men, she retained her membership in the National Woman's Party—which backed the Equal Rights Amendment—through the Second World War when she was in her fifties. It was not until she moved from New York that her formal ties to the feminist movement dwindled.

After the Intimate Gallery got under way, however, Georgia began to reap real benefits from her membership in a group. During the last half of the twenties, she had an annual solo show more often than any of the men. Knowing that her new work was going to be exhibited and reviewed regularly, she experienced a great creative outburst during the two years after the gallery opened. The critics exclaimed in amazement, and the men's respect was won. But a note of bitterness remained. "I know that many men here in New York think women can't be artists, but we can feel and work as they can," she said to Blanche. Then she added a bit sarcastically: "Perhaps some day a new name will be coined for us [women artists] and so allow men to enjoy a property right to the word 'art.'"

❖

Stieglitz had shown people Georgia's abstractions during the years when she had no shows and had talked about her constantly, so that right from the start the men in his orbit wrote about her. They echoed, in many cases, the older man's ideas and expressed them in uninhibited prose in accordance with his cult of the individual sensibility. One of the first articles was published in 1920, only two years after Georgia had moved to New York. Written by Marsden Hartley, it made her look absurd and influenced readers to view her abstractions in Freudian terms. Georgia was shocked by the essay, which was published the next year in the book *Adventures in the Arts.* "I almost wept," she recalled. "I thought I could never face the world again."

The next year, another one of Stieglitz's disciples alluded to the full-blown sexuality in her canvases. Paul Rosenfeld, a music critic whose prose was likened to "a Bacchic frenzy," wrote in the December 1921 issue of *The Dial:*

> Her art is gloriously female. Her great painful and ec-
> static climaxes make us at least to know something the

man always wanted to know. . . . All is ecstasy here, ecstasy of pain as well as ecstasy of fulfillment. . . . In her,
the ice of polar regions and the heat of tropical spring
tides meet and mingle. Greenland's icy mountain abuts
on India's coral strand. . . . Her masses are . . . like
great concentric waves that spread outward and outward
until they seem to embrace some sea. . . . The entire
body is seen noble and divine through love. . . . This art
is . . . a prayer that the indifferent and envious
world . . . may be kept from defiling and wrecking the
white glowing place. . . .

The day that Georgia read Rosenfeld's article, journalist Hutchins
Hapgood found her in a fury. Just as it made her cringe to exhibit her
pictures before strangers, she found it painful to read such words about
herself and confessed in a letter to Mitchell Kennerley later in the
decade that they made her shiver and gave her "a queer feeling of
being invaded." Hapgood was bemused and gently explained that she
shouldn't be upset because such prose really revealed more about the
writers than about her. Since she needed a defense against the invading
words, she clung to his explanation. "When people read erotic symbols
into my paintings," she learned to say, "they're really talking about
their own affairs." The explanation was less than a perfect shield,
however. A decade later she threatened to quit painting if Freudian
interpretations continued to be made, and throughout the years she
tried to ward off offending words in other ways.

There was another side to being written about, nonetheless. *The
Dial* had reproduced her painting *The Black Spot* with Rosenfeld's
article. She was ambitious, and it was a way for her work to be known.
"*The Dial* used to publish one man painter and then another," she said
afterwards. "I was so pleased to have 'the boys' publish my work. It
was then that I thought maybe I could make a living as a painter."

With people gossiping about whether Georgia was oversexed, like
her pictures, Philadelphia collector Albert Barnes said that if he were
Stieglitz he would feel obliged to defend her honor. But Stieglitz, who
once described her as warm-blooded but chaste, continued to feel that
purity resulted from paring an emotion to its essence. "She is absolutely
clean-cut like a crystal," he liked to say. "They're the pure artists—I
don't believe they ever put down a stroke with the idea of the public."
He also realized that the whispers meant that people were interested

in her work, and he urged her to ignore them. And in spite of her dislike, Stieglitz had Hartley's article and the writing of others regularly reprinted in her exhibition catalogs for many years.

A lot of the wordy hyperbole centered on her bright "emotional" colors. "When I entered the art world, the men weren't very happy about it," she remembered. "You weren't supposed to paint yellow pictures, and you weren't supposed to paint pink pictures." She had observed the infinite chiaroscuro of black and white in Stieglitz's photographs, and she was said to have acknowledged that his color sense was more subtle than hers. One time in 1922, she decided to silence the men's talk that her forte was light colors by doing a painting in somber browns. Predictably, when Stieglitz hung it prominently in a show, it was praised and sold immediately. She had appeased them, Georgia thought, and had satisfied herself by proving she was able to beat the men at their own game.

That same year, when plans for her first solo show in the twenties were under way, she wrote to a Chatham friend, Doris McMurdo, who lived in Charlottesville, that she wasn't excited about it because of all the work and, especially, the anticipated publicity that had been "stupid" in the past. But in her practical middle western way, she also understood that the written word traveled farther than a painting. "I don't like publicity," she wrote Doris. "It embarises [sic] me . . . but as most people buy pictures more through their ears than their eyes— one must be written about and talked about or the people who buy through their ears will think your work no good . . . and won't buy— and one must sell to live."

In the flyer for her 1923 show, in which she explained her ambivalence about exhibiting, she revealed that she was not entirely uninterested in what the critics would have to say. "And I presume, if I may be honest, that I am also interested in what anybody else has to say about my paintings and also in what they don't say because that means something to me too," she wrote. But after the show, she was unpleasantly surprised at the way reviewers "misinterpreted" her abstractions as erotic. Vowing to set the record straight, she made sure most of the pictures in her 1924 show were realistic or, as she put it, "on the ground." These pictures included a generous number of white and yellow calla lilies.

Georgia had worked from flowers ever since her childhood painting lessons in Wisconsin, and they were a recurring motif with powerful overtones. Her roots were in the soil of America, and she felt a stronger pang when a bud uncurled than when another skyscraper pierced the New York sky. During the winter months when she was in the midst of the city's loud tumult and ugliness, she found refuge in the stillness, silence, and loveliness of a flower. "When you take a flower in your hand and really look at it," she once said, cupping her hand and holding it close to her face, "it's your world for the moment. I want to give that world to someone else. Most people in the city rush around so, they have no time to look at a flower. I want them to see it whether they want to or not."

She liked to tell about the day she stopped in a museum to see a favorite collection of paintings and noticed a small Fantin-Latour still life of a cup, saucer, and spoon that was new to the group. In the oil a tiny flower perched in a teacup, and it seemed to be the exquisite perfection of a blossom's beauty. Interested in turning away from her "misinterpreted" abstractions in favor of representational images, she felt the impulse to paint a flower like that herself, but she hesitated. "If I could paint the flower exactly as I see it no one would see what I see because I would paint it small like the flower is small," she later explained. Then it occurred to her to paint a flower so huge that it would *make* New Yorkers stand still and contemplate it. The idea amused her, she said, so she gave it a try.

As with the story she liked to tell about never painting anything small after being scolded by the nun at Sacred Heart, this tale too, one suspects, does not reveal the whole truth. It served, instead, to deflect questions away from consideration of a deeper subconscious level, perhaps one that was not entirely known to her. Other people, like Edward Steichen, had created flower close-ups, and there were many of them in Oriental prints that she had seen. She also had great enthusiasm for the colors of flowers. She like to observe closely the hues of a tulip bud as it matured, for instance, before she painted its flower. Once at Lake George she planted a bed of purple petunias in order to study the color blue more minutely. In the thirties she attempted to explain why she had painted a big white flower:

> The large White Flower with the golden heart is something I have to say about White—quite different from what White has been meaning to me. Whether the flower or the color is the focus I do not know. I do know

that the flower is painted large to convey to you my experience of the flower—and what is my experience of the
flower—if it is not color.

She completed her first enormous flower painting in 1924, and
then allowed Stieglitz into the room to see it. He stood in the doorway,
a skeptical look on his face. "Well, Georgia," he snorted, "I don't
know how you're going to get away with anything like that—you
aren't planning to show it, are you?" Although he often said he believed
in artistic experimentation, Georgia remembered that she usually had
to convince him to go along with a new direction. He used to remain
apprehensive until the reviews came in, when her new course was
usually vindicated. Typically, when her giant flowers were first exhibited in 1925 in the Seven Americans show, reviewer Edmund Wilson
stated in the *New Republic* that she had outblazed the work of the men
around her.

Her gigantic flowers, which were painted frontally and reveal-
ingly, much the way Stieglitz photographed her, had the effect of
firmly diminishing the human beings who stood in front of them. "The
observer feels like Alice after she had imbibed the 'Drink Me' phial,"
wrote a reviewer in amusement. "It is as if we humans were butterflies,"
said another, and "this is a chastening thought." However whimsical
the remarks, the size of the bloom relative to a member of the human
race precisely reflected the relative importance of nature and mankind
in the artist's eyes.

As time went by, Georgia seemed to need to paint a flower—like
a "boutonnière for Gargantua," in another reviewer's phase—for it to
really exist for her. Lilies, jonquils, daisies, irises, sweet peas, morning
glories, poppies, forget-me-nots, marigolds, poinsettias, camellias, zin-
nias, amaryllis, lilacs, carnations, primroses, hibiscus, larkspur, or-
chids, sunflowers, petunias, jack-in-the-pulpits, and many more were
singularly reborn in paint. Often they were presented like butterflies
pinned open or lit from within, much like Stieglitz's clouds.

The black-garbed artist had a particular penchant for the unusual
blackish (actually deep purple) pansy, petunia, and other dark blooms—
as if they were the self-portraits that some viewers claimed them to
be. Although a source for purchasing a bulb of the rare black iris
eluded her and she only found it in New York florist shops for a few
weeks each spring, she painted the flower again and again for many

years. Her 1926 version was an elegant rendering of tonguelike, velvety, purplish-gray petals uncurling into "an abyss of blackness into which the timid scarcely dare peer," teased Henry McBride. Its powerful center of inner gravity, however, seemed a good deal like her own.

❖

She had successfully dramatized her flowers—and, incidentally, herself—to New Yorkers, but she was upset at the reason for her success. The fact that she was a woman still seemed to overshadow everything else. Her strong personality charged her flowers with a bolt of electricity, observed Edmund Wilson, like that "peculiarly feminine intensity" women give to their clothes. And despite her best efforts to be realistic and defuse the Freudian talk, her trembling, feathery, unfurling petals reminded people of genitalia just as the abstractions had done. Large, engorged stamens and corollas suggested male genitals, while dark recesses ("soft, enormous caves," said *Time* in 1928) that invited penetration strongly suggested female vulvas. One woman who owned a big O'Keeffe flower painting was shocked to discover someone teaching a child the facts of life from it. When she hastily rehung it in her bedroom, a friend remarked, "Oh, I'm so glad you moved that vagina out of the living room."

Georgia complained that the experience of women artists was "not confined to one phase of life," and noted that when men—Hartley and Demuth, for example—painted flowers, theirs were not interpreted erotically. Again, she charged that any sexual iconography was simply in the heads of the viewers. "Well—I made you take time to look at what I saw and when you took time to really notice my flower you hung all your own associations with flowers on my flower and you write about my flower as if I think and see what you think and see of the flower—and I don't," she later wrote for an exhibition catalog. In her old age she still insisted that none of what people saw was in her own mind. "I don't think my subconscious is all that crazy!" she declared.

O'Keeffe believed that she painted the way she did because, like any artist, she had an original way of seeing things, not because she was a female. She felt that the psychological interpretations trivialized her work. To many people her "emotional colors and "erotic" shapes were the personal statement of a woman rather than the universal statement of an artist. Her paintings showed "a womanly preoccupation with sex," one man wrote. "O'Keeffe was being a woman and only secondarily an artist." Sometimes Georgia tried to affect nonchalance. "Wise men say it isn't art!" she declared to Helen Appleton Read. "But what of it, if it is children and love in paint?"

The controversy resulted in a large element of the public going to her exhibitions to see what "Woman" was saying rather than to see art. Some also went for a feeling of psychic infusion—the same reason people went to hear Stieglitz talk. "Psychiatrists have been sending their patients up to see the O'Keeffe canvases," reported *The New Yorker* in March 1926. "If we are to believe the evidence, the hall of the Anderson Gallery is littered with mental crutches, eye bandages, and slings for the soul." It added that people "limp to the shrine of St. Georgia and they fly away on the wings of the libido."

In those years, attitudes toward sex were affected by the novels of D. H. Lawrence as well as by Freudian theories. Through Mitchell Kennerley, Stieglitz received one of the early censored copies of *Lady Chatterley's Lover*. Since Georgia's paintings had been called the counterpart of Lawrence's glorification of the truth of the senses ("She reveals woman as an elementary being, closer to the earth than men, suffering pain with passionate ecstasy and enjoying love with beyond-good-and-evil delight," said the *New York Times* in 1927), Lawrence wrote from Switzerland in 1928, asking Stieglitz how Georgia liked the novel. (Georgia answered Lawrence immediately, telling him she liked it.) Stieglitz called the book "grand and barbaric," adding that Georgia was much too straightforward to have been shocked or embarrassed by its eroticism.

In a milieu that venerated Lawrence's emphasis on eroticism, O'Keeffe's work was usually admired. In *The Brown Decades*, published in 1931, Lewis Mumford explained that Georgia was

> the poet of womanhood in all its phases: the search for
> the lover, the reception of the lover, the longing for the
> child, the shrinkage and blackness of the emotions when
> the erotic thread has been lost, the sudden effulgence of
> feeling, as if the stars had begun to flower, which comes
> through sexual fulfillment in love: all these are the sub-
> jects of her painting. . . .

He continued:

> she has invented a language, and she has conveyed di-
> rectly and chastely in paint experiences for which lan-
> guage conveys only obscenities. Without painting a single
> nude, without showing a part of the human body, she
> had magnificently embodied passion, sexual life, woman-
> hood, as physical elements and as states of mind.

The critics spent a great deal of time debating whether a woman
was able to be a great artist and specifically, how O'Keeffe ranked.
Whereas women had traditionally painted with delicacy and precious-
ness, Georgia painted with an unusual degree of versatility, power,
and individuality. "O'Keeffe's song is direct and affirmative, free of
introspective agonies, devoid of the feminine cringe and giggle," wrote
art critic Louis Kalonyme near the end of the decade in *Creative Art*
magazine. In 1928 Helen Read took up the proposition of female
greatness in *Vogue* magazine, writing that just because most men or
women don't reach greatness, it doesn't mean that either sex is in-
capable of it. O'Keeffe, she wrote, was an important painter not because she depicted for the first time what it was to be a woman in
love, as the men put it. Naturally, her female perspective infused her
personality, but, more importantly, her artistic viewpoint was unique
and her technical ability was superb.

The men usually ranked her at the top of the female class—as the
greatest woman painter in America—rather than in relation to her
male contemporaries. She was hailed in purple prose as the epitome
of emancipated womanhood—the flowering of the "Feminine Principle"—and placed on a pedestal by herself. She felt uncomfortable
with this separate-class status, realizing that it was very much second
best. Ever since her egalitarian childhood in Wisconsin, she had been
used to competing with males as an equal—and to winning. "The men
like to put me down as the best woman painter," she said angrily in
1943. "I think I'm one of the best painters."

As great deal of the rhetoric from the male critics fit neatly into
their fantasies about females. "I guess I'm full of furies today—I wonder
if man has ever been written down the way he has written women
down," she wrote to Sherwood Anderson. The men had difficulty
understanding her because she was unschooled in their intellectual
theories and uninfluenced by their male traditions, suggested Blanche

Matthias. She added that they wrote in superlatives "until the reader grows weary of the aura and hungers for the bone structure." Georgia once wrote Mabel Dodge Luhan, praising what she had written about the actress Katharine Cornell, and saying she wished Mabel would write about her work because the men were unable to do it.

Stieglitz's disciple Waldo Frank, a short, dark, round-faced, hot-blooded writer, tried in his way to rescue her from the rhetoric. "If this town were a bit simpler, a bit less impure, it might be at home with her simple purity," he wrote in his book *Time Exposures*. "If it were less daft on polysyllables, it might hear her monosyllabic speech." He wrote another time: "When she is silent, she smiles. And that smile is not often understood by the sophisticated men and women who swarm about the studio of Stieglitz. It is not understood, because it is so simple." For this reason, she was often misunderstood, he added. Although he said her paintings weren't Freudian, he did call them "often crudely direct" like peasant art, and he called her the "archetype of the eternal peasant." Then he went on to describe the midwestern Georgia as a wide-hipped "glorified American peasant . . . full of loomy hungers of the flesh [and] star-dreams . . . [with] Celt eyes [and] a quiet body."

After Henry McBride visited an exhibition, Stieglitz and a group used to wait up in a restaurant until the first edition of the next day's newspaper came out with his review. At first, like the others, McBride found Georgia's work full of Freudian implications, but she applauded his humor. Whenever she read one that she particularly liked, she used to write him a note of thanks and invite him to dinner. They became friends and corresponded from the midtwenties until the time of his death at the age of ninety-four in 1962. In one letter she praised him for helping to make a place for modern art, as Stieglitz had done. Another time, when he had a cold, she wrote him some words of sympathy on the back of the announcement of her current show—seemingly, a not-so-subtle reminder to review it.

Her efforts seemed to pay off despite the fact that he was well aware of the degree of calculation involved. Delighted when his mention of her before two other women being reviewed in the same article got her a two-column headline in the Sunday art section of the *New York Sun*, she told him she liked to be first or not mentioned at all. After his review of her 1927 show, she thanked him enthusiastically, and closed on a teasing tone of false-deprecation:

as usual [I] don't understand what it is all about even if
you do say I am intellectual. I am particularly amused
and pleased to have the emotional faucet turned off—no
matter what other ones you turn on. . . . And all the ladies who like my things will think they are becoming intellectual—It's wonderful. . . . It is a grand page. I really
feel much relieved because I am terribly afraid of you.

The next year she was particularly gratified when he defended her
work against overanalysis, and when he wrote that "to overload [her
paintings] with Freudian implications is not particularly necessary."

After her 1923 show, McBride had noted that she "is interested
but not frightened at what you will say, dear reader, and in what I do
not say." As the decade wore on, she increasingly expressed her indifference even to that. She claimed that she rarely read reviews—
even a 1929 *New Yorker* profile about her—so she would not have to
"recover" from them. Another tactic of hers was not to read a review
until long after everyone else had, in order to minimize its effect.
Rereading McBride's columns in 1939, she laughed and laughed at
his irreverent humor, saying she had "a strange oily skin" that protected
her from reviews until she was able to laugh at them.

Fortunately, her self-confidence was not dependent on the critics'
strange kind of praise, and her sense of the absurd helped to deflate
the superlatives. Lavish praise "warms her about as much as fireworks
in the air of winter night," observed Waldo Frank. Her honesty also
made her recognize that her image of herself was totally different from
theirs. "The things they write sound so strange and far removed from
what I feel of myself—" she wrote a friend, "they make me seem like
some strange unearthly sort of creature floating in the air—breathing
in clouds for nourishment—When the truth is that I like beef steak—
and like it rare at that."

From time to time she got exasperated with those who harped
on the exaggerated size of her flowers, and she tried to reason with
them. Once, when asked why a flower was so big in a picture with
the East River in the distance, she demanded of her questioner why
he didn't wonder that the river was so small—the blossom was actually
life-size whereas the river was not. Her irritation persisted, and in
1941 she made a similar point in a letter to the art editor of the *New
York Times* about a painting with a flower in the foreground and a
mountain in the background. "Such things don't make sense except

painting sense," she wrote. "I don't expect them to. I don't mind if you say it is a tiresome painting—that is a matter of personal opinion—but it is not an enlarged flower."

She liked to have a show for herself before mounting a public one, as she had done in 1915 when she first decided to paint for herself. Then "I have already settled it for myself," she candidly stated in her book, "so flattery and criticism go down the same drain and I am quite free." Her ability to form a protective cocoon around herself was critical, because if she had cared about public opinion or if her delicate creative process had become too self-conscious, it would have been destroyed. She knew she must keep painting and portray her vision whether or not her contemporaries understood it.

However strong her instinct for survival, the talk did inhibit her from painting quite as many giant flowers as she might have through the years, she admitted in the forties. In 1954, when she greeted art critic Emily Genauer while carrying some flowers, Miss Genauer exclaimed, "How perfect to meet you with flowers in your hands." Still acutely sensitive about the subject, O'Keeffe snapped, "I hate flowers—I paint them because they're cheaper than models and they don't move!"

❖

Around the time of their marriage, Stieglitz's brother Leopold sold his brownstone, and Alfred and Georgia, who had lived there in the winters from 1920 to 1924, had to find another place to live. At this time Lee offered to give his elder brother $250 a quarter, and in return, Georgia might paint him a picture of Lake George. Stieglitz had lived in midtown Manhattan most of his life, so they shunned the artists' Bohemia, Greenwich Village, and, for a while, they lived in a small East Side apartment at 38 East Fifty-eighth Street. During this time, Georgia watched the steel skeleton of the Shelton Hotel go up on Lexington Avenue and Forty-ninth Street. The first skyscraper in the nieghborhood, it would dwarf massive Grand Central Station a few blocks to the south.

From time to time Georgia wondered what it would be like to live way up in the sky. New York was preeminent for having the tallest buildings in the world, and its people were living and working higher in the air than ever before. One day, perhaps after having ridden up in one of the Shelton's six elevators to an observation terrace, she became eager to take rooms in the ultramodern brick skyscraper, to sleep and paint high above the nerve-jangle cacophony of the city sidewalks and shadowed streets, up in the sky, the infinite space, which had fascinated her so much in the West.

Rooms at the Shelton were available for between seventy and— for a large elegant suite—two hundred and fifty dollars a month. Although the rooms cost less than at a first-class hotel, Georgia and Alfred were afraid that the rent would be a financial strain for them. But after Georgia's shows in 1923 and 1924, they must have felt more confident that she would be able to sell an occasional painting.

It's interesting to note that Georgia wanted to continue to live without a kitchen of her own. She was familiar with the writings of the visionary feminist and socialist Charlotte Perkins Gilman, who had proposed that buildings be equipped with facilities for communal cooking, cleaning, and child care so as to free women from domestic drudgery—and the Shelton provided all but the last of those services. At the time, Georgia had taken on more responsibility in running the Lake George household half the year, and she most likely didn't want to be burdened with similar duties in the winter as well.

Stieglitz was also interested in the idea of living in a skyscraper. He thought that New York, where he was firmly rooted, was both a giant heartless machine and the most phenomenal spectacle in the world. In his mind, Manhattan's thrusting spires symbolized the raw energy of America. Living in the Shelton would give him a magnificent overview of his native land's youthful civilization. So, in 1925, Stieglitz and O'Keeffe settled in rooms on the highest floor of the Shelton and stayed there throughout the decade. On December 9 he wrote Sherwood Anderson that: "We live high up in the Shelton Hotel— for a while—maybe all winter—The wind howls and shakes the huge steel frame—We feel as if we were out at midocean—All is so quiet except the wind—and the trembling shaking hull of steel in which we live—."

Originally planned as a residential hotel for twelve hundred men, the Shelton had game rooms, lounges, and other public spaces that were decorated like a genteel men's club. Sturdy overstuffed furniture, Oriental rugs, crystal chandeliers, ornate fireplaces, and oak paneling gave the place a baronial look. Georgia chose a northeast corner suite, number 3003—north for good painting light and east for the river view. Thirty flights above the frenetic activity of the streets and with a gargoyle-type creature jutting out above their windows, the suite consisted of two small, low-ceilinged rooms and a bath.

The Shelton's other residents noticed the two artists because of their dramatic, compelling appearance. When they breakfasted at the simple wooden tables in the sixteenth-floor cafeteria, Stieglitz's rich, resonant voice would carry throughout the room, and strangers would linger to listen. And watching Georgia glide across the black-and-white tile floor carrying her tray, diners would later remember her grace, as well as her ramrod-straight back and freshly brushed hair. Dorothy Brett, who sometimes breakfasted with Stieglitz and Georgia on her visits to New York, reminisced: "Georgia, her pure profile against the dark wood of the paneling, calm, clear; her sleek black hair drawn swiftly back into a tight knot at the nape of her neck; the strong white hands, touching and lifting everything, even the boiled eggs, as if they were living things—sensitive, slow-moving hands, coming out of the black-and-white, always this black-and-white."

Having abandoned the idea of having a child, and approaching her fortieth birthday, Georgia began planning precisely every detail of her daily existence to eliminate anything unnecessary to art. Writer Frances O'Brien described a visit to Georgia's rooms in the Shelton in the *Nation*, for an issue dated October 12, 1927:

> In an apartment on the twenty-eighth [sic] floor of the Shelton a woman sits painting. A tall, slender woman dressed in black with an apron thrown over her lap. Beside her is a glass palette, very large, very clean, each separate color on its surface remote from the next. As soon as a tone has been mixed and applied to the canvas its remains are carefully scraped off the palette, which thus always retains its air of virginity.
>
> It is late afternoon and even in this high place the room is growing dusky. The artist does not seem to know this. She goes on painting carefully, swiftly, surely—and she and the canvas and the glass palette are one world having no connection with anything else in existence. And then the telephone rings.
>
> "Hello, Georgia? This is ———" "Hello, how are you? Would you mind calling up a little later after the light goes?" And the chastened caller ponders the twi-

light outside his window and wonders how even on a
twenty-eighth floor one can go on painting. . . .

In her tidy pale-gray room with furniture draped in off-white fabric
she carefully wrote on cards the colors she used in a painting. The
glass or enamel tray she used for a palette had a separate brush for
each color so a hue would not be muddied. She set new goals for
herself and became absorbed in solving various technical problems
after the critics had given her high praise for her technical virtuosity.
Sometimes she painted a picture so it could be hung any way—with
any of the four sides uppermost. To her own surprise, she also accomplished the feat of painting a finished canvas from the upper left-hand
corner to the lower right without going back. She tried to figure out
a way to convey the appearance of rain and snow as they fell away
from her skyscraper window to the pavement below—but she admitted
that she never made it look just right. After the last light finally faded,
she liked to descend to the sidewalks and take a walk.

In order to paint, she felt she needed simplicity around her, to
help keep her head clear and uncluttered. Her creative process involved continually locating an intense feeling about something, exploring it, and then trying to grasp it more completely by transmitting
it to canvas. Every experience was potential material, even outside
the world of nature. In the summer of 1927 she was operated on in
New York's Mt. Sinai Hospital for a benign lump in her breast. She
tried to stay conscious on the operating table for as long as possible,
afterwards painting *Black Abstraction*, her memory of the appearance
of her arm and the surgeon's light as she faded under anesthetic.
Increasingly, as she concentrated on her task day after day, year after
year, things outside her focus fell away. As she became more absorbed
in the crystallization of the moment of pure emotion, her personality
took on more of the "Whiteness" that Stieglitz admired so much.

For years Georgia had stitched most of her simple clothes out of
the finest fabrics, often sewing when she wanted to think. She made
luxurious white silk blouses, white cotton nightgowns with white embroidery, and petticoats edged with white lace. In cold weather she
donned a black wool coat with a collar that buttoned up to her chin
and black gloves of the best leather. At one time, she sported a pair
of black bloomers under a tentlike black tunic. Throughout the years,
when asked the reason for her monotone clothing—odd for a painter—

she gave several, all with some truth to them. Once she said that if she began to choose colors to *wear*, she would have not time to pick any to paint. Another time she explained that she was so sensitive to color that if she wore a red dress, she would feel obliged to live up to its flamboyance. She claimed she liked being cloaked in anonymity. "There's something about black," she remarked. "You feel hidden away in it." Deadly-serious black also served to transmit the message that she was not to be treated frivolously or flirtatiously. Also, she must have realized that if all her clothes were one color, they would match and she would achieve a look of maximum elegance with a minimum of time and money.

Out their windows to the northwest Georgia and Alfred were able to see the steep gabled green roof of the Plaza Hotel, the treetops of Central Park, and the cliffs of New Jersey across the Hudson River. To the east they could watch barges slowly float up and down the East River, automobiles inch across the Queensboro Bridge, and factory smokestacks emit plumes of soot on the opposite bank. And there was the unobstructed view of the sky: Georgia was able to see the rain moving in from the west just before it enveloped the city, as well as clouds at dusk suffused with a sunset blaze.

Their three windows, although not large, also provided a rapidly changing panorama of Manhattan feverishly, aggressively rising higher into the sky. Around the Shelton, steel beams and girders of new skyscrapers were shooting up everywhere. Some structures stopped below their thirtieth-story windows and others continued on above them. All the construction was accompanied by the sound of a dull roar of the metropolis, pierced by the screech of metal on metal and the hammering of automatic riveters like a machine gun fusillade.

One of the most amazing new towers was the Chrysler Building, which soared to a height of seventy-seven floors by the time it was finished in 1929 in a record nineteen months. Its splendid, shining chromium crown was topped by a silver needle that seemed to prick the stars. Georgia was able to watch the building take form—as well as other skyscrapers to the south, such as the Empire State Building— from the Shelton's solarium and various roof terraces. She was particularly interested in the American Radiator Building, which she saw when she walked on Forty-second Street. It was built of black brick and decorated with gold leaf that was lit at night so its pinnacle looked like a lump of glowing coal.

By evening millions of artificial lights transformed the view from their windows into high visual drama—an exciting, futuristic glimpse into the space age of the twentieth century. "At night it looks as through [the Shelton] reached to the stars, and searchlights that cut across the sky back of it do appear to carry messages to other worlds," wrote Henry McBride after a visit. From the couple's perch, friends liked to watch yellow and red auto lights threading slowly up and down Lexington Avenue, traffic lights blinking from red to green, and the letters of electric neon signs bouncing and bobbing in their nimble urban dance.

Partly to emphasize the view, Georgia left the windows uncurtained and the little rooms as bare as possible. "The door opened and I entered a room as bleak as the North Pole," wrote a newspaper reporter for the *Brooklyn Eagle* who gained entry in 1928. "It might have been a cloister or the reception room of an orphanage, so austere was it, with its cold gray walls, and its white covers over dull upholstery. There was no frivolous pillow, no 'hangings.' The only spot of color was a red flower on an easel. There was not an inch of cretonne or a dab of china anywhere. It seemed all windows—windows overlooking housetops, steel framework, chimneys, windows to the east through which the panorama of the river and bridge came flooding."

Besides her own paintings propped on easels, usually turned to the wall when visitors came, there were a few deep easy chairs that Stieglitz liked. Over the years, Georgia might display a bit of coral, some shells, pebbles on a table, dried grass in a vase, or a green plant in a white pot. Besides being Georgia's long-standing preference, the simplicity of the room was also practical. In addition to having little time or money for "decoration," Georgia needed a neutral space in which to conceptualize her dazzling colors. When the *Eagle* reporter asked in bewilderment, "Don't you like color?" Georgia's face broke into a grin. "Color does something to me," she replied, and she tried to explain why she needed to paint in a colorless room. "I like an empty wall because I can imagine what I like on it," she said another time.

Surrounded by the glitter of Manhattan in the winter, Georgia began to toy with the idea of painting it. Although she spent as little time in the metropolis as possible, she always spoke of New York as looking just the way a city should look. Also, after she married Stieglitz, she seemed ready to deal with "his" world in her art and, indeed, seemed to echo some of his thoughts about it. "I realize it's unusual for an artist to want to work way up near the roof of a big hotel in the heart of the roaring city, but I think that's just what the artist of today needs for stimulus," she told Blanche Matthias near the middle of the decade. "You have to live in today. Today the city is something bigger, more complex than ever before in history." Then she added a thought of her own that must have been playing around the edges of her mind. "And nothing can be gained from running away. I couldn't even if I could."

At first Stieglitz and the other men objected to the attempts of the Wisconsin farm girl to paint the manmade city, which was, they argued, essentially alien to her. Stieglitz pointed out that even the male painters had difficulty with the subject. Nature was the feminine sphere, they told her, not architectural subjects requiring structural draftsmanship. But Georgia, not about to be told what to paint and used to ignoring what she didn't want to hear, went ahead anyway. In the rooms, visitors often glimpsed a flower on one easel and a skyscraper on another: the juxtaposition of Georgia's inner and outer worlds. Realizing that Manhattan was Stieglitz's turf, Georgia mischievously painted the letters spelling "Stieglitz" into an urban landscape where, in reality, a neon sign flashed the words "Scientific American."

Many of her Manhattan paintings gave off the feeling of claustrophobia and of a choking absence of air. Moonlit clouds were slashed by towering buildings, the sun struggled to break through smokestack fumes, sharp-edged skyscrapers darkened the sky. In *City Night*, painted in 1926, a little white moon appeared crushed between gigantic, looming, menacing, black walls. Most of her New York oils were nightscapes, in which her peopleless city was illuminated by a reddish malevolent glow coming from the millions of colored lights. Whatever visual excitement she may have felt about New York, her red-shrouded paintings refected her fundamentally uneasy tolerance of city life. "One can't paint New York as it is," she remarked to Blanche Matthias at the time, "but rather as it is felt."

For the Seven Americans show of 1925, the year she began to exhibit her giant flowers, Georgia thought she had found the perfect place in the gallery to display her first New York picture. Stieglitz, however, refused to let her hang it and she became furious. The next year, when she had a show of her own, she insisted that the painting be hung on a wall between two windows. She always remembered that, the day of the opening, it was the first painting to be sold, and for the respectable price of twelve hundred dollars. "From then on they *let* me paint New York," Georgia recalled sarcastically. She got her final revenge when Henry McBride wrote a few years later that an O'Keeffe cityscape was "one of the best skyscraper paintings that I have seen anywhere." However, she only remained interested in painting the city for a relatively short five-year period, and only about twenty skyscrapers are recorded as having been painted by her between 1925 and 1929.

❖

Stieglitz had said repeatedly that Georgia's paintings often came out of a moment between them—out of their lifeblood, like children. After Georgia created a painting, she would turn it over to him, its guardian, so that he might find a foster parent who would take it, appreciate it, and care for it tenderly. Consequently, a collector who wanted to own an O'Keeffe had to measure up to Stieglitz's high, subjective standards. Stieglitz bluntly rejected buyers who didn't come up with a good enough reason for wanting an O'Keeffe. Once, when a lady without the "right" explanation wanted to buy a painting of a pansy, Stieglitz hurriedly wrote another collector, begging her to save the pansy from the first lady's insensitive clutches—and he even offered to throw in a smaller O'Keeffe to clinch the deal.

One of the collectors who measured up was Duncan Phillips, a Washington, D.C., millionaire who owned a gallery devoted to modern art. A slight man with clear blue-gray eyes who loved good conversation, Phillips went to most of the annual exhibitions at the Intimate Gallery. By 1926 he owned three paintings by O'Keeffe, whom he described as possessing a "vivid personality and extraordinary skill." That same year, he exhibited his O'Keeffes in a show that included paintings by her old Art Students League classmate, Eugene Speicher, who had teased her about ending up a schoolmarm while he became a famous artist. It must have been a very sweet victory for her when their paintings hung side by side in such an esteemed collection.

Stieglitz's unconventional sales methods maddened many patrons of the arts, however. In early 1927 Stieglitz boasted that he had sold

John Marin's *Back of Bear Mountain* to Phillips for six thousand dollars
when, in fact, two other Marins had been thrown in as "gifts." Stieglitz
defended pricing the works of living Americans on a par with European
masters by arguing that high prices were the only thing that made
materialistic Americans respect art. Actually, he delighted in per-
suading wealthy Americans to part with their dollars for their coun-
trymen's art. (Even though he took no commission, usually about a
fifth of the proceeds of each sale went into the gallery rent fund.) He
set prices impulsively, often asking a buyer what he was willing to pay,
allowing payment in yearly installments. Once he persuaded a dowager
to pay what a new Rolls-Royce would cost her. "She's a poor girl," he
used to say about Georgia. "She is doing something nobody has done
before. If you want these flowers, you must give her an equivalent [to
them] in terms of money."

One also suspects that he set prices high so collectors couldn't
afford to take away too many O'Keeffes. By the late twenties, Georgia
had painted about three hundred paintings and "lost" only a third of
them to buyers. Neither Georgia nor Stieglitz liked to part with a
picture, but eventually the thought of some principle—such as the
inability of anyone to really "possess" an O'Keeffe—or the need for
money prevailed, and one or two were sent out into the world. At
first Georgia only cared about selling enough to meet her minimal
living expenses and to go on working. But she recalled that later,
when her horizons expanded, she had to prod Stieglitz each spring
into parting with a few of their "children."

As the decade came to a close, there was a sense of optimism
everywhere—even in art. In 1927, thirty-six new O'Keeffes were exhibited in Georgia's midwinter show. In the first few days a half dozen
paintings were sold, ranging in price from a few thousand to six thousand dollars and totaling seventeen thousand dollars—so Stieglitz extended the show to the end of February. Ten years earlier, when
Georgia had borrowed a thousand dollars to live on for a year in New
York, she had never dreamed that she would be able to earn a living
with her paintbrush alone. But in the winter of 1927, realizing with
a start that she had been wrong, she slowly began to readjust her
thinking.

The next year she again had her usual show after Christmas, but
it was covered at length in *Time* magazine for the first time. Then she
made a stupedous sale, which caused her to surpass even her earnings

of the previous year. An American who lived in France, who wished to remain anonymous, offered to buy six small calla lily panels, painted in 1923, for the extraordinary sum of twenty-five thousand dollars (equivalent to about two hundred thousand dollars today). It happened quite spontaneously, as things often did in the gallery. The collector had asked the price of the lilies, and Stieglitz, annoyed, had snapped an outrageously high price in order to change the subject. No one was more astonished than he when his price was calmly accepted. After the initial shock wore off, Stieglitz satisfied himself that the businessman sensed the lilies' genuine worth, quite apart from their monetary value, and he made him promise to hang them in his home and not to sell them during his lifetime. Then Stieglitz allowed him to make his grand "gesture," as Stieglitz called it, and take the lilies to France.

Georgia had painted the calla lily because she liked the stiff waxy bloom's tight formation and lack of leaves. Her rendition included a series of single long-stemmed lilies in a vase, uncurling delicately to reveal phallic orange stamens. Stieglitz dubbed them "the Immaculate Conception" because of their virginal sensuality, which also flowed through many of her other canvases. Teenagers at a Catholic school near the gallery found two of the lily panels so alluring that they used to play hooky to go gaze at them, and they would innocently talk about getting the religious fathers to buy them for the church.

Stieglitz was delighted by his transatlantic coup and, characteristically, he began telling everyone about it, even writing McBride about the news. For many years, American millionaires had journeyed to France to buy European masters, and American artists had streamed to Paris to study art. France had exerted such a great influence that American art had suffered, Stieglitz believed. "I want to let Americans know that there are artists outside of France—artists right here in America," Stieglitz had said only the year before. . . . The artist comes along, living in a world of his own creation, and he immediately becomes a disturbing element. . . . America wants everything standardized." Now Stieglitz was able to say that, for the first time, France was coming to America for art. Paintings by a young American woman, who had never set foot in Europe, were going into a French parlor for a respectable price. But, most important of all, Stieglitz now felt that his commitment to America and its first generation of modern artists was justified.

On April 16, 1928, the story of the sale appeared in a small paragraph in the *New York Times*. Shortly afterwards, the city tabloids picked up the news and heralded the sum as the largest ever paid for so small a group of paintings by a living American artist. Charles Lindbergh had made his solo flight to Paris the previous spring, and Stieglitz, according to news reports, called Georgia the "Lindbergh of art" because she, too, had the no-nonsense buoyant American spirit that made her go after what she wanted—and get it. Seeing herself described in the newspapers as an all-American overnight success, Georgia reluctantly agreed to see a few reporters, who had been deluging her with requests for interviews, to set the record straight.

Lillian Sabine of the *Brooklyn Eagle*, expecting to find an artist overjoyed at her sudden riches, reported that Georgia was barely cordial, but she decided that, since the artist seemed sincere, she would respect her reticence. Throughout the interview, Georgia rarely smiled, and when she didn't like a question she brushed it aside with a comment such as, "Oh, that doesn't make any difference." The interviewer admitted in her article that at times she felt an overwhelming desire to crawl inside a large lily resting on an easel opposite her. She also confessed that she lacked the nerve to ask the reserved artist the thing her readers really wanted to know—what she was going to do with the jackpot that seemed to assure her lifetime financial security.

Georgia insisted on talking about the long years of tedious work that had led up to the sale, and that no one had noticed. "Success doesn't come with painting one picture," she told Miss Sabine. "It is building step by step, against great odds." She tried to explain to another interviewer that she had been successful, in fact, because she had *not* gone after success—because she had been free to ignore the tastes of professional dealers and painted the way she genuinely wished.

The newspapers didn't seem to hear what she was saying, however. The magazine section of the New York *Evening Graphic* published her photograph, greatly blown up, and under it splashed the headline: SHE PAINTED THE LILY AND GOT $25,000 AND FAME FOR DOING IT! The article began: "Not a rouged, cigarette smoking, bob-haired, orange-smocked Bohemian, but a prim ex-country schoolmistress who actually does her hair up in a knot is the art sensation of 1928!"

Another article mentioned irrelevantly that, besides wearing her hair in an unfashionable style, she favored long, out-of-style skirts. The newspapers' view of her were much less flattering than the ones in the art magazines, which tended to praise her lavishly for her ethereal creative spirit, as if she were one of her beautiful esoteric paintings. For Georgia, who had turned forty the previous November, this was her first taste of widespread newspaper publicity off the art page, and she thoroughly disliked it.

In April, stunned by the sale, she had fled to the cold, rainy Maine coast, only returning to New York in May to pack and depart with Stieglitz for Lake George. Whereas she flinched from the publicity, Stieglitz loved all the commotion. He announced through the newspapers that he would display the lilies for a few days in May before they left their homeland for good. During the brief exhibit he stood guard over them, repeating the story of their sale to anyone who was interested with his usual variation in detail but loyalty to the essential truth. The tension between him and Georgia was not eased any when he strained his thumb and became helpless during packing. Arriving at the lake, Georgia still felt dazed. For once she had difficulty tackling domestic chores that got the household running, and she felt no urge to paint.

7 ❖ Lake George

From the first year Georgia and Alfred were together, they had left New York every spring for Lake George. Usually they took the train, but sometimes they departed on the Hudson River night steamer from the Forty-second Street pier. The steamer took them upriver to Albany, where they boarded a morning train to the village of Lake George at the southern tip of the mountain-rimmed lake, which Georgia once called the most beautiful lake in the Adirondacks.

In 1920 Stieglitz's mother had become an invalid as a result of a stroke (she died in autumn 1922), and Oaklawn, the cavernous family estate, was sold. Up a steep hill from Oaklawn was a dilapidated farmhouse, a former pig farm that the Stieglitzes had purchased years before to clear the summer breeze of its unpleasant downwind aroma. It had been used for overflow guests, and Georgia and Alfred also used to stay there when they wanted seclusion. With Oaklawn gone, each member of the Stieglitz family began to donate money to turn the farmhouse into a comfortable country home. The renovation was supervised by Alfred's younger sister, Agnes, and her well-liked husband, George Engelhard, who oversaw the gardens and the grounds.

Soon the rambling house—surrounded by several little sheds, a tall flagpole, and a weathered barn—had a coat of fresh white paint. Its porch, which had early Victorian lacy carvings in the corners like wooden spider webs, overlooked the lovely island-studded lake and the wooded hills on the opposite shore, where the sun first appeared in the morning. A meadow, which was allowed to grow wild with high grasses, sloped from the farmhouse to a ridge of trees on the edge of the lake.

When Stieglitz and O'Keeffe arrived in the spring, they usually collapsed in exhaustion. They would slowly recover from the frenetic pace of the Manhattan winter, napping and trying to unwind. Early spring was chilly in northern New York State, but the perfumed lilacs with their heart-shaped leaves were starting to open among clumps of green pine and white birch. "Everything is very green—soft spring yellow green—the grass is soft and tall—waving—we only cut it for hay later," she wrote to Henry McBride. "The grape shoots are velvety pink—" In her element in the country, Georgia reveled in such activities as picking wild strawberries and hunting for watercress in the streams.

Since the couple always arrived weeks before the others, Georgia helped the cook and handyman open the house for the season. She used to clean the oil stove, wash floors, paint furniture, put the rowboat in the lake, and, in the first few years, plant corn and other vegetables. The help admired the way the former farmgirl cleaned a room without getting herself disheveled, and Stieglitz was amazed that she attacked housework with the same intensity and perfectionism with which she painted. In effect, she was so glad to get to the country that even housework was sometimes a welcome change. "As a matter of fact, I rather like it after the nightmare of New York," she admitted in a letter to Sherwood Anderson, adding that she also enjoyed being alone with Stieglitz. "I am having my few days of the year when there is no one around and I can really breathe—I don't know why people disturb me so much—they make me feel like a hobbled horse."

Then June came, the lush fields became dotted with white daisies, and the entourage of relatives and friends whom Stieglitz thrived on began to arrive. Groups formed to climb Prospect Mountain, one of the small mountains behind the farmhouse to the west—a four-hour excursion that Georgia liked to make daily. Sometimes guests hiked to a particularly beautiful spot on the mountainside where a large grove of white birches grew. Guests used to take the family's dinghy for a row, sometimes around tiny Tea Island, a few hundred yards offshore. Others dozed or chatted in the hammock and rocking chair on the porch, or took in the horse races in nearby Saratoga.

When the sun got hot, Georgia liked to strip off her heavy woolen socks and sweater and slip on a black tank bathing suit and rubber cap and swim off the little sandspit created by a mountain stream as it trickled into the lake. At times there was lighthearted fun. Once Stieglitz, one of the first photographers to use the hand camera creatively, snapped a picture of Georgia standing thigh-high in the lake, playfully pulling the wet hair of a hefty male swimmer. Another time he recorded the whole family munching corn on the cob while Georgia mugged at the cameraman.

Stieglitz did much of his photography in the summers now, surrounded by guests, whom he often used for models. Georgia, the only person he considered meticulous enough to touch his photographic equipment, used to "spot," or cover with India ink, the dust specks on his negatives. Then he began to print in a darkened little shack, a former potting shed, outside the kitchen door and near the flagpole.

In 1920 an old wooden weatherbeaten shed, originally built for dancing and later used for housing cows, was fixed up for Georgia's use. Stieglitz took a snapshot of her and his niece, Elizabeth Stieglitz Davidson, repairing its roof. The picture shows a lean, tanned Georgia, stripped to her chemise and bloomers, with her white stockings rolled below her knees in the summer heat, grinning under a floppy black hat. Her "shanty" up a steep incline in a field five minutes from the farmhouse, also had an outside platform facing north where she liked to paint. One of the few people invited to the shanty was Dorothy Schubart, the young wife of Alfred's nephew and a painter herself. Once when Georgia and Dorothy were painting green apples in the shanty, they left in a hurry for lunch. Upon returning, they discovered that a cow had wandered in, had munched the apples, and knocked over and stepped on Georgia's white china palette. The cow remained in evidence, mooing mournfully. Despite the smashed palette, the two women had a good laugh and shooed the cow out.

Georgia liked to spend an entire summer day dozing, reading, walking, or painting. Each year Stieglitz waited with bated breath until she gave signs that she was sufficiently rested and ready to begin to paint again. Then she went off by herself to the shanty, to a tiny upstairs bedroom in cool weather, or she set up a table, chair, and umbrella outside. Sometimes she tied a wooden tray around her waist for holding her paints and brushes. She often began with small, tentative, warm-up paintings, patiently doing the same tiny flower, leaf, or seashell over and over again.

After Labor Day, when most of the friends and relatives had departed, the languid mood of summer disappeared and the days took on a sense of urgency. Autumn days at Lake George had a crisp northern edge to them—a warning to O'Keeffe and Stieglitz that the cold would soon drive them back to the city. The sun shone for fewer minutes each day, but it burned with a hard, brilliant light. The sky was often dark with heavy, low, gray clouds that were blown in rapidly over the mountains. Reflecting them, the lake blackened and steamed in the cold air. Meanwhile, the wind gusted, rattled windows, and shook the farmhouse at night. The cicadas screeched with a shrill pulsation, as if they sensed that a frost would soon silence them. Canada geese, flying in formation, honked over the lake. Maple trees blazed fiery red and then began to lose their leaves as the mountains slowly turned brownish-purple except for patches of evergreens. When the thermometer suddenly plunged, Georgia used to hurry with a kettle of boiling water to pour over the pipes to keep them from freezing.

She thrilled to the fierce moods of the northern autumn the way she had to the violent weather of the Texas plains. She came to feel that autumn was *her* time for painting. She was rested, often alone with Stieglitz, and with many feelings and images stored from her summer out-of-doors. In October 1919 she had difficulty becoming inspired by nature because the weather had been dismal, gray, and soggy for weeks. One night, however, a burst of northern lights lit up the night sky for an hour—and it was all she needed to set her off on a marathon streak of rapid oil painting. These were the times the former pupil of William Merritt Chase, who had been taught to paint a picture a day, worked very quickly, sometimes completing a painting in half a day. Many of her finest Lake George paintings were done at this time of year in October colors, such as *Lake George with Crows* painted in 1921. Her output could be prodigious. In the fall of 1921, for example, she returned to the city with a harvest of twenty-five oils. When the light faded in the late afternoons, she lit the lamps, sewed, and prepared canvases for the next morning.

While Georgia painted, Stieglitz photographed, printed, or sat at his big desk in the downstairs sitting room and wrote his voluminous letters. He used to pause to tend the furnace or to walk a mile down the hill to the village post office with his black cape flapping and to return with the day's mail. He didn't want O'Keeffe to pause while "she still had paintings in her," as he put it, and he pushed her to work steadily until the last daylight was gone. She teasingly called him a slave driver, but she knew that he would prepare to move back to the city when she stopped painting. She was content in the country, but he was forlorn without talk and ached for the life of Manhattan. When the tug got too strong, he visited New York for a few days and then returned to Georgia's side. Finally, the inevitable: They picked a date, usually in November, to leave the lake. Georgia sadly began to pack her clothes into a trunk, and their books, letters, photographic equipment, and paintings into parcels for the train ride south to the city.

❖

As the years went by, Georgia found herself in an increasingly difficult, untenable position during the summers on what everyone came to call "the Hill." A highly individualistic person who needed uninterrupted hours of privacy in order to paint, she had to share a home with her in-laws, their children, and their children's children. There was Leopold, Alfred's brother, his wife and their married daughters, Elizabeth and Flora, and their six grandchildren. Lee's identical twin brother, Julius, founder of the chemistry department at the University of Chicago, visited with his family in the summers. Then there was Alfred's sister Agnes Engelhard, her husband, George, and their daughter, Georgia. And, finally, there was Alfred's youngest sister, Selma and her family.

Selma Schubart was a sultry, temperamental, dark-eyed beauty. One of the first women to drink and smoke in public, she dabbled in art, verse, and singing. She was elegant and liked to wear the jewels given her by her many prominent admirers, such as opera singer Enrico Caruso, whom she entertained at the lake and introduced to O'Keeffe. In the early years, Selma brought her ferocious little lapdog to the hill. It was a Boston Terrier named Prince Rico Rippe and a gift from Caruso, which tried to bite everyone in sight. Although the dog never bit Georgia, she adamantly refused to stay in the same house with the animal, and a bitter feud developed between the two willful women. "Sel" eventually relented, and in time they became friendly.

Once in a while one of the visitors was an O'Keeffe relative, often Ida O'Keeffe. Ida began to study nursing at Mt. Sinai Hospital in New York after the United States entered World War I, and she got a degree in 1921. A blunt, active, robust woman, she shared her older sister's love of the outdoors and enjoyed filling the farmhouse with the wildfowers that she gathered every day. Too independent-minded to marry, she had broken off an engagement during the years she taught art in Virginia. At Lake George she developed and unreciprocated crush on the writer Paul Rosenfeld, and a teasing, flirtatious friendship with Stieglitz. Although Stieglitz once confided to a friend that he found the O'Keeffe sisters "a queer lot," Ida's infectious laugh amused him and he found her remarkable. The household celebrated her thirty-fifth birthday with a frosted cake and gales of laughter late in October 1924.

Ida continued to paint and to study art at Columbia Teachers College when she had the time, and some of the results interested Stieglitz. Georgia didn't allow his admiration to go too far, however, and he never exhibited Ida's work. Rivalry had existed between the two eldest O'Keeffe girls since their childhood, when the grown-ups thought that affectionate little Ida was the more artistically talented of the two. At Chatham Ida had also had her drawings published in the yearbook, but she had the habit, when drawing, of stopping often to rub her pain-ridden hands, which friends attributed to "nerves," and which may have been a nervous reaction to competition with her older sister. In adulthood she annoyed Georgia by remarking from time to time that all she needed was her own Stieglitz to put her on the map as an artist. Even while a private nurse, she continued on her own to have occasional shows throughout her life. Georgia believed that up to her death in 1961, Ida still considered herself the more gifted O'Keeffe.

But the photographs Stieglitz took of Ida and Georgia at Lake George tell the real story. Although the sisters' bone structures and fan-shaped eyes were strikingly similar, everything else was different. The way Georgia arranged her hair, chose her clothes, and even the amount of flesh on her cheeks indicated her precision and the paring down of her personality so she could focus on art. Whereas Georgia combed her hair straight back, wore simple dark clothes, and stayed slender, Ida cut and waved her hair in the fashion of the day, wore commonplace printed dresses, had gained a few extra pounds, and smiled incessantly in front of the camera. Georgia seemed to be willing herself to become extraordinary, while Ida remained ordinary in a natural, pleasing way.

Georgia, who had only a lukewarm sense of kinship with her own brothers and sisters, had none with the Stieglitzes. Once when one of Elizabeth Davidson's small daughters called her Aunt Georgia, she felt a flash of anger, slapped the child across the face, and cried, *"Never call me Aunt Georgia!"* The children, forever underfoot, were a constant source of tension. Once little Frankie Prosser, the blond son of the family cook, crayoned on one of Georgia's canvases. Another time three of Leopold's granddaughters were playing Indians in the woods near Georgia's painting shanty. Hearing the shanty door slam shut with a loud bang, they scampered to the window to investigate and saw Georgia hastily trying to cover her naked body. Apparently, she had been painting in the nude—the way she used to paint in the Fifty-ninth Street studio when it was hot. When she saw their faces in the window, she screamed at them with a fury they never forgot. Afterward, she accused the little girls of "spying," but the rest of the family dismissed their behavior, calling it "exploring."

Although the Stieglitzs had loyally admired her paintings and sheltered her before her marriage to Alfred, now, in this situation at Lake George, they became the target of Georgia's frustration. Her irritation might take the form of icy remoteness. "We were a little afraid of her," admitted Stieglitz's niece Flora Straus, "because she was very intelligent, direct and critical. She asked for no mercy, and she gave no mercy." Georgia also liked to ridicule the family, along with Dorothy Schubart. After meals the two women used to go sit on a fence together and mock the mealtime conversation. "Did you hear what *he* said?" Georgia would ask about one of her brothers-in-law, and she'd laugh irreverently. But there was another, untold, side of the story, according to Georgia. "I was hard on that family," she said late in life, "but they were hard on me."

After the extended family began sharing the farmhouse on the hill, Alfred's gentle, quiet sister Agnes and her husband, the perceptive, humorous George, who was an amateur violinist, were in charge of the household and the grounds. On Sunday nights in the winter, Alfred and Georgia used to dine with the Engelhards, and everyone got along well. For four summers everything ran smoothly, until 1924, when the Engelhards and their nineteen-year-old daughter, Georgia, decided to spend the holidays in Europe.

Taking their place in the summer household were Leopold and Elizabeth, in whose New York townhouse Alfred and Georgia had lived for the past four years. "Lizzie," as Elizabeth was called, was a frugal housewife who planned bland and, in the opinion of some of the diners, unpalatable meals. That summer of 1924 her meals enraged Georgia, and she made Lizzie's life miserable. She snubbed her, jumping up from the table in the middle of a meal and sometimes even refusing to go to the table at all. Stieglitz had a kidney attack. It was a profoundly uncomfortable household, and, after the experience, Lee and Lizzie gave up sharing the farmhouse and built a house of their own on another part of the property. That decision made Georgia realize that she and Stieglitz would never have the hill entirely to themselves.

Since, in effect, Georgia had driven some of her in-laws away, so that they stopped using the farmhouse full-time, she became more responsible for overseeing the household, even though she was there to paint whereas the others were there to vacation. It was a time-consuming job, and one that she loathed. She tried to simplify household rountines by, for example, instructing Margaret Prosser, the long-time, independent-minded Nova Scotian family cook, to serve the food informally from the stove to people's plates. Georgia also began to spice the food with onions and garlic. Although all this raised a few Stieglitz eyebrows, no one dared object.

In the summer of 1926, as she was waiting for the rain to stop and the guests to leave, Georgia complained that she felt like a cat whose fur was rubbed the wrong way. She was disgusted at the amount of time spent digesting food at the lake, and, in her misery, she stopped eating and lost fifteen pounds. Finally, in late August, she was able to stand it no longer. She abruptly fled to the Maine seashore, about a hundred and seventy-five miles to the east. Surprised and worried, Stieglitz went after her. She must have told him that she would remain in Maine until the visitors were gone, because three days later he returned alone, with a cold. After delaying her departure from Maine until the end of September, Georgia finally showed up on the hill. She had evidently found precisely the inspiration and solitude she needed there—for upon her return, she set to work and finished three fine paintings in five days.

Since Alfred's brothers and sisters spent only a few summer weeks at the farmhouse now, Alfred and Georgia, who continued to spend half the year there, became its de facto owners. Little by little the people who visited were likely to be *their* friends, and in time the decor began to reflect their tastes—but not without a struggle.

When Georgia had a section of the south porch taken off to make a room lighter, there was a fuss. But when "Judith" disappeared, there was a veritable uproar. Judith was a marble likeness of the Hebrew heroine that had been carved in the 1890s and it reigned over the Oaklawn salon for years. For some unknown reason, it was transported up the hill to the farmhouse after Oaklawn was sold. Georgia and some younger members of the family detested the bust, with its silent, sneering stare, mop of frizzy hair, and one bare marble breast.

One September night in 1927 when no one was around, Georgia and young Georgia Engelhard decided to get rid of her once and for all. They dug a deep hole and, with the help of another in-law named Donald Davidson, they dumped Judith in and covered her up. When her absence was noticed, the two Georgias protested their innocence. Secretly they thought that what they had done was very funny and wondered whether future generations might find the bust and believe they had excavated Roman ruins at Lake George. In old age, O'Keeffe liked to say smugly and with obvious pleasure that Judith was still underground.

Once the detested bust had been dispatched, Georgia covered the walls of the room in which she had stood with light gray paper and painted the floor black. Slowly the farmhouse windows were stripped of their cretonne curtains to let in more light, pictures disappeared from the walls, tables were swept clean of bric-a-brac, the rooms were lit by unshaded bluish-white light bulbs, and most of the furniture— except for a few deep armchairs—disappeared. Now the farmhouse looked Spartan, but the food was sybaritic.

In spite of these changes, it was becoming increasingly difficult for Georgia to paint at Lake George, even in the autumn. Although she never cooked for the whole family, she had to cook for Stieglitz, herself, and any remaining guests after the season was over and the cook had departed. Stieglitz was well-intentioned (once he tried to bake cinnamon buns, and sometimes he attempted to dry the dishes), but he had come to domesticity late in life and had difficulty keeping his mind on it. That was the summer Georgia spent ten days in the hospital for the removal of a benign breast lump, and afterwards Lee cautiously advised her against too much overexertion, making her feel more frustrated than ever.

In search of inspiration, she would row the dinghy onto the lake at sunrise when the trunk of the big old birch tree near the dock appeared bleached white and its leaves brilliantly golden. Once she painted a view of the mountains and trees reflected in the mirrorlike surface of the lake. "The people up there live such little, pretty lives and the scenery is such little, pretty scenery," she explained, and "that's the way I felt when I painted this." She often painted her flowers and leaves enlarged, as if under a microscope, but the size of her canvases often stayed small, so that the objects seemed to push at the edges of the frames, as if the artist were trying to liberate herself from psychic and physical limitations.

She ritually painted the same chestnuts, maples, willows, and birches with green leaves, flaming fall foliage, and barren of leaves until she felt as though she knew each tree on the mountainside. She feared that she was exhausting the subjects of the lake, ponds, streams, autumn leaves, and was beginning to repeat herself. By the late twenties everything seemed either too lush, too dainty, too soft, too dark, or too detailed to her. In May 1928 she complained to Henry McBride that there was "nothing but green" at the lake, and she wondered what to paint.

Soon after she had moved to the East, she was invited to visit Stieglitz family friends who owned a comfortable old New England house in southern Maine. It was then, in the early spring of 1920, that Georgia, born and bred in the landlocked Midwest, got to know the sea. When she first compared the vast, thundering Atlantic ocean to the cozy hills of Lake George, she immediately preferred the sea, for its wildness that reminded her of the western plains. Fascinated by the swelling surf, strong salty winds, and the perfect shapes of the polished seashells washed up by the tides, she liked to walk along the deserted beaches before the summer people arrived. She liked it particularly at dusk, when she used to go down a boardwalk, through a cranberry bog and sand dunes, to watch the waves billow and break in the half-light. Throughout the decade, she returned to the seacoast almost every year when she needed to get in touch with that part of herself that propelled her to paint.

Starting in the early twenties, she was inspired to paint the sea. She did a big, bluish-green foaming wave in translucent watercolor.

She rendered the sea under a pink moon, and under stormy skies pierced by lightning. She also painted its glistening, greenish seaweed, and its purplish mussels and grayish-white clamshells, which she used to keep in a platter of seawater so their colors stayed strong. In *Wave, Night*, painted in 1928, she captured the rhythmic drama of the sea at night—a distant lighthouse beacon, the long white line of breaking waves in the inky-black water, and the crescent curve of foam on the sand. The little light breaking through the endless black line of the horizon and the dark gray sky seemed to be calling her in the gloom.

When she had suggested to Alfred in 1922 that they summer near the sea, he had laughed at the notion, even though he knew that the sea gave her something tremendous that the hill didn't. Now in his midsixties, it was impossible for him to conceive of such a radical change in his routine—to leave the land and lake he had loved since boyhood. Since she could not have a home at the seaside, she proposed near the end of the decade that they build a house of their own at the lake with the money she had recently earned from the sales of her paintings. But Stieglitz was not interested, even though it would have provided her with the privacy she yearned for. Instead, that summer of 1927 he remodeled a potting shed on the property to use as a darkroom.

❖

In the summer of 1928, relations between Alfred and Georgia were strained for many reasons. There was the publicity accompanying the sale of the lily paintings. Stieglitz refused to allow Georgia to visit relatives in Wisconsin. Georgia, other Stieglitz in-laws, and Georgia Engelhard used to go to her shanty in the evenings and make fun of the family.

Finally, Stieglitz relented and in July Georgia departed for Wisconsin where she stayed a month. Her elderly Totto aunts, Ollie and Lola, lived there, and in their eyes Georgia, whom they had helped launch as an art student, was the family pride and joy. Her brother Alexius, an engineer, who, despite his bad health, had been involved in the building of roads in the state after the war, was married and living in Madison. In addition, her sister Catherine, now thirty-three years old, the wife of banker Raymond Klenert and the mother of a small daughter, lived in Portage. That summer Georgia painted a red

Wisconsin barn and silo near Portage. She seemed to be reaching back into her early, happy Sun Prairie memories to try to remember who she was, where she had come from, and where she was going.

In her restlessness, she recalled Texas with nostalgia. She thought of the great plains as her spiritual home and wondered whether she should have left. Her teaching years, which she said she missed terribly, were "some of the happiest of my life," she told a reporter in 1928. "I'd teach now if I had the time—and if they'd let me." But since she was the greatest woman artist in the world, in the view of Stieglitz and his circle, she knew that they would make a fuss if she taught instead of giving herself completely to art. Around that time she invoked a reminiscence of a Texas theme on canvas—an intense, burning sun over bright red hills—which hung in her 1928 show.

She was keenly aware now of the differences between her own working style and that of her husband. Whereas she felt the urge to travel to find new painting subjects, he clung to the New York—Lake George axis. He relished the familiar Lake George clouds, rains, fogs and mists, whereas she increasingly felt them to be oppressive. He was to work at the farmhouse's kitchen table, but she could not tolerate people around her when she painted. Stieglitz never understood, she felt, that if someone glimpsed an unfinished canvas, it somehow— whatever his reaction—contaminated her idea and halted her work in progress. The continual, close, bizarre critiques of her work by Stieglitz's group and the New York critics felt stifling to her. And whereas Stieglitz was energized by emotional encounters, she found them enervating. "I've listened to him in intense debate with someone and wound up feeling as if I'd been beaten about the body with sandbags," she said long afterwards.

Stieglitz had frequently complained about an assortment of aches and pains. In the spring of 1923, for example, he collapsed in ex- haustion on the hill, "a little heap of misery—sleepless—with eyes— ears—nose—arm—feet—ankles—intestines—one after the other" bothering him, Georgia wrote a friend. Highly charged with both nervousness and determination, he used to suffer from indigestion due to overexcitement, and from time to time his rather frail body caved in. He was deathly afraid of germs and used to ride up to Lake George on the train with his suitcase on his lap, because he believed it was a way to ward off infection.

On returning from her visit to Wisconsin, Georgia saw that Stieglitz's health problems had gotten worse, and in September 1928 he was stricken for the first time by what he called a heart attack and Lee described as angina. Lee, Alfred's lifelong doctor ("much to his sorrow, I think" Georgia later remarked), prescribed total rest in bed for three weeks, no mental excitement, and exact amounts of specific foods. Georgia sent for nurses, but she was ultimately responsible for Stieglitz's care. He lay silently in bed, his tissue-thin skin pale, his silver hair spread out like an aureole around his head, and his voice hushed.

With a patient on her hands during her 1928 fall painting season, Georgia was unable to concentrate on art. She was distracted by annoying small duties, such as having to screen Stieglitz's visitors, mail, and phone calls, and even having to take his dictation since he was too weak to write letters. At times Stieglitz felt intensely guilty that he was keeping her from painting, and at other times he was resentful that she was not sympathetic enough toward him. For her part, she believed that if she met all his demands she would have nothing left to give. During a solitary walk when she was feeling downcast, she realized that the "thing I enjoy of the autumn is there no matter what is happening to me," and she managed to paint a picture of a hickory leaf and a daisy—a triumph over great odds, she felt.

By now, the critics were used to being hit between the eyes by the annual O'Keeffe show. For instance, after the opening of her 1926 exhibition, *The New Yorker* had written:

> We have petitioned the fire commissioner to allow us to
> paint our running gear red and to carry a clanging bell.
> We will then tear through the streets, hoping that many
> will follow. . . . For if ever there were a raging, blazing
> soul mounting to the skies it is that of Georgia
> O'Keeffe. . . . One O'Keeffe hung in the Grand Central
> Station would even halt the home-going commuters . . .
> surely if the authorities knew they would pass laws
> against Georgia O'Keeffe, take away her magic tubes and
> brushes. Americans, with their eyes on success, must not
> be dazed by the unproductive glory of immortal beauty. It
> might make them question the radiance of the legend
> goal.

The next spring, 1927, Lewis Mumford had written in the *New*

Republic that becasue O'Keeffe was an artist who continually created fresh forms, she was the most original painter in America. It was high praise, but the high expectations also created great pressure. "It's much more difficult to go on now than it was before," Georgia said. "Every year I have to carry the thing I do enough further so that people are surprised again." Henry McBride agreed in 1928 that an annual show was a real test of an artist, since it implied that there was something new to show each year.

She knew, as well, that to be the artist whom Stieglitz had unleashed and nurtured, it was essential constantly to probe, explore, and expand her consciousness to the edges of her imagination. "Making your unknown known is the important thing—and keeping the un-known always beyond you—catching—crystalizing [sic] your simpler clearer vision of life—only to see it turn stale compared to what you vaguely feel ahead—that you must always keep working to grasp—" she wrote to Sherwood Anderson. She tended to enjoy her own paint-ings very much right after finishing them, but then the feeling of pleasure used to wear off and she was impelled to look ahead again.

Increasingly, people became aware that art was her life, and that, as Stieglitz had already shown in his photographs of her, the woman and her work were integrated. Frances O'Brien had noted in 1927 that "when you look at her pictures you know that she is chiseled, ordered, and fine just the way they are." And when friends looked at her, they saw her pictures. "A strange madonna, with a fiery intensity for life, which we are not taught belongs to a madonna," wrote Dorothy Brett. "Slim, straight, in black-and-white, not mere grooming, not only *soigné*—it was more than that. It was an expression of the spirit, of the almost abstract purity of her paintings—the flowing through, the completing of her paintings in herself."

O'Keeffe was beginning to win recognition outside the Stieglitz circle, which, inevitably, made her feel more independent. In 1927, the Brooklyn Museum, which owned her work, gave her an entire room to herself in its summer exhibition of painting and sculpture. Moreover, when the trustees of the new Museum of Modern Art (including Alfred Barr, Jr., Mrs. John D. Rockefeller, Jr., and Duncan Phillips) invited her to exhibit in its second show, scheduled for late 1929, along with eighteen of the most important artists working in America, she must have known that her place among artists of her generation was secure. Although Stieglitz had doubts about her participating, fearing that the exhibition at the new museum would not be first-class enough, she went ahead and did so anyway.

Besides gaining the respect of her peers, she had become extremely popular with the general public. Versions of her giant flowers were being appropriated everywhere. They were sold in department stores, displayed in florist shop windows, and, finally, used to advertise perfume and lingerie. In addition, her financial success was so great and well publicized that the Internal Revenue Service initiated an investigation into the business side of the gallery in June 1928. (Stieglitz sent them a flyer to prove that there was no business side, and he stated that his wife paid her own taxes.)

The winter after Stieglitz's heart troubles, 1928–29, Georgia painted very little. She appeared melancholy to acquaintances. Her head looked heavy, her lips were colorless, and her eyes seemed flat, reflective, and terribly sad. Like Stieglitz, she had taken to wearing a somber black cape most of the time, as if she were in mourning, but during this period she sometimes startled people by tossing a wool cloak of a rich earth color over her black dress, as if she were trying to transform herself.

Unfortunately, her annual exhibition in the early months of 1929 came at a time when expectations were running the highest and when her new paintings were the weakest in years. Not all of the thirty-five pictures on display had been done the previous year, as was usually the case. One of an ornate pink vase in a window with a view of a smoky urban world exuded both bitter humor and a sense of confinement. The *New York Times* review gently noted that the painter was going through a time of transition and that her work was in "a fluid state, unstatic, mobile, alive with potentialities." Another critic reported that there wasn't much to say about her anymore because it had already all been said. When Robert Coates of *The New Yorker* later recalled the period, he said that her style had grown too tight "and at last the meticulousness showed a tendency to trip over itself, as one peering too closely at the minutiae before him might end by tripping over a matchstick." Georgia must have expected such low-key reactions, for she had told Henry McBride beforehand that she didn't want to exhibit again for a long, long time.

Even before their marriage, Stieglitz had known that the lake did not inspire her, and that she still dreamed about the West. As the most astute observer of her work, he must have noticed that the exultant sense of freedom in her Texas landscapes was missing from the cramped New York pictures and the subdued Lake George ones. Georgia's desire to return to the West must have been periodically ignited whenever their friends came back from vacations in New Mexico and other western states—friends like Marsden Hartley, Paul Rosenfeld, Herbert Seligmann, Paul Strand and his wife, Rebecca. Furthermore it was a time when an increasing number of Americans were buying Model T Fords and exploring the newly designated national parks in the western part of the country.

For years Alfred had talked about taking Georgia to what even he called "her America" some summer. When he had traveled as a young man (he was already then essentially an urban person) it was to visit the old civilizations of Europe. He had ventured west of the Hudson River only once, in 1900, on a trip to Chicago. Back in 1918 he had sent Paul Strand, his proxy, to collect Georgia in Texas. As he got older, he increasingly loathed change, preferring to explore the world through the large numbers of people who came to him. But after his heart attack—which came at a time when his work was mostly limited to running the gallery whereas Georgia was reaching the peak of her creative powers—she was forced to accept the obvious fact that he would never be able to accompany her to the rugged West.

In winter 1928–29, Dorothy Brett visited New York along with Mabel Dodge Luhan and her Indian husband, Tony, who all lived in Taos, New Mexico. Brett had shipped seven of her Indian paintings East for Stieglitz to see. Although he did not exhibit them, he encouraged her efforts and they became fast friends. Shy, sensitive, and partially deaf, Brett was a pretty woman with large, inquiring brown eyes. She spent many hours that winter in the gallery, where Georgia had placed a Christmas tree, sitting wrapped in a red blanket, admiring and attentive. In letters she termed the gallery "my Spiritual Home" and Stieglitz and O'Keeffe "beautiful people." Since she had taken a room high up in the Shelton Hotel, she often breakfasted with them in the cafeteria, joined them for Sunday luncheon at Longchamps (where they sipped large bowls of onion soup while she feasted on Long Island duckling), and shared Christmas dinner with them. In the spring, when she was returning to Taos, Stieglitz saw her off at Grand Central Station—but not before she had repeatedly urged them to visit Taos.

Not surprisingly, Georgia began to think seriously about spending a summer in the West, even if it had to be without Stieglitz. For the past eleven summers she had been with him and his family at Lake George, taking only occasional trips elsewhere. Although she was ready for a vacation apart from him (she had even considered Europe), Stieglitz was not so willing. Anxious about her growing dissatisfaction, he sometimes even fretted when she took an unusually long ramble by herself at the lake before breakfast.

Georgia nevertheless took stock: She was forty-one, time was passing, and she had nothing to paint on the hill. She had not painted all winter. She had been born to people used to the American tradition of pulling up stakes and heading westward in search of something better. She became quietly determined to go and, finally, Stieglitz reluctantly agreed. According to Blanche Matthias, one of Stieglitz's maxims was that "freedom is necessary to sincerity," and maybe he felt it was essential for her to go. Perhaps he was calmed by the fact that Georgia had persuaded Paul Strand's wife, Rebecca, to accompany her. Stieglitz had known Beck, the thirty-eight-year-old daughter of the backer of Buffalo Bill's Wild West Show, since the early twenties.

So at the close of her disappointing 1929 show, Georgia methodically began to pack a trunk with enough tubes of paint, brushes, and canvas to last her a few months. Then, on the first day of May, she and Beck Strand left for New Mexico.

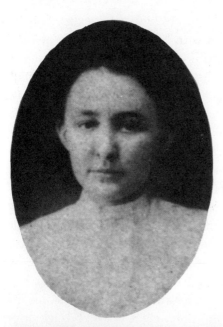

Georgia as a high school
graduate from Chatham
Episcopal Institute in 1905.

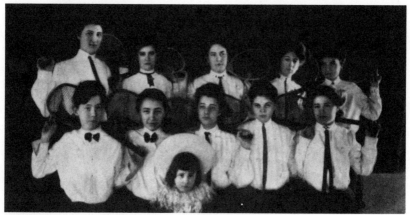

Georgia (second from left, bottom row) as a member of the Chatham
Racket Club. Courtesy of Mrs. Walter Wilson.

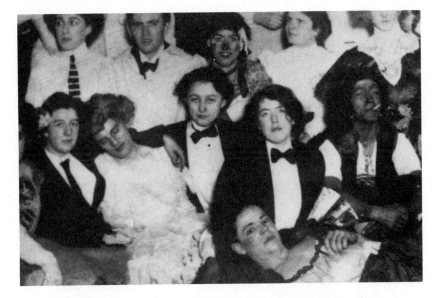

Georgia, twenty (center), and classmates at Art Students League
costume party. Courtesy of Lila Howard.

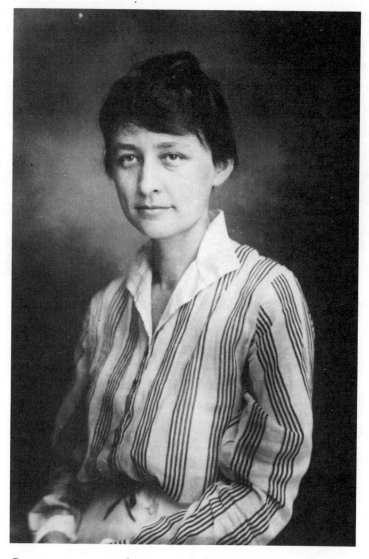

Georgia at twenty-eight, an art teacher at the University of Virginia. Courtesy of Howard Bazarre, Holsinger Collection.

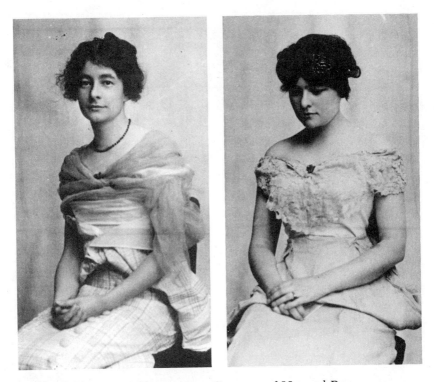

Left, Georgia's sister Ida in 1912. Courtesy of Howard Bazarre, Holsinger Collection. Right, Georgia's sister Anita in 1912. Courtesy of Howard Bazarre, Holsinger Collection.

166

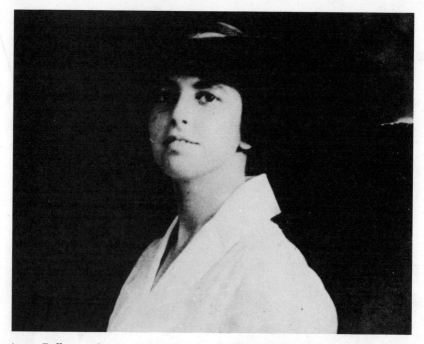

Anita Pollitzer, Georgia's lifelong friend. Courtesy of William Pollitzer.

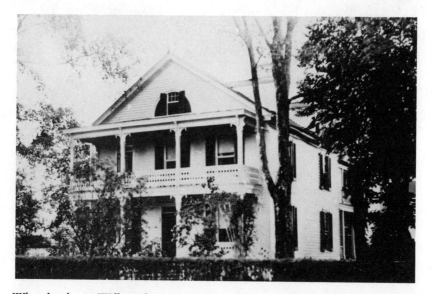

Wheatlands, in Williamsburg, Virginia, where the O'Keeffe family lived starting in 1903. Courtesy of Colonial Williamsburg Foundation.

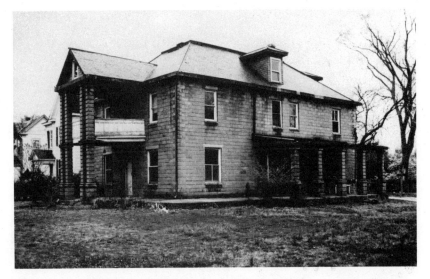

The concrete block house built by Georgia's father about 1908. Courtesy of Colonial Williamsburg Foundation.

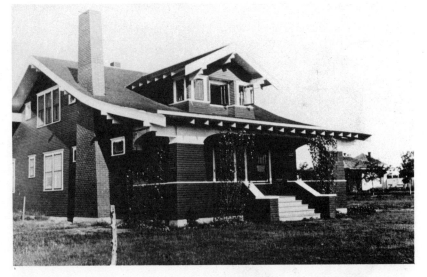

The Shirley's house in Canyon, Texas, where Georgia lived in 1917. Her room had the dormer. Courtesy of Louise Shirley.

168

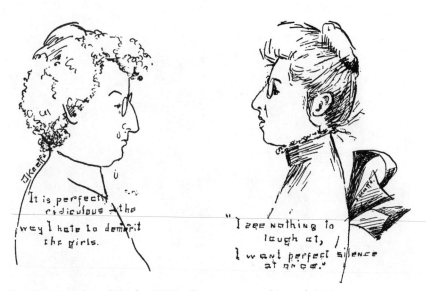

Caricatures of teachers by O'Keeffe, pp. 42 and 43 of the Mortar-Board, 1905 yearbook of Chatham Episcopal Institute, Chatham, Virginia. Courtesy of Mrs. Walter Wilson.

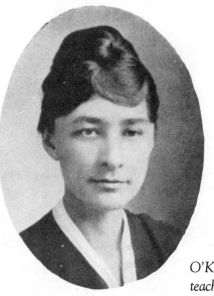

O'Keeffe as art teacher.

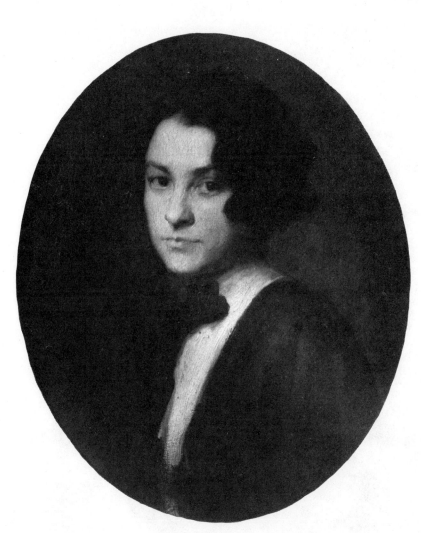

Georgia O'Keeffe by Eugene Speicher. Oil on canvas, 28 inches by 18. Courtesy of The Art Students League of New York.

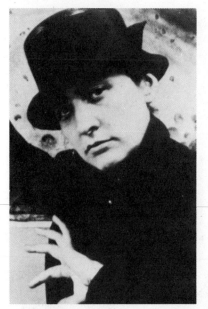

O'Keeffe by Stieglitz, c. 1918.
Courtesy of Frank Prosser.

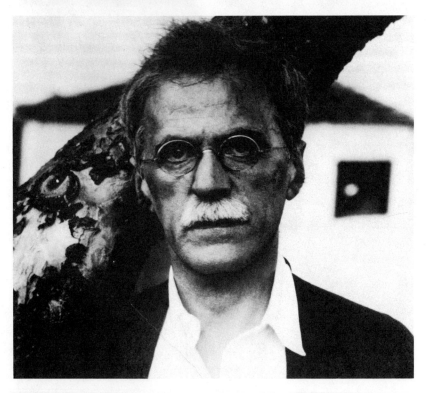

Stieglitz at Lake George, 1929. 1971 by the estate of Paul Strand.

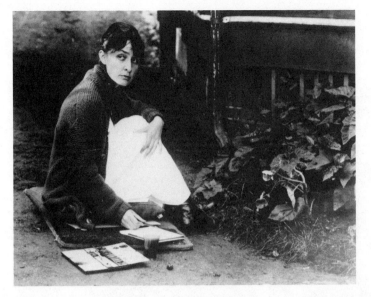

O'Keeffe at Lake George, c. 1918. Courtesy of Frank Prosser.

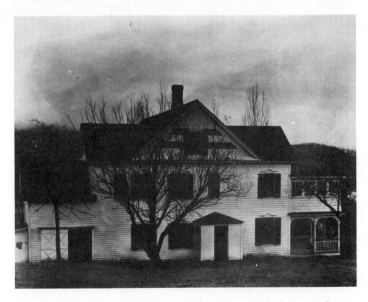

The Stieglitz summer house at Lake George. Courtesy of Frank Prosser.

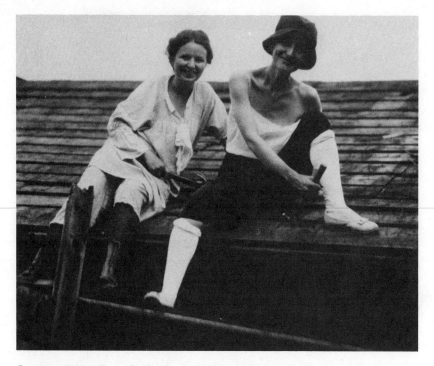

Georgia O'Keeffe and Elizabeth Davidson on roof at Lake George with hammers. Courtesy of Zabriskie Gallery, New York.

Opposite: O'Keeffe in the thirties at Lake George. Courtesy of Mrs. William Schubart.

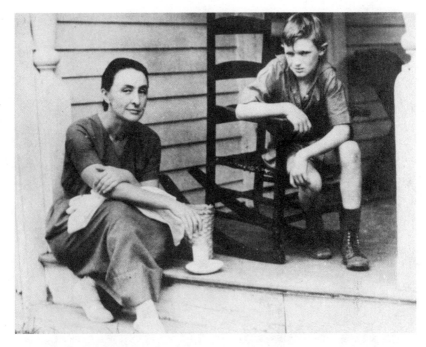

O'Keeffe and Frankie Prosser on the porch at Lake George, c. 1930.
Courtesy of Frank Prosser.

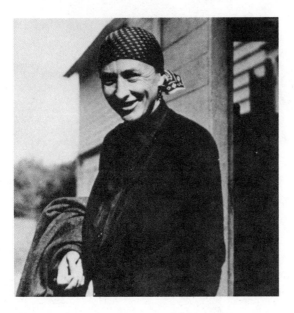

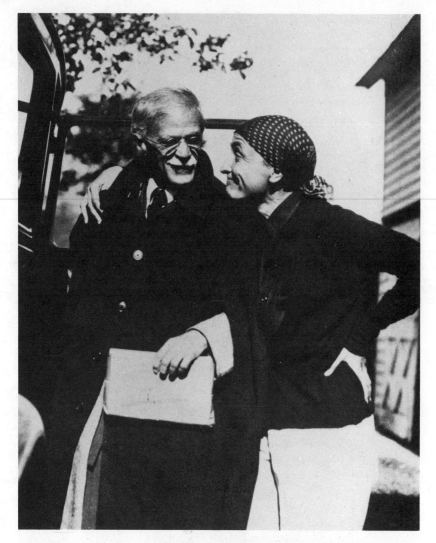

O'Keeffe and Stieglitz and her Ford. Courtesy of Mrs. William Schubart.

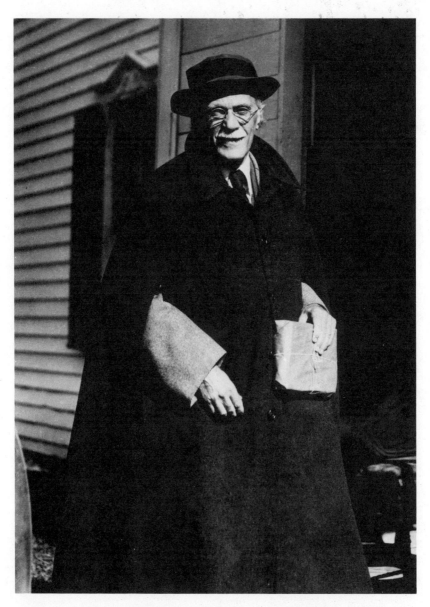

Stieglitz in cape, Lake George. Courtesy of Mrs. William Schubart.

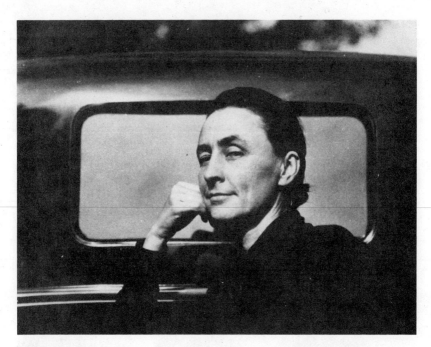

*Stieglitz portrait of O'Keeffe in front of Ford. Courtesy of Zabriskie
Gallery, New York.*

8 ❖ Taos

A few days later the train brought Georgia and Beck Strand to Santa Fe, a pretty, pink-adobe town clustered at the foothills of the Rocky Mountains. Santa Fe hadn't changed much since 1917 when Georgia and her sister Claudia first visited it on returning from a hiking vacation in Colorado. Eleven thousand Spanish, Indians, and Anglos now inhabited the tiny state capital, called by its boosters "the most metropolitan small town in American." Noted for its colorful history, art museum, high altitude, and bohemianism, it was a mecca for tourists, health seekers, artists, and escapees from bourgeois America.

On their first day in town, the two women bought tickets for a Harvey tour to the San Felipe Indian corn dance, about forty miles to the south. Georgia and Beck, who had intense sapphire-blue eyes and prematurely white hair, made a striking pair: Both had strong-boned faces and a mannish mode of dressing. Some people said they resembled one another, particularly when, at Paul Strand's urging, his wife dressed in black and acted in other ways like O'Keeffe. That summer the two women dressed in black skirts and white blouses, recalled another visitor.

When they arrived at the pueblo, Georgia spotted Tony Luhan's proud head in the crowd, leaned out the bus window, and waved to him. Mabel went running up to them and invited them to come with her to watch the corn dancers from the shaded flat roof of an Indian dwelling. When the festivities were over, they all rode back together to Santa Fe in Mabel's big car.

Fifty that year, Mabel had a small, square, determined body, bright gray eyes, and a soft melodious voice; she wore her thick chestnut hair in bangs, squaw-style, often with a girlish ribbon. At the time that Georgia had been an art student in New York, Mabel was an heiress who "collected" people in her Greenwich Village salon. After moving to Taos, she continued to invite artists and writers to visit—D. H. Lawrence and Willa Cather numbered among her guests—and she had unsuccessfully petitioned Stieglitz and O'Keeffe for years. Now she insisted that Georgia and Beck return with her to Taos, an artist's colony seventy miles to the north, where her penchant for dominating the local goings-on had led to her being given the nickname "the Empress of Mabel-town."

Georgia and Beck were reluctant to visit, because the Strands, who had been Mabel's houseguests three years before, had come back irritated by her petty jealousies and bossy ways. Although a perceptive confidante and a generous hostess, Mabel apparently was given to meddling destructively in other people's lives. Another source of discomfort for Georgia must have been the memory of what had happened a few years earlier, when she had suggested that Mabel might write about a woman's paintings more sensibly than the men. The resulting essay had been an embarrassing disappointment: Mabel attacked Stieglitz as a showman who paraded his wife's sexuality, and called O'Keeffe's pictures the "filthy" product of her sexual frustration.

Typically, Mabel was not put off by the visitors' hesitancy, and the next morning, the story goes, she arrived at their hotel and announced she had sent their trunks to Taos, so they *had* to come with her. How Mabel was able to manage this without their knowledge is hard to understand, and it's also curious that Georgia, who was so strong-willed, should succumb to such tactics. Perhaps Georgia went along because she was amused by Mabel's impudence. At any rate, soon all of them were motoring north along the road through the Rio Grande gorge toward Taos, which suddenly brought them up onto the high sagebrush-covered Taos plateau. There, as they turned back in the direction from which they had come, they saw the way the endless space receded into waves of violet and purple mountains all the way to Arizona.

Georgia and Beck were put up in the Pink House, a guest cottage across a low alfalfa-field divide from Mabel's large house (where D. H. Lawrence and his wife had stayed earlier). Georgia was also loaned an adobe studio near a stream, beneath some huge cottonwood trees. Round-shaped and with a high-beamed ceiling and corner fireplace, it had big north windows overlooking a green meadow where black-and-white Indian ponies grazed. Beyond the meadow could be seen silvery-gray sagebrush and the large, looming Taos mountains in the distance. Georgia instantly took to the beautiful secluded studio and eagerly set up her easel.

During her first days in Taos, Georgia seemed dazed, perhaps because of the intense desert light or the conflicting states of light-headness and fatigue induced by the high altitude. Soon, however, she was exultant—laughing, vigorous, and brown. She discovered that New Mexico abounded with even more wonders than the canyons and plains of Texas. Within New Mexico the altitude varied from a few thousand to fourteen thousand feet, and vegetation ranged from Sonoran cacti to alpine wildflowers. And within a few miles in any direction there was an incredible variety of geological formations—from hot springs to snowcovered peaks. Taos itself was surrounded by a vast sweep of semiarid desert, revealing the contours of the bald earth. Its dryness reduced plant and animal life to essential forms, suggestive of the way Georgia instinctively simplified her images. The place fitted her aesthetic temperament perfectly, and she was later to say that "half your work is done for you" in New Mexico. Mabel reported that in those first weeks the word "wonderful" was always on Georgia's lips. "Well! Well! Well!" Georgia used to exclaim. "This is wonderful. No one told me it was like *this!*"

The New Mexican sunlight, far more radiant than the light at sea level, often made newcomers feel that their eyes were open wide for the first time. The experience, to some, came as a startling revelation or even a spiritual awakening. "Never is the light more pure and overweening than there, arching with a royalty almost cruel over the hollow, uptilted world," D. H. Lawrence had written about Taos, saying that it had finally liberated him from mechanized civilization. "It is so easy to understand that the Aztecs gave hearts of man to the sun. . . . It is of a brilliant and unchallengeable purity and haughty serenity which would make one sacrifice the heart to it." Visual artists such as Georgia were particularly susceptible. In the searing brightness, the desert, sagebrush, flowers, and mountains shimmered in new hues before her eyes.

The thin, dry air enabled her to see farther, too, as if she suddenly had developed telescopic vision. Sometimes from the Taos highland she was able to see a half-dozen distant thunderstroms rip the summer sky at once. After dinner she liked to ride Mabel's white horse into the foothills of the mountains, sitting in the saddle as erect and graceful as an Indian. She used to rein in the horse at various vantage points to take the measure of the land, inhale the sweet sage-scented air, and watch the light fade around nine o'clock. Whereas some tourists felt overwhelmed by this lonely space in which mankind seemed irrelevant, Georgia was exhilarated by it all—the vast scale of the remote mountains, the deep silence of the land, and the empty arc of the infinte sky. It did not make her feel diminished at all. The dimensions of Lake George were cozy and those of New York vertical, but New Mexico was horizontal—and so big and open that it seemed to offer endless possibilities. "The world is wide here," she said about New Mexico in old age, "and it's very hard to feel that it's wide in the East."

At mealtimes Georgia left her studio and walked across a little bridge, took a hollyhock-lined path through the lush green field, and after climbing a small hill, entered the cool, dark dining room in Mabel's sprawling, whimsical adobe house. Mabel customarily reigned at the head of the table in an ornately carved Florentine armchair while her Indian maid, the handsome Albidia, padded softly around the table in deerskin boots, serving the food. One morning at breakfast Georgia remarked to Eleanor Young, a charming guest who wrote fairy tales, that she had seen her up very early, to which Miss Young replied, "No, I just got up. You must have seen my astrol body." Despite the entertaining company and the marvelous studio, it's unlikely that Georgia would have remained under her hostess's capricious rule for long, had not Mabel suddenly left for the East in June, only a few weeks after Georgia's arrival, to have a hysterectomy. Just as she was about to leave, torrential summer rains washed out the road, and she "insisted on rushing around to all her houses and trying to run everything and tell us what we should do—and she got very irritated and overdid," wrote another guest, Neith Boyce to her husband, Hutchins Hapgood, who was visiting with two of her children, Miriam and Charles. Neith observed that Mabel had quarrelled with all of her guests who "she wants and then gets fed up with them." Mabel finally left for Buffalo, N.Y., and while she was away, Georgia stayed on in Taos until early August.

❖

Artists had stopped to paint in Taos since the end of the nineteenth century. As early as 1914 the Taos Society of Artists organized shows of members' work for exhibition in the East. By 1929 Taos, half the size of Santa Fe, had a well-established art gallery, an art supply shop, and a summer art school.

Almost everyone in this cliquish, unconventional artists' colony had come from someplace else. There were "rich people, writers and artists who pose as Indians, cowboys, prospectors, desperadoes, Mexicans and other nearly extinct species," critic Edmund Wilson had written with only a bit of exaggeration. It was still the Wild West, in many ways. After Georgia had been there two months, a rich, eccentric resident of Taos was discovered mysteriously and gruesomely dead— an eruption of violence that for Georgia must have been a curious echo of the Amarillo murder that had happened right after her arrival in Texas. Taos boasted a gossipy little magazine, *Laughing Horse*, printed on a hand press by Willard "Spud" Johnson, which published woodcuts by local artists, stories and poems by its writers, and even, once, a hilarious spoof on its social life by D. H. Lawrence.

For the first time since she had begun to live with Stieglitz at the age of thirty, Georgia met people outside the dominion of his strong personality. At parties in Mabel's large living room, which was decked with bright Indian blankets and lit by blazing fires, she met the local characters, many of them painters who did pictures of romanticized cowboy-and-Indian life. She enjoyed the company of Spud Johnson, a slender, silent poet ten years her junior, who sometimes worked as Mabel's secretary. She also met a young man by the name of Ansel Adams who was a former pianist and who was taking photographs for the Sierra Club.

In a milieu in which the usual female attire was colorful lacy Mexican gowns, Georgia, in her black garb, stood out. One night, Daniel Rich, a young middle western tourist who worked at the Art Institute of Chicago, found himself staring at her. Despite her ascetic, aloof appearance, he thought her compelling. "That's Georgia O'Keeffe—

would you like to meet her?" Mabel asked when she noticed his glances. After they were introduced, Rich remarked that he was surprised to find her in Taos. It was her first summer, the New York artist explained. "Isn't the country wonderful?" she immediately asked. Rich, who knew O'Keeffe's work, observed that the same strong voltage of "quiet electricity" that ignited her paintings also seemed to animate the woman herself. He never forgot their casual encounter (although O'Keeffe did), and fourteen years later, the incident fresh in his memory, he gave O'Keeffe her first major museum retrospective at the Institute, where he still worked.

At another gathering Georgia noticed a husky, blond man who resembled her brother-in-law Robert Young so strongly that she felt the urge to tell him so. As it turned out, she and thirty-year-old Vernon Hunter had interests in common. An artist who had been born in New Mexico, just across the border from Texas, he knew and loved the winds and storms of the Texas plains, about which he had wonderful stories. Later, after a stint of teaching art in New York, he would return to New Mexico and, at her request, send her long, vivid descriptions of the Southwest. Although they also talked a great deal about art ("We agreed and disagreed," she said) and she enjoyed his letters, Georgia remained oddly unaware of his paintings.

During the summer Georgia went on many pack trips. One was a six-day trip on horseback to the D. H. Lawrence ranch with Miriam and Charles Hapgood and Charles Collier, the son of the influencial director of the Bureau of Indian Affairs, all in their early twenties. Dorothy Brett was living at Kiowa Ranch, three log and adobe cabins nestled among tall, whispering ponderosa pines, located fifteen miles northwest of Taos and eight thousand feet high. The ranch was a gift of one hundred and sixty acres from Mabel to the Lawrences (now in Europe), for which she had received the manuscript of *Sons and Lovers*. Georgia and Miriam slept in a primitive cabin which was invaded at night, in turn, by chipmunks and a porcupine; one night a coyote howled outside the window, frightening both women.

Georgia and "the Brett," as she was affectionately referred to, liked to ride Brett's horses up into the mountains under the cobalt blue sky. Brett was actually the Honorable Dorothy Eugenie Brett, the daughter of an English lord. She had taken dancing lessons with the royal family in childhood, but after being presented at court, she bobbed her brown hair, donned trousers and colorful clothing, and left her parents' estate on the edge of Windsor Park to study art and befriend members of the Bloomsbury group. In London she had met Frieda and D. H. Lawrence and eventually followed them to New Mexico, where she used to worshipfully type Lawrence's manuscripts. Because she was hard of hearing, she used a brass ear trumpet, nicknamed Toby. Her deafness inhibited her, making her nearly mute at times and occasionally a bit peculiar. Her eyesight, however, was exceedingly sharp, and she was observant to an embarrassing degree, Mabel once remarked. But Georgia enjoyed the Englishwoman's silent companionship and accepted her shy deference to her as the more gifted painter. One night while at Kiowa Ranch Georgia lay on a long carpenter's bench under a giant pine and watched the multitude of big stars in the black sky glitter through its branches. Afterwards she painted her memory of the tree from the unusual angle, and remained fond of the picture, *The Lawrence Tree*, throughout her life.

While Mabel was East in the hospital, Tony Luhan showed Georgia the Taos pueblo where he had been born. On several summer days she returned to set up her umbrella and easel near its brown, cubelike adobe dwellings, which were built one on top of another, and worked until blanket-wrapped Indians silently appeared on roofs to observe the sunset. In July Tony and another Indian took Georgia, the Hopgood youngsters, and Charles Collier on horseback to Bear Lake, a lovely little glacial lake on the other side of Taos mountain. They were so high up, they walked over snowdrifts above the timberline, saw masses of alpine wildflowers, and when ascending Mt. Wheeler, were struck by sheet lightning, which made their hair stand on end and gave a tingling sensation. It rained every afternoon and was so damp and cold at night that Georgia and Miriam had to share a sleeping bag to stay warm. There were also motor trips to the cliff ruins of Mesa Verde in southern Colorado, the great Canyon de Chelly of the Navajos, and even as far as the Grand Canyon in Arizona.

Both essentially silent people, Georgia and Tony shared a stillness and a love of the land—an empathy she was to feel with other Indians. Whereas Mabel's sophisticated friends joked about Tony's silences, his passion for horses, steaks, and brightly colored autos, and how he looked in formal attire, with his long black braids wrapped in purple and white cloths, hanging down his manly chest, Georgia admired his magnificent dignity. Once Tony spent a few days in New York with O'Keeffe and Stieglitz, humming songs near a window all day while

Georgia painted. When one of her sisters rushed in for a quick visit on her way somewhere, Tony began to beat his drum softly with his dark, ring-decorated fingers and to sing for her until, after four songs, she jumped up and left. "You think she hear my songs?" he asked sadly afterwards. Georgia felt, as he did, that it was a mistake to hurry through life without taking the time to listen or to see.

During the summer in Taos Georgia was playful and adventurous, freely following her impulses and doing things that Stieglitz would have scorned. One night at a rodeo, to which she had gone with Beck, Tony, and four of his pueblo pals, she drank a little bootleg whiskey. In a letter to Mabel, who had experimented with peyote, Georgia confessed that, oddly, the next morning, when all emotion was gone, she had enjoyed a state of mental clarity. It was an experience she also committed to canvas in *After the Las Vegas Rodeo*, an abstraction resembling a kaleidoscope stopped dead in its refractive spin.

She realized that New Mexico was affecting her profoundly. She felt more genuinely herself, integrated with parts of her personality that had been submerged since she left Texas. Each day was as clear to her as "the loud ring of a hammer striking something hard," she wrote to Mabel. She also wrote that something in her life was ending and another thing was beginning—she wasn't sure what, but she was taking pleasure in letting it happen. "In the magnificent fierce morning of New Mexico one sprang awake, a new part of the soul woke up suddenly," Lawrence had written about his experience in Taos. Mabel later speculated that Georgia's feverish excitement was due to the special distilled oxygen of Taos, which, she liked to say, made hearts beat faster and eyesight sharper:

> Take an exquisite sensitive mortal like Georgia O'Keeffe
> who is so specialized that she is like no one else . . .
> seems outside people's codes, customs and all folk ways—
> and suddenly lift her from sea level to the higher vibra-
> tions of a place such as Taos and you will have the ex-
> traordinary picture of her making whoopee! . . . Her
> whoopee is of the finer nerves, the more poignant vision,
> awareness few others even dream of and perceptions that
> have to remain esoteric to the majority.

❖

Georgia wanted to explore the wonderful terrain on her own. So the same month that Stieglitz sold her *Shingle and Shell VI* for six thousand dollars to a St. Louis woman, Georgia bought a black Model A Ford in Taos, presumably with the earnings, and began to learn how to drive. Tourists then did not need licenses to motor over the state's deserted dirt roads during the first months of their stays. At first Tony tried to show Georgia how to coordinate ignition, clutch, gearshift, steering wheel, and brake. One day they set out with Georgia at the wheel, the automobile jerking erratically. As they approached Mabel's closed gate, instead of braking she threw up her hands in confusion and cried, "What do I do now?" They averted disaster, but that was her last lesson with Tony, who, considerably shaken, solemnly declared she was unable to learn to drive. Thereafter, she herself despaired at times, but she was determined to master her machine.

Next to take on the task of teaching her the mysteries of driving was Charles Collier, who knew the country well. One day they motored as far as Abiquiu, about sixty miles to the southwest, where he attempted to show her a place called the Ghost Ranch, which he thought she might like. They glimpsed the area from above, driving along a dirt road on a high plain, but they did not find a road down. "This is my world, but how to get into it?" Georgia remembered thinking at the time.

Before her return East, Beck also took her turn teaching Georgia to drive, as Mabel recalled:

> Beck Strand had the dubious joy of teaching her and we all watched her lovely silver hair grow more silvery day by day as Georgia propelled the surprised machine ever faster and faster along precipices—over condemned bridges and through narrow gateways. . . . Finally we recognized that Georgia was destined to become a demon driver! Some unaccountable guardianship protected her when, catching sight of a peerless vista stretching below to the deep abyss, she reached her long arm pointing downwards and exclaiming in ecstasy: "Look at that!" made straightway for it, forgetting, with an unaccustomed experience of mechanics, that the wheels follow the hand unless one does something about it. . . . She would return after a couple of hours of frenzied velocity feeling ten years younger . . . while Beck—whose noble

friendship never wavered—would come in haggard and distraught and sinking into a chair, exclaim: "Well, I don't know what Stieglitz would say!" "Well, he's *flying*, isn't he?" Georgia would answer with zest.

Indeed, Stieglitz *was* flying. Although he was supposed to forgo any excitement because of his weak heart, he had recklessly hired a small plane to fly him around Lake George. His moods ranged from anxious anticipation of Georgia's return to depressed resignation at her absence and acute panic that she would not readjust to life in the East. He knew that the Southwest had always been her spiritual home and he remembered her reluctance back in 1918 to leave Texas to come to him. He thought of her, with her pantheistic passion for nature, as essentially "untamed," and he feared her infatuation with New Mexico might be stronger than her loyalty to him.

He spent much of the summer writing to her, as well as to Beck, Brett, John Marin (whom Mabel had invited out at Georgia's suggestion), and others, who, in response, tried to calm his worries about Georgia's health, safety, state of mind, and the type of people she was befriending. But when Miriam Hapgood, a young painter, visited Georgia's studio, she would often find her making linen shirts with beautiful even stitches for her husband which, she told Miriam, he liked very much. By July, when the orange poppies were starting to fade and the blue larkspur were beginning to bloom in Taos, his worried letters and telegrams so troubled Georgia that she reluctantly made plans to return East early. (There is a story that Stieglitz, in an act of dramatic, symbolic suicide, destroyed many of his old photographic plates and copies of *Camera Work*, which were stored in the farmhouse.) When reassured of her willingness to return, however, he magnanimously wired her not to do so until she was ready.

Georgia, meanwhile, found herself awkwardly entangled in another marriage. Since Tony was illiterate, she was asked to read Mabel's letters to him and to write his replies, which he would dictate as he sat wrapped in his blanket, his dark face mysterious and mournful. While she was away, Mabel had a fit of jealousy over Tony, whom she had heard had once again gone back to the pueblo to stay with his longtime common-law Indian wife. Mabel was also suspicious of Tony's relationship with Georgia, whose erotic nature she had written about.

Her feelings were fueled by her envy of Georgia's greater emotional balance and capacity for pleasure in contast to her own destructiveness.

Mabel wrote Tony what Georgia thought were needlessly damaging letters, which included threats of divorce. It was clear to everyone in Taos that Tony was deeply worried about Mabel and years later Georgia recalled the way he "lay like a log across her bed for days, missing her." Georgia wrote Mabel long heartfelt letters, begging her to understand Tony. "For God's sake—don't try to squeeze all the life out of him—I know from experience that it isn't a pleasant sensation"—she cautioned. Loving a person, she reasoned, meant allowing him to be himself. She had no right to keep Stieglitz from the men and women who clustered around him, she pointed out. "I think I would never have minded Stieglitz being anything he happened to be if he hadn't kept me so persistently off *my* track," she wrote.

In early August Georgia returned from a camping trip to find that Mabel had reappeared, along with Georgia's sister, Ida, as her private nurse. For several reasons, Georgia felt uneasy. Mabel was irritated that some of the trips had been led by young Collier instead of by Tony, who charged five dollars a day for each guide and each horse, which was too expensive for some guests. There were also Mabel's smoldering suspicious about Georgia and Tony. Neith Boyce observed that when Mabel returned Georgia became difficult because "she is an awful egotist and *has* to be the most important person." Tensions might have arisen between the two guests because they had fundamentally opposite reactions to the landscape. Neith was one of those who felt oppressed by the land, which she called "queer" and unhealthly, rampant with malaria, and "too stimulating nervously but not tonic."

After Georgia read her pile of letters and telegrams from Stieglitz she impulsively decided to go home. After shipping her paintings, packing a coral-colored Indian blanket as well as a silver Indian bracelet, and writing a check to cover the rent for the use of the splendid studio and some of her other expenses, she left without saying goodbye. First she had a reluctant Charles Collier drive her to see the Grand Canyon and then she left the West for Albany, N.Y., and arrived at Lake George on August 25th.

❖

By early September, Georgia and Alfred were alone together at the lake. She had returned radiant from her months in Taos, and soon her happiness had another source—her husband. Stieglitz, at sixty-five, was now in good health, tender toward her, and stretching in new directions that surprised and interested her. Besides flying, he had bought a Victrola and filled the farmhouse with the music of Beethoven, Brahms, and Bach on 78 rpm discs. Georgia felt utterly content after several years of emotional turbulence. Perhaps her brief stint playing marriage counselor for Mabel and Tony had given her insight into how two people as different as she and Stieglitz might better coexist. It seemed, as they drove to the Maine seashore for a few days and got to know each other's new selves, that their separation had renewed their relationship. Almost forty-two, Georgia felt reconciled to past disappointments in her life, and even thought that many of them had been alchemized into good luck. Her discomfort during summers on the hill, for instance, had motivated her to rediscover New Mexico. She felt that she had been very fortunate indeed.

To add to her happiness, the October weather was lovely, and, after much practice, she passed her New York State driver's test. It was also her special time for painting. Margaret Prosser came in to cook the noon meal, so Georgia had uninterrupted hours in which to paint. She was, in fact, so satisfied to be at the lake that she turned to familiar Lake George sights—such as autumn leaves and the farmhouse itself—for inspiration. She also worked on paintings she had begun in Taos, and tentatively began some new ones, feeling that she was testing new directions. She painted a passionate red-and-orange picture, probably a memory of the Southwest, over an unusually long three-day period. And, after the immense excitement of getting her feeling down, she was so drained that she collapsed in bed.

Unfortunately, newspapers from the city were bringing ominous tidings to this Eden. During the summer, the U.S. Treasury Department had issued smaller paper money, and, as if the change had been symbolic, on October 29 the stock market began to slump. By the end of 1929 it had taken a fifteen-billion-dollar drop. It's unclear whether O'Keeffe had invested her handsome earnings of the past three years in securities or deposited them in a bank. Friends assumed that her customary canniness extended to her money, since she was known to seek out the advice of her financially astute brothers-in-law.

But whether or not her own savings were safe, the financial panic must have created insecurity about future sales and threatened the couple's euphoria.

In early November the sky darkened, heavy clouds drizzled, and the mountains turned their late-autumn purplish-gray shade. Georgia mended the holes in Stieglitz's pockets and made other preparations for the return to her life in the Shelton Hotel. She hadn't been in New York since the previous April, and when they arrived the tempo of Manhattan seemed quite mad to her. She was surprised by the number of new skyscrapers that had sprouted in the sky and by the profusion of gadgets and luxuries in shop windows. Although she had vowed not to exhibit that winter, Stieglitz insisted that she have her annual show as usual after he saw the New Mexico paintings she had shipped to New York. She rushed about viewing her five paintings in the group show at the Museum of Modern Art, arranging for the new ones to be framed, and shopping. She also lunched with such friends as Helen "Reds" Dove, the wife of Arthur Dove and a promising yet timid painter whose work Georgia had arranged to be shown for the first time in New York a few years earlier, and Dorothy Brett, who was visiting New York again.

That winter large segments of the business community were going bankrupt, and Brett noticed and remarked on the frightened mood of New Yorkers. But she, as well as others, found Stieglitz and O'Keeffe relatively relaxed and untroubled, as if they were operating on a separate wavelength. They were supportive and sympathetic when in early March 1930 Brett's beloved D. H. Lawrence died in Europe.

The previous spring the Intimate Gallery had closed after four seasons because the Anderson Galleries building was sold. With the help of a loyal disciple, sometime artist Emil Zoler, and a professional packer, Stieglitz sent paintings and photographs into storage. But his friends knew that he must continue to have a gallery. Before long space was rented on the seventeenth floor of a modern tower at 509 Madison Avenue at Fifty-third Street, only a few blocks from the Shelton. In December 1929 was born An American Place, the shell of an office space with the room number 1710. As independent and feisty as ever, Stieglitz, determined to resist trends in commercial art galleries and the new Museum of Modern Art, had the following printed on a card to explain what the new gallery was *not* about:

No formal press views.
No cocktail parties.
No special invitations.
No advertising.
No institution.
No isms.
No theories.
No games being played.
Nothing asked of anyone who comes.
No anything on the walls except what *you see there.*
The doors of An American Place are ever open to all.

Past the heavy glass door of what came to be called "the Place" were one squarish exhibition room leading into another through a doorless opening, a little office, a storeroom, and a workroom. Once more Georgia took charge of the gallery's decoration. The space, which tenants were expected to furnish with carpets and wall coverings, remained bare. White shades on large west windows were rolled up from window sashes to expose mostly sky, and the rooms were flooded with light. Painted pure white and illuminated by the harsh urban sunlight, the walls looked "piercingly white" to Henry McBride. "When you enter An American Place, the first thing you feel is the quality of light. . . ." observed Dorothy Norman, a young woman who had become a frequent visitor. "There pervades the space a clear subtly fluid ever varying glow of light. Light and room are as one." Over the years some of the walls, the cement floor, exposed pipes, and radiators were painted a luminous light gray that Georgia blended by mixing many colors. Visitors marveled at the way photographs or paintings hung against her special gray seemed to float in space.

O'Keeffe's exhibition opened for five weeks in early February 1930. Two thirds of the new paintings had been inspired by New Mexico—and included such subjects as the picturesque Taos pueblo, a carved wooden Mexican virgin, and the eighteenth-century mission church at Ranchos de Taos. Practically every artist who visited Taos felt compelled to paint the massive mud-colored adobe church, which, with its thick monumental buttresses, seemed to rise out of the very earth itself. Although she had depicted many of the same subjects as the mediocre western artists, her originality saved her from banality. For instance, she had painted only a fragment of the mission wall silhouetted against the hard blue southwestern sky.

In Taos Georgia had been fascinated by the heavy, primitive, pegged crosses that mysteriously appeared and disappeared on lonely treeless knolls. Some locals speculated that the crosses marked where a Catholic had died or where pallbearers had prayed on the way to a cemetery, but others whispered that they were the crosses of the Penitentes—members of a secret religious society that had originated in medieval Spain and that practiced flagellation and even mock crucifixion. McBride joked that Georgia's three paintings of dramatic black crosses indicated she "got religion" in Taos, but what she really got there was an intuitive sense of the native people's fatalistic spirit, which stretched across the countryside "like a thin dark veil," she said. "Anyone who doesn't feel the crosses simply doesn't get that country," she told McBride. Georgia, who rarely painted anything well that she didn't deeply understand, had felt a kinship with Catholicism since those times in childhood when she was taken to Mass by her O'Keeffe relatives.

Her new subject matter succeeded in startling New York critics and in making them take notice again. In the Sunday art section of the *New York Times*, Edward Alden Jewell acclaimed the new O'Keeffes in a prominent two-column article. It was the most exciting exhibition that he had ever seen, the reviewer wrote, adding that the desert paintings looked particularly beautiful in the all-white gallery. As usual, what Stieglitz termed "a mob" streamed in, but he feared there would be few sales because of the daring nature of her new work. Admirers noted that O'Keeffe had found new inspiration but had not been overwhelmed by the scale of the great southwestern spaces like so many other painters. Yet some reviewers panned what they called her touristy themes, garish colors, and the "hysteria" of the giant crosses. It is unlikely that Georgia read many of the reviews, or, if she did, they must have seemed irrelevant in the face of her obvious, immense enjoyment of the land—and the knowledge that she would continue to paint it regardless of any negative reactions.

After feeling in tune with Stieglitz all winter, in April Georgia spent a week by herself in a Maine cabin overlooking the sea. She painted all day, every day, then walked for hours along the deserted, windy, freezing beach, and in the evening lay on the cabin floor, pensively staring into the fire. She was torn as to whether or not to leave her husband and go to Taos again for the summer. Finally, when she returned to the city, her quiet determination to go back overcame

Stieglitz's unhappiness at the idea. Before her departure, she went to Lake George to watch the spring arrive, to make the farmhouse ready for Stieglitz, and to paint six sensual oils of jack-in-the-pulpits. As she watched the woods becoming tinged with pale green, she conceded in letters that it was a lovely New England May, but, she also comprehended, Lake George was no longer her world.

9 ❖ Bones

Although the second summer Stieglitz understood better that Georgia had gone to Taos for the sake of "Art," his supreme deity, he again felt melancholy. His unhappiness now also had other roots, however. The Depression was deepening and thousands of factories stood idle, shop windows were boarded up, shanty towns had sprung up in New York's Central Park, and almost ten million Americans were without jobs. People were feeling increasingly that they were at the mercy of a sputtering industrial machine, and Stieglitz's cult of the individual sensitivity seemed irrelevant in a period of growing reliance on collective solutions.

The new mood affected the art world. Artists like Thomas Hart Benton began to paint nostalgic, regional, rural subjects, and other painters of the rapidly burgeoning radical Left turned to themes of social realism and political protest. Talk of the government subsidizing artists (the planning stage for what became Works Progress Administration grants) threatened to overshadow the kind of exclusive patronage Stieglitz prided himself on extending to a select number of artists. Criticizing the idea of involvement of government in art, Stieglitz argued that artists of an undoubtedly inferior caliber would be subsidized.

Stieglitz, who continued to place the highest value on an artist's personal perceptions, was criticized in turn as an old-fashioned individualist. In this atmosphere, Georgia's giant flowers came under fire for their social irrelevance, the interior mood they evoked, and their exaggerated individuality. Back in March 1930, before her return to Taos, Georgia had volunteered to carry the banner for Stieglitz's little band of faithfuls in a debate with Michael Gold, editor of the leftist magazine *New Masses*, perhaps because she had never thought the paintings of an ugly, harsh, urban America reflected the reality of the country. Georgia arrived in the private dining room of the Hotel Brevoort at the prearranged time, looking as serene as usual, according to the *New York World* reporter, who covered the event in great detail. "Her face, unadorned by cosmetics, with its flash of intelligent, arched eyebrows, her severely simple silk dress, her tapered, sensitive, ivory-colored hands, merged quietly into a whole, utterly simple, utterly poised." O'Keeffe turned to the rumpled, pale young radical, who looked profoundly uncomfortable. "You look more fussed than I feel, and I had expected you to be so fearless," she remarked with a little smile. "Shall we begin?"

Gold nervously chewed his cigar, gulped some tea, tore a sandwich apart, and started to talk in a choked voice. The biggest struggle of the age was that of the working class, he ventured, and "If art is alive, it is the only possible subject." Georgia calmly took a sip of tea. "When you name the oppressed, do you include women?" she asked. Only working-class women, Gold replied, intensely, and he added, "I'm afraid it doesn't seem very important to me if the pampered bourgeoise in her rose-colored boudoir gets equal rights or not." O'Keeffe responded that oppressed women of all classes were important because, in her case, she had been forced to look to male artists for models because social oppression had made for a paucity of female painters in history. "Before I put a brush to canvas, I question, 'Is this mine? . . . Is it influenced by some idea which I have acquired from some man?' . . . I am trying with all my skill to do a painting that is all of women, as well as all of me."

As the discussion continued, however, she denied that it was necessary to paint realistic scenes of women's struggles ("glorified cartoons," in her words), explaining that form, color, and pattern were more important than subject matter. Beauty enriches everyone's existence, she pointed out. Gold attacked her concern with abstract issues of technique, terming them "little tinkerings," the "psychological mewings of a bunch of ingrown decadents . . . prettified, artified evasions that are fit only to decorate the drawing rooms and boudoirs which hold the drunk parties and kept women of the rich." Then the young man suddenly added, while nervously extracting a cigarette from a case, and breaking the cigarette in the process, "Gosh, I hate to argue with a woman—you have to be polite." Georgia replied that she didn't think he had to be any more polite to her than to a man, and he flushed and offered an apology.

"You don't like flowers, do you, Mr. Gold?" Georgia continued. When he protested that he did, she said, "Well, I don't really see how you can approve them since you want all things to be useful. . . . You may be seeking the freedom of humanity, but you want to make art a tool—and the worst of it is that you must cheapen art to appeal to any mass, and your mass artists will inevitably become bad artists." Only a few appreciated a Proust, a Joyce, or a Marin in any age, she added. In rebuttal, Gold mentioned the Diego Rivera murals in Mexico, which, he said, were examples of good art that also spoke to the people. They debated some more, ignoring the little cakes on the table. "You know, I think you're a nice boy all mixed up by a lot of prejudices, defenses and hatreds," Georgia said in conclusion. "We haven't talked half enough about this. I think I'll take you to see my show, and then bring you home to Stieglitz and dinner!"

Around this period, fewer people were gravitating to Stieglitz, and some of his disciples, disillusioned with him because he attacked government subsidies of artists but lived on unearned income himself, drifted to other causes. Waldo Frank allied himself with movements on the Left, and, after the marriage of the Strands broke up in 1932, Paul Strand went to Mexico, started to take photographs of the poor, and never exhibited under Stieglitz's auspices again. (But Beck's paintings on glass of precious Victorian-style bouquets were shown from time to time at the gallery.)

Feeling abandoned by the times, Stieglitz began to spend more hours during the summer months scribbling moody letters in his Lake George den, emerging only to talk bitterly to his few unquestioning disciples (like the affected Emil Zoler, whom Georgia disliked) about the dismal fate of the contemporary artist. So pervasive was the gloom in his small circle that Georgia sarcastically dubbed Stieglitz and his remaining cronies "the Happiness Boys."

Back in New Mexico for a second summer, Georgia planned to give Mabel a wide berth and to maintain an independent existence even though she slept in the studio at Mabel's. She breakfasted at the Don Fernando Hotel in the village, ate a sandwich for lunch, and, when she was through painting for the day, was on her own for dinner. She worked hard and shunned company—even the Strands and Marins, who were also in Taos for the summer. Mabel had made it clear that she didn't want Georgia to go riding or camping with Tony. Explaining her philosophy of solitude to Brett, whom she was urging to go ahead with a controversial memoir about Lawrence, Georgia stated that one should use one's energy for work—the core of life— and ignore "the human problem." She said in another letter that the way to survive in Taos was to reduce its human beings to the size of pinpoints, the way the wide-open spaces dwarfed its "poisonous" population. A few years later, however, when she was at a safe geographical distance from "Mabeltown," she loved to make fun of its feuds.

She had become fascinated by the dry, white animal skeletons scattered over the desert, picking them up and saving them in the same spirit she had collected seashells on the beach. She insisted that the bones, baked and bleached by the burning sun, were only beautiful forms to her. "I don't think of them as *bones*," she explained, turning one delicately the way another woman might a precious gem. One day she looked at the bones in a different way—as equivalents of the desert—and knew that she would paint them. "I have wanted to paint the desert and I haven't known how," she wrote for her 1939 exhibition catalog. "The bones seem to cut sharply to the center of something that is keenly alive on the desert even tho' it is vast and empty and untouchable—and knows no kindness with all its beauty." Another time she said she liked the idea of painting bones because it was unlikely this imagery would be imitated, as her flowers had been.

There were few flowers to paint in the dry summer of 1930, and by the end of August she had collected a big pile of bones. Deciding on an impulse that she would like to take something back so she could keep working on desert subjects, she packed the bones in a wooden barrel, stuffed the colorful locally-made fabric flowers into the crevices, and shipped the barrel to Lake George. Confronted with a freight bill of sixteen dollars, Stieglitz loudly protested that it was a lot of money to pay for some old bones when times were hard. Toward the end of the year, however, he was photographing Georgia's brown fingers exploring the eye socket and teeth of a blanched horse's skull—and

Georgia was placing a white thigh bone, like an article of jewelry, on a piece of black cloth and carefully painting the composition.

Georgia had returned to Lake George and to Stieglitz in the early part of September. They found it difficult to recapture the warmth and elation they had shared the previous autumn. She disliked listening to his complaints about the decline of culture, preferring to dwell on the pleasures possible in the present. "O'Keeffe never has questioned the condition of delight—it is for her daily meal—or a walk in the world, alone," explained Marsden Hartley in her exhibition catalog a few years later. After her second summer in the desert, the hill's lushness struck her as "strange," claustrophobic, muggy, and oppressively green.

Another difference was emerging between them. Whereas Stieglitz's coterie was contracting, O'Keeffe's horizons were expanding in several directions. In December 1930, for example, she accepted an invitation to a party from Carl Van Vechten, a plump white-haired writer and photographer with a deep interest in the so-called Negro renaissance of the twenties, but declined on behalf of Stieglitz. Van Vechten, with his wife, a pretty Russian actress, lived in an apartment on West Fifty-fifth Street and frequently entertained the leading writers and artists from both the white world of midtown and the black world of Harlem.

And, despite criticism from certain leftist quarters, O'Keeffe's artistic success was continuing. Some of her New Mexico paintings appealed to the big audience newly interested in "the American scene." These and her other pictures were also being shown in numerous group exhibitions, and were being sold to museums at nearly the same high price levels that Stieglitz had established for them in the heady twenties. In 1930 the Cleveland Museum paid four thousand dollars for a painting done in Taos, a big white flower with what Georgia called a "Golden Heart." In 1931 the brand-new Whitney Museum of American Art in New York bought a tiny painting done around 1922, *Skunk Cabbage,* from the Reinhardt Galleries, and included it in the museum's inaugural exhibition. The next year the Whitney showed *Single Lily with Red* of 1928 in its first biennial exhibition and purchased two paintings—one of a white fabric flower and another of a red New Mexican hill, both painted in 1931. They bought them both from An American Place (paying O'Keeffe directly). It was a strong vote of confidence in the artist and her new themes.

Stieglitz still stubbornly insisted that the true artist did not need to travel. "Why should I go to Taos?" he once asked. "I have all the world around me on the hill." Hearing his niece Flora Straus glowingly describe the Grand Canyon to him, he gestured grandly at the clouds and loftily remarked that *he* had the sky. If he were ever to travel, the last place he would go to would be Taos. "If I wanted to commit suicide in a polite way, I would go to O'Keeffe in the high clear air of New Mexico," he explained in the forties. "My heart wouldn't stand it." Asked in old age if her husband had ever been in New Mexico, Georgia laughed out loud. "What! Stieglitz come out here where he would be fifty miles from a doctor, and not a very good doctor at that?"

Stieglitz's anxieties weren't only for himself. Although he was the one who hated automobiles and never learned to drive, he constantly fretted about Georgia's safety on the road. One of his relatives overheard him say that Georgia's auto had given her an amazing new sense of power and independence, and it was more likely this outcome that actually worried him. In the early twenties, during a self-imposed exile from the photography world, he liked to say, "There has been one who has stood by me through it all—a girl from Texas," according to photographer Edward Weston. And now he feared that the loyal girl might abandon him the way others had.

He also, as he himself sank deeper into hypochondria, continually fretted out loud about Georgia's health. He had long been terrified of germs, and now a linen handkerchief always fluttered around his mouth and nose. In winter he took to warding off viruses by wearing under his black cape a herringbone overcoat, a salt-and-pepper suit, a grayish sweater over a white shirt and black tie, and underneath everything, woolen underwear—all of which, including his flat porkpie hat, he wore inside on chilly days. His concern for Georgia was, in part, wishful thinking. "Alfred once admitted that he was happiest when I was ill in bed because he knew where I was and what I was doing," Georgia later said.

Throughout his adult life Stieglitz would become outraged when people treated his beliefs as less than gospel. When Georgia, in effect, rejected his image of her, refusing to give in to his articulate arguments that she didn't need to travel and that it was risky to do so, he grew tremendously angry and viewed her increasing autonomy as disloyalty. Defied, he was capable of being dangerous and destructive. Once, in the early thirties, he began to rage about Georgia in vulgar language in front of one of his disciples. The friend was shocked, having never heard Stieglitz speak that way about a woman before. When he started to protest, Stieglitz, still ranting, suddenly crouched before him for greater emphasis, his fist clenched and his face close to his, so that the man could see clearly the black eyes glowing and the tufts of white bristles shooting out of Stieglitz's ears and nostrils. Stieglitz was an aging, possessive husband, hurt and frightened because he was unable to fulfill the need that New Mexico met for his wife. His creativity had once been ignited by her, and, perhaps, he associated it with her and feared that his spirit would be sapped by her absence. In addition, he missed her when she was gone.

The couple's struggle was evident in photographs he continued to shoot of Georgia at the lake. Formerly he had photographed her amidst her paintings and drawings, but now he snapped her more often in the company of glinting metallic objects. From 1929 on, the photographs show Georgia with her polished black-and-chrome automobile, wearing shiny silver Indian jewelry, her hand on the steering wheel and a faraway look in her eyes. He also photographed her wrapped in a coarsely woven Navajo blanket, standing in front of the weathered barn door, and in these pictures the muscles under her brown sun-toughened, tensile skin look as hard as the old boards themselves. Yet perhaps the change in their relationship cannot be summed up so neatly, for in 1932 he shot a series of sensuous photographs of her buttocks in a heart-shaped composition—white skin around a shadowy center—strikingly reminiscent of her own *Drawing Number Twelve* of 1917, a bulbous shape on a slim stem that she later described as "maybe a kiss." Nevertheless, by the summer of 1932 Stieglitz's photographs of Georgia often caught her with an agonized glare in her eyes or a steely scowl on her face. The model and the photographer, seemingly staring one another down, were heading for a confrontation.

❖

Meanwhile, Stieglitz's interest in Dorothy Norman, a lovely, earnest young woman with smooth dark hair, was growing. They had first met in 1926 when Dorothy, who had studied art in Philadelphia before her marriage, visited Stieglitz's gallery. She was twenty-one years old at the time and pregnant. Her marriage to a handsome, temperamental Sears, Roebuck heir was difficult, and she was flattered that the great Stieglitz took the time to talk with her. Stieglitz, who once claimed that he had always been in love with one woman or another, including his own young nieces and grandnieces, continued to enjoy female company. With his own daughter in a mental institution and his second wife often away these days, he perhaps saw Dorothy as a daughter figure and delighted in her loyalty, sympathy, and adoration. In addition, he trusted her to revere the spirit of An American Place.

After Dorothy's second child was born in 1930, their friendship intensified. They met daily at the gallery except in the summer, when she left her Park Avenue apartment with her husband and children for a vacation home in Cape Cod and he went to Lake George. Stieglitz began to photograph her, working primarily at the gallery but sometimes at the Shelton when Georgia was away. The prints of Dorothy are eerily reminiscent of some of the early photographs of Georgia—both women were brunettes with grave eyes and heavy brows, distinctive profiles, and full sensuous mouths. The younger woman even posed one time in a black hat and black dress with white lapels. Dorothy's expression, however, lacked the tautness of the young O'Keeffe's as well as the direct eroticism and the flicker of amusement that had played about her lips. And whereas the earlier photographs were charged with the promise of dynamic creativity, the ambience of the Dorothy portraits, conveyed by her soft and somber gaze, was often sad.

Being photographed by Stieglitz affected Dorothy in the same way it had Georgia. She was galvanized into trying to live up to his stunning photographic image of her. "The photographs were a revelation to me. I'd be sitting there or lying there, and he'd say, 'Don't move,' and I'd hold my breath while he got his camera," Dorothy recalled. "I was completely myself with Stieglitz. There was nothing to change, no place I wanted to go, nothing I wanted to hide. My masks were elsewhere."

Dorothy was a helpmate to Stieglitz in a way that Georgia had never been, perhaps more like a traditional wife. She worked hard to free Stieglitz from such secretarial and bookkeeping chores as paying telephone bills, printing catalogs, and balancing checkbooks. More important in the period of Depression, when the market for art was nearly nonexistent and the rent fund was often inadequate, were her fund-raising skills. Anticipating the expiration of the three-year lease in 1932, Dorothy sent out letters and contacted newspapers, pleading for funds to save An American Place. By May 1932 almost a hundred people had contributed small sums and half the required amount had been raised. Soon another three-year lease was signed as the rent of fifty-five hundred dollars was guaranteed for one year. Stieglitz, who constantly agonized about the fate of the gallery, experienced its survival as an annual miracle. Deeply grateful to Dorothy for saving An American Place, he had the lease put in her name and in 1933 she was officially appointed the gallery's business manager.

Stieglitz's relationship with Dorothy was increasingly upsetting to O'Keeffe. She resented the younger woman, considering her a non-artist intruder into the circle, whereas Dorothy felt tongue-tied in O'Keeffe's hostile presence. Georgia would become enraged when Stieglitz praised Dorothy as a paragon of virtues, according to a member of the Stieglitz family. During the winter 1930–31, after two summers in Taos, O'Keeffe was irritable and unable to paint. Once again she struggled for the courage to leave for her third summer in the Southwest, but now she seemed to fear that she was losing Stieglitz emotionally. Finally she decided to go for half the season—May and June—and to return to the lake in July. In the spring, around the time she finally began to paint some lilies Stieglitz had given her, she wrote Brett, "My feeling about life is a curious kind of triumphant feeling about—seeing it bleak—knowing it is so and walking into it fearlessly because one has no choice—enjoying one's consciousness."

The previous summers in New Mexico she had gone to paint from time to time in the bald, sandy hills near Alcalde, a village in a valley about forty miles south of Taos. In 1931 she went there and rented a cottage on the H and M Ranch, which was owned by Marie Garland, a poet and painter around sixty years old and originally from New England. Georgia spent much of her time walking for miles in the arid cliffs, trying to reach the dark mesas behind them. She also spent many hours painting in her Model A Ford. She left the passenger seat back at the cottage, unbolted and swiveled the driver's seat, and propped her canvas on the back seat. Because of the auto's high windows, she had plenty of light and because of the high roof she could squeeze in a large (30" × 40") canvas. At the cottage, when she was unable to sleep in the early morning hours (perhaps because of an insistent feeling that she should be at Stieglitz's side), she used to climb up on the flat roof to watch the dawn lighten the large expanse of sky.

Stieglitz, during this time, was writing numerous letters to Dorothy, who, indeed, was possessing his imagination. He even made a rare detour outside of his usual orbit to spend a few days with her in Woods Hole, where he photographed her posing in the nude in a flower-filled meadow. As their friendship deepened, it seemed as if they might forge a creative partnership, as Stieglitz had done with O'Keeffe. Stieglitz showed Dorothy how to take pictures, and she made some fine, sensitive prints of both Stieglitz and his American Place. In 1932 he arranged for the private publication of Dorothy's poems on the subjects of love, religion, and Jewishness. Dorothy, who used to worshipfully write down much of Stieglitz's oratory, started to help edit a tribute to him, which was eventually published by Doubleday, Doran & Co. in 1934 as *America and Alfred Stieglitz: A Collective Portrait*.

In mid-July 1931 Georgia showed up on the hill as she had promised. Sometime later she moved a horse's skull for safekeeping from the kitchen table to a table in the dining room where a houseguest had draped some blue pajamas. The next morning when she was toying with her pretty fabric flowers, she was called to the door. She walked downstairs with a mock pink rose still in her hand, but then thought it would look foolish. Passing through the dining room, she glanced at the horse's head. "Almost without thinking about what I was doing, I put the flower in the horse's eye and went to the door," she recalled. "On my return, I was so struck by the wonderful effect of the rose in the horse's eye that I knew that here was a painting that had to be done."

In early October Stieglitz had returned to New York, where he continued to photograph Dorothy, again in the nude, while O'Keeffe remained on the hill with the cook, steadily painting skulls until November. This was apparently a tense time for Georgia in her marriage of eight years. Once she drove to Manhattan to deliver some paintings and irritated or embarrassed Stieglitz in some way by walking into the gallery or hotel unannounced. She returned to the lake until it was time to get her thirty-three new pictures framed for her show, which was scheduled to open two days before Christmas.

The critics were again astounded, some of them describing the skull-and-flower paintings as occult and others depicting them as surrealistic. "What will she find to top this year's splendid salutation of the dead I cannot imagine," observed a reviewer in the January 2, 1932, issue of *Art News*, "but it's a wide world and Miss O'Keeffe is not one to loiter along the way." Those who knew her well worried that the way the artificial roses, the kind that decorated New Mexican cemeteries, were gaily perched in the gaping brittle holes of what had once been ears, eyes, and nostrils indicated a morbid death fantasy or a note of bitter black humor. Henry McBride dubbed her exhibit "Mourning Becomes Georgia," and wrote that the artist dwelled on death "with the perversity of a Hamlet at the grave of Ophelia." He teased his friend, saying that her "cure for the depression is to wallow in depression." Indeed, her love of life did seem to be faltering, even if she did insist that she delighted only in the *look* of the desiccated bones with the fake flowers and that there was no idea behind them other than that of the desert. She pointed out that the cloth blossoms did not get damaged or wilt—they were "very amusing and stayed put"—whereas real flowers breathed and changed while she worked on them.

After her exhibition was dismantled in February, the gallery was hung with more than a hundred Stieglitz photographs, which included shots of a barren depression-era Manhattan, photos taken of O'Keeffe over the past decade, and the new photographs of Dorothy Norman. The show made it clear that the father of modern photography had found a face and pair of hands as important to him as Georgia's.

Furthermore, the gentle, dewy beauty of Dorothy, who was still in her twenties, contrasted cruelly with the stark, severe features of O'Keeffe, now forty-four. "Stern ancestral face full of irregularities, all definite," wrote artist Peggy Bacon, whose work Stieglitz had exhibited in 1928, about O'Keeffe at the time. "Pale with polished black hair brushed uncompromisingly back from a climbing forehead. Sharp cheek-bones, hoisted eyebrows and a long wavy nose. Structure of face bony and melancholy, enlivened by keen fan-shaped eyes and a crooked smile, generous and friendly. Delicate frame in deep black, betimes with a tragic-looking cape. Personality stripped and whittled. Conspicuous as a nun. Distinguished and restricted as Electra."

People gossiped that Stieglitz and the young Mrs. Norman were having a love affair, and, indeed, their feelings for one another were strong. When asked many years later if her relationship with Stieglitz was romantic, intellectual, or spiritual, Dorothy responded, "It was all of those."

❖

With the dismantling of the 1932 show, Georgia began to work again, but slowly and with difficulty. More than ever, personal considerations conflicted with her artistic drive, and once more she agonized about going to New Mexico in the summer. Suddenly she surprised everyone by announcing that she had decided to remain in the East during the summer months.

When the time came, she departed for Lake George to open the farmhouse and to repair the shanty. That year Stieglitz's high-spirited blond niece Georgia Engelhard, by then twenty-seven and an accomplished mountain climber and horseback rider, was also staying at the lake. O'Keeffe was diverted by the young woman's gaiety and enthusiasm, and the two joked and laughed a great deal—often at the expense of the many family members who showed up that year when their incomes were in peril. They became a constant, mischiefmaking, adventurous twosome. They hiked energetically throughout the countryside, relished the same foods, and even painted together. Georgia Engelhard was O'Keeffe's protégé for a short time, and was greatly influenced by the older woman's painting style. In fact, many years later O'Keeffe herself was unable to identify a painting as her own or the younger woman's. When Stieglitz was back in New York, they liked to lie on the farmhouse floor listening to one of O'Keeffe's favorite songs on the Victorla—Marlene Dietrich's husky rendition of "Johnny."

They also liked to drive O'Keeffe's Ford a hundred and fifty miles to the north, to Montreal, where they bought "booze," which was still illegal in the United States under Prohibition. Once they were caught and fined by border police. Since experimenting with whiskey in New Mexico, O'Keeffe liked a sip now and then even though Stieglitz disapproved. Their appetite for adventure whetted, the two women decided to motor in French Canada to the Gaspé Peninsula to look for new places to paint.

Despite Stieglitz's anxiety, they packed their paints and headed north. A photograph by Stieglitz of O'Keeffe just before she left shows her lean, tanned, grinning, a polka-dot scarf covering her hair and a black cardigan flung over her white peasant-style blouse. The women drove through the lush green farmland along the St. Lawrence River, where the soil was rich and black and the potato fields were in white blossom. They paused to paint white barns and stables and to sleep in ugly Victorian farmhouses that had bear skins nailed to their outside walls for drying. They giggled when in one house they found a wood-chuck chained next to the kitchen breadboard, presumably to scavenge for scraps. They continued on to the rocky Gaspé coast, where golden cliffs rose out of the sea, wild forests plunged into the surf, and tur-bulent tides swirled in the bays.

It was O'Keeffe's first trip outside her own country, and she was so thrilled by the beauty of the rugged coast that at the time she claimed it was as inspirational for painting as New Mexico. One night they camped on a cliff above a beach. There was a full moon, and the splendor, more than she was able to endure, made her sleepless. In the middle of the night she climbed down to the beach, where millions of birds wheeled and dived at her, making her suddenly ter-rified that she would be eaten alive. During the trip she painted green mountains, crashing waves, and the bleak but touchingly decorated mariners' crosses—memorials to young men drowned at sea.

But lodgings were meager and uncomfortable, and the climate was much more unpleasant than in the Southwest. O'Keeffe longed for the hot desert sun and complained about the Canadian cold. Finally the two women became so chilled, hungry, and tired that they found it difficult to paint, and they headed home earlier than planned. If O'Keeffe had felt compelled to continue painting the northern sea, with its harsh beauty, she undoubtedly would have found a way. But she never returned, and rarely painted the ocean afterwards.

❖

In the early part of the thirties women artists who had worked quietly for years began to exhibit more often in New York, and others received recognition in America for the first time. Between 1930 and 1932, five women artists were elected to the prestigious National Institute of Arts and Letters. Before this time the Institute had had only one female artist member, Anna Hyatt Huntington. Then Hun-tington and seventy-eight-year-old Cecilia Beaux, a portrait painter, were appointed to the even more exclusive American Academy of Arts and Letters in 1932 and 1933, respectively, and New York newspapers hailed Beaux as the greatest woman painter in America. Henry McBride and other critics championed Florine Stettheimer. In the course of the decade many other women artists had the chance to gain prominence by creating art in public spaces under various New Deal art-funding programs. The egalitarianism of the government—at one point half the participating artists were female—gave young female painters like Alice Neel and Lee Krasner the opportunity to establish themselves as artists.

Two of Georgia's sisters were also taking advantage of the expanding opportunities. Catherine, a nurse who had never had any training as an artist, became inspired to paint by her eldest sister's success. When, in late 1932, she sent her paintings from Wisconsin to the Delphic Studios in New York for a show, people were shocked. Her work, consisting primarily of close-ups of morning glories and other flowers, appeared to be almost replicas of Georgia's giant blossoms. Her show opened in early 1933 and was headlined in the *New York Times*: "Another O'Keeffe Emerges." Whatever motives lay behind Catherine's actions, Georgia was enraged and broke off all communication with her until she abandoned painting four years later.

Ida had continued to pursue her artistic talents, and in 1932, at the age of forty-two, she was awarded a master's degree in fine arts from Columbia University Teachers College. She made plans to exhibit her work at the Delphic Studios alongside the fruit and flower watercolors that her Wyckoff and O'Keeffe grandmothers had painted in the 1840s. Ida's promising work was distinct in style, and she continued to exhibit in a half dozen shows throughout the thirties. She worked in several mediums, but at one time specialized in monotypes (images on metal transferred to paper), which she made with an electric iron in her room in New York at night.

So in the early thirties Georgia was confronted all at once by a profusion of work by other women artists—even by other O'Keeffe women. Until this time she had been the most celebrated female painter among the handful of "known" women artists of the twenties working in a modern idiom. She had even been called the woman who spoke in paint for all women. It's likely that the growing recognition of other women painters threatened her sense of being exceptional, and certainly her sisters got the emphatic message that Georgia wanted to be the only O'Keeffe who painted.

Around this time an architect remarked that O'Keeffe's feelings were so big that she should be given a large wall to decorate. Since, historically, prestigious mural commissions had seldom gone to women, they rarely had had the chance to work on a monumental scale. Then during the Depression hundreds of murals were executed in public places. For an artist with a flair for the dramatically large that O'Keeffe had, the appeal of mural work was strong, and for several years she eagerly followed up each lead that might result in a commission.

Soon she had a chance to show what she was able to do. After it was learned in early 1932 that the murals adorning the walls of Radio City Music Hall, then under construction in Rockfeller Center, would be done by Mexican Diego Rivera and other foreigners, Americans protested vigorously. In response, the Museum of Modern Art promptly invited sixty-five American artists and photographers—including O'Keeffe—to submit designs for a special mural exhibition that spring. Although this was not a competition for the Radio City Music Hall commission, the many artists who entered their work hoped to win one of the contracts for the huge theater, which was being heralded as the last word in tasteful modern design.

Each artist was asked to submit a drawing for a three-part mural and to complete one large panel (seven feet high by four feet wide). Georgia hurried to finish her entry in the short six weeks before the deadline. Her mural, *Manhattan*, showed a city sky crowded by skyscraper forms and smoky plumes, not unlike her easel paintings of New York. There was more fantasy in the mural, however. A low moon drifted near a building in one panel, and large roses danced in the air in another. In the large completed central panel, a dangerously tilted skyscraper reflected the afterimage of another office tower for an intriguing interplay of geometric forms.

The Modern's mural show was a critical disaster. Reviewers attributed the disappointing results to the artists' inexperience with murals, their hurry to meet the deadline, and their use of political propaganda. (Ben Shahn's entry was *The Passion of Sacco and Vanzetti*, and others caricatured the Rockefellers and other capitalists.) Nevertheless, several critics mentioned O'Keeffe among the few contributors who showed promise. Shortly afterwards, she was approached by Donald Deskey, the designer in charge of decoration for the Music Hall, and was asked to execute a mural on the walls—the space surrounding nine round mirrors—and on the low ceiling of the theater's second-mezzanine powder room. (Deskey also asked Stuart Davis to do the men's smoking room, and the resulting work, *Men Without Women*, was later moved to the Museum of Modern Art.) Georgia enthusiastically accepted Deskey's offer and signed a contract, agreeing to a Depression-level fee of fifteen hundred dollars.

Stieglitz, however, was violently opposed to what she had done. He disapproved of the "democratization" of art and characterized the mural movement as "that Mexican disease called murals." What's more, he had complained that spring about the building of Rockefeller Center while museums were starved for funds, and he supposedly declined an offer to create a photo mural for a men's lounge in another Rockefeller Center theater. But, more importantly, he had devoted the past sixteen years to raising the price of a single O'Keeffe oil to several times the fee being offered for the entire mural, and he was afraid that the contract would ruin her carefully established market value. Georgia, on the other hand, simply longed to decorate a room at long last, and she tried to ignore his protests. She apparently felt she was in a position to oppose Stieglitz—after all, such was the stature she had attained that paintings of hers were scheduled to be included in both Museum of Modern Art and Whitney annuals that fall.

Nonetheless, a day or two after she had signed the contract, Stieglitz marched into Deskey's office, explained that he was O'Keeffe's business manager, and stated that the fee was unacceptable. Deskey replied that the contract was between O'Keeffe and the Music Hall managers, and that she was morally obliged to honor it. Stieglitz left to mull that over, but the next day he returned. As Deskey recalled it, Stieglitz said that O'Keeffe was "a child and not responsible for her actions." However, since she was extremely eager to do the mural, Stieglitz would allow her to waive the fee—but she must be paid five thousand dollars for expenses. Deskey disregarded Stieglitz's proposal, and preparations continued for O'Keeffe to paint the powder room.

During the summer of 1932 she made several trips from Lake George to New York to work on her design for the room, which was still under construction. She worried about experimenting so publicly with a mural and about the survival of her work in such a place. At first she was supposed to start work in August, but the room was still unfinished and she anxiously wondered when the canvas would be applied so she could complete her work before the theater opened in late 1932. The powder room contained hundreds of square feet of surface—much of which was on the ceiling and would be physically strenuous to decorate. Originally she had allotted at least ten weeks to do the job.

Finally in November, ignoring Stieglitz's censorious scowl, Georgia left the lake to start work on the powder room. (One member of the Stieglitz family has said that she departed in spite of Stieglitz's explicit orders that she bow out of the contract.) A few days later, and only six weeks before the Music Hall was to open on December 27, she went to the finished room with Deskey to inspect its rounded walls, newly covered with canvas. As they stood there, a small section of cloth began to separate from the wall due to defective workmanship. After months of tense waiting, Georgia's control broke. She became enraged, then hysterical, and ran out of the room in tears, according to Deskey. The next day Stieglitz telephoned him to claim that Georgia had had a nervous breakdown, was confined to a sanatorium and thus was unable to fulfill her contract. Although Georgia was actually back at Lake George, Stieglitz's intransigent will had prevailed. Deskey quickly arranged for Japanese-born painter Yasuo Kuniyoshi to paint a mural in her stead. Almost as if he were working from O'Keeffe's sketches, Kuniyoshi painted the room in dreamy gigantic foliage fronds and white flower blossoms.

In early December 1932, a few weeks after her forty-fifth birthday, Georgia returned alone to New York. Tense, drained, and despondent, she suffered from severe headaches and a hypersensitivity to noise. She felt terrified, upon venturing onto the crowded city streets, that she might lose her mind. The doctors who were called in to diagnose the ailment were not sure what was wrong. One doctor suspected that she had a weak heart—an ironic diagnosis since heart trouble was what plagued Stieglitz. Then, four days before Christmas, Georgia left their rooms at the Shelton Hotel and moved into the luxurious Park Avenue apartment where her sister Anita lived with her husband, now a partner in a Wall Street firm, and her teen-age daughter. Georgia did not improve during January 1933, and ultimately suffered from constricted breathing, loss of appetite, and an inability to walk or sleep. Finally, on February 1, in the dusk of a late winter afternoon, she was admitted to Doctors Hospital for the treatment of psychoneurosis.

In the afterglow of her first summer in Taos, Georgia had falsely imagined that she was beyond succumbing to any kind of deep hurt. Now a complex mix of problems had plummeted her into a severe depression. For one thing, she was in her midforties, a time of climacteric change for many women. Numerous needs and desires were warring within her, all of them intensified by her tension and conflict with Stieglitz. Like other people who had been in the shadow of Stieglitz's dominating personality, Georgia needed to go beyond his tight little clique. But, in spite of his age, Stieglitz was tenacious and tough. "Body tottering but determined, pursuing, crusading, charged with some high explosive which seems about to shake the structure to bits," observed Peggy Bacon of him at the time. After he had blocked her path in several directions, Georgia slid into a kind of passivity, a form of resistance that suggested she would just as soon stop living as knuckle under.

"In the valley of disarming shadows," as Marsden Hartley later described her mental state, she rested in bed. At first her only visitor was a sister, presumably Anita, and later Stieglitz was allowed to see her for one ten-minute visit a week. Eventually she began to sleep, gain weight, walk in the corridors, and, finally, to venture out alone. It's unlikely that she was psychoanalyzed: Later in life she scornfully remarked that people who underwent Freudian analysis emerged as Freudian patients, and those who went into other kinds of therapies came out those kinds of persons.

Before her discharge from Doctors Hospital, she visited her show at An American Place, even though Stieglitz had already kindly photographed it for her. Because of the time that had been taken up by her mural preparations and her illness, there were only thirteen new paintings on display. Most of them, with the exception of two white flowers that she had designed for the powder room, had been done the previous summer in Canada. Her best work from the previous few years filled out the exhibition. Interestingly, in light of the deep depression from which she had been suffering, the new pictures in the show included a painting of a Canadian cross decorated with a blood red heart and a pastel of a pink double-chambered flower called *Bleeding Heart*.

As usual, the critics gave her show lavish praise—much of which Stieglitz reprinted in her exhibition brochure. Ralph Flint in *Art News* raved that the backward look at her career showed a talent "ripe with beauty, touched by grace, buoyant with vision, sure in execution, clear as to character." During the past five years the artist had traveled a great emotional and intellectual distance from ecstatic joy to terror

of loss, acutely observed Elizabeth McCausland in the Springfield
(Mass.) *Republican*. Henry McBride lauded her seemingly effortless
technique and wrote that news of her recent illness was shocking, in
view of her masterful pictures. "In health she has always seemed so
unearthly and so unphysical as to be quite without the range of the
slings and arrows that attack us lesser mortals," is the way he began
his review. "In this case, therefore, the illness, if illness it be, must
be pure illusion—something for our friends, the Christian Scientists,
to look into. Pray they dissipate it quickly."

❖

Georgia was discharged after seven weeks in the hospital, on
March 25, in the same month that Franklin D. Roosevelt was sworn
in as President and announced that the one hundred days of economic
recovery had begun. Before checking out, she had telephoned Marjorie
Content, a thirty-eight-year-old divorcée and friend of the Stieglitz
family, and told her she had to get out of town. Marjorie and her
teen-age daughter, Sue, were going to Bermuda for the Easter holidays,
and they invited Georgia to join them. They picked her up at the
hospital, tactfully asking few questions about the nature of her illness,
and went directly to the ship.

In Bermuda they stayed in a bungalow at Cambridge Beach and
ate in the hotel dining room. While Marjorie and Sue explored the
island by bicycle, Georgia convalesced in the hot Caribbean sun,
strolled a bit along the quiet tropical lanes, and collected tiny seashells
on the beach. Compared to the grays and browns of wintry New York,
Bermuda's colors were refreshing. It was a green island dotted with
pink cottages and surrounded by a turquoise sea. Color, she was to
say in 1937, was one of the great things that made life worth living
for her. Bermuda was such a welcome change, in fact, that she extended her stay by two weeks, until the end of May.

All this time Stieglitz was frantic with worry about what he called
her "diabolical" condition, which was horribly reminiscent of his
daughter's sickness. He anticipated that Georgia would not have the
vitality to paint again for a very long time to come. Although an
astounding six thousand people had visited her last show, this was the
depth of the Depression and not one of her paintings had sold. In this
period they needed the money badly, since their medical expenses

were high. Stieglitz began to resent the onerous expense of storing his large private art collection, and he threatened to abandon to city garbagemen thousands of photographs taken by the pioneers in photography. A friend hurriedly contacted the Metropolitan Museum of Art, which accepted the photos as a gift, making them part of its permanent collection. The prints were now precisely where Stieglitz had always argued that photographs belonged.

As soon as Georgia returned from Bermuda, she and Stieglitz went straight up to Lake George for the summer. Her doctor ordered absolute quiet and no visitors—conditions she had always yearned for and had found difficult to obtain around Stieglitz. Stieglitz resigned himself to the situation because, although Georgia looked robust and beautiful to him—she had gained fifteen pounds and had a deep suntan— he saw that she still tired easily and lacked the stamina to paint. She crept along the country roads in her auto, painfully observing the cautionary speed of fifteen miles an hour. In the photographs Stieglitz took of her at the time, her eyes look vacant and flat, and she seemed to be patiently, passively biding her time.

When Homer Saint Gaudens, director of the Carnegie Institution's department of fine arts in Pittsburgh asked her in mid-August to send *Horse's Skull with Pink Rose* for the fall show, there was no response until September when Stieglitz returned the entry form late, explaining that his wife was ill.

In late autumn, when she managed a short visit to New York, she was relieved to discover that her phobias of the year before were gone. There she met with the handsome black writer Jean Toomer, one of Stieglitz's more fascinating friends, she had told Sherwood Anderson in 1924. At Toomer's request, she turned over to him the letters written to her by his young wife, Margery Latimer, the red-headed Wisconsin novelist and a friend of O'Keeffe's since the twenties, who had tragically died the year before in childbirth. Georgia's renewed acquaintance with Jean resulted in the writer visiting Lake George in December where she was spending the winter alone, except for Margaret Prosser, to avoid the stress of her marriage and the strain of Manhattan. Toomer had visited Lake George in earlier years and thought of it as a place of special artistic freedom. There were "no 'oughts' or 'ought nots' governing the running of the house except those which relate to the work of O'Keeffe, of [Stieglitz], of whoever may be his guests at the time, his fellow experiencers," he wrote. "No ought even in relation to work. No ought in relation to life—providing you do not hinder someone else. Just life."

Toomer, thirty-nine at the time, was a lanky, long-fingered, olive-skinned man who looked like a native of India. An active disciple of the Russian mystic Gurdjieff, he was both humorous and gentle. He had written *Cane,* a lyrical novel set in the American South that had been published in 1923 and had been hailed as one of the most important works of the Negro renaissance. The author, however, had rejected the idea that there was such a thing as a Negro style of writing. He refused to have his poems included in an anthology of black poetry, for example. Most of his subsequent writing was unpublished and in time he stopped writing altogether.

At Lake George, Georgia and Jean liked to drive her Ford down on the frozen surface of the lake and to walk on the wide, white expanse of ice until the bitter wind and subzero temperatures drove them back inside again. In the evenings they used to talk and laugh, amused sometimes by the antics of some kittens, and read the manuscript pages that he typed by day. The world must have seemed exceedingly pure, dazzlingly bright, and profoundly silent to them as the deep snow drifted around the farmhouse. Enjoying each other's company, they developed a fine rapport and, for Georgia, a rare degree of intimacy. At Christmastime she gave him a warm red scarf.

After he had departed for Chicago a few days after Christmas, she wrote him seven long, heartfelt, poignant letters in the first two weeks of January, letters that would last until spring. It was clear that she missed his presence acutely—the sudden rush of warmth, laughter, and virility that he had brought into her life at a time when she was unusually vulnerable and struggling to regain her vitality. "I miss you—We had duck for dinner today—Sunday—even the duck missed you," she wrote. "It seems ages and ages—and it is just a week—so many things seem to have turned over in me that it seems a very long time—" But she also realized with a surge of gratitude that his companionship had been the turning point in her illness and that she had now regained her balance. "I seem to have come to life in such a quiet surprising fashion—as tho I am not sick any more," she wrote.

Still, her strong yearning for him conflicted with her old pleasure in being alone. "I want you—sometimes terribly—but I like it that I am quite apart from you like the snow on the mountain—" she admitted. She wrote him that her favorite cat, Long Tail, had gone into heat and was stridently mewing for a tomcat. She didn't need *that*, she noted, and sometimes felt like digging a hole and burying all the cats in it. "If I sit here all evening with a feeling toward you—what can I do about it?" she asked him two weeks after he had left. "You are there and I am here—" She added that there was nothing to do but stroke her white cat, to whom she had become fiercely devoted. It slept, she wrote, soft, warm, and purring on her lap, looking striking against her black trousers and red jacket.

One night Georgia had a vivid dream in which another woman came for Toomer, and, even though he made love to this woman in the dream, to Georgia it seemed the natural thing for him to do. She awoke feeling sharply her differences with Jean and understanding the difficulties they might have if they were to get together again. Above all, she comprehended, though sadly and grudgingly at moments, that there was little room in her life for anything other than art—and certainly not the risk of love when she was trying to return to painting again. She described her feeling of fragility to Jean, using what was an apt metaphor for a farmer's daughter.

> My center does not come from my mind—it feels in me
> like a plot of warm moist well tilled earth with the sun
> shining hot on it—. . . It seems I would rather feel
> starkly empty than let any thing be planted that can not
> be tended to the fullest possibility of its growth. . . . I do
> know that the demands of my plot of earth are relentless
> if anything is to grow in it—worthy of its quality. . . . If
> the past year or two or three has taught me anything it is
> that my plot of earth must be tended with absurd care—
> By myself first—and if second by someone else it must be
> with absolute trust—. . . It seems it would be very diffi-
> cult for me to live if it were wrecked again just now.

At Christmas Stieglitz had traveled north to see Georgia for two days. In a few days, on January 1, 1934, he would be seventy, and he was now an old man with a pale, angular face and long white hair that straggled down over the collar of his black cape. As early as 1923 Georgia had remarked that she felt like a little plant Stieglitz had watered, weeded, and dug around, and this feeling had endured, even after all their conflicts. Despite their other alliances, their marriage was evolving, albeit often at a distance, into a quiet sort of respectful partnership.

In late January Georgia ventured into Manhattan for a weekend to help choose paintings for her 1934 exhibition. Then she fled back to the lake only to return the following weekend for the hanging. Although she had done virtually no work in 1933, Stieglitz loyally presented a retrospective of forty-five pictures done between 1915 and 1927. The exhibit attracted seven thousand visitors including Scott Fitzgerald's wife, Zelda. Against her doctor's wishes and accompanied by a nurse, Zelda left a mental institution in upstate New York to attend a luncheon at Scribner's, visit a show of her drawings and paintings (including vivid red poppies, white roses, and white anemones clearly inspired by O'Keeffe's anatomical flowers), and to see the O'Keeffe exhibition. "I loved the rhythmic white trees winding in visceral choreography about the deeper green ones," Zelda said of the O'Keeffes, "and I loved the voluptuous columnar tree trunk with a very pathetic blue flame-shaped flower growing arbitrarily beneath it." Zelda was also moved by what she called the "cosmic oysters" and by one "heart-breaking aspiration." The pictures "are magnificent and excited me so that I felt quite sick afterwards," she said. In fact, on the train back to the sanatorium she became so hysterical that her nurse had to sedate her.

The crowd O'Keeffe's show attracted was even bigger than the year before and, unlike the previous year, sales were good. Perhaps Stieglitz relaxed his strict standards a little, because several strangers were allowed to buy a few O'Keeffes. In March one of her Taos paintings, *Black Flower and Blue Larkspur*—magnified blossoms with light hearts like staring cat's eyes—was sold to the Metropolitan, her first sale to the prestigious New York museum. These sales relieved the couple's financial worries and helped replenish the gallery's rent fund.

Although her work was selling, O'Keeffe was still not painting. It was her longest fallow period since she had left the Art Students League twenty-five years earlier in 1908. "What annoyed me was that I've not been interested in work," she explained hesitatingly to an interviewer that March. "If I had a clue, I'd start." Even though she felt as though she had awakened from what she called "a long queer sleep," she felt so distanced from the artist in herself that she imagined denying she had painted the pictures in her own exhibition. "And when you get to that sort of place, you have to begin all over again," she said grimly. Still, her recovery was under way, and she described her sense of relief to the reporter. "When I felt well, though, I had a sense of power. I always had it," she said. "But a sense of power isn't the word. You walk down the street, I mean, and you feel so much better than anyone else you see."

Back on the hill, she suddenly grew tired of the cold and solitude, and trying to maneuver her skidding Ford over icy roads. Finding it impossible to live in New York, where she had felt "smashed to bits" during her last visit, she decided to go again to Bermuda, those "toylike islands on the glassy green blue sea," as she described it. She confessed in a letter to Jean Toomer that she just wanted "to lie in hot sun and be loved—and laugh—and not think—be just a woman . . . it is this dull business of being a person that gets one all out of shape." On the boat to Bermuda, she wrote him that she felt "petted all over" by the summery sun as she lay on the deck in a new bathing suit. She advised him to find a different sort of woman, acknowledging that she was taking herself far away from him and inevitably moving "more and more toward a kind of aloneness—not because I wish it so but because there seems no other way."

She stayed at a spacious old villa in Somerset with people she had met the previous year on the island. From the high, four-poster bed in her room she was able to glimpse the sea. She sunned herself, slept deeply, went barefoot, and immensely enjoyed being an ocean away from her old New York life and living a quiet, easy existence in the pleasant, relaxed company of young people. Although she had packed tubes of paint, she only got to the point of doing some pencil and charcoal sketches of the reddish-purple banana blossoms on the grounds of the beautiful villa and some palms and twisted banyan trees. Still, it was a start.

After leaving Bermuda at the end of April, Georgia spent three days in New York before returning to Lake George. In the city she met with Jean Toomer, who had arrived from the Midwest. She saw that he had become romantically involved with Marjorie Content, the friend with whom she had gone to Bermuda the year before. In mid-May she wrote him from the lake, saying that she wished they had been able to talk longer in New York but that, nevertheless, she was sincerely happy for him and Marjorie. Then she added, movingly, that she might have liked to share the spring with him instead of the winter, but she caught herself and concluded that now she was well and "For both of us it is very right as it is—"

When, a few months earlier, Georgia had opened a Christmas

card from Mabel Dodge Luhan, she already knew that she would be returning to the Southwest soon—if not with Stieglitz's enthusiasm, then at least with his tolerance. He knew now that even if he were able to keep her by his side, he could not eradicate her need to go, and that, in fact, his resistance would be harmful to her health as well as to her creativity. One of the factors in her gradual recovery had been his steady, generous support of her as an artist, which he expressed by such gestures as bringing her gifts of an inspirational lily or camellia and continuing to present retrospectives of her work until she was ready to do new paintings again. Whatever the price, he was committed to seeing her resume a full life of painting. Perhaps he realized that she had only defied him in order to survive as an artist.

At first she had seemed to tremble at what it might cost her in loneliness and, possibly, failure to go away from him. As powerfully driven as Stieglitz, she was unable to suppress her needs for long. "I'm frightened all the time," she admitted in old age. "Scared to death. But I've never let it stop me. Never!" Her endurance and ego had been tested by her bout with typhoid as a teen-ager, by poverty and a poor education as a young woman, and by social isolation as a schoolteacher in Texas. Her strengths and her American faith in everyone's right to self-realization had been reinforced by Stieglitz's belief in the divine right of artists to self-expression, and these had carried her through.

But as her marriage rearranged itself into a cooler kind of companionship, she did experience a deep sense of loss. "I think you're only happy momentarily," she remarked in old age when asked what the happiest years of her life had been. She amended the question to talk about her most *interesting* years. She had come through her illness and concluded that, as her friend Vernon Hunter put it in 1932, she must be "fully individuated and alone, upon a mesa."

10 ❖ Ghost Ranch

In June of 1934 Georgia headed West, almost three years after she had left New Mexico with a heavy heart to return in midsummer to Stieglitz. She motored out with Marjorie Content, who liked to camp and photograph in southwestern Indian country. They stayed at the same H and M Ranch in Alcalde where Georgia had rented a cottage in 1931. Except in the evenings when they used to cook squabs given them by the ranch manager over their wood stove, each woman went her own way. Georgia made drawings of such objects as a black eagle claw and bean necklace that she had bought in Colorado during the drive out, and Marjorie's mind was elsewhere. Her romance had quickly blossomed, and Jean Toomer was planning to arrive soon from Wisconsin and spend his time writing by the side of his dark-haired fiancée with the comely oval face.

In New York, Georgia had heard friends talk about a man who was building a house at the Ghost Ranch—the most beautiful place in the world, they said. Remembering that she had unsuccessfully tried to find it a few years before, she began to ask about it. She was alternatively told that the ranch was haunted, hard to get into, or inhabited by some old cowboys. Instead of discouraging her, the stories simply whetted her curiosity. One day when she was shopping at a little country store, she spotted an auto parked outside with the initials "GR" on it. She waited for the driver to emerge, learned that he was indeed from the Ghost Ranch, and asked for directions. The cowboy told her to follow the road northwest from Espanola, then turn where there was an animal skull—but he warned her that she might not find a skull because they were often stolen.

The next day she set out in her black roadster to search for the ranch, which was supposed to be about forty miles away. After crossing the long wooden bridge over the muddy Rio Grande at Espanola, she followed a narrow dirt road along the Chama River toward Abiquiu. The road was pockmarked by arroyos that had been carved out of the earth by violent summer downpours. After a dozen miles the road deteriorated further into a two-wheel track. She eventually motored onto a wide plain where a dark mountain loomed to the left and a row of coral-colored buttes stood like sentinels ahead and toward the right. Finally she puttered down a very steep slope onto another sea of grasslands dotted with a thirst-stunted piñons, junipers, and cedars. Fortunately, a skull was propped against a rock that day, and she steered onto the road that veered to the right. She inched across a narrow log bridge and continued until she reached low ranch buildings clustered under a lone golden mesa. She was exhilarated by the sight of the majestic valley into which she had driven and would say afterwards that she knew immediately it was where she would live.

The place turned out to be a working ranch that had just been bought by Arthur Newton Pack, a wealthy easterner and early conservationist who published *Nature* Magazine. A few years before, the Packs had vacationed at the San Gabriel guest ranch near Alcalde, hoping that the dry climate would ameliorate the asthma of one of their three children. When the owners of San Gabriel moved their operation to the Ghost Ranch, the Packs followed. They were so enchanted by the area that they built themselves a house there, and then proceeded to buy up the ranchland.

Pack soon established a fancy dude ranch—charging eighty dollars a week in the middle of the Depression—with enough little bungalows and saddle horses for twenty guests. He provided luxury in the midst of an isolated place where wild horses, wild burros, and mountain sheep were still sighted, and where coyotes and rattlesnakes were commonplace. When the ranch's small electric generator was switched off in the evening, guests had to light kerosene lamps in their cottages. The nearest telephone and telegraph wires were in the town of Espanola, forty miles away over the treacherous dirt road. Soon Pack put in a dirt airstrip for the lightweight green Fairchild plane he piloted. Meals in the main ranch house came from the vegetable garden in the surrounding green oasis, and guests often feasted on the ranch's own livestock as well as on wild duck and deer.

Upon learning that the beautiful place she had come to was a dude ranch, Georgia was skeptical. "I thought dude ranchers were a lower form of life," she later said. Nevertheless, perhaps motivated by the uncomfortable thought of being part of a threesome—with Marjorie and Jean—at the H and M Ranch, she asked if she would be able to spend a night there sometime. She was told that the following day there would be a room available for one night in Ghost House, the oldest ranch building. According to legend, a family had been murdered there, and a ghostly female presence carrying an infant returned from time to time. The phantom presumably had given the ranch its Spanish name, El Rancho de los Brujos, or ranch of the witches, anglicized as the Ghost Ranch.

Promptly returning the next day for an overnight stay, Georgia discovered with each hour that her initial delight in the ranch was confirmed, and was stronger than her doubts about dudes. During the night she was there a family suddenly departed when their son developed appendicitis. Georgia left the ranch only long enough to pack her belongings at the H and M Ranch, returning to move into the family's former rooms. On September 1, when Marjorie and Jean were married in Taos by a tipsy Spanish justice of the peace, the witnesses were Georgia and the artist Paul Jones, who lived in Espanola.

During her first weeks at the ranch Georgia hiked for miles every day, and, when she got hot, she liked to bathe in the region's narrow irrigation ditches. She motored into lonely back canyons and toward inaccessible cliffs, searching for places to paint and for ways to get her auto across arroyos. She continued to gather desert debris, such as unusual rocks, gnarled branches, and animal bones. When Pack's wrangler, Jack McKinley, would spot her striding across the grassy plain, he used to ride up to her and rein in his horse. After greeting him warmly, she always asked if he had seen any skulls. If he said yes and offered to get the skull for her, she replied that she only wanted directions so she could find it herself in its natural state. (She also probably feared the fragile bone might fracture in a cowboy's saddlebag.) After dinner ("when the shadows are long and the sun hits brightly on unexpected spots," she later wrote to Stieglitz), she liked to go up to a high mesa to watch the flaming sunset illuminate the wide valley with hot color. Afterwards she would return by moonlight.

She spent most of her time by herself, painting. She went out around seven in the cool morning, parked her black auto under a cliff or beside a red hill, and returned about five in the afternoon. In mid-afternoon it became almost unbearably hot, and sometimes the only shade was under the car. "Georgia, why don't you come in out of the heat?" guests at the ranch used to ask when they came upon her on their excursions. O'Keeffe would smile, shake her head, and continue to work. "It is very hard work to turn out anything that looks like a good painting," she admitted to Stieglitz a couple of summers later. She found she was only able to work in one place for two or three days before curious local people began stopping and asking her questions. When that happened, she drove away and painted someplace else; if the first picture wasn't done, she returned to the area a few days later.

Her artist's eye was particularly exicted by the ranch's colors. She wrote Arthur Dove that the hues were the ones they both used frequently on their canvases—browns, oranges, yellow, and violet as well as a soft green. "All the earth colors of the painter's palette are out there in the many miles of badlands," she stated in her 1939 exhibition catalog. At one time she even tried to grind the fine ocher soil and mix it with oil to make pigment, but discovered it was too sandy.

Known as the badlands because of their barrenness, the small rolling hills around the ranch were composed of disintegrating sandy silts and clay shales. The wind and rain continually shaped them into rounded knolls, quickly erasing footprints. When Georgia climbed the steep slopes it was as if she were in a newborn world where no other human being had ever been before. The hills sometimes appeared an angry purplish blood red when a cloud passed over them, and other times they were a warm, pale fleshy pink. Georgia loved the soft little hills. "A red hill doesn't touch everyone's heart as it touches mine and I suppose there is no reason why it should," she also wrote in 1939. She later confessed that she sometimes fantasized about lying nude on the dry, hot, reddish slopes.

Eastern artists at first imagined that the red hills would be easy to render because they already looked painted. O'Keeffe soon realized that this was not so: The hills were elusive and mercurial under the passing thunderheads and endlessly eroding forces of nature. Beginning in 1934, she struggled to portray their essence, experimenting on her own, and feeling that she failed many times. Sometimes she painted the hollows of the hills as if they were the curves, contours, and creases of the human body—somewhat like a Brancusi female torso with an erotic rosy flush. In 1935 she painted a little coral hill with a scraggly old green piñon clinging to it under an azure sky. In the next few years there were passionately orange, bare hills glowing like red-hot coals along with stump, a mesa, a shell, a cloud, flowers, or bones under a blue sky or a cloudy sky.

When summer was over, Georgia asked Spud Johnson, her poet friend from Taos, to drive her back East. Spud agreed since he hadn't been to New York for six years. (He later wrote a tongue-in-cheek article for the Taos Valley *News* about being "kidnapped" by Georgia O'Keeffe.) Spud was thin, with an intelligent ascetic face and expressive brown eyes, and lived in a charming little whitewashed house in Taos with his unpublished novel and poetry, books, hand press, and toy horse collection. During the days as he drove, Georgia felt comfortable enough with him to ramble on about Bermuda and other places she had visited. At night in his room he read homosexual erotica, he confessed in a journal that he habitually kept. After six days and a stop to see the Doves in upstate New York, they arrived at Lake George. Stieglitz was back in the city by then, but he traveled up to the lake to see her.

Georgia had established the pattern, rarely broken until the death of Stieglitz, of setting out from the East each spring with tubes of paint and rolls of canvas and returning in autumn with her back seat full of paintings for Stieglitz to show to the world. Sometimes she drove with a friend, like the young moustached New Mexican painter Loren Mozeley. ("Young man, will you drive me to New Mexico?" was a question she frequently posed during those years.) Other times she drove alone, sleeping in auto camps or rooming houses. She liked seeing America that way and enjoyed varying her route. Once she motored through the Dakotas, which her father had explored as a young man, and another time she took the pretty southern Appalachian route. One time she laughed out loud at the odd spectacle of two circus elephants ambling along a Kansas highway. By the time she was ninety, O'Keeffe was able to say with satisfaction that she had seen almost every corner of the United States.

❖

At Ghost Ranch, other guests have recalled Georgia as a very vigorous, extremely agile eastern artist who always looked well groomed, even in trousers. The moment anyone met her, he or she knew that the tanned woman, often dressed in immaculate white cotton—her new summer color—was "somebody." She is also remembered as a loner who clearly enjoyed her own company more than anyone else's, as someone who rarely talked about what she was painting or about anything personal, for that matter. As for Georgia, she quickly decided which vacationers she would tolerate and which she would not. Those who passed her scrutiny had good minds and strong interests or were entertaining or helpful. She coolly ignored the others, and let them know that she didn't want to waste time on them. "When you got to know Georgia, she was a very, very nice person," explained Dorothy Brett. "But she had a rather cold front that made things a little difficult for her and for everybody else. It's a horrid thing to say, but I think she was bored with people."

Although Georgia occasionally called on friends in Taos, she continued to avoid Mabeltown, much to Mabel Luhan's annoyance. It's interesting to note that she kept her distance from that subculture of creative and independent women and men even though, unlike the citizens of the small towns of Texas, they genuinely accepted her. But Georgia preferred standing apart from other artists, having had her fill of social life at Stieglitz's side, and had no patience for the follies of Taos. "I wouldn't want to live there if you gave me the country," she said in her late eighties. "It's too arty." When her interviewer exclaimed, "But you're an artist!" O'Keeffe replied, "I'll stay off by myself and attend to it."

Beck Strand had lived in Taos since her divorce and was a familiar sight in town with her silver-haired pageboy, black western hat, and black Stieglitzian cape. Georgia continued to enjoy her friendship as well as the company of Dorothy Brett, who lived more flamboyantly than ever. She dressed in colorful blouses and scarves, wore a big sombrero, kept a Mexican dagger stuck in a cowboy boot, and carted an easel around in one hand and her tin ear trumpet in the other. Georgia was amused when, at one boisterous party, Brett served her guests rice and canned spaghetti—and fashioned a tablecloth out of some draperies.

By this time D. H. Lawrence's widow, Frieda, had returned to Kiowa Ranch with her lover, a middle-aged married Italian army officer named Angelo ("the Captain") Ravagli. Georgia was astonished to discover that Frieda was a chunky, gold-toothed, guttural-voiced woman who looked more like a German hausfrau than the mate of the mythic Lawrence. "I can remember clearly the first time I ever saw her, standing in a doorway, with her hair all frizzed out, wearing a cheap red calico dress that looked as though she had just wiped out the frying pan with it. She was not thin, not young, but there was something radiant and wonderful about her," O'Keeffe recalled about Frieda, to whom she was never particularly close.

Georgia's instinct for avoiding the capers of Taos was undoubtedly reinforced by the furor that broke out over Lawrence's ashes. At Kiowa Ranch Frieda and Angelo erected a shrine to the writer out of concrete blocks and topped it with an ascending phoenix. Brett took care of the decoration of the inside and stained the shrine's round rose window glass. The following spring, in 1935, Angelo returned from Europe with the urn containing Lawrence's ashes, which were to be buried in the chapel. Mabel ardently insisted, however, that Lawrence had wanted his remains scattered over the ranch, and she threatened to steal the urn and fulfill his wish herself. To deter her, Frieda mixed the ashes with cement and made an altar. At the sunset dedication ceremony—which Mabel boycotted—a bonfire blazed, Indians danced, and, appropriately enough, a violent mountain thunderstorm crackled and flashed overhead.

At the Ghost Ranch, Georgia and Arthur Pack, who were close in age, developed a wary respect for one another that turned into a satisfying friendship. A graduate of the best Ivy League schools, Arthur was a gracious man who enjoyed people. During Georgia's first summer at the ranch, Pack's wife ran off with their children's tutor. Depressed and lonely, Arthur moved from their home to a cottage closer to ranch headquarters. In his memoir about the ranch, he recalled that Georgia "tried to be a friend—even bringing me one day as a gift a perfect drawing of a cow's skull which I then and there adopted as the insignia and trademark of the Ghost Ranch." (His personal ordeal ended happily the next summer when he met and later married a young redhaired guest named Phoebe.) Throughout the years she liked to seek him out when she wanted company, and they would talk for hours about everything from religion to ranching.

Although she preferred to eat an hour before the dinner bell rang—with the wranglers, maids, and gardeners, whose silence she enjoyed compared to the "din" created by the guests—Georgia did get to know some of Pack's classy dudes. Conductor Leopold Stokowski, who was fascinated by the Saturday night drumming and chanting of the San Juan Indians, vacationed there. Even Charles and Anne Lindbergh passed through. Many guests came from Pack's former hometown of Princeton, New Jersey. Among them was Robert Wood Johnson, a fox hunter, champion sailor, and president of Johnson & Johnson and Co., and his gay, enthusiastic wife Maggie. Georgia used to entertain them with funny stories about the goings-on in Taos. The Johnsons liked the ranch so much that they built a two-story summer house there. Maggie, who had done fashion photography with Steichen as well as wildlife photography with Pack, was fascinated by the way Georgia painted. She liked to sit in the back of Georgia's roadster and watch her paint the small mesas near their house. (In February 1940, Georgia visited the Johnsons in Nassau, where their joint yachting adventures inspired at least one fine sailing painting.)

Georgia also enjoyed the adventurous companionship of well-to-do David McAlpin, who was ten years younger than she and recently divorced. He had been collecting art since his student days at Princeton University, and he later became involved in starting the photography department at the Museum of Modern Art. During the years he summered at the Ghost Ranch, from 1935 through 1938, he and Georgia liked walking or riding together at sunrise or sunset. In a letter dated September 20, 1937, she described one of their outings to Stieglitz.

> It was the best ride I've ever had here—up and down all sorts of places that we could only get the horses to go by getting off and pulling several times—places I would never dare to go alone and cowboys wouldn't be much interested—perfectly mad looking country—hills and cliffs and washes too crazy to imagine all thrown up into the air by God and let tumble where they would. It was certainly as spectacular as anything I've ever seen—and that was pretty good—The evening glow on a cliff much higher than these here in a vast sort of red and gold and purple amphitheatre while we sat on our horse on top of a hill of the whitish green earth—There was no trail to

go back on but the one we went in on and it got dark so
I could barely see that my horse was following his own
tracks back—Then the moon came up big—almost full
and we could see out toward the trail and an easier way
home. As we got to the top of the last ridge and looked
down into the valley we had just crossed toward the
moon, it was as beautiful as anything I have ever seen—

One evening in 1935 back in New York, Dave McAlpin brought
Margaret Adams Bok, a thirty-one-year-old divorcée from Philadelphia
with three children, to the Shelton to dine with Stieglitz and O'Keeffe.
The younger woman seemed a charming person to Georgia, and the
following summer Peggy Bok visited Georgia at the Ghost Ranch, a
visit that turned into an annual tradition for the two women. Trained
as a singer, Peggy shared Georgia's love of music and learned from her
how to really see. There was much warm feeling between them, Georgia sometimes seeming to treat Peggy like the daughter she had never
had, confiding in her, and caring for her when she once had an upset
stomach at the ranch. "When are you coming?" Georgia's letters to
Peggy continually ended. When Georgia began to travel more widely,
she almost always stopped to see Peggy in Los Angeles.

In the midthirties Peggy was married briefly to Henwar Rodakiewicz, who had formerly been married to Marie Garland. A taciturn
independent motion picture photographer whom Georgia had known
for several years, Henwar was the blond son of a Polish father and an
American mother. He shared "an eye" with Georgia (as well as with
Stieglitz, who showed one of Henwar's experimental films at An American Place). One night in 1937 when Peggy and Henwar were staying
at the ranch around the time of their first wedding anniversary, Georgia
joined them and others for a magical evening outing: a drive in the
bright moonlight to a mountainside near Taos where they built a fire
and camped overnight in a little meadow enclosed by towering pines.

Ansel Adams, the tall, slender, dark-bearded photographer Georgia had first met with his wife in Taos, also spent time at the ranch.
He was fifteen years younger than Georgia and had a pleasant, tolerant
nature. In the spring of 1933 he had presented some of his early
photographs to Stieglitz, and a mutual admiration had developed between the two photographers. Stieglitz exhibited Adam's work in 1936,
and Adams later credited much of his technical expertise to the pioneer
photographer. Once, when leaving An American Place, another young

photographer muttered to Ansel that Stieglitz's talk was just "a lot of baloney." Adams gently smiled and replied that, nevertheless, it was "nourishing baloney."

Georgia's firm, lifelong friendship with Adams dated back to this time. She used to critique his photographs with the same kinds of comments that Stieglitz made, and she loaned him her auto to go photographing in at the ranch. One delightful evening at the ranch in 1937, Adams, McAlpin, O'Keeffe, and Haniel Long, the Harvard-educated New Mexican poet, unlocked the closed-up Johnson house, took the protective muslin off their superb Steinway piano, and, while Ansel skillfully played, the others stretched out on the newspaper-covered rugs and listened.

Pack liked to organize expeditions for his guests. Georgia often went along, taking her runabout or station wagon on occasion. She didn't work on such trips because drawing and painting demanded more time in one place than could be managed on a tour. Although very observant and meditative in the out-of-doors, she was never talkative in groups. When she did break her silence, it was often to express succinctly what the others were feeling. Once Pack took a group of guests to Monument Valley on the Arizona-Utah border, an enchanted region of majestic brick-red rock spires, buttes, natural arches, and shifting coral sands. On these outings, the station wagon full of camping supplies was usually driven by Orville Cox, a lean, informative guide who was one-eighth Indian, knew the Indian lands well, and spoke some of their languages. He used to search for Navajo "sings," or ceremonies, at which tribesmen gathered who had been traveling in covered wagons or on horseback from great distances from all over the reservation. These were colorful events: The women wore velvet bodices with bright full skirts, and everyone, including the haughty black-eyed men, was weighted down by glinting silver and turquoise jewelry. The night air would be lit up by hundreds of flickering yellow campfires and would throb with the murmur of voices and the beat of drums.

For Georgia, the various Indian ceremonies were numbered among life's great occasions, particularly the impressive Santo Domingo Indian corn dance on August 4, when hundreds of native men and women danced throughout the day in long undulating lines. The men painted their bodies, the women loosened their long black hair, and almost everyone carried evergreen branches symbolizing life. A male chorus provided a steady rhythmic baritone voice that, along with the pulse of the dancers' pounding feet, sounded to some like the beat of a heart.

At the annual Hopi snake dance, one dancer used to cradle a rattlesnake while another distracted it with an eagle feather. A friend thought that Georgia seemed to become a part of the primitive ritual on the lonely Arizona mesa. So much at one with herself, she was as comfortable in the company of an Indian as in that of a wealthy socialite, and as at home at an Indian rite as she would have been in Carnegie Hall. This naturalness, which enabled her to be comfortable almost any place, made her appear enigmatic to some people. Once she went with Maggie Johnson, the Johnson's chauffeur, and a wrangler to the hut of a Spanish boy to tell his anxious family that he had injured his foot. "As Georgia was telling them what had happened, she put her shawl over her head and became as one of them," said Maggie many years later, marveling at the still vivid memory.

In the summer of 1937, Ansel Adams, Dave McAlpin, Orville Cox, and Georgia made a swing through the Indian country of western New Mexico and Arizona, and an old mining town in southern Colorado. Adams took many photographs of Georgia with her black shawl around her shoulders and her black sombrero on her head. His pictures show her laughing, exuberant, relaxed—a shockingly different person from the somber one photographed by Stieglitz a few years before at Lake George. Because of one picture in which she was giving Orville a wide, warm grin, strangers later asked whether the wrangler was her husband. Explaining her rare, radiant look in that photo, Adams said that when Georgia O'Keeffe smiled, the entire earth cracked open. It was obvious that she was in her element in the West.

In spring 1938, Stieglitz had another heart attack, then a bout of pneumonia, and Georgia hired a nurse and stayed with him at Lake George until early August. Little could keep her from her southwest country anymore, however. When she finally got away, she did not have much time for painting at Ghost Ranch and only exhibited a score of new oils back in New York the next winter. In October she joined Adams, McAlpin, and Godfrey Rockefeller, a young New York businessman, in Carmel, California. They drove to Yosemite Valley, where they were outfitted with riding horses and pack mules carrying supplies for seventeen days. By then the high wilderness country of lush meadows, clear lakes, and granite peaks was dusted by a thin layer of glistening snow. Georgia observed in a letter to a friend that the yellowing aspens blazed brilliantly against the bright white snow and the hard blue sky.

❖

In Stieglitz's second one-man show at An American Place in the last months of 1934, he had hung no photographs of Dorothy Norman but displayed a half dozen new studies of Georgia—as if to say that his marriage was still intact. The economy was beginning to mend around this time, and O'Keeffes and Marins were now selling better than before. Not so much fund raising was necessary, and Dorothy spent less time with Stieglitz at the gallery. She became enthusiastic about the idea of bringing out a magazine and, beginning in 1937 and throughout the next decade, published *Twice a Year: A Journal of Literature, the Arts, and Civil Liberties.* Still devoted to Stieglitz, she dedicated her magazine to him, wrote to him in the summer, stopped by the gallery frequently in the winter, and, in 1939, bought him a cot to nap on in his gallery office.

Georgia remained very touchy about the younger woman. She barred her from the gallery when she went in to mount a show or mix her special shade of paint for the walls. In 1935, when Stieglitz accidentally switched the envelopes of the letters he was writing the two women, Georgia, who had just sat down to dine at Ghost Ranch, received a letter meant for Dorothy. It was so upsetting to her that she left the table and did not return to finish her meal. Another time, when she arrived with Dave McAlpin at a big party in the New York apartment of Nancy and Beaumont Newhall, Museum of Modern Art photography curators, she glimpsed Dorothy across the room, quickly backed out, and returned home.

Although Stieglitz continued to befriend young women and to enjoy their company, nothing as serious as his relationship with Dorothy ever erupted again. In 1940 he was once more an invalid confined to bed, his "flesh like a marshmallow, eyes of black agate," in the words of Peggy Bacon some years before, and his "soft, silver hair, wafted in all directions as by an electric fan." Lying in bed, he once mustered enough strength to whisper to his nurse, "Come close and tell me about your love life." Astonished, the nurse ran out of the room and stayed away until she was persuaded that the old man just wanted to be distracted.

Upon returning to the Shelton in early 1935, after having spent the better part of two years away, Georgia decided to move their household out of the hotel's two little rooms. Her artistic focus had shifted to the Southwest, and she had lost interest in that view of New York. In addition, she wanted more working space and, particularly when she was away, needed a housekeeper and a kitchen for Stieglitz, who was often bedridden. Now that she was painting again, they could afford the greater comforts and privacy of a real apartment.

Stieglitz, however, continued to detest change. In anticipation of their move to the Shelton more than a decade earlier, he had rehearsed the move so often in his mind before it happened that it was a long drawn-out agony for him. But Georgia persisted, and by the autumn of 1936, they had moved into a penthouse apartment at 405 East Fifty-fourth Street, only one quiet block from the East River and elegant Sutton Place. Around New York people gossiped that Georgia had managed to sign a lease for what was called "the Peter Arno penthouse," presumably where the illustrator once lived. The apartment consisted of a few large, light rooms and a wraparound terrace with a splendid view of the East River and the Queensboro Bridge.

Although Stieglitz had been unable to defeat Georgia's determination to move, he continued to act as if it were an extravagant whim. He complained that the penthouse was chilly, that her simple tastes were expensive, and that he had to take a taxi to cover the five long blocks from where they lived to An American Place. And although he wanted a railing in addition to the privet hedge and picket fence around the terrace, she declared to her friends that she wanted nothing between herself and the sky. It seemed to be *her* apartment. The Wickersham telephone number was in her name (the gallery phone was in his), and members of the Stieglitz family reasonably assumed that she paid the rent since his income was still only a few thousand dollars a year. The relationship had come full circle: She was lending him a hand, as he had once helped her.

Shortly after the move, Arthur Dove and his son, Bill, came calling. Stieglitz flung open the apartment door while Georgia hovered in the background. After greeting the visitors, he firmly marched them down the hall and into his own small room, where he settled himself in his tattered old armchair. Then he gestured to a steamer trunk beside him and loudly announced that he had not unpacked. Georgia, who had been left sitting alone in the larger room, finally appeared in the doorway and said with a little smile, "You can come in now," as Bill Dove recalls it. Then the Doves and Stieglitz got up and resettled themselves in the living room, and the talk turned to other topics.

The living room windows, which faced north and east, were uncurtained and let in a beautiful glow of light. With its white walls and minimal black-slipcovered furniture, benches, dark brown polished floors, and Navajo rugs, the room had a simple Japanese-like look that was visually exciting—especially at Easter when it was usually full of spring flowers. The decor of the room changed constantly: A stone or a skull or a shell would come out of a closet, be displayed for a few days, then disappear. When company called and Georgia didn't want to disturb her work, she used to toss a white sheet over her easel, palette, and other painting materials. As another instance of her resourcefulness, when a large table was needed, she created one from three pieces of plywood: a detachable top, made in two parts and extending to seven by fourteen feet, was supported by folding legs; it could be made half as large or dismantled completely. There was enough space to hire a Scandinavian housekeeper, who, friends recalled, cooked delicious soufflés.

On Saturday nights it was Stieglitz's habit to bring pals of his who had lingered in the gallery at closing time back to the apartment with him—often there was Emil Zoler, Louis Kalonyme, Carl Zigrosser, or Jerome Mellquist as well as Marin, Dove, and Hartley when they were in town. Sometimes the men ate at Stieglitz's favorite German restaurant, and other times they dined at the apartment. Since An American Place did not open until the afternoon on Sundays, they used to talk and argue late into Saturday night. When the talk turned to art, Stieglitz would flip his handkerchief over his shoulder for emphasis, sigh deeply, and proclaim, "They don't understand!" By the end of 1938 the Nazi military machine had annexed Austria and Czechoslovakia, and they would anxiously switch on the radio to hear the latest ominous news from Europe. Visitors often felt that Georgia, who usually sat silent and aloof in a corner, took a dim view of the "evenings," which took place more frequently when she was away. They were undoubtedly right, particularly about the nights when Stieglitz wearied early, went into his bedroom and shut the door—and she was forced to stay up and listen until everyone left.

During those years she got to know William Einstein, a young painter who had moved to New York from Paris in 1932. Although Einstein looked like an ineffectual little person, he was knowledgeable, sensitive, and a delightful conversationalist with plenty of time for the people he liked. Stieglitz was fond of him and trusted him so much that he allowed him to handle gallery paintings, gave him a show in 1936, and cited him in his will. Einstein liked Georgia as well as Alfred, and he made the effort to break through what he called her "shyness." "He is almost the only painter that I really enjoy talking with about painting, but I don't know many painters. I have a speaking acquaintance with many. I know very few," she wrote for his exhibition catalog in January 1953. When she complained to him about her reviews, he urged her to write about her work herself. And when he returned to Paris in 1938, she showed his drawings to a New York agent. "Einstein is one of us who went away to that Shangri-la that I have always heard about—France," she wrote. "However, he is one who always returns."

Einstein was eager for Georgia to meet his friend Alexander Calder, and one evening he brought the sculptor over. Soon afterwards Calder sent her a large brass brooch welded and rolled into a shape that spelled the letters "OK," and she took to wearing this ornament on all of her clothing. She continued to see Carl Van Vechten and the Stettheimer sisters, and was introduced to an assortment of creative people, like the English editor John Middleton Murry and artist Louis Eilshemius, but she kept up with few of them.

Georgia comprehended that Stieglitz was still fascinated by her work, perhaps more than anyone else. He remained her effective publicist, defending and praising her work ("her marriage knot," said a friend) constantly, and exhibiting it one or more times a year. On the other hand, it became clear that as the number of visitors to the gallery dwindled, O'Keeffe was Stieglitz's top drawing card, the artist who attracted the most attention and generated many of the sales. For this reason, he often presented her exhibits in February when attendance would otherwise have been down. The couple maintained a deep respect for one another and continued to share what had first drawn them together—a driving, motivating artistic spirit. "For me he was much more wonderful in his work than as a human being,"

O'Keeffe wrote years later for an introduction to a book of his photographs of her. "I believe it was the work that kept me with him—though I loved him as a human being . . . I put up with what seemed to me a good deal of contradictory nonsense because of what seemed clear and bright and wonderful."

When they were together at the lake in the late thirties, he liked to photograph her with ferns, daisies, apples, and strawberries in her hands, as if she were an earth mother figure—until his infirmities forced him to put down his heavy cameras for the last time in 1938. Sometimes when they were alone and feeling in harmony with one another, she was tempted to stay by his side—but then the telephone would ring, people would come to visit, he would become agitated and talkative again, and she would be very glad to retreat to the silent, sun-drenched desert.

Leaving each year was always difficult for her to arrange and often painful for both of them. Sometimes, upon leaving, Georgia must have wondered if she would find Stieglitz alive again. When asked why she was not with her ailing husband, however, she used to explain matter-of-factly that she'd be unable to paint if she sat by him and held his hand. She also said that she doubted it would actually make him feel any better, understanding that his feeling of abandonment was attributable to other sources than her departure. Regardless of her tender feelings for Alfred, she had to complete the all-engulfing artistic agenda he had set for her when they first met. And, when he wrote that he was lonely, she replied evenly that she wished he were able to be in New Mexico with her. "I've been to Lake George," she used to tell her friends, "but Stieglitz has never been in the state of New Mexico."

In her absence he portrayed himself as a martyr for "Art." He darkly explained to people that true marriage—that is, marriage based on each partner's fulfillment—is tragic because it often leads two people apart. This was especially true of a pure artist like O'Keeffe, he thought. "I don't believe she ever did anything contrary to her own inner feeling," he once said with a touch of awe. He used to sigh and admit that he would rather have six months with her than twelve months with somebody else. Each morning at Lake George, before he did anything else, he read her daily letter to him and then answered it. (By the end of their life together, they had exchanged more than 3,400 letters and telegrams.) He often sat apart from his aging clan on the hill, in the farmhouse room by the telephone, writing letters, reading, or playing the Victrola a bit. He walked a little if the sun was out. Some of the older members of the Stieglitz family criticized Georgia, calling her a selfish wife, but the younger ones accepted the fact that, as an artist, she needed her freedom.

In New Mexico, Georgia rarely spoke about Stieglitz the way other wives customarily talked about their mates; she never referred to him as "my husband," for example. Not only did she express little concern for his frail health, but she would joke about his idiosyncrasies. Most of her friends assumed she was indifferent to him and were baffled by the marriage. It seemed to be more like a sibling relationship than one between a husband and wife, and they were unable to imagine the austere O'Keeffe being Stieglitz's lover—or anyone else's for that matter. She was now almost fifty, and although she had friendships with many younger men, they tended to be much younger, contentedly married or homosexual, and any rumors of romance were generally dismissed. "I think she had enough on her hands with Stieglitz," laughed Dorothy Brett in old age. "Oh dear, they were very close, you see, very close indeed."

The relatively few letters from her to Stieglitz whose contents have been revealed indicate Brett's astuteness in this matter. For example, in eight letters she wrote during the summer of 1937, she expressed her tender concern for her husband's well-being ("You sound a bit lonely up there on the hill—It makes me wish that I could be beside you for a little while—I suppose the part of me that is anything to you is there—even if I am here—"); wifely reminders to pack the clothes brush for his trip to New York, news about mutual friends, detailed descriptions of what she was painting ("You will laugh when I say that I have two new paintings tonight that I didn't have this morning—"); her desire to share with him the beauty all around her, her joy in good friends ("I have never had a finer time with so many people at once—sort of sparkling and alive and quiet all at the same time. You would have liked it too and been a nice part of it"); her anxiety about his health ("Funny the way I sometimes get a feeling that I would like to know right this minute how you are"); and her willingness to change her plans to visit the Grand Canyon in September with Dave McAlpin and Ansel Adams in order to be with him ("You sound lonely—and I wonder should I go to the lake and have two or three weeks with you before you go to town—I will if you say so—Wire me and I will pick right up and start").

❖

Since O'Keeffe had done relatively little work her first summer back in New Mexico, her 1935 show contained only nine new drawings and paintings. By the next season she was closer to her old form. "I have only just begun!" she exclaimed. Her seventeen new pictures shown in 1936 included a golden orb of a sunflower, a soft turkey feather perched in a shiny Indian pot, and tiny, playful oils of Hopi kachina dolls. The amusing portraits—one had a black mask over a turquoise face, ruby red ears and lips, and a broken feather from its headdress over a round green eye—signaled to friends that the artist's high spirits were back.

Blossoms and bones were also back. But the flowers were no longer fake and the skulls appeared almost as mirages, especially in *Ram's Head, White Hollyhock, Hills*. Its mood of buoyancy caught the perceptive eye of Lewis Mumford, who described it in the January 18, 1936, issue of *The New Yorker*:

> The epitome of the whole show is the painting of the
> ram's head, with its horns acting like wings, lifted up
> against the gray, wind-swept clouds; at its side is a white
> hollyhock flower. In conception and execution this is
> one of the most brilliant paintings O'Keeffe has done.
> Not only is it a piece of consummate craftsmanship, but
> it likewise possesses that mysterious force, that hold upon
> the hidden soul, which distinguishes important commu-
> nication from the casual reports of the eye. . . .

To some people the hollyhock and head represented the vying forces of life and death with which the artist had grappled during her illness, and the pictures showed her "triumphant convalescence," in the words of Jerome Mellquist. O'Keeffe, typically, insisted in later years that the composition "just sort of grew together." As a matter of fact, she contrarily reversed the symbolism, pointing out that a wilting blossom should more properly depict death and a durable bone should stand for life.

O'Keeffe gained ever more momentum, and all but one of the

twenty-one paintings in her next show were new. They were exhibited early in 1937, the same year the artist would turn fifty in November. They included *Summer Days*, an oil of a deer's skull floating like a featherweight among white clouds along with a bouquet of red and yellow summer wildflowers, like a desert hallucination. Stieglitz, who was proud of her New Mexican work, although sad that she summered there, confessed to Edward Alden Jewell of the *New York Times* that he "hated" the name of that painting. It's more likely that he was disturbed by the Chagall-like euphoria of it, and Georgia herself later called it "a picture of the summertime."

In a painting she did the next summer, *From the Faraway Nearby*, an immense pair of elk's antlers soar suspended in an ethereal pinkish-blue dawn over snow-capped mountains viewed with an extraordinary clarity. Like the other pictures of skulls in the sky, this one also seemed to have been painted from an elevated vantage point, as if the artist herself were levitating on a shimmering desert heat wave. It reminded some viewers of the joyful promise of everlasting life in the message of the Christian Resurrection. In these paintings, compared to earlier works, her colors were less strident, forms were less striving, and, overall, the mood was more serene. More light than ever saturated the canvases, and there was a new sense of spaciousness. The pictures lacked a middle distance: Objects appeared either very near or very far in the crystalline desert air. Now juxtaposed with her butterfly's-eye view of enlarged flowers was an eagle's-eye view.

For years Georgia had been in the habit of revealing little about her immediate plans. So in 1937, after settling Stieglitz on the hill and packing her auto, she arrived at the Ghost Ranch near the end of July without having first notified Arthur Pack. When Pack informed her that all the cottages were full, she suggested that he move someone out to make room for her. Pack thought for a moment, then asked if she wanted to stay at Rancho de los Burros, the house he had built with his first wife three miles away from ranch headquarters. She nodded, and they went over to unlock the small U-shaped adobe house. Inside were whitewashed rooms built around a patio, and there was a bedroom with a huge window overlooking dramatic cliffs. "As soon as I saw it, I knew I must have it," Georgia said afterwards. "I can't understand people who want something badly but don't grab for it. I grabbed." She stayed there that summer with a young Spanish housekeeper named LaVerna and saw few people. She liked to talk about a big mud puddle out front that kept visitors from coming in. The large crop of paintings she did in 1937 included paeans to the house—*The House I Live In*, which had been painted from the outside, for example—as if she were a schoolgirl reporting to people back in New York on her summer vacation.

The site had been picked by the Packs for its view of a flat-topped mesa in the Jemez range, called the Pedernal, about ten miles to the southeast beyond grasslands, low scrubby trees, and a line of hills. "Look at my front yard!" Georgia soon began to exclaim to visitors, with a sweeping motion of her arm in that direction, and she gave paintings of the vista the title *My Front Yard*. The Pedernal contained a flint deposit the Indians used for arrowheads, and the Navajos believed it was the place where their legendary "Changing Woman" was born. The top of the mesa was nearly sliced off at an odd angle by erosion. O'Keeffe, who once referred to it as "a perfect blue mountain," began to use the mesa as a motif. She painted its tilting top and its slanting slopes with red hills, flowers, the moon and stars, sometimes against a blue sky and sometimes under a gray sky. "It's my private mountain," she joked in old age. "It belongs to me. God told me if I painted it enough, I could have it."

She quickly climbed the wooden ladder to the roof. To the north, great gouged cliffs rose about seven hundred feet, like a giant's fantastic sand castle, ending in saw-toothed turrets and spires. The bottom layer of the cliffs was reddish rock, two hundred million years old; it had once been dense forest inhabited by dinosaurs. Above it was a layer of fine-grained golden rock—solidified ancient sand dunes. The top layer, hard grayish-white fossil-filled gypsum and limestone, had once been the bottom of an inland sea.

Georgia soon saw that a continuous natural light show played over the face of the cliff. As the sun moved across the sky, tonalities gently shifted between pale yellows, peaches and corals, rosy reds and earth pinks, grays and blacks. Hues intensified at sunset and deepened when a thunderhead passed over the sun. All day shadows appeared, lengthened, and shortened again. She knew the sight was real, but it was so unusual that sometimes she felt as though she must be dreaming. "A pretty good backyard!" she liked to say to guests, and she boasted that the sight was unique in the state of New Mexico.

After dinner a few weeks later, she invited Peggy and Henwar Rodakiewicz, Spud Johnson, and British journalist Felix Green up to her roof; she brought up pitchers of iced fruit juice, blankets, and a lantern. It became a ritual to take friends up to the roof, and use it as a terrace. Once, years later, some houseguests heard a little voice call early one morning, "Come up! Come up on the roof!" When they stumbled up the ladder, they found Georgia, exhilarated by the sight of a frost—which had glazed the landscape a glimmering white—and the snowy Sangre de Cristo mountains far away to the east. Standing on the roof, Georgia would get the heady feeling that there was no one else in the valley.

"I've been up on the roof watching the moon come up—the sky very dark—the moon large and lopsided—and very soft—a strange white light creeping across the far away to the dark sky—the cliffs all black—it was weird and strangely beautiful," she wrote to Stieglitz after her first weeks in the house. Over the years she used to sleep on the roof in a sleeping bag in order to awaken under the vast multitude of desert stars, to watch the pale, cold moon shadows on the cliffs, and to see the first morning light touch what she called "my wonderful world."

In the greater privacy of the house, she worked hard. That first summer there she described her pesistent struggle to paint a dead, twisted cedar in the badlands. On July 29, 1937, she wrote to Stieglitz:

> Thursday afternoon—about 5— . . . I've been painting
> an old dead cedar against those purple hills I've painted
> so often. It is a tree that I made a drawing of long ago
> when I first came up here—I've been working on it yes-
> terday and today—it looks promising. It's one of those
> things I've had in my so-called mind for a long
> time. . . .

And on August 16:

> Good Sunday morning to you! . . . I think I am through
> with my tree—It is the first thing I have done that when
> I stand it by the window and look at it—then I look out
> the window—it looks like what I see out the window,
> tho it was painted a mile away. I think it really looks like
> here. Even at that I don't think it very good—I'll do it
> again.

She called one version *Gerald's Tree*, for Gerald Heard (Heard was an

Irish intellectual and spellbinding storyteller with a rich vein of humor) because he had walked and written in the sand around the cedar stump.

Georgia was introduced during that summer to British writer Aldous Huxley and his wife. Having known the Lawrences in Europe, they stayed with Frieda and her Angelito in Taos. Huxley was tall, stooped, and thin, and wore thick spectacles for his dim vision.

Georgia had always been proud of her acute eyesight, and, as an artist, she was very aware of it. She rejected sunglasses because they distorted color and abhorred the thought of needing reading glasses as she got older. For some time she had been involved with the Bates eye training method. In 1920, Dr. W. H. Bates of New York had written *Perfect Sight Without Glasses*, in which he explained his theory that poor eyesight was due to stress-related bad visual habits. He provided corrective exercises designed to relax the eyes, and some of these stressed concentration, and thus were highly psychological procedures. In the most controversial ones, disciples were instructed to flicker their eyes directly at the sun. Georgia did Bates's exercises faithfully and never did have to wear glasses, but whether the training had anything to do with that fact is hardly clear.

At any rate, in 1938 Huxley began going to a Bates teacher, possibly at O'Keeffe's suggestion. In 1942 he published a book in which he claimed that his eyesight had been so dramatically improved by the Bates method that he no longer had to wear spectacles. Despite Georgia's disdain for Huxley, inspired by the pale Englishman's dislike of the "hostile" Taos desert, she gave his book to at least one nearsighted friend.

❖

If O'Keeffe once worried that she might be eclipsed by other women artists, her fears turned out to be unjustified. Most of the critics in the late thirties continued to describe her work as masterful and miraculous, and she was included in numerous group shows from San Francisco to Paris. (Sometimes she got irritated, however, when hanging committees hung her oils in corners because they feared the drama of her pictures would dominate the room.) Whereas other exhibits at An American Place attracted sophisticated art lovers, her shows brought in the general public. To her embarrassment, the crowds included what Henry McBride called "the ladies," as well as faith healers and other spiritualists drawn to her occult skulls.

A new patron was cosmetics executive Elizabeth Arden, who defiantly refused to allow the Depression to lower her standard of living. An O'Keeffe petunia that she purchased was to be the focal point of her Fifth Avenue art deco apartment, which was decorated with satin-covered sofas and smoked-glass mirrors. When Georgia was invited to the cocktail party at which her painting would be unveiled, she asked art critic Ralph Flint to go with her, saying she didn't want to stay more than five minutes. Once she was there, however, strangers came up to her and asked, "Are you *the* Georgia O'Keeffe?" and she didn't get away before an hour and a half had elapsed. In 1936 the cosmetics magnate commissioned a large O'Keeffe painting of four white blossoms and green leaves for the Arden exercise salon in New York City. Stieglitz, who shared Miss Arden's ardor for racehorses, convinced her to pay ten thousand dollars for it.

Ralph Flint saw a startling contrast in Georgia's severe looks and the appearance of the well-preserved, bejeweled, coiffed collector, who was a decade older than the artist. Whereas Miss Arden pampered her skin with creams and lotions, Georgia nonchalantly exposed her face to the harsh southwestern sun, which had etched out her "almost aboriginal" beauty, Flint observed. For her part, Georgia once remarked that the only woman whose looks she envied were those of Mabel Luhan's Indian maid, Albidia, whose shining black bangs framed a smooth, serene face.

O'Keeffe's handsome bone structure continued to attract almost as much comment as her pictures. One photographer, who snapped her for a magazine in 1936, noted that she indifferently refrained from glancing in a mirror before he began to shoot. "Yet curiously enough, she has the basic qualities that make for spectacular beauty," he noticed. "Her high, curved forehead and hairline are similar to Merle Oberon's. Her deep-set, heavy-lidded eyes, her delicate, high cheekbones are Dietrich's."

Media coverage now began to spill over from New York newspapers and the exclusively intellectual and art publications to mass magazines, and Georgia's fame spread. In early 1938 *Life* magazine ran a photographic essay about her, and included a reproduction of her horse's head with the pink rose. A little while afterwards when Georgia went to her New York garage to pick up her auto and gave the mechanic her name, he exclaimed, "Why, I know you!" He explained, to her astonishment, that he had cut the picture out from the magazine and had attached it to his living room wall.

Maybe O'Keeffe's growing renown was bound to make her an easy target, and perhaps this is why in the spring of 1938 she drew some of the nastiest attacks of her career. After exhausting her repertoire of flowers, "your lack of technical equipment and your lack of taste lay naked and raw," wrote that believer in strict geometric abstractions, George L. K. Morris, in *Partisan Review.* *Art News* stated that she was wasting her talent by turning out her bone "formula" on a mass production basis. The next year, Georgia wrote a long elucidation for her catalog, pointing out that no one seemed to notice or understand her new subject matter, red hills. And, as if the critics had not spoken, she continued to search for skeltons where the shepherds threw their animal carcasses, and to paint ribs, backbones, teeth, and other bony parts of mules, sheep, bears. In 1943, she even did a human skull.

That same spring it pleased her greatly when John Stewart Bryan, president of the College of William and Mary in Williamsburg, Virginia, asked her to accept an honorary doctorate of fine arts. It would be the only degree she had except for a high school diploma, and Georgia replied that she was very happily surprised, and would, indeed, return to the place where she had lived as an adolescent to receive it.

For the ceremony, in May 1938, three of her sisters also went back to the town where their parents had brought them with so many hopes at the turn of the century. Anita, who owned many of her sister's paintings, took the overnight train from New York to Virginia with Georgia. Ida and Claudia, who lived in New York City and New Jersey respectively, arrived a day later. (Claudia would move to California the next year and open up a nursery school there.) Alexius, who had had a bad heart, had died in 1930 at the age of thirty-seven, leaving a small daughter and a pregnant wife. After teaching school for almost half a century, Aunt Lola had recently died. Francis had divorced and left New York to practice architecture in Havana, where, in 1936, he married a well-born Cuban woman.

Georgia declined to give a speech, but she arranged for eight of her oils to be shown. (For the occasion, Mrs. John D. Rockefeller, Jr., whose husband had begun the renovation of historic Williamsburg a decade earlier, gave her *Magnolia Blossom* to the college.) After an academic procession across an elm-shaded lawn to the graceful Sir Christopher Wren building, Bryan, in his talk, claimed, "In this quiet atmosphere [O'Keeffe's] talents for vision and craftsmanship were first given an opportunity to mature."

The truth was that her talents had matured *despite* Williamsburg, since when she lived there only her brothers were permitted to attend the all-male college. And, if the "different" midwestern O'Keeffes had been censured in those earlier days, little had changed by 1938. In the eyes of college officials, Georgia appeared to be sallow, homely, and awkward compared to the powdered, rouged southern females. Since the artist thought little about clothes, for the ceremony she had selected only a slight variation of her daily black-and-white uniform— a plain skirt, silk blouse, corduroy vest, unadorned turban, and practical shoes, topped by a double-breasted reefer coat and a pouch purse. Her reserved manner, which did not come across as gracious, was an even more flagrant violation of the southern style. "She seemed strangely hostile to the honor and not moved by it," recalled Leslie Cheek, Jr., head of the art department at the time. "She seemed to be in some other world." Nevertheless, she enjoyed all the attention, seeing old Chatham classmates and Williamsburg neighbors, and the warm Virginian spring weather as well.

❖

In the late thirties, as a result of being so widely known, O'Keeffe was approached by a number of varied commercial firms. She was one of several dozen artists from throughout the world that Steuben Glass invited to do a design for them. Georgia drew a wide-open, delicate, detailed lily, which was then engraved by a copper wheel on the bottom of six large, low, translucent crystal bowls. These were priced to sell for five hundred dollars each. "Standing before [a bowl] one recalled, somehow, those silvery edges and that strange, veinous sensibility which one had always associated with the best of her work," observed Jerome Mellquist.

In the summer of 1938, the advertising agency N. W. Ayer asked O'Keeffe to be one of its series of artists whom they were having visit Hawaii as the guest of their client, Dole Pineapple Company. In exchange, she would present Dole with two paintings of Hawaii that it could use in its advertisements. After looking over some Hawaiian travel brochures, Georgia accepted the offer—perhaps because she was intrigued by the hundreds of flora specimens growing on the islands that existed nowhere else on earth. In early February 1939, her annual exhibition hung and Stieglitz left in the care of Margaret Prosser at the penthouse, she caught a train for the West Coast, then boarded a ship for Honolulu.

From Hawaii she wrote enthusiastic letters about a tropical paradise of strange rare blossoms and gigantic green foliage. She began to sightsee eagerly and to take in everything the islands had to offer—from the steaming fissures on the top of a cold, black volcano crater to the lovely, unusual white bird-of-paradise flower. Soon she was working steadily. She painted the yellow hibiscus with its forthright stamen, the white lotus, golden plumeria, the dramatic red heliconia, and even fishhooks—but no pineapples.

There was a good reason why. After Georgia had been in Honolulu for several weeks, she discovered Dole's pineapple fields on the other side of the island—"all sharp and silvery stretching for miles off to the beautiful irregular mountains," she remembered. "I was astonished— it was so beautiful." The following day she told the young advertising man, who was responsible for helping her get around, that she wanted to live in the workers' village on the edge of the pineapple fileds since it was too far a distance to drive to each day. But Dole, abiding by the rigid island social custom of keeping the classes separate, was not about to allow its New York visitor to live with its pineapple pickers. When the advertising man said no, that the village was only for the field workers, Georgia angrily retorted that she was a worker, too, and had the right to stay where she wished. Other sharp words were exchanged, but afterwards the young man tried to smooth things over by bringing the artist a pineapple. Georgia, however, called it "manhandled" and rejected it with disgust.

Soon thereafter, on the recommendation of friends of friends, Georgia left for the island of Maui, and the lush, undeveloped island turned out to be the place she enjoyed the most in Hawaii. She stayed in the isolated little seaport town of Hana on the edge of a rain forest full of bamboo and ferns. For a spell she also lived among the field hands on a sugar plantation, where the strong smell of sugar permeated the humid air. She liked to drive a banana wagon to a nearby three-tiered waterfall that cascaded down among dense vegetation into clear pools. She also visited the beautiful Iao Valley on the other side of the island, where she painted a black lava bridge and misty waterfalls. Four of her most successful Hawaiian paintings depicted thin ribbons of frothy water slicing through great black rock formations and massive velvety-green mountain valleys.

When she returned to New York after three months in Hawaii, she decided to give Dole a small oil of a red ginger flower as well as a painting of a green papaya tree. Dole replied that it was delighted with the first painting but not with the second—the papaya advertised a rival canning company's product—and asked for a picture of a pineapple instead. Had she known she had to paint a pinapple, Georgia growled in reply, she never would have accepted Dole's invitation. Meanwhile, N. W. Ayer art director Charles Coiner telephoned Honolulu and had a huge, budding pineapple plant shipped to Georgia's penthouse by air in thirty-six hours—not an easy feat at that time. Although the artist grumbled that this was no way to paint a pineapple, she admitted that the plant's long, spiky, green blades, with the fruit growing in the center, were surprisingly handsome. She subsequently painted a pineapple bud for Dole, and the company used it as well as various other O'Keeffes in its annual report and in national magazine advertisements.

Georgia's next exhibition contained paintings of the exotic Hawaiian botanical specimens, sometimes erratically spelled, in the O'Keeffe style. In her statement for the catalog, Georgia suggested that she felt somewhat inadequate in the face of nature's bountiful splendors. "What I have been able to put into form seems infinitesimal compared with the variety of experience," she wrote. She also implied that to digest the overpowering stimuli of Hawaii required far more time than she had taken, even though she had worked from drawings, memories, and mementos on her return. "It has to become a part of one's world, a part of what one has to speak with—one paints it slowly . . ." she wrote in part. "To formulate the new experience into something one has to say takes time. Maybe the new place enlarges one's world a little. Maybe one takes one's own world along and cannot see anything else." Although Henry McBride praised the show, saying that "the world is Georgia O'Keeffe's oyster," she must have known that the standard of her tropics paintings was not up to the level set by her desert ones. At any rate, she sold none of the paintings immediately, and she rarely exhibited them again.

While she was away, Stieglitz had been a bit wary, anticipating her enthusiasm for yet another new place, but he eagerly looked forward to seeing the Hawaiian pictures. Upon her return in April 1939, however, he was dismayed to find that she was exhausted, irritable, and tense. It was more than a reaction to the contretemps over a pineapple; she had trouble eating and sleeping and was tormented by continual severe headaches. All these symptoms were ominous reminders of what had preceded her breakdown six and a half years before. Evidently, after a year of constant moving about—New York, New Mexico, California, and Hawaii—her highly tuned nerves were wound too tight, her sensory circuits were overloaded, and her system short-circuited. In May her doctors ordered her to bed and forbade any travel to Lake George or New Mexico in the near future. By summer she was beginning to convalesce. She lay on a cot in the hot sun on the penthouse terrace, surrounded by the terrace's green hedge and white picket fence. As she got better, she took solitary walks at dawn around the sooty city, seeing only her doctor and Stieglitz, who refused to go to the lake without her.

It was during this period that Georgia—along with such luminaries as Eleanor Roosevelt and Helen Keller—was named one of the twelve most outstanding women of the last fifty years by a committee of the New York World's Fair. *Sunset, Long Island*, a picture she had painted of a fiery orb suspended over undulating dunes, was the one painting chosen to represent New York State at the fair. The recognition must have been gratifying to her, and Stieglitz's unwavering sympathy and support must have had a salutary, steadying effect. By the end of August 1939, she was strong enough to travel to Lake George, and by October she was painting again. Perhaps her relatively rapid recovery this time, in contrast to her long illness in 1933, owed something to the fact that by now she was the most famous, most successful woman painter in America.

11 ❖ Abiquiu

After recovering in the East from her exhausting trip to Hawaii, Georgia was in the mood to withdraw from exotic new worlds on her return to the Ghost Ranch in the summer of 1940. "Her" familiar wide valley, she found, was as wonderful as ever. When she discovered someone else living in Rancho de los Burros—the house she felt to be rightfully hers—she offered to buy it from the Packs.

They were willing to sell because it was too isolated to be easily rented out. The subsequent deed, dated October 30, 1940, noted that Georgia's nearly eight acres were bounded on the north, west, and south by the Pack ranchland, and on the east by the Carson National Forest—all areas, she believed, that were likely to remain undeveloped because of their aridity. She was rumored to have acquired her desert ranch for six thousand dollars—the price of one important O'Keeffe oil. But whatever its exact cost, she realized that it was only a fraction of its real worth. It had been solidly built in 1933 out of eight-by-fourteen-inch mud-and-straw bricks, and had hand-carved lintels and other fine details. More importantly, Georgia liked the feeling that now something was settled, that she was able always to return to the place she loved the most. That summer she painted pictures of the first home she had ever owned—one of these, tenderly done, showed a slab of adobe wall, patio post, and chimney.

Once the house was hers, she had the iron gate dismantled, a wall or two knocked out to make a large studio, some little rooms added, and high, narrow fireplaces built. The viga, or beamed, ceilings were painted white. As with every environment she had created, in this one, too, everything was subordinated to the view. By 1943 walls in every room had been broken through and replaced by huge panes of glass. Her bedroom had entire walls of glass to the north and to the west. Georgia had always wanted a home that was made without wood and contained only functional kitchen furniture, and now her dream house was realized. With satisfaction, she told visitors, to whom the house looked like a monastery, that it had only those things she was unable to exist without. "I think a house should just be a shelter," she once remarked in a friend's beautiful home. After a few years the rooms still had little more than massive wood work tables, plain white cotton curtains and bedspreads, muted Navajo rugs, and an occasional bright red pillow or two. Everywhere were displayed her precious bones, rocks, shells, feathers, pine cones, and desert driftwood—treasures she enjoyed knowing no one valued as much as she.

In the patio, the heart of the U-shaped house, she let seeds of wild grama grass, gray-green sagebrush, and jimsonweed sprout. Believing that mankind could not improve on nature, she allowed them to grow their own ways. However, at one time, she neatly surrounded the jimson, a poisonous weed with an evening-blooming white blossom that she liked to paint, with pieces of red rock. Birds built nests in the overhanging shelter of the roof, and lizards and snakes sunned motionless on the tree stumps she had placed in the patio for seating.

When she had first summered in the house three years earlier, she had continued to eat many of her meals at the main ranch house, albeit with the help. Now, however, she began to take the extra effort of keeping house in order to maintain her cherished privacy. It was no easy job. Water had to be pumped and there was no electricity. The soil was too poor for a garden, so it was necessary to drive eighty miles over the bad, deserted road to Espanola and back for canned fruits and vegetables, or one hundred and forty miles to Santa Fe and back for fresh produce.

Sometimes even those trips were impossible to make and she was completely—and dangerously—isolated in the valley without a telephone. After summer cloudbursts, waterfalls were likely to pour down the sheer rock face of the cliffs behind her house and to roar in flash floods down the arroyos and drainage ditches, turning them into raging rivers. Sometimes the road was flooded and an auto could not get out or within a half mile of her house for several days until the waters receded. There was also the excellent chance of being bitten by a rattlesnake here, many miles from a hospital's antivenom supply. Still, Georgia disliked killing the cold-blooded creatures, and, when the one or two that lived around the house crawled onto the warm stones of a fireplace, she learned to pick them up with a shovel and toss them outside the patio. When acquaintances in New York expressed surprise that an artist was able to cope with such difficulties, O'Keeffe explained with a great deal of pride that she came from people who worked with their hands.

Yet she realized that she needed to hire someone to help with the time-consuming domestic chores so that she could be left free to paint. In 1940 she lunched at the Alcalde valley ranch of Mary Wheelwright, a Cabot from Boston—a tall, tweedy spinster in her sixties who owned at least one of Georgia's paintings. There she met Maria Chabot, a husky brown-eyed Texan in her twenties who ranched for Miss Wheelwright. Soon Georgia hired Maria to work for her. Maria, greatly admiring the way the artist lived, and sharing her sense of independence and love for the region, felt a strong personal bond. Fascinated by Georgia's work, Maria would later travel to New York and Chicago in the winter to see her exhibitions. In the summers, the capable younger woman cooked, cleaned, shopped, and cared for the riding horses that had been acquired for the season and for their several untamed Siamese kittens that had been adopted as pets. When Georgia bought a battery-powered generator, Maria was the one to start the unreliable machine after dark. Although Georgia was likely to scrub the kitchen floor at night when she was unable to sleep or to spend a day grinding wheat and baking bread, she was now generally free to paint prodigiously for eleven or twelve hours a day.

When the painting light had faded, the two women liked to ride the horses up into the high wild places that were inaccessible by car or by foot. Maria's fearless, youthful spirit tended to embolden Georgia, who was now in her fifties. Other times they drove to places where a sudden waterfall had been created by a downpour, or they camped overnight to watch a hot sunset and pale dawn illuminate a particular mesa. They also camped near the village of Abiquiu among strange grayish-white formations of ancient lava ash, which, beginning in

1940, Georgia was to paint many times, in both sunlight and shadow, calling it "the White Place."

A few years before, she had seen some dark hills marked by sandy striations—about a hundred and fifty miles drive northwest of the ranch into Navajo country. "Those hills!" she recalled afterwards. "They go on and on—it was like looking at two miles of gray elephants." It was also like looking at wonderful, natural abstract forms to her. Her eye was excited by what she saw as rolling black and silvery shapes with veins of white, pink, and gold undulating across them. The dry, desolate region contained nothing nourishing for the human body, Georgia later observed, only aesthetics for the soul—and she began to call it "the Black Place."

Georgia and Maria used to load up the station wagon with logs, water cans, food, canvas, rope, cots, tools, tubes of paint and an easel, and even the cat, and set out for the gray hills. After the dirt road ended, they inched along dry stream beds where autos had never gone before. While Maria drove, Georgia walked ahead to point the way or to tell her to brake when they had to stop to shovel sand, chop sage, or roll rocks out of the way of the wheels. They continued in this tortuous way beyond the last Navajo hogan, into the heart of what they called the "Blackness," and camped by some old cedars. After exploring the hills a bit, Georgia would begin to paint. When the weather was hot, she had to pause to drink water and to lie in the shade for a while. Once, when it was cold, she painted with gloves on and sat with her feet on a little rug. Occasionally the wind violently flapped the bandanna she tied over her hair, shook her easel, and blew her chair over when she stood up. They ate dinner at sunset, sometimes roasting venison wrapped in bacon on long sticks over the fire.

Georgia eventually painted the gray hills as often as the red ones. In the winter of 1942 she exhibited three early versions of the region— soft, unfocused, realistic gray and white hills, balanced between a bit of blue sky and tan earth. Then, a few years later, she painted the taut, masterful *Black Place III*, a play of sharp vertical zigzags and flowing horizontal forms—in dead black, snowy white, and blood red— hovering on the edge of abstraction. Five years after that, she interpreted the same shapes in pink and green. Maria used to wonder if the people who admired O'Keeffe's elegant, enamel-smooth oils ever imagined the sun, rain, wind, dust, and mud the two endured so they could be created.

Despite the hardships of living there, Georgia said in old age that all the associations with the ranch house added up to "a kind of freedom." Perhaps that was because it gave her the solitude she craved—even her mailbox on the lonely road two miles away did not have her name on it. One of her first summers at this house she noted with satisfaction that her only visitors were those who made a great effort to see her. When friends did find her, however, they usually stayed for a night or two or even longer. In the autumn of 1940, for instance she had the entertaining company of William Einstein, who had fled Paris ahead of the Nazi armies. At the ranch Einstein marveled at the mood of "excited peace" in Georgia's home.

O'Keeffe relished the feeling that she was far from the war in Europe. At this time, before the United States had entered the Second World War, she felt safe from aggressive armies because, she thought, no one would possibly be interested in her empty New Mexico valley. Dressed simply, in an old hand-sewn dress of soft red homespun cotton or wrapped in a green or a red shawl, Georgia seemed to friends to be a pillar of steady strength in a world gone mad. Finally, in November 1940, after the chamisa bushes along the roadside had turned golden and the wild purple asters had bloomed, she tore herself away from her creative, calm existence and returned to New York.

A year later, on December 7, 1941, the Japanese bombed Pearl Harbor and America entered the war. It did so in a mood of grim resignation, in contrast to the patriotic flag-waving spirit with which it had entered the First World War. At Ghost Ranch the following summer, in 1942, life became even more difficult. Ranch hands were drafted, so there were fewer men to do the hard manual labor. Since gasoline was rationed and had to be measured drop by drop in the isolated valley, horses became a necessity for getting around. Butter and meat coupons also had to be counted carefully. Although Georgia had felt far from the war only the year before, she soon suspected that it was uncomfortably close when FBI agents began snooping around the ranch. Then, after Arthur Pack received a security clearance, mysterious men who could be asked no questions began to arrive for weekends of rest from the Los Alamos atomic research laboratory forty miles away.

In the spring of 1942, the University of Wisconsin had offered O'Keeffe an honorary Doctor of Letters degree along with General Douglas MacArthur, the commander of the Pacific forces, who was stationed in Australia. Having been severely criticized in Texas for her lukewarm attitude toward war in 1917, Georgia was surprised that she was selected for the honor. In her letter of acceptance, the Wisconsin native daughter wrote university administrators that she was hopeful about America when an artist was honored alongside a general during wartime. She frankly said that to continue along on one's own path, when it was not part of the war effort, took a great deal of courage and conviction in oneself. Citing wartime shipping problems, she declined to send any paintings to Madison for the occasion.

A few minutes before the commencement ceremony, she was waiting at the entrance of the university field house for her aunt Ollie. Still an imperious, spry old lady at eighty-seven, Ollie was immensely proud of the niece she had helped get through art school. The governor of Wisconsin strolled by while O'Keeffe was waiting, and, noticing her, thought she looked small and alone as well as a little abandoned. In his speech, he joked—much to O'Keeffe's irritation—about "poor little Georgia O'Keeffe," who had been forced to find her way to the ceremony by herself. Again, as before, when she had received an honorary degree in Williamsburg, she was misunderstood and patronized by the officials. Nevertheless, she graciously shook hands with old neighbors and relatives at the reception afterwards, and even with her old Sun Prairie schoolteacher, Mrs. Zed Edison.

❖

Since their first meeting in Taos in 1929, Daniel Catton Rich had thought that O'Keeffe's talent was a marvelously original one, and had watched her career continue to develop. By the time he ran into her again in 1942 at a big party at the New York home of a prominent art dealer, he was the curator of painting at the Art Institute of Chicago, with a knack for attracting fine exhibitions. Rich and O'Keeffe sat down on a sofa together and began to talk about the natural world of New Mexico, a subject she warmed to. He described her enthusiasm for it: "Her eyes shine, she sits forward on her chair, the words pour forth and that full creative electricity which for twenty-five years has animated her art becomes suddenly apparent." They also talked about painting, and Rich ventured that it would be nice if Chicago could have an O'Keeffe show. Georgia was silent a moment and then, to his surprise, replied that she thought so too. They agreed to meet the next day and talk about it more.

Rich's subsequent announcement that the Art Institute of Chicago would present O'Keeffe's first big retrospective was considered a coup by the art world. Legend had it that Stieglitz would never allow her to have an important show outside An American Place. Undoubtedly, the subject must have been a delicate one for Georgia to broach to him because, at his advanced age of seventy-nine, he would not even be able to see the exhibition. Perhaps she pointed out that John Marin and other artists who had been under his wing had had museum shows, or that it would be valuable for her to see twice as many of her paintings hung together than it was possible for Stieglitz to show in his small quarters. Maybe she reminded him that the Institute was the Midwest's most prestigious museum and that it had included her work in two group shows. At any rate, he approved without a fuss on the condition that the museum buy an important painting and that O'Keeffe be allowed to hang her own show. It was agreed that Stieglitz would show the newest O'Keeffes in New York as usual after the Chicago exhibit. (He had the pleasure of exhibiting a delicate feather series—containing, for example, a picture of two white feathers on a coral ground.)

When Georgia arrived in Chicago in January 1943, her friends Narcissa and Clinton King (she had painted *Narcissa's Last Orchid* in 1940) feted her with a dinner of chili and beans, and then she set to work. She was unhappy with the pale violet walls in the three East Gallery rooms set aside for her exhibition, and she also disliked the lighting and the way the protective glass on her paintings reflected the light. First she insisted that the gallery walls be painted white— and then there were other demands. Three days later, most of her paintings still rested on little rubber floor mats, propped against the wall, waiting to be hung.

O'Keeffe's painstaking way with her paintings be came a topic of amused conversation at the museum. *Chicago Tribune* reporter Marcia Winn claimed that she heard the artist say to herself in a quiet voice, while gazing at her picture of the Lawrence tree, "You know, I look so nice at home in New Mexico. I do look well on an adobe. I'm always surprised at how well I look against it." Clearly, O'Keeffe identified so closely with her art, the reporter observed with humor, that she seemed to confuse her pronouns. When another reporter asked one afternoon, "Miss O'Keeffe, may I see you for a moment?" she gestured at her paintings, smiled playfully, and joked, "Of course, just look around." Marcia Winn, who described Georgia as handsome enough herself to put on display ("exquisite coin-like beauty, done almost in pale sepia, and brown hair wound around in a cornoet"), bantered, "If you were hanging yourself, you'd be meticulous too."

On the fifth day of work, the first painting went up. Small but wiry and strong, Georgia moved with a gliding grace over the highly polished museum floors in her flat shoes, easily carrying heavy paintings, some of which were weighted with metal frames. Daniel Rich had flung off his jacket and he raced around, in a blue shirt with a yellow tie, trying to help and eager to do as she wished. Finally, the combination of strain and the gray wintery weather proved too much for her. A few days before the scheduled opening, Georgia came down with a bad cold and took to bed in the Blackstone Hotel, where she was staying. The snowdrifts piled up along Michigan Avenue where the massive, marble Art Institute stood, and the preview dinner went on in her honor, without her.

On January 31, 1943, sixty-one O'Keeffes went on display in the museum where, in 1905, Georgia had been a dutiful art student. The pictures ranged from a 1915 charcoal to *Turkey Feathers and Indian Pot*, done in 1941. To Chicago viewers the clear, clean, luminous colors of her flowers, fruits, landscapes, and bones glowing in the white galleries were wonderfully refreshing in the midst of wartime. "Find the abstraction which is filled with lovely green running from dark to light, with cream and pale pink balancing its beauty, and you will find it hard not to remember the poet's admonition—'beauty is its own excuse for being,'" wrote one reviewer. Not every critic raved about her work, but "If you like her work, you love it," observed Marcia Winn, and "If you don't, you can't forget it." With characteristic self-confidence, O'Keeffe knew that her exhibit was a good one, regardless of how it was received, and, furthermore, insisted that the museum had the obligation to buy one of her paintings. Acceding, the museum chose *Black Cross, New Mexico*, painted in 1929.

For the catalog Rich wrote a long, perceptive essay about the artist that included more biographical facts about her than had ever been published before, but she seemed to trust him to get it right. Like many other people, he found it difficult to separate her art from her life. "Seen in the whole her art betrays a perfect consistency," he wrote. "It has undergone no marked changes of style but has moved outward from its center. In over a quarter of a century of painting, O'Keeffe has only grown more herself."

❖

Georgia was already a highly professional, successful artist when she arrived in New Mexico at the age of forty-one. Consequently, she shunned the regional art galleries and museums, including the state Museum of Fine Arts in Santa Fe. In the forties, the museum's directors favored sentimental western art and indiscriminately hung the work of almost every taxpayer who wished to exhibit—sometimes as many as seventy or eighty artists a year. Georgia ignored most of the other artists in the state and was quoted by fellow artists as saying that of the hundreds of painters in New Mexico, only three were any good— Andrew Dasburg, Cady Wells, and she. (Born the same year as she, Dasburg had studied at the Art Students League and in 1930 moved to Taos, where he did his Cubist-inspired landscapes; Wells, his student and a friend of Georgia's, also painted fine landscapes.)

Georgia also thought that her craft standards were higher than those of others. Painter Raymond Jonson never forgot the day she walked into his Santa Fe art supply store in 1943 complaining about the generally poor quality of stretchers, and asked whether any of his were straight. Jonson took down most of his rack of two hundred or so stretchers so she could measure each one alongside the door frame. Finally, she found eight that passed her scrutiny.

She was openly, unabashedly proud of her own work. "I still like the way I see things best," she once said to critic Ralph Flint as they left New York's Metropolitan Museum, and the remark was published in *Town and Country*. Naturally, New Mexican artists both resented her aloofness and envied her success. Their attitude was reflected in an article published in *The Santa Fean* magazine in 1941, in which her ambition was obliquely criticized but it was also conceded that "her originality is so great that even if she made a painting of a black piece of paper it would be exciting." But, the story goes, when someone suggested to the state museum director that O'Keeffe paint a Federal Arts Project mural for the museum's St. Francis auditorium, he firmly rejected the prospect of having "some so-called woman artist's bone-littered landscape" on the walls. "I'm loved," O'Keeffe remarked to a reporter in 1943, "but I suspect I'm hated in the same proportion."

She rarely deviated now from her orderly painting life, emerging from it mainly to tend to tasks of daily life. "When you work as I work, what you do is your pleasure," she said to an interviewer in 1945. Her life was bounded by the shifting hours of sunrise and sunset, and organized to provide long stretches of solitude that she shaped to her painterly rhythm. "Now we'll go out and watch the thunderstorm," she used to announce to visitors in such a way that no one dared object, as one visitor, writer Christopher Isherwood, recalled. Then they would sit in chairs on her roof for hours—"as if at a theatrical performance," he said—watching the boiling black clouds and jagged lightning bolts in the distance.

Interruptions were also sometimes allowed for the dozen or so friends she saw from time to time. She cultivated her friendship with painter Cady Wells, a charming, amusing man from a wealthy Massachusetts family who didn't work nearly hard enough, she thought. Once in a while Dorothy Brett drove down for the night and, on Georgia's ever rarer trips to Taos, she liked to stay with Beck Strand, who was by then remarried to Colorado gentleman rancher Bill James. "I know I am unreasonable about people, but there are so many wonderful people whom *I can't take the time to know*," she tried to explain to her gregarious old friend Anita Pollitzer.

These were the years when, her fame having reached a pinnacle, O'Keeffe's sense of her own worth was solidifying into a steely protective armor against unwelcome distractions and intrusions. She believed that her art and, by extension, she herself had absolute rights, and she seemed oddly unaware of the havoc this self-centered attitude could cause in others. For instance, she valued Maria Chabot, and had named a painting of two pink flowers that she did in 1942 *Maria Goes to a Party*. But when the young woman began to act in a possessive manner and to make some of her own demands, Georgia informed her that she was dismissed, even though Maria had worked for her for five summers at the ranch during the difficult war years. Georgia then hired a more compliant Spanish girl to take Maria's place.

Sometimes Georgia asked in little Wayne McKinley, son of the Packs' governess and their former wrangler, who used to ride past her house for the Pack mail each day during the war. But, inexplicably, O'Keeffe made his sister and the older children wait unhappily outside.

"Georgia O'Keeffe lives there," a Ghost Ranch cowboy used to tell riders, waving in the direction of her house and cautioning them to stay on the trail. "She has a shotgun—and she uses it." Georgia was probably amused by the warning, but a shotgun wasn't necessary. She knew how to tongue-lash celebrity hunters and other strangers "with a firmness and a finality that left them gasping," recalled Arthur Pack.

In 1935, upon first meeting Georgia, Phoebe Pack had walked right up to her and, in her youthful naiveté, had stuck out her hand and said, "Hi, Georgia!" It got their relationship off to a good start because, as Phoebe later learned, O'Keeffe often snubbed people who were awed by her. Even so, Phoebe found out that their self-sufficient, prickly neighbor was the hardest person to get along with she had ever known. Once, she recalled, Georgia spotted a large cake in the kitchen of the dude ranch. "I'd like that cake," she suddenly demanded, saying that it was her young housekeeper's birthday. When Phoebe said no and explained that the cake was for the twenty-five guests, Georgia stomped off in a rage, leaving Phoebe stunned by her presumption.

The world out of which O'Keeffe's art emerged contained no imperfect, boring, bothersome human beings. Henry McBride jokingly suggested in a review he wrote in 1941 that when she painted her southwestern "heaven," Georgia should paint some steel bars across the blue sky to keep any intruders out.

In the summer of 1943 she found a perfect pelvic bone in the mountains. She took great delight in its curious, convoluted shape and the oval hole in it, and eventually hung it as a mobile in her home. One day she impulsively held the ring of bone up to look at it—"in the sun against the sky as one is apt to do when one seems to have more sky than earth in one's world"—and suddenly saw a painting to be done. She painted the bone up close, the way she painted blossoms, sometimes from the front, sometimes from the side, and once like the curved wing of a great gull. The bony frame often acted as a telescope—focusing the eye on the endlessly receding void of sky, or what the artist termed "the blue hole." In a burst of imagination and creative energy, she rapidly painted the hollow socket with her familiar motifs—the Pedernal, flowers, the moon—trying the new shape with the old ones. And, as if unable to let the image go, she painted the pelvis red against a blue sky—and then, in the same year that atom bombs were exploded over Hiroshima and Nagasaki, she intuitively painted a fiery red bone in a hot yellow sky.

When she exhibited her pelvis paintings for the first time in 1944, they were greeted by a round of applause from viewers used to her barbaric symbols. Death was more than mere decay, she seemed to be saying. McBride, who called a pelvis picture with the moon her best picture ever, warned readers that, in the apolitical artist's mind, these were not "war pictures," just abstract forms. Nevertheless, they were interpreted as her wartime statement about bloodshed, because in an earnest essay for her catalog, in which she was trying to explain why she painted what she called "the Bones and the Blue," she confirmed the view that the pictures were painted with an awareness of world war raging around her. She wrote that she found the bones "most wonderful against the Blue—that Blue that will always be there as it is now after all man's destruction is finished."

As Georgia approached the age of sixty, people remarked more and more often on her many strong "masculine" qualities: her driving ambition, immense self-confidence, uncompromising will, intimidating presence, and her absorption in work. Stieglitz explained that she gave herself completely in her painting. Indeed, she had never lived the typical life of so many women—that of devotion to men and children. Her longing for a baby was now so buried that friends were sure that she had never wanted one, that her direction as an artist had always been clear and steady. Yet, as if a source of feeling had been severed, some of the paintings she did in the dry desert seemed sapless and rigid. There was a startling contrast between the soft, undulating pink and blue voids she created when she began to live with Stieglitz and the empty pelvic birth canal surrounded by brittle bone that she did twenty years later.

Not surprisingly, Georgia had little in common with most women and began to say she preferred the company of men. When one of her young male friends married, she was often noticeably disappointed in the bride. Scornful of traditional sex roles, in 1942 she wrote an endorsement for the National Woman's Party, which was still trying to get an equal rights amendment passed. Influenced by the example of the matriarchs in her own family, she believed that females were often more competent than males. Consequently, she felt disappointed by the inertia of her own gender in overcoming upbringings that trained them to be dependent. "I think it's pretty funny that women have always been treated like Negroes in this country and they don't even know it," she told a reporter in old age. "Even when you tell them, they won't listen." She had little respect for females who seemed fussy or silly to her, and she was likely to ignore or criticize them, and complain when their spike heels punctured her pounded dirt floors, for instance. Once, in 1940, when Dave McAlpin, Ansel Adams, and Beaumont Newhall were at her apartment in New York, they all impulsively decided to go to the nearby World's Fair. "Let me call Nancy," said Newhall, thinking his wife might enjoy going. "Oh, that won't be necessary," Georgia replied quickly, rejecting the idea.

❖

For many years, Georgia had been curious about an abondoned hacienda in the village of Abiquiu, a secretive hilltop hamlet that was sixteen miles from the ranch and completely hidden from the road. One day, after doing some shopping in Abiquiu's little general store, she climbed into the ruin through a hole in the wall that had been made by a fallen tree. Inside, she discovered the remains of a large garden, a patio with a well, a dilapidated house with a collapsing viga roof, dangling handhewn wooden doors, and adobe walls that were crumbling back to dust. She also saw a door in a long patio wall that intrigued her for reasons she never really understood.

Georgia inquired whether the Chavez property was for sale. Old man Chavez said something about wanting to turn it into a motel, then offered it to her. But this was before she had purchased her house at Ghost Ranch, and she thought the price he quoted was too high for the broken-down ruin. (She later learned that in 1826 a previous owner had acquired it for two cows—one of them with calf—a bushel of corn, and a serape.) When Jose Chavez reduced the price a few years later, Georgia was buying the ranch house instead. Shortly thereafter Chavez died and his son sold it to the Catholic church for one dollar. The church, in turn, allowed the Abiquiu Cooperative Livestock Association to use it to house the village pigs and cows.

In the early forties, having become tired of wilted and canned food, Georgia decided again that she needed the Chavez property for its water rights and garden. Because of the large age difference between Stieglitz and herself, she had in the back of her mind as well the realization that she had to prepare for a second life totally on her own.

Finally, she was still fascinated by the interplay of spaces between the door and the wall in the villa. The idea of living in two homes was not unthinkable to her since she had migrated seasonally between two places for years. It had started as early as 1912, when she taught in Texas and Virginia, and had continued throughout her New York/Lake George years. The fact that the Abiquiu house was only a few miles from Ghost Ranch was unimportant, Georgia pointed out to those who were puzzled, because one home overlooked a green river valley and the other stood amid a rosy, rocky landscape.

It also didn't deter her that the Abiquiu townspeople were of an alien culture and suspicious of her, and that the tiny village contained little more than a run-down church, several unmarked Penitente *moradas*, and a couple of bars. Two centuries before, the town had been an Indian farming pueblo. Then other Indians, who had acquired a veneer of Spanish culture as the conquerors' slaves, migrated to Abiquiu and intermarried with Spanish settlers there. There remained by the forties fewer than five hundred of their descendants, who still spoke their own Spanish dialect. A blacksmith and a butcher were among them, but most of the people were farmers or shepherds. The only Anglo was Martin Bode, a German who had married into a local family, and who was both Abiquiu's postmaster and storekeeper.

O'Keeffe began to badger the Catholic church to sell her the Chavez property, in the belief that if she wanted something badly enough, she would be able to get it. She was right. The house, surrounded by three acres of land, became hers on December 31, 1945, reportedly for ten dollars. The crumbling structure—part pueblo, part villa, part stock shed and pigpen in five different buildings—was bounded by the road from Espanola to Ghost Ranch on one side, by what the deed termed the Abiquiu pueblo on another, and on the other side an *arroyito* called El Ojito del Muerto ("the little eye of death") and a livestock corral.

Needing someone to oversee the house's renovation, she managed to persuade the previously rebuffed Maria Chabot to do it. (She later gave her a pelvis picture for her labors.) While the work was going on, O'Keeffe used to visit the site on horseback and camp there to take in the view. The renovation was a difficult job since most of the nails and boards in the area were going into the building of the Los Alamos atomic research center. O'Keeffe had raw wood brought from the mountains and managed to get some kegs of nails through her architect brother. Adobe bricks were made for the few feet added here and there to improve the building's proportions. Walls two feet thick were broken through and large panes of glass installed. Fireplaces were built in every room, and an ancient pueblo ceremonial cooking room was restored to its original state. Since she disliked furniture, Georgia had adobe benches built into the long walls of the living room. In the small dining room, a low window was created to overlook a tiny patio shaded by parallel viga poles. When the house was ready to be plastered, local workmen mixed mounds of brown mud and carried it to women who stroked it on by hand in the traditional manner, giving the pinkish, uneven, rounded walls the look of human skin. "Every inch has been smoothed by a woman's hand," Georgia remarked about the house, enjoying the way its textured softness looked against the hard desert sky.

Although O'Keeffe claimed she didn't buy the property for its hilltop view, she took good advantage of it in her large studio and small adjoining bedroom. Large sheets of glass were placed so as to overlook the tall green grass and the gentle graceful line of cottonwood trees along the river, and, off in the distance, multi-colored mesas. When she entered her new all-white studio, Georgia gazed down, as if from a mountaintop, at the sweeping expanse of the Chama River valley.

While the work was going on, she was sometimes impatient at its slowness, and other times acted tremendously pleased with the way the house was taking shape. She did not want her mud villa to be Spanish, Indian, or contemporary in character, but, rather, her own style. "I wanted to make it *my* house, but I'll tell you the dirt resists you," she would say. "It is very hard to make the earth your own." When the house was finished three years later in 1948, she called it a pleasant carapace that fit her precisely. Her friends, however, thought of the rambling assortment of eight rooms, patios, courtyards, passageways, and a garage as her private pueblo. To the villagers, it looked like a huge fortress that commanded Abiquiu's best view.

❖

Georgia continued to live the life of a Persephone, spending half the year in the bright southwestern summer and the other half in a dark New York winter. During the war, city life seemed to distress her more than usual. Manhattan was no longer the brilliantly lit, visually exciting place that she had painted in the twenties. Due to air-raid drills, its neon signs were often switched off and its skyscraper windows were blackened over. Sounding just like Stieglitz, Georgia heatedly told a reporter in 1945 that few Americans were interested in art: "What our civilization is interested in is how much they can make out of it and how fast they can make it go."

She seldom went out socially or ate in restaurants anymore, and only occasionally went to a movie as a Bates method exercise for her eyes. She saw a few people—like artist Maude Clapp and her husband, Frederick, the director of the Frick Collection. Several of her friends, including Florine Stettheimer, died in this period. She took refuge in long hours of painting, and, although she had long complained that New York was a "paralyzing" place in which to work and that she was often ill there, she did a few of her finest desert still lifes in the city. Perhaps nostalgia added to the intensity of these pictures. Eventually, she spent only four months or so in New York—around the time of her yearly shows.

She was also still returning each winter for Stieglitz's sake. Fewer tensions existed between them now, and she told a friend, "We always agree about the important things." Yet Stieglitz still felt desolate when she left each spring, so she once sardonically named a 1944 pastel of two shiny stones *My Heart*, because, she later explained with a little smile, "I thought they looked hard." But, finally, when Stieglitz's health had declined to such a point that it took all of his strength to simply sit up in a chair, she was dismayed. She wrote Henry McBride:

> I see Alfred as an old man that I am very fond of—grow-
> ing older—so that it sometimes shocks and startles me
> when he looks particularly pale and tired. . . . Aside
> from my fondness for him personally I feel that he has
> been very important to something that has made my
> world for me—I like it that I can make him feel that I
> have hold of his hand to steady him as he goes on.

When she would indicate a readiness to delay her departure, however, Stieglitz would tell her to go so she could return with new paintings and the strength for another New York winter. "How can I be jealous of a place?" he would ask rhetorically. Once he remarked to a friend that O'Keeffe's health came before his feelings because out of her vitality came her paintings. "Incredible, just incredible," he used to mutter when he saw her new paintings. Because he was more reconciled to her absences than a decade earlier, there was room for tenderness in his feelings for the woman whose uniqueness still amazed and charmed him. Even before she had left New York in the spring, he would mail her a letter that would be awaiting her arrival in Abiquiu. "O'Keeffe is *beautiful*," he told a visitor to the gallery in late 1945. "She is beautiful in every respect."

In the uncertain months after the United States had entered World War II, Georgia began to look for another apartment. She wanted a place with a bedroom for Stieglitz that was small enough to be kept warm by an electric heater should wartime fuel rationing make that necessary. She also wanted the apartment to be nearer An American Place so that if taxis became scarce, he would be able to walk there. Since Stieglitz loathed change, she searched for rooms as similar to the penthouse as possible. On October 1, 1942, after six years in the penthouse, they moved into a smaller, cheaper apartment that met Georgia's requirements. It was at 59 East Fifty-fourth Street, a block away from An American Place.

Unlike the other places she had picked, this one had no view. And without rugs, draperies, or lampshades it had a tentative, temporary, forlorn feeling. One table held an unetched crystal Steuben bowl. Usually, a lone picture hung over the mantel—a muted O'Keeffe or a little Dove, often *Rain*, Dove's tranquil gray collage of willow twigs, flecks of mirror, and rubber cement raindrops. "My home is simple, but I aim to make it simpler!" Georgia exclaimed defensively to one surprised visitor as she sat on the black sofa that blended in with her well-cut black suit and dramatized her white cuffs and strong, scrubbed, gesturing hands. Another caller, in May 1946, noticed a low white bowl holding two withered white tulips and one wide-open yellow one whose petals were about to drop. "I couldn't throw away the white ones for fear of disturbing it," Georgia explained, with her unusual reasoning, as she poured Mexican tea from a plain white teapot. "Tulips so often die so beautifully."

On the first day of 1944 Stieglitz had turned eighty. Because of his weak heart, he was now unable to walk more than very short distances. He only left the apartment to go to his post at An American Place on the days he was able to get out of bed. He would walk alone down Madison Avenue on those mornings, his black cloak draped over his frail frame and his old hat sitting on his wispy white hair—the clothes of his student days in Berlin and the happiest time of his life, he liked to say a bit bitterly, before he tried to do battle for "Art" in ignorant America. He clung to the same convictions Georgia had first heard him express in 1908, and flashes of his former self returned when he would begin articulating them. He was susceptible to mood swings—despondent one moment and elated the next—the gloominess deepened by the fact that the United States was once again at war with Germany. However, Georgia observed, "He was one of those people who enjoyed their gloom, but you could make him laugh about it."

With his undimmed dark eyes and pale translucent skin, he now looked "more saint than satyr," noted his old friend Lewis Mumford. His delight in chocolate ice cream cones and petulance when faced with a plate of vegetables for lunch made him seem a touch infantile at times. As he made his way to the gallery, deep in his own thoughts, he was oblivious to the stares of passersby, who undoubtedly saw an eccentric old man.

By the forties Marsden Hartley had left the circle and Stieglitz exhibited only Marins, Doves, and O'Keeffes. The pictures of the faithful few were also displayed in his tiny office—often Dove's charming little *A Blue Jay Flew Up a Tree*, Marin's wash of a seagull and a rough green sea under a leaden gray sky, and O'Keeffe's riveting *Black Abstraction*. In addition to these, he was surrounded, in his office, by his books, a cluttered desk, a sensuous marble female torse by Lachaise, and sometimes a red flower in a water glass. When one of the shows of the loyal three opened, he still resided over it—"an ancient prophet with white hair and dark, burning, searching eyes [who] would stand guard over the latest creations of his friends . . . as if to protect them from defilement," recalled his longtime patron Duncan Phillips.

Few people visited An American Place anymore, however, and Stieglitz sardonically called the silent rooms "my tomb." "I have been deserted," he used to say. "The paintings on the walls are orphans." European artists like Marc Chagall, Max Ernst, and Fernand Léger, who had fled Europe and come to New York during the war, did not seek out the old man who had first exhibited the work of their compatriots in America. Alone in his cubbyhole that smelled of disinfectant like a sickroom, Stieglitz often dozed on his cot, covered by his heavy cape and warmed by an electric heater. When friends did venture up to see him—often at Georgia's suggestion—he was sometimes too weak to rise. He used to tell callers despondently that his life had been wasted, often bemoaning Eastman Kodak's advertising campaign, which "degraded" his profession by promoting its camera with the slogan "You push the button and we'll do the rest."

Georgia continued to leave gallery business to him, even though he was more unpredictable than ever with collectors. In the midthirties when Maggie Johnson wanted to buy for her bedroom one of the blue morning glories Georgia had painted at Ghost Ranch, Georgia directed her to Stieglitz. He paced back and forth lecturing her until, finally, he said that although she was not able to have a baby she *could* have an O'Keeffe—for "only" fifteen thousand dollars! (Maggie left the gallery empty-handed.)

O'Keeffe didn't interfere even when, in spring 1946, a dozen unframed Marin watercolors were stolen and when, in March, her painting *The Cliffs* vanished from the gallery, followed by the disappearance a few weeks later of two other pictures of hers. Georgia didn't mention the loss of these two to Stieglitz despite the fact that her old friend Alina Weiner had bought one of them, had left it at the gallery for framing, and was skeptical of Georgia's story about "losing" it (an incident that may have injured their friendship). "I listened to so much talk about the Marins and when my first picture was taken, I wasn't going to listen any more," she explained long afterwards. She continued to focus on painting, realizing it was good fortune rather than businesslike representation that enabled her to earn a living from sales of her pictures, which Stieglitz priced around three or four thousand dollars apiece. Perhaps her nonchalance derived from the fact that she had earned enough money to buy two homes in New Mexico in six years and so she was clearly not in financial distress.

Shortly after O'Keeffe's Chicago retrospective, the Museum of Modern Art offered her another major exhibit in New York. This was the first such show for a woman painter at the Modern, although a memorial show to Florine Stettheimer would open a few months afterwards. It was much more difficult for Stieglitz to accept this show than the one in Chicago, but after a struggle of wills, Georgia agreed to the big exhibition even though it would be at a museum that Stieglitz still eyed skeptically and that was only a block and a half from her "home" at An American Place. Despite the fact that he had displayed fourteen new O'Keeffes prior to the opening of the museum show, the event made Stieglitz melancholy. He was satisfied that he had brought the gifts of the girl from Texas before the world and convinced it to recognize them, but he felt eclipsed and knew that there was nothing more he was able to do for her.

The invitation to the Modern's preview was graced by a reproduction of O'Keeffe's *Blue Lines*, the 1916 watercolor that for Stieglitz had always symbolized the potential for love between men and women. Since he never went out in the evening anymore, Georgia went without him to the gala dinner and reception held in her honor on May 14, 1946. She had carefully arranged her graying hair on top of her head for the occasion, but, unlike the other ladies, she refused to bare her shoulders in an evening gown and wore a prim black silk dress instead. Over the entrance to the galleries containing the O'Keeffes was the artist's distinctive, upright signature, reproduced in big black letters. Georgia had supervised the hanging along with James Johnson Sweeney, the elegant, intellectual Irishman who ran the museum's painting and sculpture department. The fifty-seven pictures, dating from 1915 to 1945, had been hung chronologically and sparsely on the white walls, in the understated style of An American Place.

In his review, Henry McBride took a long backward look at the career of the artist whom he had known for more than three decades. Their friendship was of such long standing that the previous year, Monroe Wheeler, a museum official, had humorously stuffed a "Georgia O'Keeffe necktie" (white steer heads on a dark ground) into the critic's pocket at a dinner party. McBride's review in the *New York Sun* began:

> The name Georgia O'Keeffe goes up in lights. Stardom!
> It is placarded on high, along with Chagall's, at the
> Modern Museum and may be read from as far away as
> Fifth Avenue. Stardom at last! It has been a long time
> coming. Or has it?

He depicted her as an artist who had been very lucky. He recalled the time in 1921 when Stieglitz had exhibited his portraits of her and she became notorious in art circles. With Stieglitz showing her prolific, inspired output every year from 1923 on, he went on, the momentum of her career was maintained. He explained that her seccess was also aided by the easy-to-like "suavity, serenity and extreme finish" of her style. The retrospective, he concluded, placed her "securely in the top postion among women artists." O'Keeffe, for once, resented his review. She disliked the lady-artist label, and she probably didn't care much for his playing up her good fortune and playing down her diligence and genius.

A sour note was sounded by critic Clement Greenberg's hostile review in *The Nation*. This champion of the emerging abstract expressionists attacked the lack of correct intellectual underpinnings in the work of the early American modernists and wrote that the importance of O'Keeffe's "pseudo-modern art is almost entirely historical and symptomatic." Her work is "little more than tinted photography. The lapidarian patience she has expended in trimming, breathing upon, and polishing these bits of opaque cellophane betrays a concern that has less to do with art than with private worship and the embellishment of private fetishes with secret and arbitrary meanings."

In early June 1946, Georgia departed for Abiquiu as usual, traveling for the first time by air, leaving Stieglitz in the care of a housekeeper. Stieglitz lingered in New York for weeks afterwards, going to the gallery, even though the season's last show had been dismantled and the walls were bare. He was going through his usual anguish at the necessity of changing his routine in order to escape the summer heat and retreat to Lake George. Although his cedar trunk was packed, he was still at the gallery on Saturday, July 6, when he felt a sharp spasm over his heart and lay down on his cot. That afternoon when Beaumont and Nancy Newhall dropped by with an ice cream cone for him, he was still lying there. He asked them to read to him once again the review of O'Keeffe's retrospective by James Thrall Soby, Sweeney's boss at the Museum of Modern Art. (Soby had written that the show eliminated any doubts he had had about O'Keeffe as a painter.) Afterwards, the Newhalls helped Stieglitz home.

A doctor eased Stieglitz's pain with a shot of morphine, and he spent the next few days in bed. On Tuesday evening he was well enough to dine in his bathrobe and slippers with his good friend Jerome Mellquist. On Wednesday morning he arose before seven—earlier than usual—and got dressed to go to An American Place, but as he walked from the bathroom to the living room, he was felled by a stroke. He had gripped the wall molding of the hallway to keep from falling, leaving grayish fingerprints, then slumped to the floor unconscious. He was found by Andrew Droth, the elderly gallery handyman, who arrived with the mail at the apartment around noon. An ambulance was called, and Stieglitz was admitted to Doctors Hospital at 1:05 P.M.

In New Mexico Georgia's car was flagged down by the boy who

worked in the Espanola telegraph office, and she was given the telegram telling her Stieglitz had had a cerebral thrombosis and was in a critical condition. She drove directly to the Albuquerque airport and caught a flight going east. On arriving at the hospital, she found him in a deep coma and learned that the prognosis was poor because of his advanced age of eighty-two. By late Friday night he was rapidly sinking. He stopped breathing at 1:25 A.M. on Saturday, July 13, 1946, having succumbed to a brain hemorrhage rather than the weak heart from which he had long been suffering.

On the same day Georgia signed the undertaker's papers and determinedly began looking for a pine coffin in order to bury Stieglitz with simple dignity. Somehow, although it was a Saturday in summertime New York when most businesses were closed, she succeeded. She detested its pink satin lining, however, and sat up late into Saturday night tearing it out and replacing it with a plain white linen one. On Sunday a quiet memorial service was held by a small group of mourners at the Frank E. Campbell funeral chapel on Madison Avenue. It had been Stieglitz's wish that no words be spoken or music played. In a beautiful ceremonious gesture, Edward Steichen silently placed a green pine bough on the black-draped casket. Georgia carried herself with quiet dignity and remained stoic throughout the drive with the coffin to the Queens crematorium. On the day of the funeral, obituaries in the New York newspapers noted in subheads that Alfred Stieglitz was "the husband of Georgia O'Keeffe." Thus, at her mentor's death, O'Keeffe, whose finest paintings were hanging on the walls of the Museum of Modern Art, was as well known as her famous husband.

Georgia took the ashes up to Lake George and buried them at the foot of a tall old pine beside the lake. Then she went to Fairholme, the opulent Newport mansion where her sister Anita summered with her husband. (Anita was familiar with grief, having tragically lost her only child, Eleanor, at the age of twenty-three in an airplane crash five years before.) Since Georgia was a reticent individual by nature, her grief at the loss of her partner of almost thirty years was evident only to those who were close to her. She responded to expressions of sympathy by merely acknowledging that it was a time of change for her, that she was learning to be alone in a new way. Although her years with Stieglitz had been a bittersweet mixture of stimulation and frustration, long after he "was gone," as she put it, she would admit to intimates that she missed him intensely and that she wished he could be with her in her wonderful world.

Other pillars of her world were tumbling. John Marin had been stricken by a heart attack in the spring at the age of seventy-six. Arthur Dove, who had been sickly, died a few months after Stieglitz. To recover her ballast, Georgia returned to Abiquiu in autumn 1946 and stayed until the end of November. She walked among the red hills, now whitened by snow, and painted a large lone blackbird skimming the slopes in a cloudless blue sky.

❖

While Stieglitz was alive, the subject of the disposal of his lifetime accumulation of art had come up, and he and Georgia had disagreed. Stieglitz knew, particularly after a large part of his collection was exhibited in Philadelphia in 1944, that it was a fine, valuable record of the first avant-garde generation of artists in America. He wanted it kept together as a testimony to his vision and because he thought it belonged together. Georgia, on the other hand, was sure that no institution would go along with that idea, and, if any did accept all of the huge collection, it would store rather than show the works of art. Taking the artist's view of the matter, she told him that more people would see the contemporary paintings and sculptures if they were divided up among several museums, and, finally, she stated that if he didn't like her plan, he must find someone else to give the collection away.

At Stieglitz's death, however, his short will—signed in 1937— named his wife as both the inheritor and executor of his entire estate. Suddenly Georgia was faced with the immense job of giving away eight hundred and fifty modern works of art, hundreds of photographs, and fifty thousand letters. Afterwards, when she was criticized for her decisions, she admitted that they were not Stieglitz's. "In the opinion of many of his friends and acquaintances I knew that no matter what I did could not be right, but I think he would not object too much to what I have done," she wrote in a lengthy explanatory article for the *New York Times* Sunday magazine section in 1949. "He would not mind my doing what it was impossible for him to do."

For the three winters after Stieglitz's death, she dutifully returned to the small New York apartment to fulfill her obligation to him. With the help of an earnest young assistant, Doris Bry, she saw to it that each work of art was photographed and cataloged in a meticulous, methodical way. After consulting museum curators, Georgia weeded out inferior items and made lists of which remaining items would go where, based on her wish to avoid duplication. She decided that the bulk of the art would go to the Metropolitan Museum because it was in the city Stieglitz had called home. The centrally located Art Institute of Chicago, where she had gone to art school and had held her first museum retropective, got the second-largest group. An archive was established at Yale University's Collection of American Literature, later placed in the Beinecke Rare Book and Manuscript Library for Stieglitz's voluminous collection of letters and papers. Other institutions received smaller bequests.

Among these was Fisk University, which had been founded for Negro students in Tennessee; her friend Carl Van Vechten knew the founder of its art department, black artist Aaron Douglas, and was head of the university's art committee. Perhaps, also, she chose Fisk because of her fondness for black writer Jean Toomer as well as for the generous, outgoing black Tennessee artist Beauford Delaney, whom she sketched around that time. At any rate, her gift of fine African primitive carvings and a hundred or so paintings enabled Fisk to establish an art gallery, in a renovated gymnasium, comprising one of the best contemporary collections in the South.

It was clear that Georgia cared deeply about the fate of her gift. A few days before the Fisk gallery opened in the autumn of 1949, she arrived in Nashville in her black convertible coupé along with Doris Bry to arrange for the gallery's lighting, wall colors, and the placement of the art. In the catalog she expressed the wish that everyone who saw the works of art would realize that there were many ways to see and to think, and, as a result, that each person would feel more confident in his or her own way. One evening a reporter for the Nashville *Tennessean* returned to the darkened gallery for a last look, and discovered the artist stretched out on a hard bench, wrapped in her black cape. She was unable to lock up until Miss Bry returned with the key, O'Keeffe explained to the startled newsman, who backed out in embarrassment, feeling as though he had stumbled upon a napping General Grant or, more likely, a guardian spirit of art.

Besides settling the estate, there were many other matters that distracted her during the first difficult year after Stieglitz's death, and, consequently, Georgia painted very little. In June 1947 there was a Stieglitz retrospective at the Museum of Modern Art. In the summer she was in a fever to finish the Abiquiu house and to uproot herself finally from New York and complete the transplantation to New Mexico. Unexpectedly, her Spanish housekeeper had a baby. Then paleontologists, tourists, and the press flocked to the Ghost Ranch when ancient dinosaur bones were discovered there. (After all the talk for years about *her* fascination with bones, Georgia must have been amused.)

Finally, at the end of August her old friend Henwar Rodakiewicz, who was working on a State Department film series on artists and their worlds, arrived in his Rolls-Royce roadster to do a film about her. At times she was charming with the film crew, particularly with the youngest member, daring him to eat her hottest chili peppers. But when Henwar began to make more demands on her time, sharp words were exchanged, he was deeply wounded, and their long friendship was ruptured. His short black-and-white film therefore began with footage about O'Keeffe, but ended up being mostly about the local Indians.

The summer of 1948 was easier in every way. Abundant spring rains made the native prickly yucca send up its tall, dramatic, white flower stalk, a sight so splendid that when Georgia came upon it in her walks at dusk, she thought that it deserved the name given it by mission priests, "our Lord's candlestick." She spent more time painting than the summer before. One of her pictures was a very large canvas (almost 4' × 7') simply called *Spring*—a painting, in a gentle, muted mood, of white blossoms and pale bones levitating in front of the Pedernal. Instead of shipping the canvas back to the East as she always had done when Stieglitz was alive, she kept it in New Mexico, as if there were now no reason to send it to New York.

In spring 1949 she was elected to the self-selecting, blue-ribbon National Institute of Arts and Letters, along with artist Gertrude Lathrop, E. E. Cummings, Christopher Isherwood, and several others. (Stieglitz was never elected because no category existed for photographers.) The honor was very great for Georgia, since, at the time, only 10 percent of the Institute's members were women. Aside from the occasions when she had received her honorary degrees, this was the first time she was recognized by a group composed of both men and women of distinction.

By the end of the third winter's work on the Stieglitz estate,

Georgia was impatient to conclude the time-consuming job, resume her painter's life, and move permanently to New Mexico. One day after returning from Abiquiu, she walked into the apartment and answered the ringing telephone. It was her old Chatham classmate, Susan Wilson. When Georgia told her that she planned to move to New Mexico, Susan cried, "But when will we see you?" Keeping in touch with old school chums was hardly a consideration in her decision to leave the East, and she casually replied, "Oh, we'll see each other." (But the two friends never did see each other again, and when Susan invited Georgia to Chatham's seventh-fifth anniversary in 1969, Georgia never even answered her letter.) Just before she departed from the city where she had lived part of each of the last thirty years, O'Keeffe painted a picture of the Brooklyn Bridge, as if it were something she had always meant to do and had never gotten around to before. Then, at the age of sixty-one, she gave up the apartment on East Fifty-fourth Street and moved to Abiquiu in time to watch spring arrive.

After Stieglitz's death, Marin and O'Keeffe made an attempt to keep An American Place going, but, not surprisingly, they understood that no one could fill his shoes. In autumn 1950, O'Keeffe exhibited her work there for the first time since his death. Her best work of the preceding five years—only thirty-one paintings because so much of her time had been spent working on the estate—was also the gallery's final show. The occasion was a solemn one for the remaining members of the Stieglitz circle who gathered to note the end of a significant era in American art.

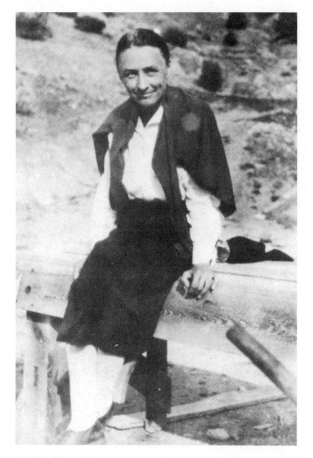

O'Keeffe in Taos, 1929. Courtesy of the Museum of New Mexico.

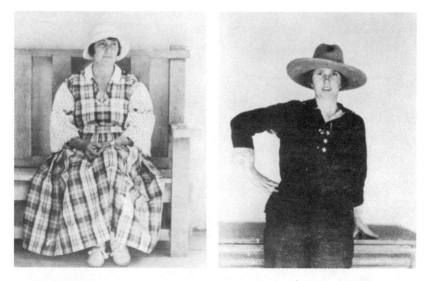

Mabel Dodge Luhan (left) and Dorothy Brett. Courtesy of the Museum
of New Mexico.

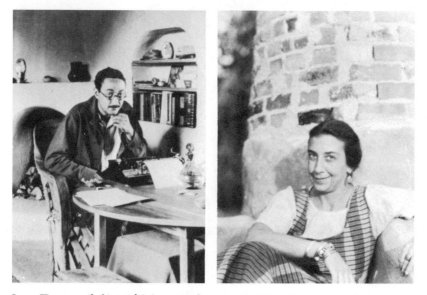

Jean Toomer (left) and Marjorie Content in New Mexico, in the early
thirties. Courtesy of Marjorie Content.

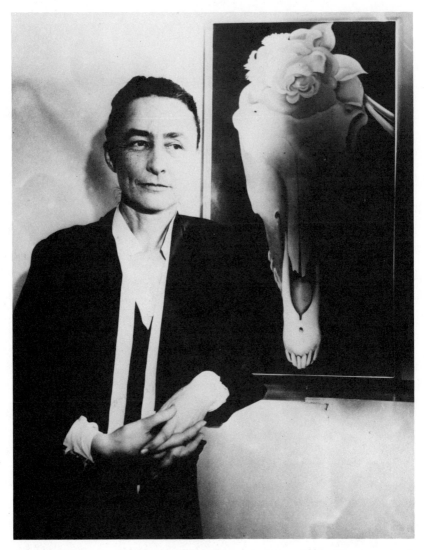

O'Keeffe and one of her skull painting, 1931. United Press International Photo.

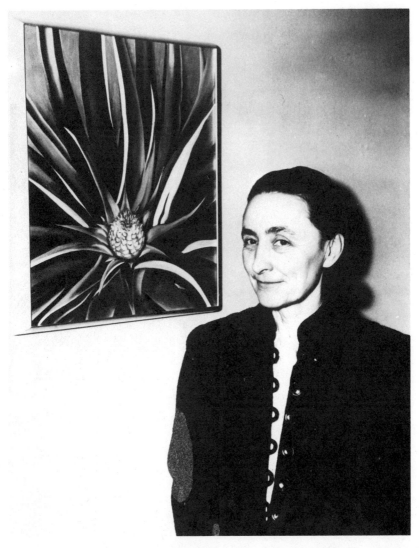

O'Keeffe with painting of pineapple done for Dole Pineapple Company.
Courtesy of Castle and Cooke, Inc.

276

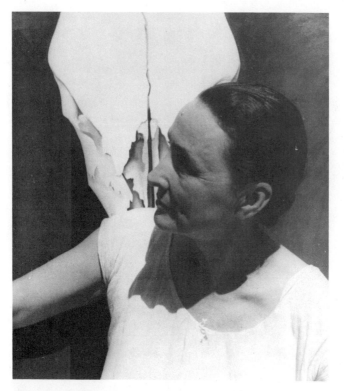

Carl Van Vechten portrait of O'Keeffe. Courtesy of the Library of Congress.

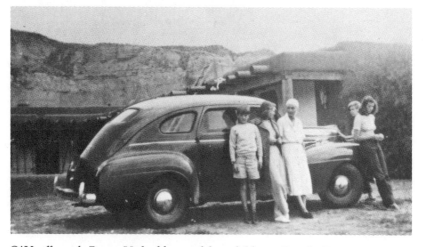

O'Keeffe with Peggy Kiskadden and her children, Derek, Benjamin, and Welmoet Bok, at Ghost Ranch in 1941.

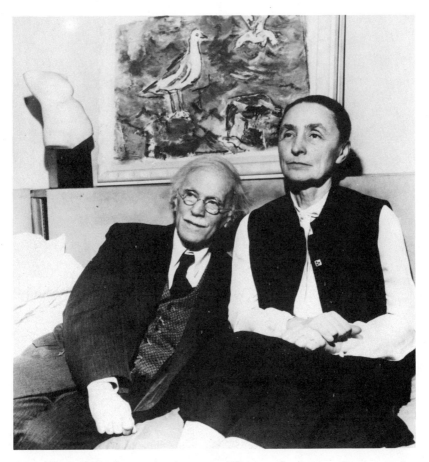

O'Keeffe and Stieglitz at An American Place in the forties. Courtesy of the Bettman Archive, Inc.

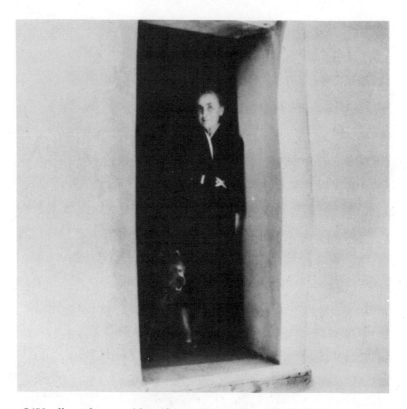

O'Keeffe with one of her chows. Courtesy of Todd Webb.

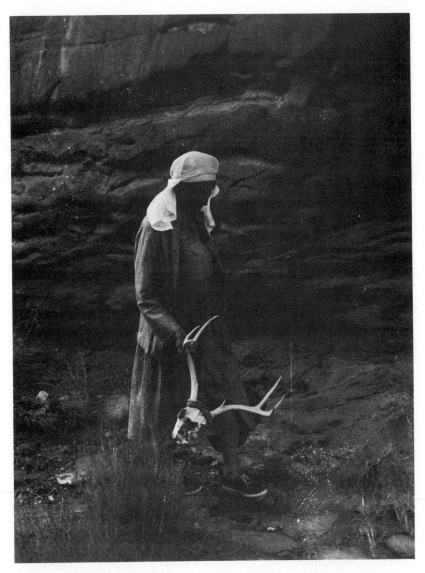

*O'Keeffe with new found antlers in Glen Canyon, August, 1961.
Courtesy of Todd Webb.*

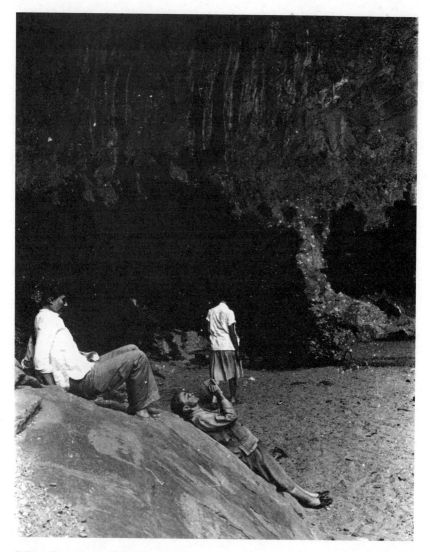

O'Keeffe with Tish Frank and Doris Bry in Glen Canyon. Courtesy of
Todd Webb.

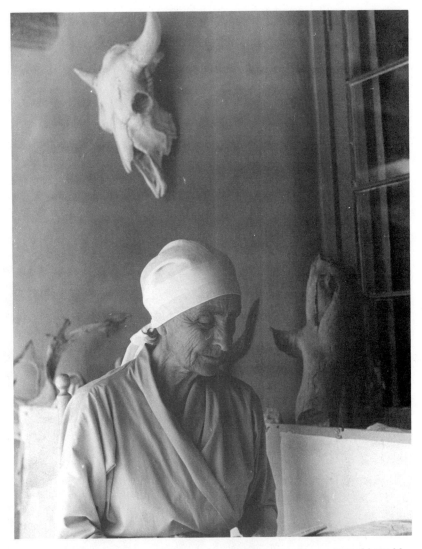

O'Keeffe on the portal at Ghost Ranch, 1962. Courtesy of Todd Webb.

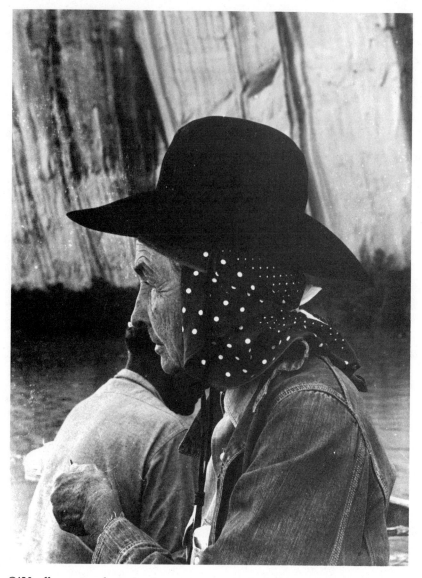

O'Keeffe rowing the raft after running out of gas, Glen Canyon.
Courtesy of Todd Webb.

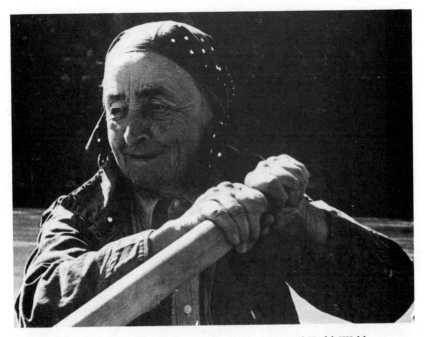

O'Keeffe floating through Glen Canyon. Courtesy of Todd Webb.

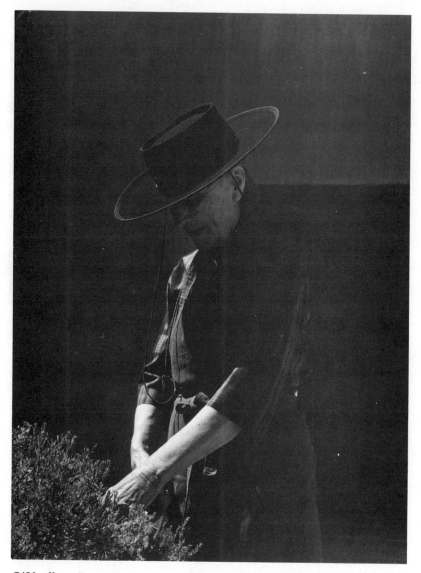

O'Keeffe in Patio at Abiquiu, 1963. Courtesy of Todd Webb.

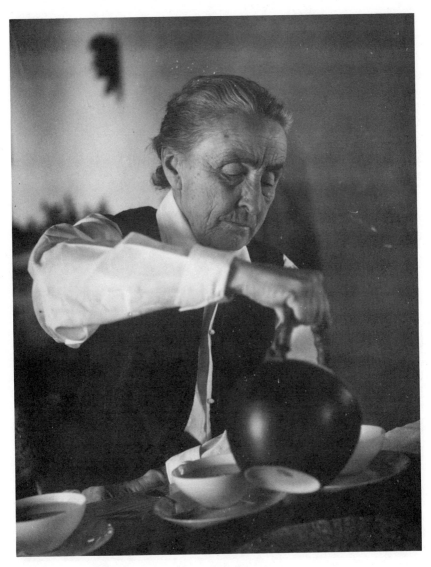

Pouring tea, 1962. Courtesy of Todd Webb.

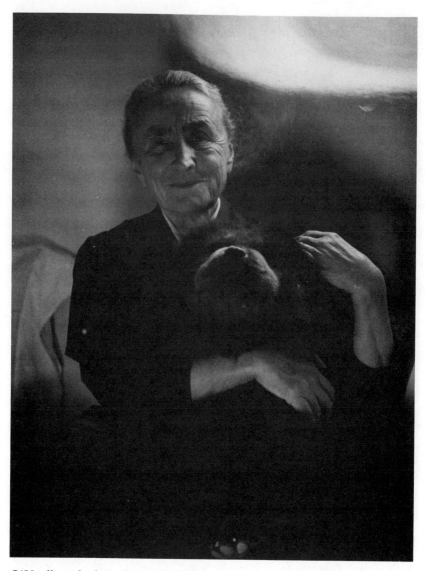

O'Keeffe with chow dog called Beau, 1961. Courtesy of Todd Webb.

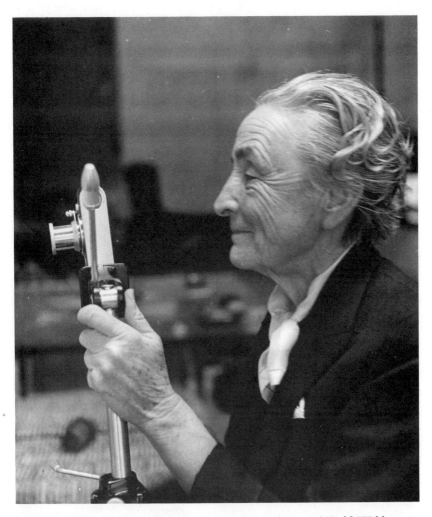

O'Keeffe with her Lieca at Abiquiu, 1966. Courtesy of Todd Webb.

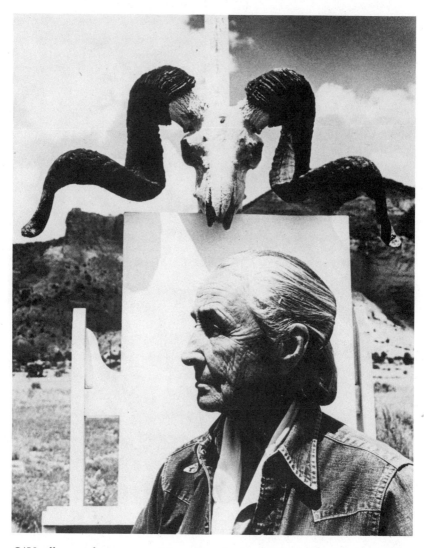

O'Keeffe at eighty-one, at Ghost Ranch. © Arnold Newman, 1968.

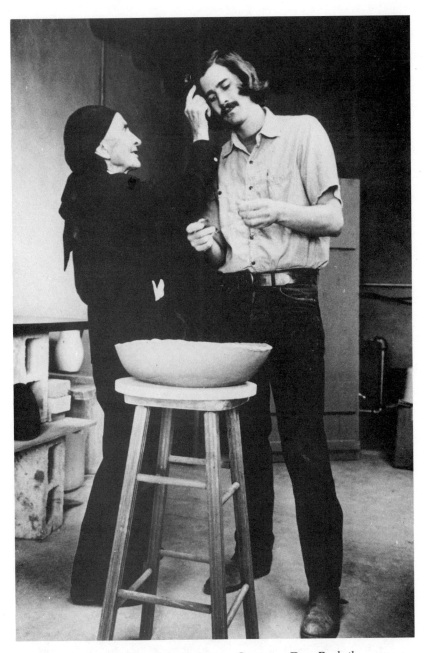

O'Keeffe and Juan Hamilton in 1975. Courtesy Dan Budnik.

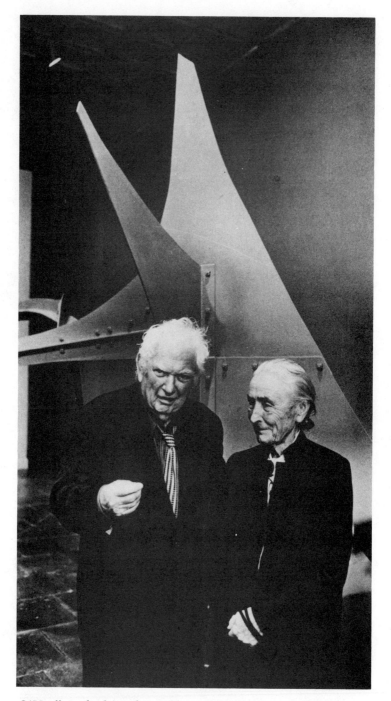

*O'Keeffe and Alexander Calder at his Whitney retrospective in
1976. Gorton, New York Times Pictures.*

12 ✤ Roads

The decade after the end of her alliance with Stieglitz, the somnolent fifties, was a rather secluded, stagnant time for O'Keeffe as an artist. To begin with, she had to learn to deal with the public, art dealers, and others by herself. Starting with her very first show in 1916, Stieglitz had shielded her from the commercial side of the art world, which he had also taught her to distrust. It was a world in which she had never had much interest. Consequently, she decided to put a great distance between herself and the New York art scene and to ignore what she called the "queer things" written about her. She pledged not even to deny or correct errors because that would just call attention to them. In fact, she hinted that she took pleasure in the myths the press perpetuated about her because they created a safe public persona behind which she could hide her real self.

Still, after her last exhibition at An American Place she was forced to face the unpleasant fact that she needed to choose an agent. In the thirties, Stieglitz had lent "his" artists' works to group shows organized by Edith Gregor Halpert at the Downtown Gallery, which was located in a narow brownstone mansion on East Fifty-first Street near Fifth Avenue. The gallery had begun modestly in Greenwich Village in 1926, and was one of the few still dedicated to Americana, American artists, and the best in modern American art. A Russian-born woman with heavy dark eyebrows, Mrs. Halpert was a well-known dealer and a respected businesswoman. Among the artists she represented at one time or another were Charles Sheeler, Max Weber, Stuart Davis, Yasuo Kuniyoshi, and Ben Shahn. By loaning her pictures, Stieglitz had given her the nod as much as to anyone, and so it was natural for O'Keeffe to settle at her gallery. The works of the deceased Dove and Demuth were there, and John Marin had been lured by the promise of a room in which his work would be on continual display. In the Halpert gallery, therefore, O'Keeffe would be the sole female in a group of male artists, as usual.

It was easy now for Georgia to lower the extremely high visibility she had due to Stieglitz's assiduous cultivation of interest in her work during his lifetime. After Stieglitz's death she no longer needed to exhibit each year to earn her living. During the fifties she only had three solo shows—and only one of these presented recent work—under Edith Halpert's auspices, reflecting, in part, her relatively sparse and minor output in this period. Also, the Downtown Gallery exhibits received little publicity, especially in comparison to the big museum retrospectives she had during the forties. Her first show there in the early months of 1952—pastels she had done throughout her career—received only a one-paragaph notice in the *New York Times*, which said little more than that she was "an enigmatic and solitary figure in American art." And, since she no longer lived within earshot of art world gossip, it was easier for her to ignore whatever reviews she did get.

In April 1958, fifty-three small watercolors were exhibited at the Downtown Gallery that Georgia had done quickly and intuitively between classes when she was teaching school in 1916 and 1917. With their few bold, simple, spontaneous strokes of bright color, the washes, mostly of lush Virginia mountains and fiery Texas skies, verged on the edge of abstraction. Most of the leading painters of the fifties, like Jackson Pollock and Willem de Kooning, worked in rapid, vigorous brushstrokes with random splashes of vivid color, much the way the young O'Keeffe had executed her washes. Her early watercolors, presented in a New York milieu dominated by the abstract expressionists, seemed more "modern" than her later, more formal, representational oils. Consequently, the Downtown Gallery attempted to link the washes to the roots of the modern abstract movement.

In fact Fairfield Porter, a painter himself, called O'Keeffe's work the earliest example of the California School, particularly its immaculate surfaces and portrayal of light. " 'From the Plains,' which represents a huge expanse of red and yellow sky, and which is only the latest of a series beginning in 1919, has the scale of emptiness and Romanticism that is seen in different ways in the work of such native Westerners as [Clyfford] Still and [Ad] Reinhardt. And her division of space in 'In the Patio' has in it some of the design of Rothko. These painters may or may not have been influenced by O'Keeffe, but she did come first, and our present familiarity with these painters should help us to see O'Keeffe's work freshly again, with its sense of the immensity of space."

Most people didn't see the link, however, perhaps because the men's abstractions were much bigger and more chaotic than the delicate O'Keeffes. Instead, the abstract expressionists overshadowed the first group of American modernists, and O'Keeffe was usually dismissed as being merely a figure of historic interest. (In the fall of 1958 the Metropolitan Museum devoted a room to her paintings in its show of fourteen American "masters" dating from colonial times.) In fact, the virile canvases of a young generation of males created an inhospitable climate for a lone female—a situation symbolized by de Kooning's violent, slashing series of grotesque women. Seen in this context, it's possible that O'Keeffe's withdrawal from the art scene was partly motivated by her self-protective instinct. Well aware that her work had fallen out of fashion, she wrote Henry McBride that she didn't expect it to be liked, and that she would keep painting in her own way. But without a prominent group to champion her, she became more secretive and remote.

While the Manhattan art world was pursuing abstract expressionism and forgetting about O'Keeffe, she was discovering, to her pleasant surprise, that her first winters in New Mexico were even better than the summers, she wrote enthusiastically to a friend. She would gaze down from her white Abiquiu studio at the cows and horses grazing among the appealingly warm, muted, mellow grays and tans of the winter cottonwoods and dried grasses in the Chama River valley, where a dark mesa loomed to the east and a jagged, pinkish one stood to the west. During the few frigid midwinter weeks, when the nightime temperature plunged to twenty degrees below zero, she found that the severe cold generated a better kind of excitement for her than the city ever had. She wrote to her friend Frances Steloff, who had visited a few months earlier, that "in the morning my north window is a white forest of frost to the top sometimes." Snow dusted the high mesas and capped the dried tan chamisa along the roadsides with white crowns. In her studio a fire crackled with pungent piñon wood, and her superb stereo system played the early instrumental music of Monteverdi and Bach. At night she liked to read in bed, but she often left unread the Sunday *New York Times* to which she had a subscription. By March gusty spring winds turned the air pink with dust as, she wryly observed, her neighbor's topsoil blew into her garden, and hers blew into someone else's.

During these years she used to order books from Frances Steloff, who ran the Gotham Bookmart in New York, and send her packages of chile. Georgia often asked for hard-to-find titles for herself and others, including a Smithsonian report on the Zuni Indians, Greek plays, poetry, and books about gardening, Spain, South America, cooking, Asia, and the Middle East.

She was glad in autumn 1952 to hire a deaf housekeeper to whom she didn't need to talk, because out of the silence emerged some fine new paintings, inspired by her New Mexico life. She painted the head and horns of the handsome, half-tame antelope that was shot after it had tragically gored the Pack's governess to death. (Arthur Pack had flown it to the ranch years before and had fed it by bottle before setting it free; the big buck used to frighten Georgia so much that she slept with an iron poker beside her bed.) As she painted the tangled bare branches of wintery cottonwood trees, which resembled soft gray clouds, she experimented with a new blurred style. Now that Stieglitz was not there to react to a new painting direction, she asked McBride to take a look at the cottonwood canvases she had shipped to the Downtown Gallery prior to her show of new work in 1955. Whatever his response was, it was a theme she did not carry further after the exhibit.

Her painting habits had been set as early as her days at Chatham, when during some classes she had romped around the art studio, and during others had concentrated so deeply that she was oblivious to everything around her. When she first began to live with Stieglitz, he had fretted when she was not painting. But she had dismissed his anxiety, sure of her own rhythm, which was governed by inspiration, instinct, and impulse. Although she was not the type of disciplined artist who deliberately goes to a studio each day to paint, she did prepare for the moment when she would feel ready to begin. She stretched canvases and tacked them to supports or primed canvases with a white undercoat. A half-dozen blank canvases—which she jokingly called "the hopefuls"—usually stood ready in her studios.

She learned to respect the weeks or months it took for an idea to germinate, waiting in quiet expectation as the painting crystallized in her mind's eye. "I know what I'm going to do before I begin, and if there's nothing in my head, I do nothing," she explained. She knew that if she started on an image before it was ripe, she would end up destroying the canvas and beginning again. She also learned not to talk about what she might paint for fear of losing her impetus.

Her visual ideas came in various ways. "I have the kind of mind that sees these shapes," she said once. "I know what some of them are from. Many have realistic landscape or natural bases, but others are just beautiful shapes that I see in my mind." She wasn't sure about the source of some of her most powerful abstractions, such as the colliding curves and rectangles of *The Black Spot* done in 1919. But memory or dream shapes such as these, often in rhythmic curves that were repeated like musical sounds, tended to be more real to her than objects she saw in the actual world. Some forms, like certain spirals, reappeared in her work thoughout her life like a private artistic dialect.

When she didn't find a shape in her head, the rich lode of her inspiration was, of course, the natural world, in all its profound mystery and infinite loveliness. She painted out of her passion for the sky, the moon, the sunlight, the hills, the desert—and the many small flowers, stones, and bones she found there, which she enlarged out of sheer enthusiasm, McBride once observed. "Why paint something if you don't love it?" she asked rhetorically another time. "I suppose you have the right to call me a romantic painter." Sometimes she viewed her paintings as a favor returned for what nature so generously gave her.

By the time she began to paint a canvas, it was mostly a matter of methodically putting down the picture already in her head. Although she conceived an idea intuitively, she allowed for only the minimum of "accidents" in its realization. Usually she made a preparatory drawing. Then she searched through her color samples, carefully recorded on pieces of cardboard, for the correct pigments to mix and place on her large palette. She painted rapidly yet meticulously, pausing only to eat, and usually she was finished with a small canvas by the time the daylight faded. Those were her best days. When a canvas was very large, however, and took longer than a day to paint, she seldom saw anyone or went anywhere until it was done, turning it to the wall if the housekeeper or anyone else entered her studio. Or, if she was dissatisfied with the result, she sometimes stubbornly worked off and on for months, painting the same canvas over and over—even though she knew that it was probably useless because her best pictures were usually those she painted the fastest.

For a long time she had liked to sleep in the patio of the Abiquiu house. Its high walls made her feel as though she were enclosed in a square box and covered with a starry lid. She was still fascinated by its door and, inevitably, began to paint it. This severe, serene, sun-drenched series of patio pictures, which she did over a fifteen-year period, reflected the silent, stripped-down life lived within the patio walls. The firmly closed black patio door, both impenetrable and mysterious, suggested the artist's secretiveness, but, ironically, made the public more curious about her and about what was behind the door. (The door led to the storeroom for her paintings.)

She struggled over her patio-door paintings, hoping each time "to get it right." First she painted a dark square in a long pinkish rectangle, placed between a line of beige earth and a slice of blue sky. Next she painted a diagonal shadow dissecting the wall and door, then did a version with fluffy clouds overhead, another with stepping stones underfoot, and finally one with big snowflakes and another with a green leaf drifting into the patio. Although she resolutely painted *My Last Door* in 1954, she then felt compelled to continue for another six years. "It's a curse—the way I feel I must constantly go on with that door," she sighed to art historian Katharine Kuh. She painted it from the side, through window panes, then switched its color to green and to red. As in her enigmatic paintings of darkened doors and windows of Lake George and Gaspé barns, the artist seemed to be struggling with the issue of the degree to which she wanted to shut out the bothersome world or to let its rewards and honors come in.

Many viewers wondered why her canvases were full of inanimate objects and void of human life. With a few exceptions, such as birds in flight over Palo Duro canyon, Lake George mountains, and New Mexican hills, O'Keeffe never painted living creatures. "I have sat for so many artists that I would never ask anyone to do the same for me," she used to explain. Then she sometimes added, a great deal more honestly, "I've always believed that I can get all that into a picture by suggestion. I mean the life that has been lived in a place."

Although she had made evocative pencil portraits in her youth to please people, she was not interested enough in human beings to go on. One exception was the free-spirited artist Beauford Delaney, who posed in order to get out of his unheated Soho studio, and whom she enjoyed enough to make several drawings and pastels of his head. Usually, however, she seemed to distrust such reactions to people; in her book she observed that some people she loved made her see nothing, while others about whom she cared little made her see shapes. Even her close friends sometimes experienced a shiver when they stood in front of a picture empty of human life, and a few of them felt that her canvases were increasingly cold and calculated as time went on. "Miss O'Keeffe's works are steeped in solitude and insist . . . that their creator is the last (or first) human being on earth," wrote a reviewer in 1961. "It is a kind of paradox that such a feeling of detachment can be combined with a passion for nature."

O'Keeffe never made a firm distinction between representation and abstraction the way other people did, and she always went back and forth between the two approaches. What was objective to her was sometimes nonobjective to others and vice versa, and she applied nonobjective principles to realism, as Arthur Wesley Dow had taught. Some people wondered whether she had absorbed the twentieth-century concept questioning the existence of an absolute truth. The idea— inherent in Einstein's theory of relativity and Freud's theory of the unconscious—had been discussed by Stieglitz and his friends during her young adulthood in New York. Although she paid little attention to such talk, she must have perceived the underlying attitude of uncertainty. Once, after telling an interviewer that a realistic picture must function abstractly, she suddenly laughed at what she was saying and amended it by adding, "Of course, what I've just said isn't true because you may want a picture of a tree just botanically rather than as an artist!"

From girlhood on she had done paintings in series as a way of slowly exploring a subject, of seeing it from various angles and in different lights, she explained at one time. As she went along, she ruthlessly simplified her image so that it often lost its resemblance to the reality of the initial object. "Nothing is less real than realism— details are confusing," she was quoted as saying as early as 1922. "It is only by selection, by elimination, by emphasis, that we get at the real meaning of things." The last picture in a series was often just what she conceptualized as the subject's core, so "It can be nothing but abstract, but for me it is my reason for painting, I suppose," she said another time.

Repetition also came from her compulsion to express her vision again and again as well as from her perfectionist drive to do it better. "I don't like anyone else's paintings, not even my own half the time," she remarked once. Rather than discouraging her, her "failures" tended to keep her going and trying new approaches. "Oh, look at that!" marveled a young woman poet at the picture of a pelvis and an egg form hanging in her house. "That isn't what I wanted," replied O'Keeffe. "What did you want?" asked the young woman. "Well, it wasn't that. That was one of my failures—and some of the cliffs were failures too. That's one thing that has always kept me working. It's not good enough—you must always remember that with your poetry—it's *not* good enough. It's very good, but it's *not* good enough."

In her mind, a series was never finally finished; rather, the paintings just tapered off when she lost interest in them or her conviction flagged. One evening at the ranch in 1958, she was waiting for a friend while leaning against the ladder to the roof and gazing at the darkening Pedernal. "I saw that the moon was white and high," she remembered, and "the sky a magnificent green." She had toyed with the idea of painting a wooden ladder, and suddenly she visualized the painting to be done. The resulting *Ladder to the Moon* made one believe that it was easily possible to journey from the mesa, up a ladder floating in a turquoise sky, to a bright half-moon. It is not entirely clear why the dreamlike picture never led to other pictures like it. One clue is that after it was done, the concept seemed so bizarre, she confessed to Daniel Rich, that it made her laugh and wonder if she were losing her mind.

As she worked in her gray and, later, white rooms, colors came to her very clearly. "Color is as intimate to her as the musical note that passes through the ear to innermost organs of sense," Herbert Seligmann had written in 1923. She thought in color the way others, Stieglitz, for example, thought in words, and she joked in the late thirties that she hoped to give up reading and writing with the help of the telephone, dictaphone, and radio. Despite the fact that she had a strong, vivid, and distinctive writing style, she said that words were often false, meaningless, and limited. Pigment, on the other hand, was trustworthy yet unexplored terrain in which new tonal

variations were still to be mined. Thinking that her color vocabulary—
which ranged from gleaming blacks to a vaporous white—was superior
to the English language, numerous times she was adamantly reticent
about her work, unwilling to try to describe it in words. "I see no
reason for painting anything that can be put into any other form as
well," she once said, explaining that she preferred to paint her feeling
about something rather than to talk about it. She used to tell frustrated
interviewers that she didn't like to think in words, that words were
"inelastic." Once when asked why she painted skulls, she said that
she was unable to explain in words and would have to paint a picture
to explain it. "Probably I would do a picture with another skull in it
and then where would we be?" she asked with a little smile. Sometimes
her humor left her entirely. "The meaning is there on the canvas,"
she snapped at critic Edith Evans Asbury in 1968. "If you don't get
it, that's too bad. I have nothing more to say than what I painted."

Placing lines, masses, symbols, and colors together so they spoke
eloquently—this was her natural idiom. Her genius lay in her ability
to create a tongue that translated her intense feelings of "dumb ec-
stasies and nameless fears, even for sounds like the roar of gigantic
wheels that throb in one's head as one awakes from ether," as Lewis
Mumford wrote in *The New Yorker*, referring to *Black Abstraction*. When
she explored the vibrations of the color blue, for instance, she could
awaken deadened feelings in viewers with her cobalt tones and lead
their imaginations into "almost unknown relationships with life," Blanche
Matthias said in 1926. It was clear that O'Keeffe's skilled conscious-
ness-altering cryptography, constantly enriched by her fertile imagination, could confront the viewer's senses on a gut level. For this
reason, she disliked it when her symbols were intellectualized, because
it dulled a painting's emotional impact.

Her technical virtuosity, which probably reached its height when
she was in her forties, had been remarkable from the start. "The best
O'Keeffes seemed wished upon the canvas—the mechanics have been
so successfully concealed," McBride wrote in 1933. "Her brushwork
has grown, if possible, still more elusive in its myriad delicate nuances
of tone and blendings of color," added Edward Alden Jewell in a 1937
New York Times review. Also a perfectionist about her craft, by the
end of her career she had left some of her paint samples in the sun
for thirty years to test their color fastness. She also took the highly
unusual step of paying restorers herself to repair cracks, fingerprints,

and the marks caused by warped stretchers on those paintings of hers that belonged to other people.

Perhaps her high standards for herself were what led to her mixed feelings about her first big retrospective. "You know, an exhibition is a strange thing," she said at the time. "You end up loving yourself and hating yourself at the same time." These severe standards also led her to destroy about forty inferior O'Keeffes when she moved to New Mexico after Stieglitz's death. Some had cracked paint, but, more importantly, she said she was tired of weighing the merits of artwork. "Of course I destroyed my old paintings," she said defensively when asked about it. "Do you keep all your old hats?"

She had always liked to experiment with frames, and at various times they ranged from gaudy to minimal to nonexistent. Her 1938 show, for example, included paintings with elaborate frames in the style of the ones designed by her friend Florine Stettheimer, who loved lavish decoration. Georgia was likely to buy a piece of bronze used to adorn a Victorian table in a New York secondhand furniture shop, then have a craftsman copy and make a filigree metal frame that would jut around a picture like embroidery lace. Once she framed a New Mexican sunflower so the rhythm of its petals was repeated in the scalloped frame.

O'Keeffe also used to design extremely simple frames, and these satisfied her the most. She placed a thin piece of silver leaf, which appeared as a hairline of light, along the edge of a canvas to hold the glass and visually to project the picture out from the wall. Sometimes she had a narrow chromium frame coppered so it wouldn't cool her hot southwestern colors, or had it partly burnished to harmonize with the color and mass on the canvas. From time to time she used no frames at all, but continued the painting on the canvas wrapped around the edge of the stretcher—a technique that became popular in the sixties long after she had first tried it in the forties.

Because of her indifference to words, she usually let other people name her paintings, although some titles clearly sound like her own phraseology. She disliked painting her name on the front of a canvas like other painters. She preferred the hand of the artist to recede into invisible brushstrokes and wanted nothing to mar a painting's perfect surface. As far as identification was concerned, she felt that her style was signature enough. Once when a stranger asked why she didn't sign her paintings, she replied impatiently, "Why don't you sign your face?" When a completed picture met her standard, she sometimes would draw a small star on the back and write "OK" inside it instead.

❖

Her periods of solitude were interrupted by visits from friends, particularly over the Thanksgiving, Christmas, and New Year's holidays. On Thanksgiving in 1950, for instance, Spud Johnson and Dorothy Brett drove the hour and a half down from Taos to share Georgia's customary very early dinner at five o'clock (their hostess didn't like to sleep on a full stomach). In high spirits, the three old friends devoured part of a nine-pound turkey with chestnut stuffing, cranberries, fresh watercress, home-grown strawberries, and claret—all described afterwards in delectable detail in Spud's journal. Brett, who now had the assistance of a battery-operated hearing aid, had set off her tight white curls and bright red lipstick with a scarlet fur-trimmed quilted coat and furry boots, much to Georgia's amusement. "I do enjoy my trips down to Georgia," Brett wrote a month later to Frieda Lawrence. Her home "is warm and cozy, and it's so peaceful, and heaven help me, civilized." The visit was also inspirational, for Brett painted a picture on her return to Taos, possibly one of her colorful evocations of Indian dances.

Before they departed, Georgia took her friends for a walk in the White Place, where erosion-resistant rocks balanced on spires of softer stone. Spud, like his hostess, was a great walker and acutely observant. He used to return with his pockets full of odd rocks and other findings that had escaped even Georgia's sharp eye. Afterwards, he jokingly wrote in his little publication *Laughing Horse* that she had arranged the hard rocks on the clay pinnacles in order to paint them that way. "Georgia is so simple and genuine—so alive and interested in such fundamental things as rocks and food, people and mountains, color and sound and taste and feeling—that it's both stimulating and satisfying to be with her," he wrote in his journal. For her part, O'Keeffe as always enjoyed the company of the now balding Spud, who used to sit silently at parties, puffing on his pipe, with a reserved, enigmatic look on his gaunt face.

The visit was so successful that Brett and Spud returned a few weeks later for Christmas. Georgia had put one big Christmas tree in the Abiquiu patio and another by the fireplace in the living room.

On Christmas Eve they lit nine traditional bonfires on a cliff, made mulled wine, and went to the festive midnight Mass at the little Abiquiu Catholic church, where the tradition was to go to parishioners' homes for *posole* afterwards. On Christmas day, in the afternoon, they drove to the deer dance at the Taos pueblo, where dancers wrapped in deer hides—complete with heads and antlers—pranced about with sticks representing front legs.

Visitors also came from what Georgia began to call "the green country" outside the Southwest. Among them was her sister Claudia, who was a teacher in Los Angeles, and others included Doris Bry, Anita Pollitzer, and Peggy (Bok) Kiskadden. Sometimes several of Georgia's neighbors also dropped in—perhaps the black-garbed local priest and the nuns in their flowing white robes and black veils. Houseguests often stayed at one house while O'Keeffe lived in another—so they wouldn't be underfoot, she candidly explained. In the fall of 1952 she painted at the ranch while her friend of twenty years, William Einstein, and his French wife stayed in the Abiquiu house. Einstein had returned to America with pictures he was going to exhibit in New York. O'Keeffe's continuing fondness for him was evident in the lengthy, equivocal statement she wrote for his exhibition catalog— even though she hadn't seen his new work and she had always thought that he was a terrible painter.

For a change from what she called her stereo's "mechanical music," in the winter of 1956 she attended a Budapest String Quartet concert in Los Alamos. Afterwards, she went backstage to greet Mischa Schneider, whom she had met in New York in the forties. She had made such a powerful impression on the young Russian-born cellist then that he remarked to her at the concert that it was impossible to forget her face. She invited him and his brother, Sasha, to lunch at the ranch the next day. It was Mischa's birthday so she opened a bottle of good wine, and Sasha played "Happy Birthday" on his violin as well as some marvelous Bach. For Georgia this gay, alive afternoon with the musicians was a rather rare experience in her life. She enjoyed it immensely and felt a pang of nostalgia for her old life with Stieglitz.

Some casual callers around this time found her extremely formidable, remote, and self-contained. They remarked on the way her iron-gray hair was tightly knotted, the razor-sharp edge of her wit, and the antiseptic whiteness of her New Mexican cotton dresses. Only her hooded eyes hinted of any lightness of spirit, they noted. One afternoon she seemed more interested in the large, luscious strawberries that acquaintances from Santa Fe had brought than in anything else. Evidently her mind had long ago been cleared of social trivialities so she could focus on art, and she was bored and irritated by chitchat that didn't directly connect people to one another.

One weekend Spud Johnson brought along a handsome, effusive boy. Georgia disliked the young man and called him "the blond one" rather than by his name. One afternoon as she put on a record, she told the boy bluntly, "You won't like this music—why don't you go into your room and read your book?" The boy gushed that what he *really* wanted to do was to see a particular drawing of O'Keeffe's again, and he began to rave about it. "Look here," she reported acidly, reading his mind precisely. "I seldom lend my work—and I *never* give it away!"

No matter how glad she was to see friends, she was usually ready to be left alone once more after they were gone. After a short period of adjustment, sometimes tinged with loneliness, she settled into solitude again and was content. She did not feel alone under the big sky, perceiving it rather as a companion. Once she had closed up the apartment and moved out of New York, she admitted to a friend that she didn't need many people in her life, and, in fact, she remarked on another occasion that she would be happy in a world without other human beings. The seclusion of her life in New Mexico might make her odd, she conceded, but if she enjoyed herself, then she supposed that it didn't much matter.

She was to have a kind of companionship, in any case. At Christmastime in 1952 a friend, said to be the head of the nearby San Juan Indian pueblo, presented her with two Chinese chow puppies for her protection. Although she claimed she felt no need for watchdogs, the puppies amused her. They seemed to fit right into the wintery landscape with their fluffy coats, plumed tails, and confident coyotelike trot. Soon she became devoted to them. They lay outside her studio by day, slept in her room at night, and trailed her on her walks. For the sake of the dogs, she had a snake fence built at the ranch and began to kill the rattlesnakes around the house—severing their heads with a hoe. She even stopped painting in her car because, she explained in 1960, she didn't have the heart to leave her canine companions behind and she was unable to work with them along. And, this woman who was not a joiner eventually began to pay dues to the International Chow Society.

At first her friends were afraid that the fierce chows would attack her. She admitted that possibility but rather took pleasure in their ferocity and nailed up "Beware of the Dogs" signs at both houses. "They bite very well," she said once. "I've seen more than one pair of shoes fill with blood." (This from the woman who had refused to stay at Lake George when Stieglitz's sister, Selma, brought along her fierce little dog.) The dogs were termed "vicious monsters" by the Abiquiu priest after they bit a village woman who was protecting her child from them. One time at the ranch they were out for a walk with Georgia when they saw Phoebe Pack in the distance and went galloping and yelping toward her. Phoebe, who was carrying chunks of raw meat, was terrified. As the chows charged closer, she threw the meat as far from her as possible to divert them. When Georgia finally strolled up, Phoebe explained what had happened. "Phoebe, that's all right," Georgia said, unaware of her neighbor's fear and thinking of her dogs devouring the meat. "It won't hurt them." As the years went by, Georgia raised two more fierce chow puppies, Bobo and Chia, and as they aged she replaced them with others, Jingo and Inca, that were equally ferocious.

Meanwhile, changes threatened to disturb her peaceful existence. After World War II, the Packs spent more time in Tucson, Arizona, where it was easier for them to educate their children but from where it was naturally harder to manage Ghost Ranch. By the fifties they decided to give the ranch to the United Prebyterian Church, saying nothing of their decision to Georgia. One evening in 1955, when church officials were meeting with the Packs to finalize the deal, she got wind of what was going on. Stunned, then outraged because she believed that years ago Pack had promised her the right of first refusal if he ever decided to give up the ranch, she rushed to her car, quickly drove the few miles to the Pack house, and slammed on the brakes.

"Arthur," she cried as she burst into the living room, "what's this I hear about your giving the ranch away? If you were going to do that, why didn't you give it to me?" A sudden silence followed, after which Pack tried to introduce her to the shocked churchmen and to explain that they planned to put the ranch to good use. "Humph!" she snorted, realizing that the deal was sealed. "Now I suppose this beautiful place will be crawling with people and be completely spoiled. I never had any use for Presbyterians anyhow!" So angry she could barely continue to speak, she stormed out the door again. Matters weren't helped any when one of the first ministers assigned to the ranch, which became church conference center, greeted her with the words, "Hello, girlie, how are you?" "*Nobody*," O'Keeffe said afterwards, calls me 'girlie.'" She decided to act as if the invading Presbyterians did not exist.

Georgia also began to complain bitterly about the increasing intrusions of cars, trucks, airplanes, and tourists into "her" silent valley after the war. In the fifties the road to the ranch was paved, electricity came in, and telephone poles stood in the red hills where the only previous sign of civilization had been rough wooden crosses. Georgia herself for many years refused to install a private telephone. When she needed to call someone, she was content to use the pay phone on the porch of Bode's store, even though her voice was inaudible if the wind was howling. When she finally relented, bending to pressure from neighbors and friends, she had the telephone hidden in a closet. She was outraged when a small, low building ("something they call a museum," she said contemptuously) designed to house educational exhibits of native animals, plants, and minerals was erected between her ranch house and the view to the south. Then, with the planning of a large flood-control dam for the area, the old road near the Chama River was replaced by a four-lane highway that was closer to the ranch buildings. For the first time it was possible for her to hear passing traffic and for sharp-eyed travelers to spot her home from the road.

She had other difficult adjustments to make as more of her friends died during the decade: John Marin in 1953, Ettie Stettheimer in 1955, Frieda Lawrence in 1956, and then Mary Wheelwright, Aunt Ollie Totto—at nearly one hundred and two—and her brother-in-law, Robert Young, in 1958. Learning that Young had committed suicide in January in the billiard room of his Palm Beach, Florida mansion, Georgia flew to New York, where an exhibition of her work was about to open. Young's body had been brought north in his private railroad car, and Georgia stayed with Anita in the Waldorf Towers. Young had been chairman of the board of the New York Central Railroad at the time of this death. Financially astute and as iron-willed as her oldest sister, Anita in time began to wage a battle with the railroad's directors in a dispute over her late husband's railroad shares, and then she successfully fought Young's Texas relatives, who contested his will, in which he had left her everything. Having spent years giving away her husband's works of art, Georgia did not seem to approve of Anita's attitude. When she returned to New Mexico shortly thereafter, she dropped by the home of Young's cousin, Robert McKinney, and his wife, Louise. "I just want you to know that Anita and I are not one bit alike!" Georgia exclaimed, then stalked off again.

One of her greatest solaces during this difficult decade was the garden at her Abiquiu house. When she first began to live there, she used to rise at dawn to work in the soil during the growing season, much the way her father had done on the Wisconsin farm in her childhood. She began a pattern of living in the village in winter and spring until the garden was planted, then moving to the ranch for summer and autumn. She had the deeded right to open irrigation gates once a week and to flood the garden until it resembled a lake divided by raised paths. At first she planted the ordinary vegetables, but over the years she raised a great variety of exotic ones too. Shade for tender sprouts was provided by fig, almond, and mulberry trees. She also planted, on a steep hillside to the east of the house, a terraced fruit orchard containing apricot, peach, and apple trees.

Like everything else she put her hand to, the garden was remarkable. It was going to be an organic garden, she decided, and when grasshoppers invaded, she brought in turkeys to eat them, instead of using insecticides. She spent hours discussing soils, seeds, fertilizers, vitamins, minerals, and other substances with neighbors, and she learned how to dry, freeze, pickle, store, and can her harvest. Deeply interested in preserving the nutrients in food, she devoted a great deal of thought to her diet. She sipped tea at dawn, then ate a big breakfast that usually contained meat, snacked in midmorning on homemade yogurt or skimmed-milk health drink, lunched at noon on a soufflé and salad or something similarly light, and dined again, sparely, in the evening on little more than fruit and cheeses. As a result of this fare, her weight stayed steady at one hundred and twenty-seven pounds, and her health was better than in earlier years.

Her meals were delicious. She enjoyed reading cookbooks in bed at night before she fell asleep. She had always loved the strong flavors of garlic and raw onions, and particularly the sweet taste of chile the moment before the sensation of hotness hit. She searched for wild herbs and consumed basil and marjoram from her own herb garden, spreading them on homemade bread with sweet butter. She bought eggs from one farmer, milk and cream from another, and superb southwestern beef butchered to her specifications. One weekend in the midfifties when Spud Johnson, Dorothy Brett, and another Taos friend, ce.

Clarly, she relished fine food.

Shortly after the Christmas of 1950 that she had spent with Spud and Brett, Georgia and Spud decided to join Eliot and Aline Porter on the trip they planned to take to Mexico in the spring. Georgia had first met the Porters in New York in the midthirties when Eliot, then a physician who taught biochemistry at Harvard, showed his photographs to Stieglitz. After Stieglitz had exhibited Porter's nature photographs in late 1938, the younger man gathered up the courage to quit his Cambridge teaching post and to move to New Mexico and devote himself to photography.

Like almost everyone who knew Spud, Georgia felt a little sorry for him. Since he had little money, she offered to pay his way if he would drive her. He was a perfect companion because he was tolerant in a good-natured way, responding mildly and with humor to what people said and confining his expressions of irritation to his journal. He also knew Mexico well, having been there in 1922 with his friends Witter Bynner and Frieda and D. H. Lawrence. For Georgia, at the age of sixty-three, this trip was a real adventure. Before they left Abiquiu in February 1951, Spud helped her to choose which clothes she should pack. They decided to take her jeep station wagon instead of her the roadster in order to accommodate all her luggage—her suitcases of clothes, shoes, and painting materials as well as an icebox of food and a tiny gas stove for picnics.

Tensions with the Porters began to surface before the trip had gotten very much under way. Georgia had neglected to get auto ownership papers, so the first day the Porters, who had already said goodby to their three small sons and were eager to get going, drove on ahead for a few miles in their car. After getting the necessary doucments in Santa Fe, Georgia and Spud caught up with them. At the end of each day's drive toward Mexico City, Georgia insisted that everyone dine with her around five o'clock, even though the others would have preferred to change their clothes and have a drink first. When the two cars got into the busy Mexico City traffic, they lost each other, which Spud confided in his journal was probably due to a deliberate move on the Porters' part, since Georgia's domineering attitude irritated Aline, a striking young blond painter from Boston. When Spud and Georgia accidentally ran into the Porters ten days later in another Mexican city, they decided to return home separately.

Georgia was astounded by what she saw in Mexico. Even at the Mexican border, while she and Spud waited for their tourist cards, she was so interested in the muralist she had spotted at work that she climbed a nearby ladder to question him. From Mexico City they drove on to Cuernavaca, then further south to Oaxaca, in a volcano-ringed valley they found similar to Taos in its beauty. Georgia sketched in the beautiful gardens of the old hacienda outside of town where they stayed, and they went sightseeing in nearby Indian villages. She was fascinated by the peasants' markets, and, usually followed by a bored and resentful Spud, who carried her bundles, she bought calico, baskets, flowerpots, serapes, fluted green pottery, black teacups, and other handicrafts throughout the trip. However annoyed he became, Spud stayed politely and loyally by her side, he wrote in his journal, so she wouldn't get lost or feel abandoned.

Upon their return to Mexico City, they called on Rose and Miguel Covarrubias, whom Georgia had met in Taos in 1929 and probably had kept up with at Carl Van Vechten's parties. The gregarious, hospitable couple had lived in New York before moving to a colorful hacienda in the artists' colony of Coyoacán, twenty-five miles outside of Mexico City. In the twenties and thirties, Miguel had been a popular illustrator for such magazines as *Vanity Fair* and *The New Yorker*, and had even caricatured Georgia as "the lady of the lilies." By the fifties he had become director of dance for the Mexican National Institute of Fine Arts. The well-connected Covarrubiases took the Americans to an impressive ballet rehearsal, to plays and museums, and to see the Diego Rivera and José Orozco murals. They met Rivera, an artist with wild black hair and smooth Latin manners, as well as his wife, who particularly interested O'Keeffe. Frida Kahlo was Jewish-Mexican, a mock-primitive painter who dressed in ribbons, jewels, and traditional Mexican costume. A cripple at forty, as a result of a traffic accident in her youth, she often painted self-portraits and scenes straight out of her stormy marriage to Rivera.

Rose Rolanda Covarrubias, a handsome Spanish-Irish dancer and photographer who had been born in Los Angeles, had written and illustrated two books with her husband on Central American art and anthropology. The two were extremely knowledgeable about ancient Mayan sites. Before long Rose and Georgia decided to fly to the Yucatán peninsula together to see them. One dawn in Chichén Itzá the two women left their straw-roofed hut and climbed up into a temple, holding on to a chain, to watch the sunrise break over the dense green jungle, which was as wild and wonderful as the sea, Georgia observed.

In early March Georgia telegraphed Spud from the Yucatán to meet her at the Covarrubiases' home in four days so they could start for home. After a stop in Guadalajara, Georgia and Spud crossed the border into south Texas to see Big Bend National Park. In Texas Georgia met a man who reminded her of an old beau from Texas, and she reminisced aloud about her longtime love of the plains, wondering whether she should have stayed, after all, in what she still called her spiritual home, the Texas Panhandle. Then, via the Carlsbad Caverns in southern New Mexico, they returned to Abiquiu. After covering five thousand miles in six weeks, Georgia was satisfied that she had seen the broad rivers, rugged mountains, and dark-skinned craftsmen to the south of her. It was the beginning for her of a thirst for travel that would not be satiated for the next dozen years.

With Stieglitz gone, there was nothing to stop her from venturing off. She usually traveled in the spring when dust storms were likely to swirl over New Mexico. In the early fifties two of her artist friends who lived in different parts of France—William Einstein and the sculptor Mary Callery—had visited her and no doubt urged her to finally see Europe. Georgia had first become friends with Mary Callery when the latter exhibited her brightly painted metal sculptures in New York in the forties. A tall blond with gray eyes in a square face, Callery had an uninhibited wit and a boisterous sense of fun. After a visit to Abiquiu in 1945, she had fallen in love with the American West and moved to Montana for a few years. By the early fifties, however, she was back in Paris.

In the spring of 1953, when she was sixty-five, Georgia set out for Europe for the first time. In her youth France had been the mecca for artists, and had cast its long shadow over the first generation of modern American painters. Europe was the home of the first avant-garde artists, the place where Stieglitz had studied photography and where Marin, Dove, Hartley, and the others had learned about art.

Indeed, as an art student Georgia might have followed the European-bound exodus if her father had been well-off or if her beau had taken her with him to Paris. Instead, forty years later, she carefully packed her black and white city clothes, donned one of her expensively cut black suits, and departed for two and a half months in the fabled continental capitals.

In Paris she dutifully toured the Louvre, where she favored the simple Fra Angelicos and the serene Buddhist sculptures. She was stunned by the spiritual power of the cathedral in Chartres as she stood in pools of colored light cast by its glittering stained-glass windows. In Aix-en-Provence, where Einstein lived, she coolly observed Cézanne's Mont Sainte-Victoire, the subject of many heated discussions within the Stieglitz circle in the twenties. O'Keeffe refused to meet the great Picasso, whom Mary Callery knew. "I didn't care very much about looking at him, and I'm sure he didn't care about looking at me. I don't speak French, so we couldn't talk," she reasoned afterwards. "My companion thought it was heretical, but if you can't talk, what's the point?" Since they would have been able to chat through a translator, her reluctance suggests a continuing apprehensiveness in regard to awkward social situations or, possibly, her empathy for another artist's privacy. Later she admitted that she had no desire to return to France, thus confirming the impression that her indifference to Europe as a student had been as much a matter of temperament as circumstance.

Just before leaving Europe, she visited Spain. She usually disliked looking at other artists' paintings because she tended to dissect their techniques critically rather than to enjoy naturally her fellow painters' visions. In the Prado in Madrid, however, she was surprised by the pleasure it gave her to look at the works of El Greco, Velázquez, and, especially, Goya. She admired the way the shadowy, dingy Goyas were lit by a mysterious force, and, despite the brutalities he depicted, she decided that she liked Goya as much as any Western artist. It was as if she felt a kinship with his somber Catholic spiritualism, which had something in common with the mentality that produced the menacing mood in her paintings of New Mexican Penitente crosses. She also adored the Spanish bullfights. In fact, she enjoyed the spirit of Spain so much that she returned the next year for a three-months stay, accompanied by a young woman named Betty Pilkington, the daughter of the Abiquiu service station owner.

She was also fascinated by the savage spirit of Peru, where she spent two months in spring 1956 with Betty Pilkington. While she was in Lima, she heard a story that she never forgot about a hotel just erected on the lakeshore. On the day the hotel's electricity was turned on for the first time, the embankment collapsed and the brightly lit hotel slowly sank under the dark waters of the lake. "I've never seen nature so absolutely terrifying," she said of Peru afterwards. "The mountains shrouded in evil, gray mist, the strange and remote Indians with terrible secrets in their eyes. Natural calamities everywhere." Along with Mexico and Spain, she put Peru on her list of the best places in the world to visit.

On her return, she tried to paint what she had seen from her working sketches, color notes, and memory. It was a struggle, perhaps because she was breaking her own rule of only painting what she knew best. She threw away many of these canvases. One picture, however, painted in 1957, survives. Called *Misti—A Memory*, it shows what the artist termed a "watermelon-shaped" volcanic peak in the Andes, painted with its conical top rising above horizontal cloud layers. Her paintings of other places in other countries have gone unrecorded and virtually none have been exhibited or reproduced, even though she talked with friends about painting such sights as the trained white Lippizzan horses of the Spanish Riding School in Vienna that moved, she noted, like music.

Georgia undertook a three-and-a-half-month trip around the world with a small tour group early in 1959, at the age of seventy-one. First she visited Blanche and Russell Matthias in their hilltop San Francisco apartment, which had a sweeping view of the bay. A widely traveled couple, they told her what not to miss. Blanche also took her sightseeing in Chinatown and to her elegant country club for luncheon, where the artist's black nunlike garb startled the other ladies. (Georgia, who told friends that she liked *them* to wear color, once had a graceful red dress of Blanche's copied for herself in gray silk.) The two friends also shopped in San Francisco's finest stores for china and glassware, which were shipped back to Abiquiu—as well as for woolen panties for Georgia that they finally located at Macy's.

Next she flew west to Asia—Tokyo, Hong Kong, Taiwan, and other places in the Far East. The Orient seemed oddly familiar to her, but for a good reason. As a young woman she had been drawn to the tranquil Japanese prints in Arthur Wesley Dow's large collection. Later she pored over the old Japanese wood blocks of her friend Louis Ledoux. Christopher Isherwood had observed that her life in New Mexico was Zen-like in its utter simplicity. Something about Abiquiu resembled Oriental vistas; even the stunted sagebrush with its ancient-looking bark and gnarled branches was reminiscent of bonsai. "Sometimes the light hits the mountains from behind and front at the same time, and it gives them the look of Japanese prints, you know, distances in layers," Georgia herself observed. In addition, she had enjoyed reading translations of the poetry and prose of Japan and China, and even loved Chinese food. In time even her clothing began to look like the traditional Japanese kimono—the loose, sashed garment that was crossed in front and had full sleeves.

As O'Keeffe had once turned to the art of Asia when her contemporaries looked to cubism before the First World War, she now turned to it again at a time when the abstract expressionists were dominating the American art scene. She made special trips to see Asian art in museums all over the country, from San Francisco to Kansas City to New York. The dignity, harmony, and craftsmanship of Chinese painting still appealed to her strongly, and she declared it to be the best painting in the world.

This admiration became one of her links with Witter Bynner, a distinguished Harvard-educated academic and minor New Mexican poet who had traveled in China, translated Chinese poetry, and collected Chinese art. The two were close in age, both friends of Carl Van Vechten, and near neighbors, yet they saw each other only a few times a year. Bynner was a night owl and she was very much a day person. When she drove to Santa Fe to shop, she was usually back in Abiquiu by noon, the time that he usually arose.

Her round-the-world trip also included stops in Southeast Asia—Saigon, Bangkok, Phnom Penh—and seven weeks in India, where she traveled from steamy Bombay to cool Kashmir in the foothills of the Himalayas. She joked that she had been afraid to visit India for years because so many of her acquaintances had become addicted to Eastern religions. One of the first to be converted had been Stieglitz's niece, Elizabeth Stieglitz Davidson, who had invited Hindu holy men to Lake George in the thirties. Although Georgia, of course, was not converted, she became fascinated by the Indian philosophy of profound acceptance.

When she flew from Asia into the Middle East in early May 1959, she felt the shock of leaving one world and entering another. The feeling was intensified when she arrived in Rome, where, repelled by the grandiose scale of Christian art in the Vatican, she cut her visit short. "The cherubs on the wall of the Vatican—dreadful," she declared. "Those big naked things. Bigger than a man. Everything is Rome was like that to me—extraordinarly vulgar." When she had the chance to travel again in the autumn of 1960, it was to Asia that she returned for six weeks—primarily to see the chrysanthemums in Japan and to tour Angkor Wat in Cambodia and view other sights she had missed the year before. "I prefer the Far East to Europe," she explained with a touch of humor. "I like the dirty parts of the world."

She loved to fly into the vital, vertical metropolis of New York, which she had once painted from the top of one of its skyscrapers. "It always seems so vast and sparkling," she said, adding that it seemed like a real city compared to the cities in the rest of the world. Yet now that she lived in earthen, firmly grounded homes, she could not imagine living up so high in the sky, or anyplace in a city, for that matter. She confessed that Manhattan's tempo and violence frightened her now. She usually lingered in New York for a few days to see the art, to take care of business, and to visit old friends. The world seemed big to her now, she used to tell people, but they found her enlarged as well. "It was quite wonderful to watch the way she deepened," Blanche Matthias recalled. "It was so honest—there was no borrowing."

Yet she was always glad to arrive at the little Albuquerque airport. When asked why she traveled so much, she would reply that she wanted to see if she lived in the right place. Photographing her in her home in 1956, Yousuf Karsh asked why she lived in such a remote spot. "What other place is there?" she replied. After seeing the world, she decided that her beloved Abiquiu was as good as any place on earth—despite the postwar intrusions of traffic and people. She spoke of her love for her beautiful valley as an addictive, intoxicating, delightful disase. "It's the most wonderful place in the world," she stated matter-of-factly in 1960. The only place close to it, she said, was the ancient city of Petra in the Middle East, which was so isolated that it was necessary to charter a plane, drive, ride horseback, and hike to reach it—and then one had to spend the night in a cave. After a number of years, her understated Abiquiu living room, in which black and white Indian blankets covered the banquettes and white draperies concealed her bookcases, began to reflect her travels. Besides a Mayan head or two in wall niches, there was now an open hand of Buddha on a thick glass coffee table among the stones and bones.

13 ❖ Clouds

During the decade after Stieglitz's death, Georgia enjoyed being out of the hot light of publicity. But as a result of her dropping out of sight, many of her old admirers didn't know whether she was still painting or not, and a new generation did not recognize her name. Finally, in 1957, *Newsweek* featured O'Keeffe, the last linchpin of the Stieglitz circle, in its "Where Are They Now?" column. Then in December 1958, *The Saturday Review* published an article by an art collector who claimed that the prices of O'Keeffe paintings had unexpectedly fallen from previous price peaks into a "devastating decline."

In a letter to the editor on the artist's behalf, Daniel Catton Rich quickly and emphatically denied the assertion. Rich, who had just left the Art Institute of Chicago to direct the Worcester Art Museum in Massachusetts, had recently asked O'Keeffe to exhibit under his auspices in New England. She had already visited the museum that autumn, but had apparently not yet made a decision. In his letter, Rich said that interest in O'Keeffe's work was oddly immune to fashion, and that she stood alone among her generation as an artist whose prices had remained steady. In light of all this, however, Georgia acquiesced to having a major museum show for the first time since Stieglitz's death.

The decision made, Georgia had taken off on her around-the-world trip. This was in early 1959, right at the time that jet-airline passenger service was initiated. The Space Age had dawned: During the previous year, the news of Russian and American man-made satellites orbiting the globe had been flashed across the nation's television screens. A few short years later, an astronaut would be spinning around the planet in a matter of minutes, and the artist of the floating bones and flowers would remark that her fantasies were coming true. Born in the horse-and-buggy era, she'd been sixteen when the Wright brothers had made their brief Kitty Hawk flight, and thirty-seven when she moved to the top of a skyscraper. Now in her seventies, she was anxious during the takeoff of the jet, but her fear vanished once she was airborne and was replaced by fascination at the extraordinary spectacle of the earth from thirty thousand feet.

She was surprised to see so many rivers, tributaries, and deltas undulating through the earth's deserts. "The rivers actually seem to come up and hit you in the eye," she said to Katharine Kuh. She penciled tiny inch-and-a-half-square sketches in a kind of shorthand on scraps of paper that she kept in her purse. When she got home, she made large charcoal drawings from them that were strongly reminiscent of some of her 1915 charcoals but without the inner tension of the earlier sketches. Then she proceeded to paint oils of the remembered rivers, painting hard and well once again in anticipation of the important upcoming exhibition. Because of their bold, unusual colors, which had emerged from the artist's imagination, the dreamy ribbons of river meandering through flattened landscapes were given such titles as *It was Yellow and Pink* and *It was Red and Pink*. The orgy of color included rich, bright, inventive tones of blue with pinks, greens, and grays, as well as greens with pink, yellow, and orange.

Meanwhile, plans for the Worcester exhibition were going ahead. In his letters, Rich asked O'Keeffe for ideas and opinions at each step along the way, making his own suggestions delicately. After sending her a color sample of the light gray walls and a floor plan of the two proposed galleries, he asked how many paintings she thought should be hung. O'Keeffe sent him photographs of nineteen new paintings for possible inclusion, and he accepted all but three. Then when he and his wife and daughter visited Abiquiu in July 1960, the two picked the rest of the forty-three paintings from Georgia's twenty or so notebooks containing photographs and transparencies of her work.

Although O'Keeffe tried to be considerate of the museum director, she caused some difficult moments. She bluntly asked him if the museum was going to buy one of her paintings for its collection, hinting that it had that obligation. (The museum did not buy one.) Then a few months before the scheduled autumn 1960 opening, she inquired if the date could be changed because she might want to return to Japan. (Rich moved the opening up by a few weeks so she was able both to supervise the hanging and take her trip.)

Georgia spent many hours in the spring and summer of 1960 writing letters, putting paintings on new stretchers, framing, packing and shipping, with only the assistance of sometimes unreliable local helpers. Because it was such arduous and tedious work, she vowed it was the last time she would ever exhibit. Exhibitions were one of the necessary evils of her life, she said. "For most people a show is a joy," she explained. "For me it's a headache, and it's the kind of work an artist shouldn't be doing."

Her first major exhibition in fourteen years contained a great deal of new work and lured New York art critics to Worcester. More than a third of the show's paintings had been executed since 1946—and a good many in the past two years, during the time plans for the exhibit were under way. The pictures included a painting of the lovely hearts of two orangey poppies, created in 1950, as well as *White Patio and Red Door* of 1960, a stark composition of reddish geometric blocks that measured a very large 16' × 28'.

Some reviewers were mystified by the seemingly abstract, writhing shapes of rivers and other forms, even though the artist told one viewer that they were almost photographically real. As he had in 1943, Rich emphasized that O'Keeffe's work was an organic whole, and he encouraged the hanging of early and late works together to show recurring motifs. Her work always has "the same lucidity, the same elegance, the same renunciations and the same inner richness, regardless of theme or period," he wrote in the catalog as if he were describing her personality. Then he concluded:

> Frequently when on a new tack the artist will express uncertainty as to where her "so-called mind" (as she humorously refers to it) is taking her. At seventy-two O'Keeffe can still surprise herself. I have a feeling that she will continue to surprise all of us for quite some time to come.

Although Georgia had always disliked being interviewed and meeting her public, she deliberately tolerated both in Worcester. She even serenely presided over a small press conference of art critics the day before she flew to Japan. In her interviews, however, she managed for the most part to avoid discussing herself or her work, instead raving about her life in Abiquiu and repeating old stories about herself as if by rote. On her return from Asia she was delighted to learn that her public reappearance had been successful—a half dozen national magazines had taken note, some published lavish color reproductions of her work, and *Newsweek* hailed her as "the grand old lady of painting."

Then the following summer *Look* ran photographs of elderly women whom they proclaimed to be "Ageless Beauties": Isak Dinesen, Edith Sitwell, Katharine Cornell—and Georgia O'Keeffe. Georgia's photogenic face, her presence and style, still made for the same kind of impact before the camera as forty years before. Now her lines and wrinkles—on the expressive face of someone who had an intimate knowledge of solitude and endurance—appeared deliberate and even beautiful.

After her Worcester show was dismantled in December, twenty of her newest drawings and paintings were exhibited in spring 1961 at the Downtown Gallery in New York. It would turn out to be her last appearance there. For a long time, tensions had been building between O'Keeffe and Edith Halpert. Georgia had complained that her pictures were damaged, that they were priced too low, loaned too frequently, and that the wooden frames Mrs. Halpert placed around her paintings looked like "fence boards." Halpert, in turn, considered O'Keeffe "difficult," especially when the artist demanded that the gallery walls be repainted white prior to her shows. Those who knew both women well speculated that the clash between two temperamentally opposite women with such dominating egos was inevitable. By 1960 many of the best O'Keeffes were retained by the painter rather than consigned to the Downtown Gallery. Doris Bry, who had helped O'Keeffe settle the Stieglitz estate, would step into Halpert's shoes a few years later.

Because of her recent fascination with rivers, as she had seen them from the air, it seemed natural for Georgia to decide to join a river raft trip in late August 1961. The float down the upper part of the Colorado River, which snaked smoothly through southern Utah with a minimum of white water, was organized by Eliot Porter. Porter, now in his sixties, with a forelock of straight brown hair that habitually fell into his shy, spectacled brown eyes, had become a photographer of wide renown. The rest of the group included Doris Bry, photographer Todd Webb, one of Mabel Dodge Luhan's granddaughters named Tish Frank, and a half dozen other people.

During the ten-day, one-hundred-and-eighty-five-mile trip, they were baked by the sun, frozen by the cold, and drenched by thunderstorms. Georgia gamely donned sneakers and climbed agilely on and off the large rubber rafts when they stopped to camp on sandbars. She refused to accept help in handling her sleeping bag and other equipment and once even helped to row. "If I can't do it myself, I shouldn't be on the trip," she used to state as she tried to adjust to the group. At night she liked to angle her sleeping bag carefully toward a view of pleasing rock forms, of stars visible through a boulder opening, or of a graceful branch silhouetted against the nightime sky. Once she joined the others in watching an eclipse of the moon.

At times she resembled a part of the landscape herself (particularly when she wore the sundress that was the same color as the ocher rocks), her brown face looking as deeply etched with lines in the shade of her black sombrero as the darkly creased cliffs. She would break her meditative silence to say, "Isn't it fine?" and the simple remark, specific and clear, seemed to say all there was to say about Glen Canyon's sandstone walls soaring above the muddy river. Since all her senses were completely alert and tuned to the splendors around her, her perceptiveness heightened the experience for others. "Georgia feels and sees the space and what it does to you, and allows you to feel and see it too," observed one member of the group, who added that knowing the artist had been a deeply personal, profound experience.

Since there was no time to paint on the trip, Georgia asked Eliot Porter to take her back on another river trip immediately afterwards. In the following few years, as the river, backed by the Glen Canyon dam, slowly rose to hide much of the canyon's beauty, she returned more than a half dozen times. She viewed such wonders as Music Temple, a big dark cavern with a slit of an opening to the sky, Mystery Canyon, a bulging soot-black cliff, and the spectacular Hidden Passage canyon. In her studio she tried her hand at painting what she had seen, although she did not seem sure enough of the results to exhibit them. A group of *On the River* and *Canyon* paintings from this period show interplays of flat waterways, sometimes plowed by a raft's oar, and steep rock walls.

Georgia and Eliot, who had been casual acquaintances for thirty years, became great friends on the trips. "Look at Eliot!" a member of the group once exclaimed as he scurried up a cliff ahead of the others with a heavy load of camera equipment on his back. "Oh, that's because he has an idea," explained Georgia admiringly. The two would collect rival piles of the rounded, polished riverbed rocks and, amidst a lot of good-natured bantering, raid one another's cache in fun. One evening Porter discovered a small, flat smooth black beauty without a blemish that everyone agreed was the absolutely perfect rock. Their teasing became a trifle tense when Porter realized that O'Keeffe seriously coveted it, but he said it was for his wife, Aline, who was at home.

O'Keeffe had treasured pebbles she came upon at Lake George, on the seashore, and in mountain streams, and had displayed them in her New York apartments. In New Mexico, where a wide variety of minerals lay near the abandoned mines, she enjoyed taking visitors on all-day rocking excursions. She always discovered a new stone with delight and, long afterwards, remembered exactly how it had looked the moment she first saw it. Once she picked up a stone outside her hotel in Cambodia and carried it in her pocketbook halfway around the world.

She was uninterested in classifying rocks by their geological names, just enjoying the look of their hard, definite shapes and the feel of their polished, silken surfaces. She placed her rock treasures around her home like precious gems—some in a glass dish in the living room, hundreds on a stone slab in the patio, and a few dramatic black ones on a mantel.

Months after Eliot had discovered the prize stone, Georgia joined the Porters for Thanksgiving in their home in Tesuque, on the outskirts of Santa Fe. They had displayed the perfect black stone on their dark-slate coffee table to see what Georgia would do. When she thought no one was looking, she slipped it into her pocket. According to one version of the story, she put it back, and the Porters later gave it to her as a gift. According to another version, she secretly took it home and, in time, they told her to keep it. At any rate, she kept the stone, displaying it on a shelf above her narrow white bed. Evidently, she was still the same person of whom Stieglitz had said long ago: "When she wants something she makes other people give it to her. They feel she is fine and has something other people have not."

❖

In the early fifties O'Keeffe had painted some realistic pictures of the landscape and the highway, U.S. 84, which linked her to the world. In one direction it led to her Abiquiu home and the Albuquerque airport and, in the other, to Ghost Ranch and the county seat of Tierra Amarilla. It was a road that Georgia had driven countless times, and she instinctively knew the motion of each curve, rise, and dip as it cut through red rocks and swept through wide plains and the green river valley. In 1963 O'Keeffe turned from her fascination with rivers to focus on the sweeping movement of the pavement. *The Winter Road* gracefully interpreted the highway slicing through a cold white world via the motion of a single brown calligraphic stroke, "Rivers and roads lead people on," O'Keeffe remarked about her latest subject matter.

In Texas long ago she had painted washes of the liberating space of western sky, and when she moved to New York she never forgot that sky. In the twenties she sometimes ended letters to Taos acquaintances by asking them to salute the big sky for her, explaining that the sky was the best part of anywhere. "I suppose I could live in a jail as long as I had a little patch of blue sky to look at," she said in 1968.

When she began to jet around the world, her sense of freedom as related to the endlessly expanding skies became apparent once again. She was excited by the spectacular twentieth-century airplane-window view of the high, snowy, sunlit clouds formed by pure ice crystals in the thin blue air, and she decided they were something to paint. One of the first oils was a picture of a solid, white mass of clouds on the bottom two-thirds of a large canvas, and then, above it, the sky. As she went on to other oils, the cloud bank was broken up into colliding, chaotic cloudlets. Next, she placed more blue space between the little clouds—and they started to look like an inviting path of stepping stones into infinity.

Sheer size seemed integral to the cosmic concept in the artist's mind. Perhaps painting large was also a challenge she was unable to resist in an era of enormous paintings. In 1965, at the age of seventy-seven, she launched the largest painting of her long career—24' × 8', or a total of one hundred and ninety-two square feet of canvas— as if this were the mural she had always yearned to paint. Its dimensions were determined by those of the inside wall of her double garage at the ranch, where she planned to execute it.

After the drawing was done and the roll of specially ordered oversize canvas had arrived from New York in the spring, she was impatient to start. Rather than wait for a friend to fly out in summer to help her stretch the giant canvas, she decided to prepare it immediately. Then for four grueling days, she labored with her handyman, Frank Martinez, a lean, leather-skinned, black-haired Abiquiu native, whom she had doggedly taught to stretch smaller canvases to her perfectionist standards. The two finally succeeded, and the gigantic canvas was ready to be primed with white paint.

Georgia began the painting around June, rising early each dawn and continuing all day, and finally washing her brushes around nine each summer night when the last light dimmed. It was a race to the edge of nervous exhaustion that was fueled by sheer grit and iron willpower. It was also a race against the calendar, which daily was bringing shorter days and colder weather to the unheated garage. She climbed a ladder to reach the top of the canvas, then alternately stood or sat on a ten-foot platform, a table, a box, the floor, then sat in a little Mexican chair, until finally she worked on the bottom edge by lying on the ground, despite the threat of rattlesnakes that could come into the open garage. In the course of her work she had the solid garage doors replaced by windowed ones that let in more light, and she made plans to install a wood-burning stove if necessary.

Over the telephone she told a friend that the biggest painting of her life was probably "silly." But her real feeling was indicated by the fact that she liked to climb a little red hill behind the ranch just before sunset, when the sun cast a hot golden glow over the valley, to look back at and admire what she called her "cool square" in the garage. During those minutes the celestial blues, milky whites, and pale pinks of the painting radiated a glacial light that appeared wonderful to her.

The day it was finally finished, in the autumn of 1965, she felt the sudden need to show it to someone. Her relationship with the neighboring Presbyterians had begun to thaw after the leadership was taken over by Jim Hall, a tall, lanky, ecological-minded minister with wavy white hair and a laconic manner. O'Keeffe telephoned the Halls, her nearest neighbors, and got Ruth Hall, who said she would be right over. The long horizon of the huge painting seemed to stretch forever, with orderly, cottony clouds calmly floating—without touching—in a spacious paradise. To the artist's amusement, Ruth stood speechless before the chunk of heaven that her awesome neighbor had captured and grounded in her garage.

Perhaps her drive to finish *Sky Above Clouds IV* was attributable, in part, to another upcoming retrospective—this one in Texas. Although Georgia had hated the bother and worry she had had with the Worcester show, she must have decided that it had all been worthwhile. The new exhibition, in spring 1966, would be the biggest exhibition of her lifetime, for which ninety-six works would be shipped to the Amon Carter Museum of Western Art in Fort Worth from among the forty or so museums and numerous collectors who owned her work. As usual, O'Keeffe made many demands, for example, requesting that the wood paneling in the airy museum designed by Philip Johnson be covered by false white walls, and that workmen handling her paintings wear white gloves. In the end, her old friend James Johnson Sweeney, then director of the Museum of Fine Arts in Houston, helped hang her pictures sparingly on the walls, in much the same way the two had spaced them at the Museum of Modern Art twenty years earlier.

Georgia was seventy-eight now, and on opening night she looked diminutive, particularly when dwarfted by her mammoth clouds. But her iron-rod posture and regal bearing gave the impression of great strength and stature. Her dark brows, which had become more noticeable as her hair became increasingly white, gave her face a severe, scowling look when she was not smiling. And although her bone structure was now less defined under her aging skin, her jawline remained as hard as the Abiquiu cliffs. Much of the evening she was surrounded by ladies with beehive hairdos who had adorned themselves with flowery gowns, high heels, elegant furs, and Indian jewelry. In her tailored black suit, with a spot of silver glinting at her throat, she looked like a nun or, rather, like a mother superior who had wandered into the party by mistake. But under her heavy, arc-shaped eyelids, her eyes gleamed with amusement and a touch of triumph. On the walls around her were the curvaceous, opulent shapes and the incomparable rich colors of her life's work—and real finery of her vivid imagination.

O'Keeffe's stunning cloud panorama was received with a degree of incredulity and skepticism, however. Critic Peter Plagens shivered before it as if, he wrote in *Artforum* magazine, the clouds were icebergs bobbing in an arctic sea. He also wondered whether the artist had consciously adopted the dramatic optical tricks of the new op artists. Other people observed that the celestial purity of her work was due to her detached and isolated life in the desert, where she continued to take no art students and lived with two fierce chows. Like one of her fleecy clouds, she seemed to levitate above the concerns of most mortals as she immersed herself in the grandeur of nature. At the opening she went up to Ted Reid, her student from long ago in Canyon who had come from north Texas to see the show, and she asked him how he liked the cloud painting. "What is it?" he replied. A onetime pilot who had seen clouds in many forms, he didn't connect the abstract cloudscape with what he knew of the sky's vapors. But she didn't seem to care. "Go find one which you like better," she smilingly instructed.

In the mind of Plagens, who was more amazed that Georgia had survived as a woman artist than by anything else, her formalism dated her. "Miss O'Keeffe's works, for all the sweep and scale, are of an old-fashioned stripe: objects of quiet delight and contemplation," he observed. They fit no ready niche, and, indeed, Georgia joked that the critics had tried to place her in every movement that came along—expressionism, precisionism, regionalism, surrealism, and all the rest—until pop art came along, and then they gave up.

Afterwards, the exhibition traveled to Houston and then part of it went to the University of New Mexico in Albuquerque. It was the first time the artist had exhibited in the state that had inspired her for almost forty years, and, as a result, only well-traveled New Mexicans knew her legendary work. Not surprisingly, the show was the object of intense curiosity. More than two thousand New Mexicans jammed the opening, with two hundred a day streaming in until, by the time it was extended for another week, seven thousand people had viewed it. Meanwhile, Georgia had flown to London with her sister Catherine to see the British museums.

❖

In the sixteenth century Spanish explorers had glimpsed the golden afternoon sunlight on the earthen walls of the Rio Grande pueblos, and the legend had drifted back to Europe that there were seven cities of gold in the New World. The Spanish returned to search in vain for gold, but they left many descendants and their strong cultural imprint, especially in Abiquiu. Since Georgia had first stopped by the hilltop village three decades earler, many of its most energetic young people had left, until the population was halved to two hundred and fifty. Now its sharply rutted, rocky dirt plaza was habitually silent except for the distant wail of an infant, the bark of a mongrel, or the Latin rhythms from a bar radio. Bode's grocery store had moved down the hill to the side of the highway, and grass grew out of the roofs of some of the remaining adobe homes. The most substantial structure on the square was the church of St. Thomas the Apostle, where a huge white cross rose above broken glass on a pedestal in the front. Inside was an uneasy mixture of manufactured religious art and charming folk crafts. Off the plaza to the east, evergreens and a century-old tree thrust over O'Keeffe's well-maintained wall, creating a flash of yellow in the autumn.

Abiquiu was still a stronghold of the group of religious zealots who believed in gaining atonement through physical suffering. During Lent, when they were most active, Georgia liked to peer through a crack in the wall to watch the slow procession of mourners, who paused to pray at stations of the cross and dragged a cross and a "cart of death" to an unmarked chapel outside the village. She was fascinated—as she had been by immigrants' Sunday rituals in Sun Prairie and by the gloomy expression of Hispanic Catholicism in Spain, South America, and the Southwest. There is a story that the artist, who was tight-lipped regarding what she knew about the sect, was at one time granted permission to join the procession for three stations of the cross before she was made to turn back. In any case, she like to climb onto her roof to listen to the Penitentes' strange song of grief, which was chanted repetitively through the night to the accompaniment of the high note of a tiny flute and the dull thuds of cactus whips. The sounds reminded her of the mournful lowing of cattle in Amarillo years ago, and when, in 1954, she painted a searing orange and yellow picture, possibly an equivalent of the moving Penitente dirge, she named it *From the Plains II*.

At the same time, Abiquiu had one of the worst reputations for violence in New Mexico, a state famed for its lack of gun laws. Bitter family feuds over such matters as land titles persisted, and there was still dissension over the land that had come to be called the Ghost Ranch. After early explorers had driven Indian buffalo hunters from the area, the Spanish king gave more than fifty thousand acres of it to a loyal lieutenant in 1766. Then when the United States annexed the region in 1848, the heirs began to be taxed. Slowly the land, eventually traded and subdivided many times, was confiscated—usually in lieu of taxes that the impoverished shepherds, living in one of the poorest counties in the nation, were unable to pay. Finally in 1929 many conflicting title claims were bought up by one owner, and the Ghost Ranch came into being.

During the politically active sixties, anger among the Spanish-American people built up over the lost land grants in northern New Mexico. Buildings were burned, gunshots were heard in the night, Ghost Ranch was threatened with seizure, and eventually adjoining U.S. Park Department land was occupied by local protesters. Finally in June 1967, the charismatic Chicano political leader Reyes Tijerina and armed followers charged the county courthouse in Tierra Amarilla with the intention of taking the district attorney through a citizen's arrest. Instead, they captured hostages and wounded a state policeman in the chest. One of the hostages was a wire service reporter, and the story made front-page news around the country. The National Guard rushed in tanks, helicopters, and hundreds of soldiers with loaded guns, who stayed until the violence subsided in a few days. One day at the height of this tense period, a Roman Catholic priest, the Reverend Ralph Pairon, was lecturing parishioners in Abiquiu when a bullet tore throught the window. That was enough for him. The priest fled Abiquiu forever, leaving the church keys at the post office.

A little while later his replacement, Father Robert Kirsch, was sent to Abiquiu. One evening after he had been in the village for a short time, he heard screams coming from the parish house. He rushed over and found boys drinking and fighting, and girls lying on the floor bleeding. An informal, blunt, burly Irishman, Father Bob quieted things down with a few well-aimed punches. Later, he took eight young men to the district attorney's office and had them booked on felonious assault charges. Parishioners were shocked by the priest's forthright actions, and the young men were frightened by the possibility of jail. However, once he felt he had the situation firmly in control, Father Bob dropped the charges.

At first, when Georgia had moved in alone behind her high Abiquiu wall, townspeople were a little afraid of the unsmiling stranger, who strode confidently about in an ankle-length black dress and black hose, carrying a walking stick and trailed by two ferocious dogs. Superstitious villagers nervously wondered whether she was a witch. Their suspicions were further aroused when they heard about her eerie skulls and bones—and a coiled snake skeleton in a recessed glass case, which once caused an Indian visitor to remark that everything in her home seemed alive, as if with supernatural spirits. Way back in the thirties Peggy Bacon had drawn a caricature of Georgia with an unmistakable resemblance to Charles Addams's spooky cartoon character named Evil. Forty years later a Chicago journalist shuddered as she passed the elk skull and antlers at O'Keeffe's gate and deemed the placed the home of a "sorceress."

Georgia did not improve matters by staying loftily distant from her neighbors' Catholic faith and adamantly refusing to speak their Spanish language, forcing them to use their poor English with her. She explained that it embarrassed her to speak Spanish badly, but, in fact, when she had traveled in the Gaspé region years before, she'd admitted that she was glad not to know French and waste time in small talk. Also, she seldom uttered the words "thank you" to the shifting staff of natives who worked in her kitchen and garden for low wages, and she rarely entered their homes. One longtime employee noticed that she treated them differently from Anglos and came to the conclusion that she didn't really like the Spanish people, but only found them useful.

Much of the townspeople's resentment was due to jealousy, however. She appeared fabulously wealthy in their eyes as the owner of two fine homes and two cars simultaneously—one a black car and the other often a white luxury one: For example, in the sixties she had a white air-conditioned Lincoln Continental, which was followed by a white Mercedes Benz in the seventies. This impression was reinforced by certain incidents, such as the time a neighbor, who had found a small discarded O'Keeffe oil in the town dump, learned he was able to use it to secure a loan of twelve thousand dollars.

Perhaps tall, vivacious, black-haired Dorothea Martinez, who cooked, cleaned, washed, and ironed for O'Keeffe for almost twenty years, worked for her longer than anyone else. One day at Christmastime in 1951, Georgia suddenly appeared at her door. "Come over to my house, right now!" she demanded of the surprised Dorothea, explaining that her housekeeper had quit in a fit of pique while she had houseguests. The idea of a job in Miss O'Keeffe's house appealed to Dorothea because she thought it would enable her to earn some money, improve her English, and meet interesting people. So when she finished washing her dishes, she went over. Her new employer was so demanding and difficult, however, that after three days she almost quit. In time a truce was established as Dorothea learned to say no with a glare from her flashing dark eyes that, she claimed, could send Georgia back to her studio. (Dorothea refused, for example, to go out to the "lonely" ranch, since it was away from her home and her husband, Frank, who also worked for O'Keeffe.)

Georgia didn't ask the townspeople to try to understand her, her art, or her disciplined daily life. She was regretful when a neighbor who used to visit in the mornings with her children had to be discouraged from doing so because it interfered with her time in her studio. As the years went by, Georgia realized that a deep cultural gap had not been bridged, and that she and her neighbors would never comprehend one another. She merely hoped for peaceful coexistence. Although the proud villagers were usually courteous to the old lady who lived behind the high wall, most of them stubbornly ignored her, and, after two decades in Abiquiu, she remarked that she still felt like a newcomer.

Yet in her own way, Georgia tried to be a good citizen. When she discovered that her well had the only pure water in town, for instance, she spent thousands of dollars to provide the village with a system that pumped water from the mountains. She funded the purchase of equipment that made it possible for the local television station to pick up educational programs. And after dark, when the little boys who played in the plaza knocked on her gate, she would invite them in. As she got to know them, she outfitted them with Little League baseball uniforms, balls and bats, and sent them to games in her car. Sometimes she became interested enough in a boy to hire him to prime her canvases and go camping with her or to send him to private school in Espanola or to the University of New Mexico. In return, however, she expected him to do things gratefully for her, and she became irritated if her demands were resisted.

The boys jealously refused to allow the youngest children to tag along to Miss O'Keeffe's, and they claimed that she did not like girls. Nevertheless, one day spirited Rosie Trijillo, aged twelve, decided to find out for herself if this was true. With her younger sister, Rosie knocked on Miss O'Keeffe's formidable gate. Georgia answered the door and politely invited the two little girls inside. She led them into her studio, gave them crayons, and let them sit on the floor and draw. At lunchtime, much to Rosie's amazement, she invited them to eat with her—and the girls tasted the best fried bananas of their entire young lives.

Georgia had heard the boys talking wistfully about having a gymnasium, and she was genuinely concerned that her neighbors had little to do at night. Perhaps she remembered her pleasant childhood evenings at the Town Hall community center near the O'Keeffe farm in Sun Prairie. In any event, she decided that the village should have a recreation center. In 1967, exactly one day after the arrival of Father Bob Kirsch, she sent word that she wished to see him. When he didn't appear, she telephoned. "I'm Georgia O'Keeffe," she began. At first the priest pretended that he didn't know the name, then he claimed that he was too busy to see her, until, finally, he made an appointment with her for three weeks hence. When he arrived at the ranch on the agreed date and got out of his car, her two snarling chows leapt at him. "Watch out! They'll bite you," she cried. "If one bites me, you'll only have one dog left," the priest shouted back as she hurriedly collared the dogs and brought them inside.

The ruddy-faced priest, who was known to wear disheveled black habits, and the dignified, immaculately dressed artist sat down to talk. Georgia explained that she wanted to have a building erected and give it to the church. At first Kirsch, thinking about the church's crumbling adobe dust that drifted into the chalice as he celebrated Mass, was unenthusiastic. But when it became clear that she had no interest in paying for repairs to the church, he agreed to administer the construction of the building that she had in mind. Meanwhile, she graciously let him use rooms in her Abiquiu house for resting and reading away from his small, shabby priest's quarters.

Soon, however, O'Keeffe and the priest were involved in something of a power struggle. Although she wanted to donate the building to the church for tax purposes, she didn't seem to want the parish to control the use of the community center, Kirsch believed. She wanted to pick its board of directors, but he insisted that married couples be elected by the parish. And when she balked at spending an extra few thousand dollars for a wooden floor, perhaps because she had lived for so long without one herself, he went to the Arthur Pack Foundation for the additional funds. Father Bob thought that she was manipulative after she called the archbishop to complain about him. "You can't buy a priest for sixty thousand dollars," Father Bob would tell her, referring to the estimated cost of the structure. "Uncle Sam is building it at your suggestion," he also said, emphasizing the tax write-off benefits of the gift.

Nevertheless, once the beige metal building was finally erected next to the church, the priest admitted to great if grudging admiration for O'Keeffe and her "brilliant" mind. He said that he used to enjoy sparring with her, and he believed that she liked to tangle too. And when Saturday night dances were held in the gym, he was glad when she allowed him to act as her escort.

❖

In the sixties, the bestowal of awards on her by the larger society increased to a rate of about one a year. Perhaps the most prestigious was her election in 1962 to the seat vacated by the death of E. E. Cummings on the fifty-member American Academy of Arts and Letters, the nation's highest honor society for people in the arts. Elected along with her, to fill vacancies created by the deaths of her old classmate Eugene Speicher and others, were painter Thomas Hart Benton, sculptor Jacques Lipshitz, historian Bruce Catton, and writer Lillian Hellman. She joined a very exclusive group of only five women members, of which she was the only painter and that included Pearl Buck and Marianne Moore. The tribute to her noted that she had "created original symbols for old experiences, sometimes too intimate for more direct revelation. She endows whoever looks at one of her paintings with a kind of clairvoyance—in the sense not only of absolute clarity of vision but also of a perception of things far beyond the painted canvas." When Jim Hall congratulated her, she replied, "Well, at this stage I just think it's funny." However gratified she may actually have been by the recognition, she publicly played down such honors, often remarking that it seemed odd to be lauded for just living her life.

As she began to exhibit widely again, *Vogue* published a thoughful paean to her by the art critic E. C. Goossen in March 1967, a few months before she turned eighty. "It was their spring fashion issue, and you turned page after page of beautiful young things leaping though the hay before coming to eight pages—eight pages!—of this old face," she said. "I thought that was rather grand." The next year *Life* featured her in a heavily illustrated cover story that emphasized her picturesque western life-style. Conscious of her image, she tried not to talk when posing for photographers so she wouldn't be snapped with her mouth open. But she saw the humor in that, too. "It would be terrible if I got a double chin," she joked to a photographer who was focusing on the famous profile in 1970.

The public became aware of an elderly artist who was obviously vigorous and vibrant in her self-made world. Visitors to her home came away feeling that they had never met anyone who was happier with her life. Stieglitz's niece, Flora Straus, stopped by with her son in 1962 for a few hours, and Georgia insisted that they stay to see the ranch and spend the night. "She had to show us her triumphant way of life," Flora recalled, adding that Georgia once again seemed like the same young woman who long ago had been wildly enthusiastic about the view from the thirtieth floor of the Shelton Hotel.

Georgia remained unusually agile for her age, scampering up ladders and over hills with a sure, quick step in her small flat slippers, often black Ferragamo shoes. "Miss O'Keeffe, you walk just like a fourteen-year-old Indian girl," Jim Hall remarked, reining in his horse as their paths crossed at the ranch one day. Traditionally, old people tended to stay relatively active in the salubrious, dry climate of New Mexico. In the thirties the doctor and lawyer with the longest practices in the United States were said to be New Mexicans. But Georgia was more likely to credit the retention of her catlike grace to sessions with Ida Rolf. Dr. Rolf believed that a properly aligned body, achieved by pressing on sheaths of soft connective tissue, eased chronic tension and enhanced feelings of well-being. In the forties, when she was tense and tired from the work of settling Stieglitz's estate, Georgia began going to Rolf in New York for treatments, and later she invited her to Abiquiu in order to undergo strenuous massages.

As O'Keeffe's face became familiar to yet another generation, she guarded the privacy of her life more fiercely than ever. She only consented to install a telephone with an unlisted number in the sixties—

for the sake of her Abiquiu neighbors, she said, since they needed another subscriber before the telephone company would put in lines. When strangers on airplanes and in other public places recognized her much-photographed face, she was embarrassed, irritated, and sometimes rude. One time she went to the Santo Domingo corn dance in a wraparound dress cinched by a dramatic hand-tooled belt of silver X's. A man came up to her and asked, "Aren't you Georgia O'Keeffe?" She appraised him coolly for a moment, then replied "No!" leaving him totally speechless and neatly deflated. When unwelcome callers ventured to ask her what she was painting, she was likely to snap, "Nothing—because I'm talking to you!"

A few of her old friendships deteriorated, due in part to her intractability. She tended to become disgusted with friends who, in her judgment, didn't stay true to the best in themselves. As the aging Dorothy Brett became fatter and more eccentric, Georgia lost her desire to see her, even though she was one of only a few old friends who were still alive. Perhaps the saddest break was the one with Spud Johnson. Georgia and Spud had talked about where he would bestow his journals and other papers, and she had put him in touch with the curator of the Stieglitz archive at Yale's Beinecke Library. But when the curator visited New Mexico in 1965, Spud, seemingly having forgotten his promise to meet with him, was in Nebraska. Georgia apparently never forgave him, and at the time he died three years later he was still deeply hurt that he had not heard from her since then.

The life she protected so passionately was one she continued to feel the urge to pare down to essentials. Once, when visiting a peacock breeder with Daniel Rich, she asked for one tail feather, but the owner insisted on giving her three. As they drove away, she studied the feathers carefully, then tossed two of them out the car window. "I wanted only one," she said firmly. She complained about the bother of having two homes and wistfully talked about living in a tent in the desert, opening its flaps, and letting everything inside blow away. When a fire destroyed the uninsured paintings and Indian blankets of New Mexican acquaintances, she telephoned them the next day and remarked that she had often wished for a fire to free her of possessions. The Abiquiu house, where a jade plant had grown into a huge thick-trunked tree in the living room, still represented a kind of worldly responsibility that she resented. She felt she was happier and painted best at the smaller, simpler ranch, which she had made hers with far less effort.

Painting, of course, remained the essence of her life. "Why of course I'm still painting!" she exclaimed to a New York newspaper interviewer at the age of seventy-five. "I'm not old or worn out." No such thing as "retirement" existed when life and work were so interlocked. Since she had less stamina now, however, she was likely to go to bed as early as seven o'clock on painting days. Around this time she described her life to writer Lee Nordness:

> One works because I suppose it is the most interesting
> thing one knows to do. The days one works are the best
> days. On the other days one is hurrying through the
> other things one imagines one has to do to keep one's
> life going. You get the garden planted. You get the roof
> fixed. You take the dog to the vet. You spend a day with
> a friend. You learn to make a new kind of bread. You
> hunt up photographs for someone who thinks he needs
> them. You certainly have to do the shopping. You may
> even enjoy doing such things. You think they have to be
> done. You even think you have to have some visitors or
> take a trip to keep from getting queer living alone with
> just two chows. But always you are hurrying through
> these things with a certain amount of aggravation so that
> you can get at the paintings again because that is the
> high spot—in a way it is what you do all the other things
> for. . . . The painting is like a thread that runs through
> all the reasons for all the other things that make one's
> life.

After her exhibitions in the Southwest in the midsixties, Lloyd Goodrich, the white-haired, dynamic director of the Whitney Museum, sent O'Keeffe a flattering letter inviting her to show at the Whitney. The Whitney had owned her work since the early thirties, had exhibited O'Keeffes in numerous annuals, and had wanted to give her a major show for some time. After being assured that she wouldn't have to do any of the exhausting work of putting the show together after Doris Bry was brought in as guest curator, she gave the go-ahead for yet another retrospective—the first in the New York art capital since Stieglitz's death in 1946, twenty-four years earlier. Afterwards the show would travel to Chicago and San Francisco.

As plans for the exhibit got under way, she felt the impetus to return to the theme of rocks, which she had first painted—brown, pink, red—during her bone period. She lovingly traced the form of a nearly round, glossy black stone in much the same way she had zeroed in on a pear, a fig, an avocado, or a blackish blossom fifty years before. When painted myopically near, the small rock appeared voluminous against a blue sky and as potent as a volcano.

As usual, she worked smoothly with museum officials as long as they did precisely as she wished. Goodrich traveled to Abiquiu to see O'Keeffe's world as well as to see certain of her paintings. Originally planned for 1969, the Whitney retrospective was postponed for a year, to October 1970, because she insisted on having the largest floor, the fourth, for her one hundred and twenty-one works. She also demanded that a lengthy catalog be ready a month before the opening, since there was virtually nothing about her in print. Lloyd Goodrich planned to hang the O'Keeffes chronologically. "You hang by the idea and I hang by the eye," O'Keeffe objected when she learned this, and she promptly decided to supervise the hanging herself.

On opening night one heard the same words used for her—"patrician" and "elegant," for example—as were used to describe her paintings and drawings. The artist looked handsome in a dove-gray silk suit and blue velvet shoes. At her throat she wore the spiral brooch crafted by Alexander Calder, which had been copied in silver to harmonize with her whitening hair. One of the hundreds of people at the opening was an old beau from her days at the Art Students League, George Dannenberg. O'Keeffe shook hands with the old man, as she did with everyone else, but for some reason Dannenberg was disappointed by the encounter. "All I remember is that she had on purple shoes," he remarked sadly afterwards. "Someday we'll meet again."

When the exhibition traveled to San Francisco, she took Blanche Matthias to see it, explaining each picture carefully because her friend's eyesight had dimmed. When they got to her new oil of a rock, *Black Rock with Blue*, Blanche paused and, with a flash of acumen, remarked that it was the most beautiful picture of all. A little smile crept around the corners of Georgia's mouth. She was used to saying that she had never surpassed her early work, but with the rock she had done what she aimed for. "It was the last thing I did," she said to Blanche, "and the best."

Reviewers noted similarities between her work and that of a group of younger painters of the past decade—painters like Kenneth Noland and Ellsworth Kelly, who tended to simplify forms, define edges, focus on a single object, and work in a few colors. (O'Keeffe herself especially admired Kelly's pure colors and clean forms, and once joked that she mistook one of his paintings for hers.) The interest of art historians and critics in this minimalist style helped to draw attention to her work at a time when American artists were being treated like cultural heroes.

To O'Keeffe's astonishment, her retrospective was immensely popular with a generation of people young enough to be her great-grandchildren. As her works traveled to the Art Institute of Chicago and to the San Francisco Museum of Art, they set new attendance records that left every other painter behind except for Andrew Wyeth. At her crowded opening on the West Coast, O'Keeffe was handed flowers and treated like a celebrity. It was evident that her visual vocabulary was once again affecting many viewers far more deeply than that of a merely regional talent or a historical figure, as some critics had characterized her in the fifties. She was back in the mainstream of the modern art movement again.

14 ❖ Shadows

One day in late 1971 Georgia suddenly realized, to her shock and horror, that her eyesight was no longer sharp, She hurried to the phone. "My world is blurred!" she cried in panic to an old friend who immediately rushed to her side. In the next few months, enraged by her terrible loss and sudden helplessness, she visited many eye specialists. It turned out that, at the age of eighty-four, O'Keeffe had lost her central vision and retained only peripheral sight—an irreversible eye degeneration found among the elderly.

As a visual artist whose life had always revolved around her sight, it was an outrageous irony for her to suffer the same fate as Mary Cassatt and lose what was most precious to her. Her exceptionally keen vision had been a source of pride to her since early childhood. In middle age she had tried to protect her eyesight by doing the Bates eye exercises. As she aged, her darting, sparkling, blue-green eyes, hooded in loose skin, reflected her lively mind. Now in old age, she was unable to bring into precise focus many of the images that made her solitary life so gratifying and she stopped painting.

She began to use a magnifying glass that she sardonically called "my eye." She wrote Blanche Matthias that Abiquiu was lovely, or rather, she amended the statement to explain to her sightless friend, it was lovely in her mind's eye, since she now saw it best with her memory. O'Keeffe had "talking records" ordered for her as well as a subscription to the large-print edition of the *New York Times*.

One autumn day at the ranch in 1973 she heard a knock. At her kitchen door was a tall young man in his late twenties, with a brown moustache and a long ponytail, who worked at the Presbyterian conference center. He inquired whether she had any jobs for him to do. O'Keeffe was accustomed to having young strangers drop by. ("What can you say to visitors, especially to aspiring artists?" she used to ask. " 'Go home and work!' " Or else, " 'Nobody's good at the beginning.' ") Used to turning them away, she replied negatively to this caller, and he began to walk away. Then she remembered that she had some paintings that needed to be wrapped for shipping, so she called him to come back. She noticed that he spoke in an educated manner, learned that he was able to type, and before long began to rely on him to do odd jobs around the house. "He came just the moment I needed him," she recalled gratefully a few years later.

Soon after she hired Juan Hamilton, O'Keeffe had telephoned Jim Hall and asked him to come over to fill her in on him, to find out whether he was trustworthy. Hall, who knew about Hamilton's family, told her that Hamilton's father was a Presbyterian missionary and educator, and that Juan had been brought up in Ecuador, Colombia, and Venezuela before the family returned to New York when he was fifteen. After graduating from college in Nebraska, he studied sculpture at Claremont Graduate School in California. Then he married a fellow student, moved to Vermont, and built a house while working as a potter. When the marriage broke up two years later, a friend of the Hamiltons wrote Hall and asked whether Juan would be able to stay at Ghost Ranch, which was in a region with a Hispanic culture that was close to the one of his boyhood. Hall agreed and Hamilton arrived in spring 1972 and soon went to work in the kitchen of the conference center. Hall concluded his account by saying that he believed Juan could be trusted.

Juan, divorced and in debt, reminded O'Keeffe of "a wilted leaf." The hippie invasion of Taos and other northern New Mexican towns a few years before had left her disgusted with young people who shrugged off hard labor. After she learned that Hamilton was a potter, she told him that if he was going to stay around he must get back to his own work. Soon he was working with clay on O'Keeffe's kitchen table, and, slowly, asymmetrical pots began to take shape, sometimes finished with blackish-brown patinas. They looked strikingly similar to her paintings of magnified, bulbous black rocks, which she believed she was no longer able to paint. O'Keeffe, who always had a strong tactile sense, enjoyed the feel of their forms, in the same way she liked rubbing a smooth river rock between her fingers.

O'Keeffe decided that the young man had the same deep vein of creativity in him that was so dominant in her and that she had shared with Stieglitz. So, for virtually the first time in her life, the famous artist who had never formally taken a student became deeply interested in someone else's artistic development. She encouraged Hamilton and placed some of his heavy-bottomed urns with tiny mouth openings in her white-carpeted Abiquiu studio on top of black filing cabinets along with her shells, stones, and other treasures.

Soon Hamilton quit his job at the conference center and went to work for O'Keeffe on a full-time basis. He bought land that had a small adobe house on it in the hamlet of Barranca, a few miles west of the village of Abiquiu in the direction of the ranch. O'Keeffe urged him to focus on his pottery and, at the same time, began to build a career for him, as Stieglitz had done for her. Five years after they met, he had his first show at the Robert Miller Gallery in New York, where he exhibited fourteen vessels (all dating from the time he went to work for her). Announcements of the show were mailed to O'Keeffe's well-connected acquaintances, and most of Hamilton's works were sold—including two to New York's Metropolitan Museum.

Previously, O'Keeffe had shown little interest in ceramics. As a Chatham schoolgirl, she had told a classmate that she disliked the "dirty" feel of clay on her fingers. At Columbia Teachers College she received only an average grade in a clay modeling class. Then, after a sole piece of sculpture she had done was exhibited by Stieglitz at 291 in 1917, the piece was said to have been destroyed. During her travels in later life, she usually avoided the ceramics rooms in museums.

Consequently, when she allowed Hamilton to teach her how to make hand-rolled pots, it represented a complete change in attitude. Experimenting with clay gave her a chance to get back to work in a medium that relied as much on touch as on sight. As she began to make something again, she discovered that her urge to create was still as strong as ever. Relieved and excited, she had a kiln built at the ranch for firing the pots. She became so interested in working in three dimensions that, after visiting the sculpture park of her friend and collector Harriet Bradley in Milwaukee, she worked for a while with cardboard models of a ten-foot white form that she envisioned erecting at Ghost Ranch with the help of Hamilton.

As time went on, however, O'Keeffe became frustrated by her slow progress in clay. "The clay controls me, I can't control it," she complained. "I can't make the clay speak like Juan can make it speak." Furthermore, the bending made her back ache, and she accidentally smashed one of the first pots she finished. One day she grabbed a brush from the hand of a girl who was doing some varnishing at the ranch. "I just *have* to hold a brush in my hand!" she exclaimed. In fact, she was gradually working her way back to painting. She realized that, even with her dimmed eyesight, she had more control with a brush of paint than with coils of clay, and she began to work in watercolor, and even in oil, again.

In October 1976, O'Keeffe and Hamilton went to Washington, D. C., to tend to some business relating to the Stieglitz photographs at the National Gallery of Art and to discuss the possibility of an O'Keeffe museum in New Mexico under the auspices of the Smithsonian Institution. On a brilliantly sunny autumn day they walked to the Freer Gallery to see the Chinese paintings and then continued walking all the way to the Lincoln Memorial. Then O'Keeffe, just a month short of eighty-nine, rested on a rock near the reflecting pool and gazed up at the soaring white Washington Monument, which punctured the clear blue sky. Suddenly she visualized a painting to be done. The resulting series of oils, titled *From a Day with Juan*, clearly depicts the midsection of a grayish obelisk. The third oil in the sequence, painted in 1977, thrust into space with a fierce, defiant joy.

In the spring of 1977, when Juan and Georgia were visiting the wooded farm of Georgia's friend Esther Underwood Johnson in Oldwick, New Jersey, they saw an unused barn studio full of fine artist's materials belonging to her son. "Why not come paint?" Juan asked O'Keeffe. They both began to work in watercolors with big brushes, enjoying themselves immensely. Her view of the orchard out the bathroom window, *Pink and Green Spring*, evoked with sensitive and sure strokes a row of bright apple-green trees with a soft pink space vibrating in between them. She also did a group of blue watercolors— round balls and evenly balanced slashes—surprisingly like the more taut ones she had executed in the summer of 1916, and, indeed, one of them was named *Like an Early Abstraction.*

O'Keeffe's tenacious instinct for survival had enabled her to make the immense adjustment necessary for her to paint with shadowy vision. She even courageously and proudly remarked that her new way of seeing light, shadow, color, and line was "interesting," and that it gave her new painting ideas. Hamilton and other people encouraged her to do anything to keep on working, reminding her that Matisse, although bedridden, kept going by cutting brightly colored paper with scissors. O'Keeffe learned to take tubes of paint to her housekeeper, to ask her to read out loud the names of the colors on the labels, and then, with the information memorized, she would return to her studio. She also adopted the centuries-old practice of hiring studio assistants to execute her ideas. She would direct an assistant to hold a piece of twine or a yardstick against a canvas so she could visualize a form (sometimes by peering through binoculars from across the studio), then she would have him draw the shape in charcoal, mix the paints, and do some of the background brushwork himself.

In 1980 a controversy arose about whether she should publicly acknowledge such help. It began when a young assistant, John Poling, claiming that he only wanted to set the record straight, stated that he had collaborated with O'Keeffe on several oils in the obelisk series, one of which was reproduced in *ARTnews.* O'Keeffe sharply disagreed with the idea of admitting any help, even though the color modulations of the oils show less subtlety than her earlier paintings. "Mr. Poling was the equivalent of a palette knife," she said. "He was nothing but a tool."

Her other senses, still extraordinarily acute, enabled her to largely camouflage her handicap and precisely detect what was going on around her. She remained surefooted, heard the faintest sound, and discerned each of the spices in her food. In her great pride, she rarely spoke of her crippled vision, and some visitors were unaware of it, particularly when she pointed out sights with her cane. Other people wondered how much she actually saw since her sight seemed to fluctuate considerably. Sometimes she groped for a doorknob, but at other times she noticed when a small reproduction of one of her paintings was wrong side up. "She doesn't miss a thing," observed her sister Claudia wryly. One of her college-age housekeepers even suspected that her partial blindness was a game she played in order to hoodwink everyone around her.

Despite her diminished powers as an artist, in the summer of 1982 she had the pleasure of astonishing the public again. In one of the rare times that an O'Keeffe sculpture had been exhibited, an eleven-foot, organic spiral of cast aluminum, painted black, dominated a sculpture show of twenty American sculptors at a San Francisco museum. Its prototype was a two-foot white plaster version made in 1945. When O'Keeffe visited the exhibition, leaning on Hamilton's arm, she "saw" the show by letting Juan guide her hand over the forms. As the two slowly toured the gallery, a faint smile appeared on her face. She was heard to remark that she bet Noguchi had expected that *he* would get top billing.

Most of the time she seemed sweeter and more feminine now than at any time before in her long life. Some friends attributed her apparent mellowing to a graceful aging eased by growing fame, whereas other people attributed it to the closeness with Hamilton. At his urging, the woman who had often worn deadly-serious black since early adulthood began to wear colors in public—turquoise, maroon, dark green in pure Amish cotton, silk, or velveteen that fabric artist Carol Sarkisian usually had stitched into kimonos.

Juan had entered O'Keeffe's life when she was despondent over her dependency and her inability to paint. Now she was immensely thankful to him for getting her back to work, as she had been grateful to Jean Toomer during her period of depression in the thirties. The friendship with Hamilton also helped relieve the loneliness of old age, and he even helped her to laugh at her increasing frailties and forgetfulness. By enabling her to enjoy life and to paint again, he seemed to sustain her will to keep going. The two liked to tease one another and to crack jokes, sometimes at the expense of O'Keeffe's admirers. In this respect, she was not very different from the younger Georgia who used to ridicule the teachers in Texas, her in-laws at Lake George, and the artists and writers of Taos. Once, when they called on Carol Sarkisian and her husband Paul, a well-known artist, who lived in an old school in Cerrillos, New Mexico, Juan put on roller skates and began to wheel around their gymnasium. Suddenly he swooped down, lifted the delicate O'Keeffe up in his arms, and whirled her around the floor. She giggled with merriment, in the way Patsy O'Keeffe might have behaved at the Art Students League, before the need to earn a living forced her to revert to her underlying seriousness.

The relationship between O'Keeffe and Hamilton appeared to consist of many elements: man-woman, parent-child, artist-artist— roles all inspired by sincere respect and genuine affection. O'Keeffe often primped before Juan arrived. She would light up in his entertaining company and was delighted by his remarks. "She's in love with him," stated Jane Oseid, a blond college student from California who helped keep house for O'Keeffe for a year until the summer of 1977. O'Keeffe's attachment to Hamilton worried several close relatives and old friends, one of whom observed that throughout history powerful old ladies had frequently sought the allegiance of a younger man to give them the illusion that they were desirable again. "Juan's the son she never had, and the lover she repressed the need for," the friend surmised.

Their affection, her coquettishness, and his possessiveness eventually led to persistent rumors that O'Keeffe and Hamilton were married. For a while, not even O'Keeffe's closest friends, who remarked that O'Keeffe had always been a law unto herself, knew for sure. It was said that she was greatly amused by the gossip. When Hamilton was asked directly by a reporter in the fall of 1978 whether the rumors were true, at first he replied, "No comment," thereby further fueling the stories. A few months later, however, he publicly denied the marriage talk as O'Keeffe had habitually done in private. What he really needed, Hamilton observed to a reporter for *People* magazine, was a twenty-three-year-old Georgia O'Keeffe. A few years later he did marry a young woman and have children. "Take good care of my grandmother," he would say to the household staff as he headed out the door.

❖

From the first, Hamilton had encouraged O'Keeffe to be more receptive to interview requests and other offers that streamed in, and his assistance made it easier for her to consider them. After New Mexico's governor Jerry Apodaca took office in 1975, a young cultural aide, Allan Pearson, suggested turning the anteroom outside the governor's office in Santa Fe into a gallery for state artists. Despite O'Keeffe's longtime aloofness from the local art scene and her reputation for rarely lending paintings, Pearson invited her to be the first artist exhibited in the Governor's Gallery. To his astonishment, Hamilton telephoned six weeks later to say that they would drive down to see the space. O'Keeffe and Hamilton approved it, and they began to make plans for her second show (albeit a minuscule one of only twelve paintings this time) in her home state.

The reticent painter had been ambivalent about William Einstein's idea that she write about her work herself because she had never thought of herself as a "word person," despite the fact that she had always exhibited a distinctive, lucid, and compelling writing style in her letters. Nonetheless, she began to write down a few things at the time Einstein made the suggestion until he returned to Paris and there was no one to prod her. She fell back on quoting Sir Joshua Reynolds, who had said that an artist should sew up his mouth. "I think it's very silly to talk about myself like this," she objected to an interviewer in 1934. "I don't approve of it at all." Although she occasionally had written essays for her exhibition catalogs, she declined to do so for her retrospectives in Chicago and New York in the forties. Then in the seventies, after one of her secretaries discovered the old notes she had written down for Einstein, Hamilton began to urge her to continue.

Because of Hamilton's encouragement and her growing interest in publicity, she overcame her old reluctance to write about herself, and agreed to write a book about her art for mass distribution. She asked Juan, despite his lack of publishing experience, to oversee its production—to be her eyes for her. She was one of a very few important painters with no major book about her work, and for this reason she was able to win a rare degree of contractual control over the design and color plates of the first edition of her book from her publisher, Studio Books, a division of Viking Press in New York. As work on the book progressed, Viking editors traveled to Abiquiu to get her approval of the transparencies, layout, and proofs from the actual printing plates.

Her anxiety over the venture ended when the first copy of the signed and numbered edition of *Georgia O'Keeffe* arrived in Abiquiu in the fall of 1976, and the first glowing review was read to her over the telephone from New York. Priced at seventy-five dollars, the book contained more than a hundred reproductions—some of paintings never before shown publicly—and was outselling the latest Andrew

Wyeth book by Christmastime. Opened, the huge book measured an awkward two feet across, as if the artist had deliberately meant to challenge the public to learn, as she put it, "how paintings happen."

How they happened was told in startlingly effective, simple, short Anglo-Saxon words that combined to create vivid, evocative images. Old friends commented that the novella-length narrative—in which she focused on beautiful objects and amusing predicaments in her quest to be genuinely herself—was in the artist's true voice. Reviewers, however, were sometimes puzzled. In his review for *The New Yorker*, art critic Sanford Schwartz described her tone as oddly "casual and regal" at the same time, a voice that kept the reader in a quandary as to whether the artist was being "sarcastic, deliberately funny or just direct." He continued, in words that perceptively characterized her personality: "Her voice is hauntingly off-key: it is always a shade too remote, too headstrong, or too naive."

While production of the book was under way, O'Keeffe allowed a television crew to spend five days filming her world, in October 1975. After turning down earlier offers from other film makers, she had accepted the one from Perry Miller Adato of National Educational Television in New York because she had offered her the chance to speak for herself. She was uncomfortable as usual answering questions about herself during the filming, so that sometimes she replied to obvious or familiar ones with barely concealed impatience, particularly while walking in the snowy Black Place, with the youthful camera crew trying to keep up with her rapid pace.

But when the completed, award-winning paean to her was aired two years later on her ninetieth birthday in 1977, her humor and courage plainly glowed throughout it. She flew to Washington, D.C., the day before her birthday to see the film and to attend a reception afterwards at the National Gallery of Art, where some of her paintings and Stieglitz photographs of her were on display. "O'Keeffe sailed through it all with an inner composure so pervasive, and so catching, that the entire affair acquired an unlikely mellow air, a public ceremony improbably turned into a genuine celebration," observed a newsman at the mobbed event. The film was widely acclaimed and often re-broadcast.

Then, in the autumn of 1978, fifty-one photographs of her, taken by Stieglitz many years before, were displayed at the Metropolitan Museum in New York. The *New York Times* art critic Hilton Kramer hailed the exhibtion—which contained some nudes never before shown publicly—as "an extraordinary event, quite the most beautiful and moving photographic show in recent memory," thus recalling the enthusiasm with which a portion of the photographic portrait had first been received in 1921. O'Keeffe and Hamilton had made their selection from five hundred prints, after spreading them out on a large table in Abiquiu, to assemble the document of the famous liaison between the young painter and the master photographer. Once O'Keeffe became so lost in memories stirred up by her younger image that, when she walked by a mirror, she was surprised to remember that her hair had turned white. But most of the time she felt far removed from the dark-haired young woman in the photographs with the full, firm flesh.

Although in old age her earlobes and nose seemed accentuated and the characteristic rise of her left eyebrow and the curl of her lip more pronounced, other things remained the same. When a Chatham school chum saw a snapshot of the wrinkled, aged artist, she exclaimed that she had seen exactly the same direct intense gaze on the chubby face of teen-age "Georgie" seventy years before.

Memories of her marriage to Stieglitz seemed to come flooding back to O'Keeffe as she studied the photographs. In her brief but provocative text for the handsome book that accompanied the photographic exhibit, she hinted at the powerful attraction she and Stieglitz had had for one another and the bitter struggles that the prints so clearly revealed. Stieglitz's old friend Herbert J. Seligmann had been angry that she had expressed her debt to Stieglitz so sparingly in her art book and in the television documentary. But in the book of Stieglitz's breathtaking photographs, O'Keeffe wrote that thirty years after his death she still had the same respect for his work that had been responsible for cementing her alliance with him during his lifetime. As she passed the age of eighty-two, Stieglitz's age at his death, she liked to reminisce about him fondly, telling young photographers amusing stories that illustrated the intensity with which he photographed. When she was younger, she had had to suppress her impatience with her elderly husband's numerous ailments, but now that she was subject to chest pains herself perhaps she felt more compassion. O'Keeffe permitted plans to be made by Hamilton and a young art historian, Sarah Greenough, for a Stieglitz retrospective in early 1983 at the National Gallery of Art and for an accompanying book to beautifully reproduce her husband's photographs and quote from his letters. In a grand gesture of respect to Stieglitz, his ninety-five-year-old widow made the trip from Abiquiu to attend the opening.

Soon after he began to work for her, Hamilton was handling her mail, screening her telephone calls, and getting involved in her business and personal affairs. Not unlike Stieglitz and the irritating, idiosyncratic way he sometimes stood between O'Keeffe and the public, Hamilton also had a way of sometimes being an undiplomatic emissary. Although she had never had easy relations with the people of Abiquiu, mattrs got worse, and in the summer of 1977 someone printed obscenities about the elderly woman and her young man on her high adobe wall. Once when he sensed hostility toward him from one of O'Keeffe's old friends, he jumped into her black Volvo and angrily drove off in the direction of Colorado. Incidents such as these caused some of O'Keeffe's friends to worry that he was forcing her to choose between him or them. O'Keeffe, however, was supposed to have remarked that she had always liked difficult men.

Undoubtedly, the most serious casualty of O'Keeffe's relationship with Hamilton was her thirty-year alliance with Doris Bry. After having helped O'Keeffe settle the Stieglitz estate by the early fifties, Bry had continued to handle estate matters and to care for the O'Keeffe paintings stored in New York. (Also involved with the Stieglitz photographs, Bry had written the catalogue for the 1958 Stieglitz retrospective at the National Gallery of Art.) After serving as guest curator for O'Keeffe's 1970 retrospective at the Whitney, Bry edited and published *Georgia O'Keeffe Drawings*, a portfolio of ten drawings signed and numbered by the artist, which was reissued in 1974 in another elegant limited edition, along with the artist's brief descriptions, entitled *Some Memories of Drawings*. Several years after O'Keeffe's break with Edith Halpert, Bry had begun to act as the artist's agent, negotiating the sales of paintings and representing O'Keeffe to the public. Like Stieglitz, Bry rarely loaned a painting, avoided selling to art dealers or to speculators, and carefully kept prices high by placing relatively few O'Keeffes on the market during a year and saving the best pictures for the best collections. She often insisted that potential buyers agree to various conditions, such as the artist's right of refusal if the painting came up for resale, barring loans to group shows, specifying it be hung on a white wall, retaining reproduction rights, consulting on reframing and repairs, and other matters. Bry later claimed that she did "just about anything except paint the paintings so [O'Keeffe] would be free to paint."

As Hamilton became more and more important in O'Keeffe's life, he began to negotiate the sale of paintings without Bry's knowledge. In 1975, for example, he and O'Keeffe sold two paintings to a Chicago art dealer. One was priced at half its worth and the other at double its value, in Bry's opinion, and the sale was made without safeguarding reproduction and resale rights—all of which threatened to ruin the market that Bry had established, she believed. Tensions mounted and in the spring of 1977 O'Keeffe dismissed Doris Bry, the woman who had fiercely guarded her privacy for years, and promptly sued for the return of her paintings and other property that were stored by Bry in New York vaults.

In Georgia's affidavit, sworn in June, the painter claimed that her problems with her agent were longstanding and finally had become "intolerable," although Bry disagreed with that interpretation of her relationship with the aging artist. "I am genuinely sorry that the relationship between us is over," she said, "but it is entirely the result of Miss Bry's insistence on dealing with my paintings as though they were her own and acting toward me as though I was working for her."

O'Keeffe may have mellowed in recent years in some respects, but she was still extremely willful. The atmosphere around the artist now became distinctly Machiavellian, owing to all the secrecy, rumors, intrigue, speculation, and vying for influence as court papers were sealed.

Doris Bry countersued, arguing that she had an unbreakable agreement with O'Keeffe. In August 1978 a New York federal court judge dismissed that argument but left unsettled Bry's further claim that she had been more than an art agent, and therefore she was entitled to more than an agent's 25 percent commission. Beginning in the fall of 1977, a lengthy period of taking depositions began in preparation for a trial. Bry remarked bitterly that were she able to life her live over again, she would not devote it to Georgia O'Keeffe. Five years later the artist and agent reached a private settlement and the suit was dismissed.

On the opening night of the pottery exhibition in New York in the fall of 1978, Bry had notice of a lawsuit served against Hamilton, alleging that he had influenced the aging artist to turn against her former agent, and citing thirteen million dollars in damages. Hamilton subsequently filed a countersuit, charging Bry with damaging his name. O'Keeffe came loyally to his defense, believing by now that she had to choose between her long-time dealer and the young potter. "Juan has done so much more for me than she was ever able to do," she said. "We've done a great deal of good work together."

Some years earlier, O'Keeffe had realized she must make plans for her estate after her death—for her homes, books, art collection, and, of course, her own paintings—her ethereal dreams "constructed of steel," in the words of a critic many years ago. In the summer of 1979, O'Keeffe revised her will again, naming young Hamilton—"my friend"—her executor, instead of Doris Bry, and deeded him the ranch. She also bequeathed him a generous number of her oil paintings, watercolors, drawings, and pastels. She divided another fifty-two works between eight museums around the country. Other powers were granted to Hamilton, such as the right to give away the remaining O'Keeffes in the residual estate to charitable institutions. He would become owner of her books, records, and other personal property as well as papers not going to the Beinecke archive at Yale University and photographs and prints not given to the National Gallery of Art. Gifts of money were granted to neighbors, friends, and employees, but none to relatives. Then the 91-year-old artist signed the will with the large and barely legible penmanship of a blind person. The will was amended in November of 1983 and again in August of 1984; changes strengthened Hamilton's claim to the estate, as O'Keeffe's signature became more tremulous, sprawling, and childlike. In fact, after her death, several of her relatives would legally challenge the amended will, charging that it was never the elderly artist's true intention to give her residual estate—worth millions of dollars in art work alone—to Hamilton personally instead of to museums, universities, and other tax-exempt organizations.

❖

In the wake of the television documentary and a paperback edition of O'Keeffe's book about her art, there was a resurgence of articles about the artist in newspapers and mass magazines, and reproductions of O'Keeffes began to appear everywhere. Her wash of a red canna graced the jacket of an art book about watercolors, one of her cow skulls appeared on the jacket of a publication about American painting, a shell showed up on the cover of a biology textbook, and her blackbird gliding over snowy hills was reproduced on UNICEF greeting cards. "I'm getting to be publicity-mad," O'Keeffe remarked to a friend around that time. Then, in the winter of 1978–79, a giant brown banner heralding the photography exhibit—reading "GEORGIA O'KEEFFE—A PORTRAIT BY ALFRED STIEGLITZ"—flapped outside the Metropolitan Museum of Art on Fifth Avenue.

Whenever she ventured anywhere she was received as a celebrity—even, occasionally, in faraway Abiquiu. Since its start in 1973, the music-loving artist had generously assisted the summer Santa Fe chamber music festival, allowing it to reproduce a different O'Keeffe on its advertising posters every year. In the summer of 1977 O'Keeffe was driven to a festival performance held in the orchard of the Ghost Ranch conference center, and arrived a few minutes late. As she walked to her seat with her friend, virtually every head in the audience swiveled in her direction and away from the musicians flanked by posters of her lovely, wide-open purple petunias. A few years later the festival commissioned a young composer, John Harbison, to write a piano quartet and he dedicated it to her.

O'Keeffe continued to wear the mantle of fame uneasily, however. She found it embarrassing to be called "great," she confided to Bryn Mawr students in 1971. Around that time amateur historians and town boosters in her birthplace of Sun Prairie named a park for her and naïvely asked her to donate a painting to their tiny historical museum. But after what they interpreted as a series of rebuffs (capped by her refusal to ride in their bicentennial parade), the park was abruptly renamed for someone else.

Pilgrimages began to be made to Abiquiu by such well-known personages as Andy Warhol and Joan "of Arts" Mondale. Pete Seeger played her a song on a flute he made from a bird's leg she had given him on an earlier visit. The fashion designer Calvin Klein arrived by helicopter to find her wearing a cream cardigan with black bands he had left on her doorstep five years before. A collector of her work, Klein revealed that her photograph was in his bedroom, and he called the visit "a religious experience." Photographs taken of Klein at the ranch, including some when he posed like a dazed lover in her bedroom, were later used in advertisements for his clothing.

To ward off all the people seeking her out, O'Keeffe kept changing the unlisted telephone number of her private party line, which rang in both houses. Unannounced visitors found that she was still unpredictably gracious or emphatically rude. "I've wanted to meet you for years," exclaimed one young artist outside her gate in 1970. "Well, here I am. What do you want to know?" replied O'Keeffe, inviting her in and, with a gentle tug of her caller's long, loose, hair, advising her to protect it from the sun.

But another time she mockingly sat with her back to two young admirers while a friend pretended to be the famous O'Keeffe. Sometimes she walked right up to gaping tourists, one hand on her hip, and rendered them speechless by demanding, "And what can I do for you today?" She loved to tell about the time she opened the gate to a stranger, who asked to see Georgia O'Keeffe. "Front side!" she declared, then turned and announced, "Back side!" then turned again and said, "Goodbye!" and slammed the gate.

Remarking that she had been happiest before she moved to New York, when she had the freedom of anonymity, O'Keeffe resented the bag of mail that arrived each day from museums, art dealers, students, historians, and ordinary people who sensed something in her paintings they vaguely yearned for. ("Oh, my, they do go on," she was likely to sigh when her fan mail was read to her, indifferent as always to lavish praise.) She hired part-time secretaries to cope with the two-foot stack of letters on the sagging table in her studio and complained that the Abiquiu house was like a New York office. Most of the time she made the effort to reply politely to requests in three brief, carefully worded sentences—although she also admitted to throwing much of the mail into the wastebasket sometimes.

"It's the last time I'll do this—I'd rather sleep," she had complained when she went to Chicago in 1967 to receive an award from the Art Institute of Chicago art school. Yet ambivalence actually marked her attitude toward the laurels the world extended to her, and she continued to make trips to collect honorary degrees that were bestowed on her seasonally by such prestigous Ivy League institutions as Harvard and Columbia universities. In a sense she remained the daughter of the aristocratic Ida Totto who had been eager to raise her family above its farm origins, but on the other hand, her sharp, satirical, outsider's eye mocked the pretensions surrounding academic pomp and polite chitchat. "She was dignified to all appearances but mischievous and even a bit nasty in conversation," recalled Lilli Hornig, an educator and the wife of the president of Brown University which awarded O'Keeffe a degree "but actually [she] seemed to love all the pageantry of Brown's unusual festivities and took part in the long march down the hill."

Her equivocal attitude was also evident in the photograph she chose for the back of the jacket for her art book. In it, she and a chow stood with their backs to a camera held by Hamilton, one hand on her hip and the other on a cane. She relished the pose, calling it "a prize," and explained that she and her dog were looking at the future. But others wondered. "There is an unattractive Cheshire Cat archness about it, as if O'Keeffe were being sporty with her own public image, and with her public, as she is with the cane," wrote critic Sanford Schwartz.

When it was suggested to the National Park Service that O'Keeffe's Abiquiu home become a national historic site, the Park Service rejected the idea. New Mexico Congressmen persisted and in September, 1980, the secluded site was approved by Congress, funds were appropriated, and the Park Service was ordered to accept the gift. Meanwhile, the villagers of Abiquiu became alarmed that the museum would threaten their isolation with an invasion of tourists and traffic. When an environmental impact study for controlled access by tourists in vans did not quiet their concerns, O'Keeffe, who easily sympathized with their desire for privacy, asked for the repeal of the legislation and directed Juan Hamilton to give the walled villa to a charitable or other institution after her death. In another gesture of good neighborliness to those she had lived among for almost forty years, she gave fifty thousand dollars towards a new village elementary school on Christmas Eve of 1982.

For some time prices of her paintings had been escalating. As the stock market took off in the late sixties and her pictures were about to break into the six-figure bracket, she was tight-lipped about her prices. "You are not going to get that out of me!" she declared to a reporter in 1968. "I have gone with the market. I doubt there are many that get more. But the market is ridiculous now, fantastic." Ever mindful of Stieglitz's stern lectures that she not undersell herself in dollar-conscious America, she usually refused to negotiate her prices, which had been high since her headline-making sale to the mysterious Frenchman in 1928. In March 1973 her *Poppies* of 1950, owned by the Edith Halpert estate, set a new O'Keeffe auction record when it sold for one hundred and twenty thousand dollars at Sotheby Parke

Bernet Galleries in New York. Prices for O'Keeffes continued to steadily climb and, twelve years later, Sotheby's set another record when it sold her *White Rose-New Mexico* of 1930 for more than one and a quarter million dollars, as prices promised to soar even higher.

The notoriety surrounding her high prices was not without some hazards, however. In 1972 a group of prominent artists, including O'Keeffe, contributed paintings and other works of art to an auction run by two Manhattan art galleries to raise money for the McGovern for President campaign. Shortly thereafter the press reported that O'Keeffe's small abstraction was the highest priced in the group, at forty thousand dollars. As a result of being publicly associated with President Nixon's political opposition, O'Keeffe earned a place on the White House enemies list, along with hundreds of other loyal Americans. "I'm delighted!" said this utterly American artist when the list was made public. "I think that's a very good place to be." She didn't stay in presidential disfavor long, however: Five years later President Ford awarded her, and twenty-one other people, the nation's highest civilian honor, the Medal of Freedom. In the early eighties James Stieglitz, her greatnephew, pleaded guilty to criminal charges of forging O'Keeffe's signatures on phony lithographs of her work.

As the artist made plans for her paintings after her death, she expressed the desire to buy back some of her best work. She also initiated a lawsuit to recover three small O'Keeffes that she remembered disappearing from An American Place a few months before Stieglitz's death in 1946. The paintings had turned up thirty years later in an art gallery in Princeton, New Jersey run by an art dealer named Barry Snyder. While the paintings were stored in a bank vault, a long legal battle began. O'Keeffe at first lost her cause in the New Jersey lower court, next she won on appeal, and then Snyder appealed to the New Jersey Supreme Court which, in the summer of 1980, ordered a new trial to establish if the paintings were actually stolen and if O'Keeffe had been negligent in not reporting them missing for many years. It looked like it would be the first major art theft case to go to trial in more than a decade, and it was viewed in the art world as one that might establish more clearly who owns stolen art. But the legal question was never resolved. O'Keeffe and Snyder reached an out-of-court settlement, which reportedly arranged for each to keep one painting and sell the third, *Cliffs*, at auction and split the proceeds.

O'Keeffe had long shunned the state-owned Museum of Fine Arts in Santa Fe, fearing a lack of security and professionalism, and, consequently, for many years its lone O'Keeffe was a small, dark, moody Lake George landscape willed to it by Rebecca Strand James. In late 1980 O'Keeffe sent the museum a large donation to help it buy one of her important paintings for their collection. When the board of directors hesitated over the four hundred thousand dollar price tag for one of her favorite paintings, *Summer Days*, the artist withdrew the offer and sold it instead to Calvin Klein for a million dollars. As museum officials planned a renovation, some of them hoped she would consider an O'Keeffe wing or, at least, an inaugural exhibition; although the artist was willing to consider the latter, she withdrew her cooperation after misunderstandings with museum officials. O'Keeffe's 1979 will had directed her executor to give works to the Museum of Fine Arts and to University of New Mexico, but in August, 1984, they were dropped from the will. At the time of her death two years later, only four works by the state's greatest living artist were in public collections in New Mexico. After it became apparent that the institutions might challenge her intent to disinherit them, state officials worked out an agreement with Juan Hamilton to give the state museum and university paintings worth one-and-a-half million dollars in lieu of estate taxes.

❖

At the end of the activist sixties, the feminist movement had taken hold with another generation of American women. The visibility of women artists grew dramatically as they protested their neglect by museums and galleries. In 1970 the militant Women Artists in Revolution (WAR) demanded equal space for women's art in the Whitney annuals, and, to drive their point home, demonstrators scattered eggs and tampons around the museum. In time, women were organizing feminist galleries, exhibitions, and art schools for one another. One of the most notable events was the creation of Womanhouse, a Los Angeles mansion where feminist imagery was used to mock traditional female roles, such as a "Nurturant Kitchen" covered with latex fried eggs resembling breasts. Many of the growing number of young female artists, searching for an artistic heritage, had the face of Artemisia Gentileschi, a seventeenth-century Italian painter, stenciled on their tee-shirts.

O'Keeffe, however, was no longer the schoolteacher who had read the radical feminist writers of her day, the suffragette who had been forbidden by law to vote until she was thirty-two, the woman artist who had spoken before the National Woman's Party, or even the feminist who had debated with political radical Michael Gold. In old age an artist with boxes of establishment honors neatly stacked on shelves in her Abiquiu house, she felt discomfited by the "undignified" behavior of the young feminists.

Also, activism had never been her style. In 1926 she had told Blanche Matthias, as she would tell Dorothy Brett a few years later, that focusing on one's work was the most important thing. "She tried for more than her potentiality," Blanche had written about her friend. "Most of us only dream that perhaps we have one, and growl because the family or daily grind of life keeps us from finding out about it. 'Too much complaining and too little work,' says O'Keeffe." Fifty years later O'Keeffe repeatedly said that if the young artists worked more and complained less, there would be more of their paintings and sculptures to hang in museums and galleries. "You have a chance to get what you want if you go out and work for it," she would say. "But you must really work, not just talk about it."

Quietly outworking "the boys," of course, had been her strategy in the twenties. Surrounded by the men who flocked to Stieglitz, she painted largely in isolation from artists of her own sex. Although she never forgot how women had jammed her shows then, because they intuitively understood the "woman feeling" in her paintings, she was mindful of Henry McBride's warning as early as 1923 that she would "be besieged by all her sisters for advice—which will be a supreme danger for her" as an artist. Later in life the proudly independent artist did not seek out alliances with peers who were a generation or two younger, such as New York's Louise Nevelson and Helen Frankenthaler, or even Agnes Martin, who lived in a nearby New Mexican village. Consequently, in the seventies O'Keeffe did not sympathize with the desire of young women for female solidarity.

Although she believed that the men had never understood her work, she recalled that, nonetheless, they had helped her tremendously. "Women never helped me," she once declared in old age. "The men helped me." Perhaps she forgot that few women art critics and museum curators were in a postion to help her as much as Stieglitz. Not remembering and not feeling obligated to other women, O'Keeffe came to resent those who tried to appeal to her through feminism—and when feminist Gloria Steinem arrived in Abiquiu with a bouquet of red roses, O'Keeffe refused to see her.

Georgia did remember, however, that being labeled a woman artist in the twenties was synonymous with being called second-rate. She refused to participate in Peggy Guggenheim's landmark show of women's painting in 1943 at her Art of This Century gallery in New York, dramatically declaring at the time—"I am not a woman painter!" In the seventies some among the young generation of feminists pointed out that O'Keeffe had created an essentially female iconography of deep recesses and centered images, as in the magical *Abstraction Blue* of 1927, in which a searing white light beam bisects a turquoise and midnight-blue bulbous shape, which vaporizes into gossamer pink and gaseous blue. When feminist artist Judy Chicago pointed out that O'Keeffe's flowers were symbols of femininity it must have been disturbingly reminiscent, for Georgia, of the turgid Freudian exaggerations penned by Stieglitz's friends when she first began to exhibit. As a result, a half century later, she had no desire to cooperate with films and exhibits about women artists.

Nevertheless, her New York retrospective in 1970 and her inclusion two months later in the show of women artists at the Whitney brought her to the full attention of the young of her own gender. In their eyes, O'Keeffe was an intriguing role model: a lone, strong, prolific woman whose self-reliant, close-to-nature way of life in New Mexico embodied many popular counterculture values. What's more, her individualistic painting style often made untried artists more acutely aware of how art is created through the prism of personality and helped them understand their own inner-directed artistic processes.

The charisma of O'Keeffe's public image inspired an outpouring of portraits, dances, songs, and poems by numerous young people. Artist Mary Beth Edelson, for instance, created a black-and-white poster she called *The Last Supper*, portraying O'Keeffe as Jesus or, in Edelson's words, "the great mother goddess" of women artists. In 1979 O'Keeffe was the only living woman to be included in Judy Chicago's *The Dinner Party*, a tribute in embroidery and porcelain place settings to thirty-nine important women throughout history. O'Keeffe's pink and gray plate, with a fathomless dark cavity, rose off the table higher than any other plate, symbolizing, in Chicago's view, her almost-successful aspiration to be entirely her own woman. It was clear that, regardless of her aloofness from the feminist movement, she, more than anyone else, was "probably nearer to the inner dream of women who want to learn to see as women," in the words of middle western writer Meridel LeSueur, who had been inspired by O'Keeffe's exhortation to create "as a woman" since the twenties.

Despite her diffident public stance, O'Keeffe was in fact interested in the gifted young women she got to know personally. When she received an award from Bryn Mawr in 1971, she encouraged the art students at the women's college. "Paint what's in your head, what you are acquainted with," she urged them. "Even if you think it doesn't count—and for some of you it may not—doing something that is entirely your own may be pretty exciting." And when Carol Merrill, a secretary in her twenties from Albuquerque, wrote her an exceptional letter, O'Keeffe invited her to visit. After waiting a year and a half to gather up the courage, Carol responded and was told to appear on a particular Sunday afternoon and stay for an hour. As it turned out, O'Keeffe spent all afternoon with the attractive, perceptive young woman, who aspired to becoming a poet. Among other things, they talked about health food and looked at the artist's collection of rare books, including signed editions by E. E. Cummings and two uncut first editions of James Joyce's *Ulysses*.

After that, Carol often spent weekends in Abiquiu, typing and cooking for O'Keeffe for wages. When she told the artist that she wrote poetry, O'Keeffe asked where she had been published. The pragmatic question galvanized the young woman into working on her poetry more diligently, into keeping her journal more assiduously, and, eventually, into publishing—among others, a poem about the inspirational O'Keeffe—and, in time Carol became a college teacher of English. Like Stieglitz, O'Keeffe had the capacity to be a powerful clarifier to those around her. Her directness was a kind of disturbing truth serum, which quickly got to the core of the matter at hand.

Carol, who came from Tulsa, Oklahoma, had never been anyplace like O'Keeffe's two homes, where everything—the white marble Saarinen table, black leather Eames chair, black Calder mobile, small Dove oils, Hiroshige snow scene—was, as she put it, so "carefully considered." "Everything is done with full attention," Carol marveled, even to the precise way O'Keeffe folded a silk scarf or a linen handkerchief. "She's not thinking of anything else. She's right there folding that napkin. That's the form she's observing." Like others, Carol found it difficult not to imitate O'Keeffe's deliberate, self-assured, and grace-ful gestures. Also, like many others, she was fascinated by the way O'Keeffe lived fully in the present, with complete awareness of every moment. "One day we were walking out in the cliffs when everything seemed so—different," Carol recalled. "There's something about that woman. It isn't just charisma, and it isn't just personality. I think it's other levels of consciousness."

Once O'Keeffe had declared to Arthur Pack that she was self-sufficient and, therefore, did not believe in God. But, at the same time, it was always obvious that her spirituality went extremely deep. Evangelical Christians found a sense of God in everything she painted, for instance. For her part, O'Keeffe liked to claim that she could convert someone to Catholicism because she understood the attraction of the faith so well, but then she usually added that she could not believe because of her intellectual reservations, particularly about the position of women in the church. In 1966, when Benedictine monks completed a stunning small chapel in a biblical-looking, profoundly silent canyon near the ranch, she became curious about the monastery, and then, impressed by its aesthetics, began to attend the services there from time to time.

Early on Easter Sunday a few years afterwards, O'Keeffe and Carol Merrill arose at 2:30 A.M., ate lightly, donned long woolen black cloaks against the nightime chill, and headed for the Benedictines' isolated monastery in the artist's Volkswagen bus. Once they entered the chapel and found places to sit on the split-log benches, O'Keeffe seemed to merge with the medieval mood created by the incense, flickering candles in wooden troughs, simple carvings on the rock altar, and Navajo rugs on the stone floor. As the dawn sky lightened, eyes gazed upward through a large glass window to a high cliff where a white cross had been placed. At the end of the Mass, the two women, one old and one young, both with handsome, broad-boned faces, arose to leave with the other worshippers. As they passed one of the tunic-clad priests, he inquired if they were mother and daughter. O'Keeffe was greatly amused, but, in a way, he was right—Carol was momen-tarily the daughter, or granddaughter, of Georgia's choice.

❖

In her nineties, Georgia continued to get up at dawn and do

exercises learned from Ida Rolf. After breakfast, she often went into her studio and brought out mail and articles to be read to her by the housekeeper on duty. Sometimes, when she was at the ranch, she walked with the housekeeper and her chows, or, in Abiquiu, she walked around the garden or the driveway, clocking her distance by moving a pebble after each revolution. Her steady strides were not those of a nonagenarian, and, when she was rested, she sometimes startled people by looking decades younger. From time to time she sat motionless in the strong desert sun and asked those around her to describe the appearance of the passing clouds.

From Juan Hamilton and the other young men and women who worked day or night shifts and shared her meals, O'Keeffe learned what was on the minds of the younger generation. She tried Earth Shoes, considered the theories of Buckminster Fuller, and inquired about the effects of marijuana. (She remarked once that she had no desire to smoke pot and alter her finely tuned sense of reality.) Fascinated by the heated waterbed of an old Taos friend, she lay down on it one day when visiting—and promptly took a nap.

She went to bed at sundown, summer as well as winter, since at her great age her body often became utterly exhausted. Before she slept, one of her housekeepers read to her for an hour or two from a book or one of the magazines to which she subscribed, such as *Smithsonian*, *New West*, or *Prevention*. She lay with her eyes closed, seemingly asleep, but the next day she was able to recall entire passages almost word-for-word from what had been read to her. Due to her age, she only dozed off for two or three hours during the night.

From time to time she saw old friends in New Mexico and around the country, such as a visit with Ansel Adams, when she went to his photographic exhibition in Tucson, Arizona. At first she declined the invitation to Alexander Calder's retrospective at the Whitney in the fall of 1976, but changed her mind when she unexpectedly needed to go to New York on business. (She was glad she went, for Calder died shortly afterwards.) Since she had the habit of telephoning friends at dawn after long wakeful nights and detaining visitors for lengthy conversations, some people observed that she was lonely. Loneliness, however, was not an emotion that the proud O'Keeffe admitted to. When asked by a journalist if she was lonely, she pointed out that she talked to her dog, her housekeeper, and, in between, she worked and walked. "What else is there?" she asked. "I can do everything I have to do better here because I don't have anyone to bother me," she said in another conversation. "People bother me."

In the autumn of 1978, the four surviving O'Keeffe siblings—Georgia, Anita, Catherine, and Claudia—gathered in Abiquiu. Each a distinct individual, the sisters were linked to one another by common childhood memories. Throughout her life, Georgia's relationship with each sister had sometimes been stormy, because of their moments of envy and hers of competitiveness. This was especially the case with the multitalented Ida, who had called herself a painter until the time of her death from a stroke in Whittier, California, in 1961. "We were never a close family," admitted Catherine, the only grandmother among the four elderly women (with a granddaughter named Georgia), a peppery woman with sparkling blue eyes, who lived with her retired banker husband in Portage, Wisconsin. "We got along if we didn't see too much of each other."

Proud, stern Anita, who rarely visited New Mexico, was a wealthy widow who usually wintered at Montsorrel, her Palm Beach estate, and summered at Fairholme, her Newport mansion, until her death in the winter of 1985. She left her homes, art collection, and most of her $20 million fortune to the Robert R. Young Foundation and gifts of cash to servants and socialite godchildren. By mutual agreement, Anita and Georgia left each other out of their wills. Interestingly, her ten O'Keeffe oils and five pastels—dating from Lake George flower and leaf studies of 1924 to a New Mexico cottonwood scene of 1954—excluded characteristic southwestern landscapes, further suggesting her distaste for her sister's Southwest. At the age of ninety-seven, Georgia was too frail to attend the Rhode Island funeral when Anita was buried beside her daughter and husband.

It was the youngest sister, Claudia, to whom Georgia remained the closest until Claudia's death in the autumn of 1984. Ever since the days in Texas when Georgia was charged with Claudia's care after their mother's death, the relationship between the two sisters had been a mixture of caring and conflict. "Families are the work of the devil!" Georgia had anxiously exclaimed long ago when her teen-age sister went horseback riding without telling her. In adulthood Claudia became a slim, athletic, affable nursery school teacher who remained single and owned a home in Beverly Hills, California. After her retirement, Claudia appeared in Abiquiu each spring to oversee Georgia's large vegetable garden. She often arrived in a white Cadillac, accompanied by a fluffy lapdog (which Georgia contemptuously called "the spider") and her Cuban maid (inherited from the sisters' deceased brother Francis).

Claudia occasionally appeared tongue-tied in the company of her famous sister's circle of distinguished callers, and her stays in Georgia's home were not always easy. Sometimes she seemed to provoke her older sister, as when, believing that Ida never got her just due as an artist, she helped arrange an exhibit of her work in Santa Fe. Most of the time during Claudia's visits the sisters lived apart, one at Ghost Ranch and the other in the village. "I'm going to the ranch because we fight like cats and dogs," Claudia once remarked to a visitor after Georgia arrived at the Abiquiu house. Although Claudia worried from time to time that she had little importance for her sister except for her service of managing the garden, she was still drawn back to Abiquiu for half the year out of deep loyalty and unspoken love for the sister who still took responsibility for her.

Looking back, Georgia liked to say that she did what she wanted in life and it just worked out—as if she were merely lucky that she discovered the Southwest, that Stieglitz became interested in her, and that people liked her paintings from the start. But that explanation, with the implication that she played a passive role, is too easy. Besides her abundant artistic gifts, her triumph as an artist demanded a clear-eyed, unconflicted will. "I've always known what I've wanted—and most people don't," she declared once.

O'Keeffe was close to the truth another time when she mused that perhaps her success was also due to a streak of aggression in her, or, in her words, to having "taken hold of anything that came along that I wanted." In girlhood she had deliberately decided what kind of person she wished to be, and then she carefully conformed everything to that goal with unrelenting willpower, in the same conscious way that she cultivated a habit of neatness. She devoted her life "to the relentless pursuit of the self . . . [and] step by step was able to extract through the hard won discipline of her inner life a way to reveal her experience," observed one of her peers when she was given a gold medal by the American Academy of Arts and Letters.

Her laserlike focus on painting required sublimations so that she might channel her intense emotions into expression on canvas. As long ago as 1915 she had lectured the more impetuous Anita Pollitzer on the virtues of self-control. Just as she tidied up her studio before inviting anyone in, so she presented an uncomplicated facade to the world. Instead of introspective art talk, much of her conversation remained down-to-earth. "You meet her and you think she's all simplicity," observed a friend of forty years, who added that Georgia's inner landscape was extremely complicated and characterized by numerous repressions.

When O'Keeffe first moved to Manhattan as a young woman, she had not been as sure of herself as she eventually became under Stieglitz's tutelege. But she had arrived with enough assurance to accept what he had to give—an inspired image of herself. As she matured, her healthy ego—necessary to her early attempts to draw in her own way—was exaggerated into a brand of narcissism that is not unusual in an artist, and perhaps is even essential. Her self-assurance, tinged as it sometimes was with an almost adolescent arrogance and gaucherie, suggested that a key piece of her personality had been locked into place when she left Wisconsin at the age of fifteen. One day in the thirties, after she had returned to New York and failed to telephone a certain friend, she ran into her at a party. "Oh, I didn't call you because there was nothing I wanted from you," she blurted out. Her straightforwardness, however, was also her saving grace. Even people who became most exasperated by her egocentricity respected the fact that it, too, was undisguised and as magnified as her other qualities. "Considering that she is a genius, she is a remarkably fine and honest person with shortcomings as we all have," summed up the friend she had failed to telephone after time had mellowed her feelings. Like many others, she was left with admiration for and fascination with the unique O'Keeffe.

Besides having a rich talent, ambition, assistance, and virtually no doubt about the validity of her vision, O'Keeffe had the brains to match her artistic gift and to guide its flowering. Simone de Beauvoir wrote that one is not born a genius, one becomes a genius—and the lives of most women make that evolution impossible. With careful thought, O'Keeffe planned her life so that nothing would impede her development as an artist. Although she hesitated and stopped painting several times during her life, "every stop she took was solid," her old friend Blanche Matthias observed. O'Keeffe herself did not attribute her accomplishment as much to native genius as to extremely hard work and the courage to take risks. She compared her existence to balancing on the thin, sharp blade of a knife where, she long ago decided, it was worth a misstep if she was enjoying herself.

In old age O'Keeffe's passion for Ghost Ranch remained as powerful as it was on the day she first glimpsed it more than forty years before, even though with time the sandy red hills seemed to have shrunken somewhat, and the golden cliffs appeared to have eroded slightly. Each autumn, her traditional season for painting, she liked to linger at the ranch on the road marked "Road Closed Dead End" until the cold drove her out. Then she had the white curtains drawn tight against the curious and moved "downtown," as her young staff jokingly called the house in the village. "I store my belongings, sleep and work in Abiquiu," she once explained, "but I do my living at the ranch." She still climbed the ladder to the roof to take the measure of her majestic valley, which she had crisscrossed many times on foot and on horseback. "Living out there has just meant happiness," she declared, adding she could not get enough of it. "Sometimes I think I'm half mad with love for this place." She still talked about the past when asked about it—the exciting years of the twenties in Manhattan and the early days at Ghost Ranch—but she tried not to dwell on memories or on past regrets. Her laments were about rapidly developing New Mexico. She abhorred the grotesque structures built to carry high-tension wires across her beloved mesas and plains, dwarfing telephone poles and the little crosses of the last Penitentes.

She vehemently scorned the fear of death, but one of her oldest friends suspected that the idea of death was actually intolerable to her. She liked to say that she planned to be reincarnated as a blond with a beautiful soprano voice. "I would sing very high, very clear notes," she said, "without fear." It was undoubtedly not easy for someone as alive as O'Keeffe to accept the fact that someday her ashes would be mingled with her lovely rosy hills, and she would no longer be able to enjoy her world. "When I think of death, I only regret that I will not be able to see this beautiful country anymore," she remarked, then added hopefully, "unless the Indians are right and my spirit will walk here after I'm gone."

As Georgia became increasingly frail in her late nineties, Juan Hamilton helped her purchase a house in Santa Fe, where she reluctantly moved to be near intensive medical care. On the morning of March 6, 1986, when it became apparent that her strength was failing, she was brought to nearby Saint Vincent's Hospital where she died a few hours later at 12:20 P.M. At the age of ninety-eight, O'Keeffe had been in reasonably good health until her body suddenly yielded to complications of old age. When the news of her passing reached the village of Abiquiu just before dusk, a villager began to ring the bells of the little adobe church of St. Thomas the Apostle. The sounds pealed across the river valley, which was beginning to green in the early spring. O'Keeffe's body was cremated the next day, and, at her request, no funeral or memorial service was held, and her ashes were scattered in the landscape with which she will be forever identified.

Sources

Chapter One

Sources, other than those attributed below, include Claudia O'Keeffe, Catherine (O'Keeffe) Klenert, June (O'Keeffe) Sebring, and Mrs. Charles W. Totto. I am indebted to the Reverend Carl Tiedt of Sun Prairie for his manuscript dealing with O'Keeffe family history.

2 "Why . . . beautiful?"—Charlotte Willard, "Georgia O'Keeffe," *Art in America*, October 1963.

5 Wedded . . . bride—*Sun Prairie Countryman*, February 28, 1884.

7 "little . . . child"—Helen Renk, "Georgia O'Keeffe—Sun Prairie Native," *Sun Prairie Star-Countryman*, September 2, 1948.
"I was not . . . all"—Mary Daniels, "The Magical Mistress of Ghost Ranch, New Mexico," *Chicago Tribune*, June 24, 1973.

8 "I had more . . . sight"—Renk, "Georgia O'Keeffe . . ."

9 Jessie Flint—Jessie Flint Williamson to author, September 8, 1977.

10 "She seemed . . . him"—Renk, "Georgia O'Keeffe . . ."

12 "When two . . . knows everything"—Ibid.

14 "I think . . . painting"—Georgia O'Keeffe, *Georgia O'Keeffe*, New York: Viking Press, 1976.
"I decided . . . care"—Mary Braggiotti, "Her Worlds Are Many," *New York Post*, May 16, 1946.

20 "The barn . . . years—"—Letter from O'Keeffe to Mitchell Kennerley, January 20, 1929, Kennerley Collection, Manuscript Division, New York Public Library.

Chapter Two

Other sources include Susan Young Wilson, Claudia O'Keeffe, Catherine (O'Keeffe) Klenert, as well as several Williamsburg residents, notably Duncan Cocke. For much of the material about Chatham Episcopal Institute, I am indebted to a manuscript by Frances Hallam Hurt of Chatham, Virginia.

24 "The most unusual . . . was perfect"—Christine McRae Cocke, "Georgia O'Keeffe as I Knew Her," *The Angelos* (Kappa Delta sorority publication). November 1934.

25 "I started . . . it"—Amei Wallach and Tom Zito, "Georgia O'Keeffe," *Albuquerque Journal*, November 13, 1977.
"her exuberance . . . hands"—Coche, "Georgia O'Keeffe as I Knew Her."
"When . . . want?"—Ibid.

26 "Singing has . . . paint"—" 'I Can't Sing So I Paint!'" *New York Sun*, December 5, 1922.

26 Her easel . . . intently—Cocke, "Georgia O'Keeffe as I Knew Her."

29–30 "the students . . . highly"—Art Institute of Chicago school catalog, 1905–06.

32 "Georgia was great fun . . . her"—John Henderson to author, May 25, 1977.

34 "Everyone called . . . O'Keeffe"—Lila Wheelock Howard to author, September 28, 1977.

35 "a rustle . . . arrived!"—Ronald G. Pisano, *The Students of William Merritt Chase*, Huntington, N.Y.: Heckscher Museum, 1973.
"There . . . fun"—Georgia O'Keeffe, *Georgia O'Keeffe*, New York: Viking Press, 1976.
"It doesn't . . . school"—Ibid.
"The essential . . . *that?*"—Mary Lynn Kotz, "A Day with Georgia O'Keeffe," *Art News*, December 1977.

36 "One instructor . . . public"—Georgia O'Keeffe, "Stieglitz: His Pictures Collected Him," *New York Times Magazine*, December 11, 1949.

37 "I . . . stood"—Ibid.

38 announced in the local newspaper—*Virginia Gazette*, August 31, 1907.

38 "Rather . . . all"—Ernest Watson, "Georgia O'Keeffe," *American Artist*, June 1934.

39 "They made . . . me"—Ralph Looney, "Georgia O'Keeffe," *Atlantic Monthly*, April 1965.

39–40 "O'Keeffe . . . aroused"—Helen Appleton Read, "Georgia O'Keeffe—Woman Artist Whose Art Is Sincerely Feminine," *Brooklyn Eagle*, March 2, 1924.

40 "If . . . could"—Jerry Tallmer, "Daily Closeup: The Silver Lining," *New York Post*, October 17, 1970.
"There . . . time"—Daniel Catton Rich, *Georgia O'Keeffe*, Chicago: Art Institute of Chicago, 1943.

41 "We loved . . . tired"—Mrs. Ashton Dovell to author, May 26, 1977.

42 "Georgia . . . adventure"—Marsden Hartley, *Adventures in the Arts*, New York: Boni and Liveright, 1921.

Chapter Three

Other sources include several Charlottesville residents as well as Mrs. Arthur Macmahon, Mrs. James Ariail, William Pollitzer, and Marie Rapp Boursault.

44 "curiously uninteresting"—Arthur Young to author, August 1, 1978.

"It seemed . . . own"—Jerry Tallmer, "Daily Closeup: The Silver Lining." *New York Post*, October 17, 1970.

46 One of the newspapers that ran headlines about the scandal—*Amarillo Daily News*, September 17, 1912, and subsequent issues.

47 "That . . . emptiness"—Anita Pollitzer, "That's Georgia," *Saturday Review*, November 4, 1950.

48 "I'd . . . space"—Calvin Tomkins, "The Rose in the Eye Looked Pretty Fine," *The New Yorker*, March 4, 1974.

49 "A nice-looking young man . . . gone"—Iantha Bond Hebel, *Badger History*, February 1957.

51 "Filing . . . me"—Mary Lynn Kotz, "A Day with Georgia O'Keeffe," *Art News*, December 1977.

52 "There . . . independent"—Pollitzer, "That's Georgia."

52 "Her colors . . . else"—Ibid.

53 "radiant . . . emotions"—Dorothy Norman, *Alfred Stieglitz: An American Seer*, New York: Random House, 1973.

54 "a Japanese . . . rudeness"—Mahonri Young, *Early American Moderns*, Watson-Guptill, 1974.
   "were like . . . core"—Mabel Dodge Luhan, *Movers and Shakers*, New York: Harcourt Brace, 1936.

55 "I was liking . . . me"—Letter from O'Keeffe to Anita Pollitzer, August 1915, Museum of Modern Art press release, May 1946.
   "I had . . . anything"—Charlotte Willard, "Georgia O'Keeffe," *Art in America*, October 1963.

56 "verve . . . Miss O'Keeffe as teacher"—Letter from Margaret Davis Benton to author, March 15, 1978.

57 "I had . . . out"—Ralph Looney, "Georgia O'Keeffe," *Atlantic Monthly*, April 1965.

58 "a little man"—Letter from O'Keeffe to Pollitzer, February 10, 1916, America Literature Collection, Beinecke Library, Yale University.

59 "Hibernating . . . anything one wishes"—Letter from O'Keeffe to Stieglitz, February 1, 1916, MOMA press release.

59–60 "I believe . . . express yourself?"—Letter from O'Keeffe to Pollitzer, summer 1915, MOMA press release.

60 "This thing . . . there"—Carol Taylor, "Lady Dynamo," *New York World Telegram*, March 31, 1945.
   I grew up . . . own—Georgia O'Keeffe, exhibition catalog statement, Anderson Galleries, January 29, 1923.
   "I feel . . . disgusted"—Letter from O'Keeffe to Pollitzer, October 1915, MOMA press release.

61 "It was . . . walk"—Taylor, "Lady Dynamo."
   "I was . . . myself"—Georgia O'Keeffe, *Georgia O'Keeffe*, New York: Viking Press, 1976.
   "The thing . . . way"—Letter from O'Keeffe to Pollitzer, January 4, 1916, MOMA press release.

62 "I was struck . . . said"—Pollitzer, "That's Georgia."

63 "I always . . . up"—Modern Honors First Woman," *Art Digest*, June 1946.
   "purest . . . while"—Letter from Pollitzer to O'Keeffe, January 1, 1916, Beinecke Library.

64 I had just . . . game—Letter from O'Keeffe to Pollitzer, January 4, 1916, MOMA press release.

64–65 Mr. Stieglitz . . . tell you—Alexander Eliot, *Three Hundred Years of American Painters*, New York: Time, 1957.

65 I put . . . distance—Letter from O'Keeffe to Stieglitz, February 1, 1916, MOMA press release.
"Some . . . lovely"—Ibid.

66 "incredible . . . smiled"—Aline Pollitzer Weiss to author, April 19, 1977.

68 "For . . . much"—O'Keeffe, *Georgia O'Keeffe*.
"Do . . . idiot?"—Herbert Seligmann, *Alfred Stieglitz Talking*, New Haven: Yale University Library, 1966.

69 "But . . . baby"—Jean Evans, "Stieglitz—Always Battling and Retreating," *PM*, December 23, 1945.
"Such a scuffling . . . got it"—Henry McBride, "Curious Responses to Work of Miss Georgia O'Keeffe on Others," *New York Herald*, February 4, 1923.
"Never . . . today"—Henry Tyrrell, "New York Art Exhibitions and Gallery News," *Christian Science Monitor*, June 2, 1916.

Chapter Four

Other sources include Louise Shirley and Mr. and Mrs. Ted Reid.

71 Swayne quotations—Mattie Swayne Mack to author, June 11, 1977.

72 "Because . . . it!"—Emma Jean McClesky Smith to author, June 15, 1977.

75 "I can't . . . beautiful!"—Vivian Robinson, "Artist's Journey to the Top Began at West Texas," *Amarillo Globe-Times*, August 27, 1965.
"a long . . . sky"—Georgia O'Keeffe, *Georgia O'Keeffe*, New York: Viking Press, 1976.
"The light would begin . . . came"—Calvin Tomkins, "The Rose in the Eye Looked Pretty Fine," *The New Yorker*, March 4, 1974.

77 "It was . . . pleased"—Anita Pollitzer, "That's Georgia," *Saturday Review*, November 4, 1950.

77–78 "The recent . . . woman"—Henry Tyrrell, "Esoteric Art at '291,'" *Christian Science Monitor*, May 4, 1917.

79 "Well . . . woman"—Jean Evans, "Stieglitz—Always Battling and Retreating," *PM*, December 23, 1945.
For . . . again—Hutchins Hapgood, *Victorian in the Modern World*, New York: Harcourt Brace, 1939.

82 "From then . . . back"—Sheila Tryk, "O'Keeffe," *New Mexico*, January-February 1973.
"What does . . . red?"—Herbert Seligmann, *Alfred Stieglitz Taking*, New Haven: Yale University Library, 1966.

83 "The war . . . ground"—Letter from O'Keeffe to Anna Barringer, undated, Barringer Collection, Alderman Library, Univeristy of Virginia.

85 "the vague . . . moment"—Letter from O'Keeffe to Sherwood Anderson, undated, Anderson Collection, Newberry Library, Chicago.

Chapter Five

Other sources include members of the Stieglitz family who do not wish to be identified, Herbert Seligmann, and Blanche Matthias.

87 "I was born . . . obsession"—Alfred Stieglitz, exhibition catalog statement, Anderson Galleries, February 7, 1921.

88 "uncommon beauty . . . every moment"—Sue Davidson Lowe, *Stieglitz: A Memoir/Biography*, New York: Farrar, Straus, Giroux, 1983.

90 "They were . . . happy"—Flora Stieglitz Straus to author, April 4, 1977.

91 "Alfred . . . family"—Jean Evans, "Stieglitz—Always Battling and Retreating," *PM*, December 23, 1945.

92 "I believe . . . believe"—Djuna Barnes, "Giving Advice on Life and Pictures," *New York Morning Telegraph*, February 25, 1917.

93 "Isn't he . . . about that"—Susan Young Wilson to author, May 31, 1977.

94 The flesh . . . intercepts—Poem was published in MSS, March 1922.

95 "Can you . . . the woman"—William Dove to author, June 22, 1978.
"I know . . . time"—William M. Milliken, "White Flower by Georgia O'Keeffe," *Bulletin of the Cleveland Museum of Art*, April 1937.

96 "Once Stieglitz . . . it"—Dorothy Seiberling, "Horizons of a Pioneer," *Life*, March 1, 1968.

96 "spiritually . . . Stieglitz?"—Georgia O'Keeffe, "Can a Photograph Have the Significance of Art?" MSS, December 1922.
"is always . . . time"—Letter from O'Keeffe to Sherwood Anderson, undated, Anderson Collection, Newberry Library, Chicago.

97 "I was . . . about"—*Georgia O'Keeffe: A Portrait by Alfred Stieglitz*, New York: Metropolitan Museum of Art, 1978.

99–100 the article by Georgia Engelhard—Georgia Engelhard, "Alfred Stieglitz: Master Photographer," *American Photography*, February 1945.

100 O'Keeffe . . . own—Sanford Schwartz, "Georgia O'Keeffe Writes a Book," *The New Yorker*, August 28, 1978.
"whenever . . . many"—Letter from Alfred Stieglitz to Paul Strand, Nov. 17, 1918, in Sarah Greenough and Juan Hamilton, *Alfred Stieglitz: Photographs and Writings*, Washington, D.C.: National Gallery of Art, 1983.

101 "You see . . . round"—Mary Lynn Kotz, "A Day with Georgia O'Keeffe," *Art News*, December 1977.
"registered . . . delicacy"—Jerome Mellquist, *The Emergence of an American Art*, New York: Charles Scribner's Sons, 1942.
"considerable . . . ever"—Henry McBride, "Photographs by Alfred Stieglitz," *New York Herald*, February 13, 1921.

102 "Stieglitz . . . beloved"—Waldo Frank et al., *America and Alfred Stieglitz*, New York: Doubleday, Doran, 1934.
"He . . . so"—Hutchins Hapgood, *Victorian in the Modern World*, New York: Harcourt Brace, 1939.
"There came . . . personality"—Henry McBride, "O'Keeffe at the Museum," *New York Sun*, May 18, 1946.

103 "intimate . . . ill"—Howard M. Jones, *The Letters of Sherwood Anderson* (letter dated June 12, 1924), Boston: Little Brown & Co., 1953.

104–105 Georgia . . . nunnery—Henry McBride, "Curious Responses to Work of Miss Georgia O'Keeffe on Others," *New York Herald*, February 4, 1923.

105 "long head . . . humor"—Peggy Bacon, *Off with Their Heads*, New York: Robert McBride, 1934.

106 "an ascetic . . . emotions"—Helen Appleton Read, "Georgia O'Keeffe—Woman Artist Whose Art Is Sincerely Feminine," *Brooklyn Eagle*, March 2, 1924.

107 "I have . . . forms"—Letter from Stieglitz to Mitchell Kennerley, September 9, 1923, Kennerley Collection, Manuscript Division, New York Public Library.
The Stars . . . Womb—Poem, "A Portrait—1918," was published in *MSS*, March 1922.

108 "His belief . . . days"—"Georgia O'Keeffe's Show an Emotional
    Escape," *Brooklyn Eagle*, February 11, 1923.
    "Unlike . . . choice"—Blanche Matthias, "Stieglitz Showing Seven
    Americans," *Chicago Evening Post, Magazine of the Art World*, March
    2, 1926.

Chapter Six

111 "There is . . . no force"—Herbert Seligmann, *Alfred Stieglitz Talking*,
    New Haven: Yale University Library, 1966.
    "They were . . . together"—Arthur Young to author, April 2, 1978.

112 "Privacy . . . having"—Waldo Frank et al., *America and Alfred
    Stieglitz*, New York: Doubleday, Doran, 1934.
    "smoldering . . . subsided"—Hutchins Hapgood, *Victorian in the Mod-
    ern World*, New York: Harcourt Brace, 1939.
    "widely . . . though"—Peggy Bacon, *Off with Their Heads*, New York:
    Robert McBride, 1934.

113 "And when you find . . . Jehovah"—Waldo Frank, *Time Exposures*,
    New York: Boni and Liveright, 1926.
    "When she . . . them"—Marsden Hartley. *Adventures in the Arts*,
    New York: Boni and Liveright, 1921.
    "What . . . see?"—Blanche Matthias to author, November 22, 1978.
    She . . . "as is"—Blanche Matthias, "Stieglitz Showing Seven Ameri-
    cans," *Chicago Evening Post, Magazine of the Art World*, March 2,
    1926.

114 "He had faith . . . beings"—Georgia O'Keeffe, "Can a Photograph
    Have the Significance of Art?" MSS, December 1922.

115 "like . . . affair"—Seligmann, *Alfred Stieglitz Talking*.

116 "He also enjoyed . . . this"—Georgia O'Keeffe, "Stieglitz: His Pictures
    Collected Him," *New York Times Magazine*, December 11, 1949.
    "He was the leader . . . game"—Ibid.

117 "That girl . . . do"—Seligmann, *Alfred Stieglitz Talking*.

118 "All . . . painting"—Grace Glueck, " 'It's Just What's in My Head,'"
    New York Times, October 18, 1970.
    an art magazine—*The Art World & Arts and Decoration*, December
    1918.

119 "Women . . . it"—"Georgia O'Keeffe's Show an Emotional Escape,"
    Brooklyn Eagle, February 11, 1923.
    "I've had . . . own"—Carol Taylor, "Lady Dynamo," *New York World
    Telegram*, March 31, 1945.

"I would listen . . . talking"—Dorothy Seiberling, "Horizons of a Pioneer," *Life*, March 1, 1968.

120 "All . . . much"—Barbara Rose, "O'Keeffe's Trail," *New York Review of Books*, March 31, 1977.
"I am not . . . feeling"—Matthias, "Stieglitz Showing Seven Americans."
"One can not . . . work"—Ibid.
"I seemed . . . country"—Edith Evans Asbury, "Silent Desert Still Charms Georgia O'Keeffe, near 81," *New York Times*, November 2, 1968.
"He would . . . see"—Calvin Tomkins, "The Rose in the Eye Looked Pretty Fine," *The New Yorker*, March 4, 1974.
"If . . . together"—*Georgia O'Keeffe: A Portrait by Alfred Stieglitz*, New York: Metropolitan Museum of Art, 1978.
"His mind . . . down"—Tomkins, "The Rose in the Eye . . ."

122 "It was . . . beautiful"—Dorothy Brett, "Autobiography: My Long and Beautiful Journey," *South Dakota Review*, Summer 1967.
"You . . . something"—Matthias, "Stieglitz Showing Seven Americans."
"There were more . . . take notes"—Henry McBride, "Modern Art," *The Dial*, May 1926.

123 "I almost . . . again"—Glueck, " 'It's Just What's in My Head.'"

123–124 Her art . . . place—Paul Rosenfeld, "American Painting," *The Dial*, December 1921.
"a queer . . . undated"—Letter from O'Keeffe to Mitchell Kennerley, undated, Kennerley Collection, Manuscript Division, New York Public Library.
"When . . . affairs"—Glueck, " 'It's Just What's in My Head.'"
"*The Dial* . . . painter"—Mary Lynn Kotz, "A Day with Georgia O'Keeffe," *Art News*, December 1977.

125 "When I entered . . . pictures"—Mary Daniels, "The Magical Mistress of Ghost Ranch, New Mexico," *Chicago Tribune*, June 24, 1973.
"I don't . . . to live"—Letter from O'Keeffe to Doris McMurdo, July 1922, Chatham School, Chatham, Virginia.

126 "When you . . . or not"—Mary Braggiotti, "Her Worlds Are Many," *New York Post*, May 16, 1946.
"If . . . small"—Georgia O'Keeffe, exhibition catalog statement, An American Place, January 22 to March 17, 1939.
The large . . . color—William M. Milliken, "White Flower by Georgia O'Keeffe," *Bulletin of the Cleveland Musuem of Art*, April 1937.

127 "The observer . . . phial"—James W. Lane, "Notes from New York," *Apollo*, April 1938.

128 "an abyss . . . peer"—Henry McBride, "Georgia O'Keeffe's Recent Work," *New York Sun*, January 14, 1928.
"Well . . . don't"—Georgia O'Keeffe, exhibition catalog statement, 1939.

129 "Wise men . . . paint?"—Helen Appleton Read, "Georgia O'Keeffe—Woman Artist Whose Art Is Sincerely Feminine," *Brooklyn Eagle*, March 2, 1924.
"Psychiatrists . . . libido"—Murdock Pemberton, "The Art Galleries," *The New Yorker*, March 13, 1926.
"she reveals . . . delight"—"In New York Galleries: Georgia O'Keeffe's Arresting Pictures . . . ," *New York Times*, January 16, 1927.
"grand and barbaric"—Letter from Stieglitz to Kennerley, fall 1928, New York Public Library.
"the poet . . . obscenities"—Lewis Mumford, *The Brown Decades*, New York: Dover, 1931.

130 "O'Keeffe's . . . giggle"—Louis Kalonyme, "Georgia O'Keeffe: A Woman in Painting," *Creative Art*, January 1928.
Vogue—Helen Appleton Read, "The Feminine Viewpoint in Contemporary Art," *Vogue*, June 15, 1928.
"I guess . . . down"—Letter from O'Keeffe to Sherwood Anderson, undated, Anderson Collection, Newberry Library, Chicago.

131 "until . . . structute"—Matthias, "Stieglitz Showing Seven Americans."
"If it . . . speech"—Frank, *Time Exposures*.
"When . . . simple"—Waldo Frank, "Georgia O'Keeffe," *McCall's*, September 1927.
"often . . . peasant"—Ibid.

132 as . . . you—Letter from O'Keeffe to Henry McBride, January 16, 1927, McBride Collection, Archives of American Art, Smithsonian Institution.
"to . . . necessary"—McBride, "Georgia O'Keeffe's Recent Work."
"a strange oily skin"—Letter from O'Keeffe to McBride, July 22, 1939, Archives of American Art, Smithsonian Institution.
"warms . . . night"—Frank, *Time Exposures*.
"The things . . . at that"—Letter from O'Keeffe to Kennerley, undated, New York Public Library.

132–133 "Such things . . . flower"—Letter from O'Keeffe to art editor, *New York Times*, February 23, 1941.

133 "I have . . . free"—Georgia O'Keeffe, *Georgia O'Keeffe*, New York: Viking Press, 1976.

"How perfect . . . move!"—Emily Genauer, "Art and Artists: Arts and Flowers Theme of New Show," *New York Herald Tribune*, April 18, 1954.

134 "We live . . . we live"—Letter from Stieglitz to Sherwood Anderson, Dec. 9, 1925, in Greenough and Hamilton, 1983.

135 "Georgia . . . white"—Frank, *American and Alfred Stieglitz*.
In . . . painting—Frances O'Brien, "American We Like: Georgia O'Keeffe," *The Nation*, October 12, 1927.

137 "There's something . . . it"—Taylor, "Lady Dynamo."
"At night . . . worlds"—McBride, "Georgia O'Keeffe's Recent Work."

138 "The door . . . flooding"—Lillian Sabine, "Record Price for Living Artist," *Brooklyn Eagle*, Sunday magazine section, May 27, 1928.
"I like . . . it"—Anita Pollitzer, "That's Georgia," *Saturday Review*, November 4, 1950.
"I realize . . . I could"—Matthias, "Stieglitz Showing Seven Americans."

139 "One can't . . . felt"—Ibid.
"From . . . New York"—Ralph Looney, "Georgia O'Keeffe," *Atlantic Monthly*, April 1965.

143 "I . . . standardized"—L. L. Stevenson, "Stieglitz Hides His Famous Photographs in Strike to Help Young Artists," *Detroit News*, May 8, 1927.
"Success . . . odds"—Sabine, "Record Price for Living Artist."
Not a rouged . . . 1928!—Vladimir B. Berman, "She Painted the Lily and Got $25,000 and Fame for Doing It!" *New York Evening Graphic*, May 12, 1928.

Chapter Seven

Other sources include members of the Stieglitz family who do not wish to be identified, Frank Prosser, and Dorothy Brett.

146 "Everything . . . pink—"—Letter from O'Keeffe to Henry McBride, May 11, 1928, McBride Collection, Archives of American Art, Smithsonian Institution.
"As a matter . . . horse"—Letter from O'Keeffe to Sherwood Anderson, undated, Anderson Collection, Newberry Library, Chicago.

150 "a queer lot"—Letter from Stieglitz to Rebecca Strand, September 1924, American Literature Collection, Beinecke Library, Yale University.

151 "I was hard . . . . me"—Dorothy Seiberling, "Horizons of a Pioneer,"
   Life, March 1, 1968.

154 "The people . . . this"—" 'I Can't Sing So I Paint!'" *New York Sun*,
   December 5, 1922.
   "nothing but green"—Letter from O'Keeffe to McBride, May 11,
   1928, Archives of American Art, Smithsonian Institution.

156 "some of . . . me"—Vladimir B. Berman, "She Painted the Lily and
   Got $25,000 and Fame for Doing It!" *New York Evening Grahpic*,
   May 12, 1928.
   "I've . . . sand bags"—Seiberling, "Horizons of a Pioneer."
   "a little . . . other"—Letter from O'Keeffe to Anderson, undated,
   Newberry Library.

157 "much . . . I think"—Deposition by Georgia O'Keeffe, October 14,
   1976, *O'Keeffe vs. Snyder*, Superior Court of New Jersey, Mercer
   County.
   We have . . . goal—Murdock Pemberton, "The Art Galleries," *The
   New Yorker*, March 13, 1926.

158 "It's much . . . again"—Lillian Sabine, "Record Price for Living Art-
   ist," *Brooklyn Eagle*, Sunday magazine section, May 27, 1928.
   "Making . . . grasp"—Letter from O'Keeffe to Anderson, undated,
   Newberry Library.
   "when you . . . are"—Frances O'Brien, "Americans We Like: Georgia
   O'Keeffe," *The Nation*, October 12, 1927.
   "A strange . . . herself"—Dorothy Brett, "Autobiography: My Long
   and Beautiful Journey," *South Dakota Review*, Summer 1967.
   the most important artist—The group included John Marin, Charles
   Demuth, Yasuo Kuniyoshi, Maurice Sterne, Max Weber, Eugene
   Speicher, John Sloan, Edward Hopper, and others.

159 "a fluid . . . potentialities"—"Georgia O'Keeffe," *New York Times*,
   February 10, 1929.
   "and at last . . . matchstick"—Robert M. Coates, "The Art Galleries:
   Mostly Women," *The New Yorker*, May 25, 1946.

160 "my Spiritual Home"—Letter from Dorothy Brett to Spud Johnson,
   January 11, 1929, Johnson Collection, Humanities Research Center, University of Texas.
   "beautiful people"—Letter from Brett to Johnson, January 25, 1929,
   Humanities Research Center.

Chapter Eight

178 "filthy"—Mabel Dodge Luhan, "The Art of Georgia O'Keeffe," American Literature Collection, Beinecke Library, Yale University.

179 "Well! . . . *this!*"—Mabel Dodge Luhan, "Georgia O'Keeffe in Taos," *Creative Art*, June 1931.
"Never is . . . to it"—D. H. Lawrence, "New Mexico," *Survery*, May 1, 1931.

180 "The world . . . East"—Amei Wallach, "Georgia O'Keeffe," *Newsday*, October 30, 1977.
"insisted on . . . with them"—Letter from Neith Boyce to Hutchins Hapgood, dated 1929, American Literature Collection, Beinecke Library, Yale University.

181 "rich . . . species"—Edmund Wilson, *Letters-on Literature and Politics*, New York: Farrar, Straus & Giroux, 1977.

182 Rich anecdote—Daniel Catton Rich, "I Met Her in Taos," *Worcester Sunday Telegram*, October 30, 1960.
"we . . . disagreed"—Georgia O'Keeffe, "Friends Pay Tribute to R. Vernon Hunter," *New Mexican*, May 22, 1955.

184 "You . . . songs?"—Michaela Williams, "Georgia O'Keeffe, 80, Revisits Chicago," *Chicago Daily News*, June 17, 1967.
"the loud . . . hard"—Letter from O'Keeffe to Mabel Dodge Luhan, undated, Beinecke Library.
"In the . . . suddenly"—Lawrence, "New Mexico."
Take . . . majority—Luhan, "Georgia O'Keeffe in Taos."

185 "What . . . now?"—Sheila Tryk, "O'Keeffe," *New Mexico*, January-February 1973.
Beck . . . zest—Luhan, "Georgia O'Keeffe in Taos."

187 "For God's . . . sensation—"—Letter from O'Keeffe to Luhan, July 1929, Beinecke Library.
"I think . . . track"—Ibid.
"she is . . . person"—Letter from Boyce to Hapgood, 1929, American Literature Collection, Beinecke Library, Yale University.
"too . . . tonic"—Letter from Boyce to Hapgood, July 18, 1929, American Literature Collection, Beinecke Library, Yale University.

189 Brett noticed and remarked on—Letter from Dorothy Brett to Spud Johnson, December 28, 1930, Johnson Collection, Humanities Research Center, University of Texas.

190 "When you . . . as one"—Dorothy Norman, "Camera Work" *Camera*, December 1969.

191 "Anyone . . . country"—Henry McBride, "The Sign of The Cross," *New York Sun*, February 8, 1930.

Chapter Nine

Other sources include Herbert Seligmann, Dorothy Brett, Flora Straus, Dorothy Norman, Andrew Norman, and Marjorie Content Toomer.

194 O'Keeffe-Gold debate—Gladys Oaks, "Radical Writer and Woman Artist Clash on Propaganda and Its Uses," *New York World*, March 16, 1930.

196 "the human problem"—Letter from O'Keeffe to Dorothy Brett, May 4, 1930, American Literature Collection, Beinecke Library, Yale University.
"poisonous"—Letter from O'Keeffe to Brett, April 7, 1931, Beinecke Library.
"I have . . . beauty"—Georgia O'Keeffe, exhibition catalog statement, An American Place, January 22 to March 17, 1939.

198 "O'Keeffe . . . alone"—Marsden Hartley, exhibition catalog statement, An American Place, January 4 to February 27, 1936.
"strange"—Letter from O'Keeffe to Brett, September 10 1930, Beinecke Library.

"Why should . . . hill"—Georgia Engelhard, "Alfred Stieglitz: Master Photographer," *American Photography*, February 1945.
"If I . . . stand it"—Jean Evans, "Stieglitz—Always Battling and Retreating," *PM*, December 23, 1945.
"What! . . . that?"—Mary Daniels, "The Magical Mistress of Ghost Ranch, New Mexico," *Chicago Tribune*, June 24, 1973.
"There . . . Texas"—Dorothy Norman, *Stieglitz Memorial Portfolio*, New York: Twice-a-Year Press, 1947.
"Alfred . . . doing"—Leo Janis, "Georgia O'Keeffe at Eighty-Four," *Atlantic Monthly*, December 1971.

199 "maybe a kiss"—Georgia O'Keeffe, *Some Memories of Drawings*, New York: Atlantis Editions, 1974.

201 "My feeling . . . consciousness"—Letter from O'Keeffe to Brett, April 7, 1931, Beinecke Library.

202 "Almost . . . to be done"—Harold Butcher, "Georgia O'Keeffe," *Santa-Fean*, September-October 1941.

203 "What will . . . way"—"Exhibitions in New York: Georgia O'Keeffe, An American Place," *Art News*, January 2, 1932.
McBride review—Henry McBride, "Skeletons on the Plains,, *New York Sun*, January 2, 1932.
"very . . . put"—Isabel Ross, "Bones of Desert Blaze Art Trail of Miss O'Keeffe," *New York Herald Tribune*, December 29, 1931.

"Stern . . . Electra"—Peggy Bacon, *Off with Their Heads*, New York: Robert McBride, 1934.

208 "that . . . murals"—"Metropolitan Buys 3 Works in City Art Show," *New York Herald Tribune*, October 29, 1934.
a child . . . actions"—Letter from Donald Deskey to author, November 7, 1978.

210 "Body . . . bits"—Bacon, *Off with Their Heads*.
"In . . . shadows"—Marsden Hartley, exhibition catalog statement, 1936 O'Keeffe show.
"ripe . . . character"—Ralph Flint, "1933 O'Keeffe Show a Fine Revelation of Varied Powers," *Art News*, January 14, 1933.

211 "In health . . . quickly"—Henry McBride, "Georgia O'Keeffe Exhibition," *New York Sun*, Janaury 14, 1933.

212 "No, 'oughts' . . . life"—Waldo Frank et al., *American and Alfred Stieglitz*, New York: Doubleday, Doran, 1934.

213 "I miss . . . time—"—Letter from O'Keeffe to Jean Toomer, January 3, 1934, Special Collections, Fisk University Library.
"I seem . . . any more"—Ibid.
"I want . . . mountain—"—Letter from O'Keeffe to Toomer, January 17, 1934, Fisk University Library.

214 "If I . . . here—"—Letter from O'Keeffe to Toomer, January 15, 1934, Fisk University Library.
My center . . . now—Letter from O'Keeffe to Toomer, January 10, 1934, Fisk University Library.

215 "I loved . . . afterwards"—"Jazz Age Priestess Brings Forth Painting," *New York Post*, April 3, 1934.
"What annoyed . . . start"—Archer Winsten, "Georgia O'Keeffe Trying to Begin Again in Bermuda," *New York Post*, March 19, 1934.
"a long queer sleep"—Letter from O'Keeffe to Luhan, December 26, 1933, Beinecke Library.

215–216 "And when you . . . see"—Winsten, "Georgia O'Keeffe Trying to Begin Again in Bermuda."

216 "smashed to bits"—Letter from O'Keeffe to Toomer, February 8, 1934, Fisk University Library.
"toylike . . . sea"—Letter from O'Keeffe to Toomer, March 5, 1934, Fisk University Library.
"to lie . . . shape"—Letter from O'Keeffe to Toomer, February 14, 1934, Fisk University Library.

"petted all over"—Letter from O'Keeffe to Toomer, March 5, 1934, Fisk University Library.

"more . . . way"—Ibid.

"For . . . is—"—Letter from O'Keeffe to Toomer, May 11, 1934, Fisk University Library.

217 "I'm frightened . . . never!"—Mary Lynn Kotz, "A Day with Georgia O'Keeffe," *Art News*, December 1977.

"I think . . . momentarily"—ABC-TV interview, broadcast November 11, 1976.

"fully . . . mesa"—Vernon Hunter, "A Note on Georgia O'Keeffe," *Contemporary Arts of the South and Southwest*, November-December 1932.

Chapter Ten

Other sources include members of the Stieglitz family who do not wish to be identified, Marjorie Content Toomer, Loren Mazeley, Beaumont Newhall, David McAlpin, and Maggie (Johnson) Eily.

220 "I thought . . . life"—Sheila Tryk, "O'Keeffe," *New Mexico*, January-February 1973.

"when . . . spots"—Leter from O'Keeffe to Alfred Stieglitz, exhibition catalog, An American Place, December 27, 1937, to February 11, 1938. (Letter dated August 16, 1937.)

221 "It is . . . painting"—Ibid.

"All . . . badlands"—O'Keeffe, exhibition catalog statement, An American Place, January 22 to March 17, 1939.

"A red . . . should"—Ibid.

223 "When you . . . people"—Dorothy Brett to author, July 26, 1977.

"I wouldn't . . . attend to it"—ABC-TV interview, broadcast November 11, 1976.

224 "I can . . . about her"—Calvin Tomkins, "The Rose in the Eye Looked Pretty Fine," *The New Yorker*, March 4, 1974.

"tried . . . Ghost Ranch"—Arthur N. Pack, *We Called it Ghost Ranch*, Abiquiu: Ghost Ranch Conference Center, 1966.

225 one fine sailing painting—*Brown Sail—Wing and Wing* of 1940.

It was . . . seen—Letter from O'Keeffe to Stieglitz, September 20, 1937, 1937–38 exhibition catalog.

227 "a lot of baloney"—Willard Van Dyke to author, May 3, 1978.

229 "flesh like . . . fan"—Peggy Bacon, *Off with Their Heads*, New York: Robert McBride, 1934.

231 "You . . . now"—William Dove to author, June 22, 1978.

232 "He is almost . . . few"—Georgia O'Keeffe, Associated American Artists exhibition catalog statement, January 1953.
"Einstein . . . returns"—Ibid.
"For me . . . wonderful"—*Georgia O'Keeffe: A Portrait by Alfred Stieglitz*, New York: Metropolitan Museum of Art, 1978.

234 O'Keeffe letters—From the eight letters from O'Keeffe to Stieglitz, July 29 to September 30, 1937, 1937–38 exhibition catalog.

235 "I have . . . begun!"—Edward Alden Jewell, "Georgia O'Keeffe Gives an Art Show," *New York Times*, January 7, 1936.
The epitome . . . eye—Lewis Mumford, "Autobiographies in Paint," *The New Yorker*, January 18, 1936.
"triumphant convalescence"—Jerome Mellquist, *The Emergence of an American Art*, New York: Charles Scribner's Sons, 1942.
"just . . . together"—ABC-TV interview, broadcast November 11, 1976.

236 "a . . . summertime"—Ibid.
"As soon . . . grabbed"—Leo Janis, "Georgia O'Keeffe at Eighty-Four," *Atlantic Monthly*, December 1971.

237 "It's my . . . it"—Amei Wallach, "Georgia O'Keeffe," *Newsday*, October 30, 1977.

238 "I've been . . . beautiful"—Letter from O'Keeffe to Stieglitz, August 26, 1937, 1937–38 exhibition catalog.
Thursday . . . time—Letter from O'Keeffe to Stieglitz, July 29, 1937, 1937–38 exhibition catalog.
Good . . . again—Letter from O'Keeffe to Stieglitz, August 16, 1937, 1937–38 exhibition catalog.

240 "almost aboriginal"—Ralph Flint, "Lily Lady Goes West," *Town and Country*, January 1943.
"Yet curiously . . . Dietrich's"—A. Pinchot, "Not in the Picture: Sidelights on Celebrities," *Delineator*, May 1936.

241 "your . . . raw"—George L. K. Morris, "Art Chronicle: Some Personal Letters to American Artists Recently Exhibiting in New York:" *Partisan Review*, March 1938.

242 "She seemed . . . world"—Letter from Leslie Cheek, Jr., to author, November 16, 1977.
"Standing . . . work"—Mellquist, *The Emergence of an American Art*.

243 "all sharp . . . beautiful"—"Pineapple Story," *Art Digest*, March 1, 1943.

244 "What . . . experience"—Georgia O'Keeffe, exhibition catalog state-
        ment, An American Place, February 3 to March 17, 1940.
    "It has to . . . else"—Ibid.
    "the world . . . oyster"—Henry McBride, "Georgia O'Keeffe's Hawaii,
        New York Sun, February 10, 1940.

Chapter Eleven

Other sources include several of O'Keeffe friends and members of the Stieglitz family who do not wish to be identified.

249 "Those . . . gray elephants"—Robert Hughes, "Loner in the Desert,"
        Time, October 12, 1970.

250 "a kind of freedom"—Dorothy Seiberling, "Horizons of a Pioneer,"
        Life, March 1, 1968.
    "excited peace"—Letter from William Einstein to Alfred Stieglitz,
        September 7, 1940, American Literature Collection, Beinecke
        Library, Yale University.

251 "Her eyes . . . apparent"—Daniel Catton Rich, *Georgia O'Keeffe*,
        Chicago: Art Institute of Chicago, 1943.

252 "You know, . . . it"—Marcia Winn, "Front Views and Profiles,"
        Chicago Tribune, January 22, 1943.

253 "Miss O'Keeffe . . . around"—Georgia O'Keeffe," *Marion (Ind.)
        Chronicle Tribune*, January 23, 1943.
    "exquisite . . . too"—Winn, "Front Views and Profiles."
    "Find . . . being"—Eleanor Jewett, "O'Keeffe Show Unexcelled in
        Beauty, Color," *Chicago Tribune*, January 31, 1943.
    "If . . . it"—Marcia Winn, "Georgia O'Keeffe—Outstanding Artist,"
        Chicago Sunday Tribune, February 28, 1943.
    "Seen . . . herself"—Rich, *Georgia O'Keeffe*.

254 "I still . . . best"—Ralph Flint, "Lily Lady Goes West," *Town and
        Country*, January 1943.
    "her originality . . . exciting"—Harold Butcher, "Georgia O'Keeffe,"
        Santa-Fean, September-October 1941.

255 "I'm loved . . . proportion"—W. W. Hercher, "Greatest Woman Art-
        ist Exhibits Paintings," *St. Paul (Minn.) Pioneer Press*, January 23,
        1943.
    "When you . . . pleasure"—Carol Taylor, "Lady Dynamo," *New York
        World Telegram*, March 31, 1945.
    "as if . . . performance"—Christopher Isherwood to author, Novem-
        ber 19, 1978.

"I know . . . *know*"—Anita Pollitzer, "That's Georgia," *Saturday Review*, November 4, 1950.

256 "with . . . gasping"—Arthur N. Pack, *We Called It Ghost Ranch*, Abiquiu Ghost Ranch Conference Center, 1966.

"I'd . . . cake"—Phoebe Pack to author, April 2, 1978.

"heaven"—Henry McBride, "Georgia O'Keeffe's Heaven," *New York Sun*, February 1, 1941.

"in . . . world"—Georgia O'Keeffe, exhibition catalog statement, An American Place, January 11 to March 11, 1944.

257 "most . . . finished"—Ibid.

257–258 "I think . . . won't listen"—Grace Glueck, " 'It's Just What's in My Head,'" *New York Times*, October 18, 1970.

258 "Oh . . . necessary"—Beaumont Newhall to author, August 31, 1977.

260 "I wanted . . . own"—Seiberling, "Horizons of a Pioneer."

"What . . . go"—Taylor, "Lady Dynamo."

261 "paralyzing"—Isabel Ross, "Bones of Desert Blaze Art Trail of Miss O'Keeffe," *New York Herald Tribune*, December 19, 1931.

"I thought . . . hard"—William Clew, "43 Paintings to Be Shown," *Worcester Evening Gazette*, October 3, 1960.

I see . . . on—Letter from O'Keeffe to Henry McBride, undated, McBride Collection, Archives of American Art, Smithsonian Institution.

262 "O'Keeffe . . . respect"—Jean Evans, "Stieglitz—Always Battling and Retreating," *PM*, December 23, 1945.

"I couldn't . . . beautifully"—Mary Braggiotti, "Her Worlds Are Many," *New York Post*, May 16, 1946.

263 "He was one . . . it"—Seiberling, "Horizons of a Pioneer."

"more . . . satyr"—Lewis Mumford, *Findings and Keepings*, New York: Harcourt Brace Jovanovich, 1975.

"an ancient . . . defilement"—Marjorie Phillips, *Duncan Phillips and His Collection*, New York: Little Brown, 1970.

"I have . . . orphans"—Evans, "Stieglitz—Always Battling . . ."

264 "I . . . more"—Deposition by Georgia O'Keeffe, October 14, 1976, *O'Keeffe v. Synder*, Superior Court of New Jersey, Mercer County.

265 McBride review—Henry McBride, "O'Keeffe at the Museum," *New York Sun*, May 18, 1946.

266 "psuedo-modern . . . meanings"—Clement Greenberg, *The Nation*, June 5, 1946.

268 "In the opinion . . . do"—Georgia O'Keeffe, "Stieglitz: His Pictures Collected Him," *New York Times Magazine*, December 11, 1949.

271 "But . . . you?"—Susan Young Wilson to author, May 31, 1977.

Chapter Twelve

292 "an enigmatic . . . art"—Stuart Preston, "Picasso's Diversity: Work of Several Periods—Sculpture—O'Keeffe," *New York Times*, February 24, 1952.

293 " 'From the Plains' . . . space"—Rackstraw Downes, *Fairfield Porter: Art in Its Own Terms 1935–1975*, New York: Taplinger Publishing Co., 1979.
    "in the morning . . . sometimes"—Letter from Georgia O'Keeffe to Frances Steloff, Dec. 9, 1953, Berg Collection, New York Public Library.

295 "I know . . . nothing"—N. Heller and J. Williams, "Georgia O'Keeffe: The American Southwest," *American Artist*, January 1976.
    "I have . . . mind"—Mary Daniels, "The 'Real Painting Country' of O'Keeffe," *Chicago Tribune*, September 28, 1975.
    "Why . . . it?"—Harold Butcher, "Georgia O'Keeffe," *Santa-Fean*, September-October 1941.
    "I suppose . . . painter"—Henry Seldis, "Georgia O'Keeffe at 78: Tough-Minded Romantic," *Los Angeles Times, West magazine*, January 22, 1967.

296 "It's . . . door"—Katharine Kuh, *The Artist's Voice*, New York: Harper & Row, 1962.
    "I have . . . place"—Daniel Catton Rich, *Georgia O'Keeffe*, Chicago: Art Institute of Chicago, 1943.
    "Miss O'Keeffe's . . . nature"—"Exhibition at Downtown Gallery," *Arts*, May-June 1961.

297 "Of course . . . artist!"—ABC-TV interview, broadcast November 11, 1976.
    "Nothing . . . things"—" 'I Can't Sing So I Paint!'" *New York Sun*, December 5, 1922.

298 "It can . . . suppose"—John I. H. Baur, *Nature in Abstraction*, New York: Macmillan, 1958.
    "I don't . . . time"—Phoebe Pack to author, April 2, 1978.
    "Oh look . . . enough"—Carol Merrill to author, August 10, 1977.
    "I saw . . . green"—Grace Glueck, " 'It's Just What's in My Head,'" *New York Times*, October 18, 1970.

"Color . . . sense"—Herbert Seligmann, "Georgia
O'Keeffe'American," *MSS*, March 1923.

299 "I see . . . well"—William M. Milliken, "White Flower by Georgia
O'Keeffe," *Bulletin of the Cleveland Museum of Art*, April 1937.

"inelastic"—Blanche Matthias, "Stieglitz Showing Seven Americans,"
Chicago Evening Post, Magazine of the Art World, March 2, 1926.

"Probably . . . be?"—Allen Keller, "Animal Skulls Fascinate Miss
O'Keeffe, but Why?" *New York World Telegram*, February 13, 1937.

"The meaning . . . painted"—Edith Evans Asbury, "Silent Desert
Still Charms Georgia O'Keeffe, near 81," *New York Times*, November 2, 1968.

"dumb . . . ether"—Lewis Mumford, "The Art Galleries," *The New
Yorker*, January 21, 1933.

"almost . . . life"—Matthias, "Stieglitz Showing Seven Americans."

"The best . . . concealed"—Henry McBride, "Georgia O'Keeffe's Exhibition," *New York Sun*, January 14, 1933.

"Her brushwork . . . color"—Edward Alden Jewell, "Georgia O'Keeffe
Shows New York," *New York Times*, February 6, 1937.

300 "You know . . . time"—Marcia Winn, "Front Views and Profiles,"
Chicago Tribune, January 22, 1943.

"Of course . . . hats?"—Michaela Williams, "Georgia O'Keeffe, 80,
Revisits Chicago," *Chicago Daily News*, June 17, 1967.

301 "I do . . . civilized"—Letter from Dorothy Brett to Frieda Lawrence,
December 28, 1950, Frieda Lawrence Collection, Humanities Research center, University of Texas.

"Georgia . . . with her"—Spud Johnson journal, November 26, 1950,
Johnson Collection, Humanities Research Center, University of
Texas.

302 "mechanical music"—Letter from O'Keeffe to Blanche Matthias, February 6, 1956, American Literature Collection, Beinecke Library,
Yale University.

304 "They bite . . . blood"—Leo Janis, "Georgia O'Keeffe at Eighty-Four,"
Atlantic Monthly, December 1971.

"Phoebe . . . them"—Phoebe Pack to author, April 2, 1978.

"Arthur . . . anyhow!"—Arthur N. Pack, *We Called It Ghost Ranch*,
Abiquiu: Ghost Ranch Conference Center, 1966.

310 "I didn't . . . point?"—Williams, "Georgia O'Keeffe, 80, Revisists
Chicago."

311 "I've never . . . everywhere"—Janis, "Georgia O'Keeffe at Eighty-Four."

"watermelon-shaped"—"Where Are They Now?" *Newsweek*, May 13,
1957.

312 "Sometimes . . . layers"—Beth Coffelt, "A Visit with Georgia O'Keeffe," *San Francisco Sunday Examiner & Chronicle*, April 11, 1971.

313 "The cherubs . . . vulgar"—Charlotte Willard, "Georgia O'Keeffe," *Art in America*, October 1963.
"I prefer . . . world"—Grace Glueck, " 'It's Just What's in My Head,'" *New York Times*, October 18, 1970.
"It was . . . borrowing"—Blanche Matthias to author, November 22, 1978.
"What . . . there?"—Yousuf Karsh, *Portraits of Greatness*, New York: T. Nelson, 1959.
"It's the most . . . world"—William Clew, "43 Paintings to Be Shown," *Worcester Evening Gazette*, October 3, 1960.

Chapter Thirteen

Other sources include John Marin, Jr., Mitchell Wilder, Otto Pitcher, Lloyd Goodrich, and various friends and neighbors who do not wish to be identified.

315 "devasting decline"—Wilfred May, "Does Rembrandt Pay Dividends?" *Saturday Reivew*, December 6, 1958.

316 "The rivers . . . eye"—Katharine Kuh, *The Artist's Voice*, New York: Haper & Row, 1962.

317 "For me . . . doing"—Ibid.
"the same . . . period"—Daniel Catton Rich, *Georgia O'Keeffe: Forty Years of Her Art*, Worcester, Mass.: Worcester Art Museum, 1960.
Frequently . . . come—Ibid.

318 *Look*—"Ageless Beauties," *Look*, July 4, 1961.

320–21 "When she . . . not"—Herbert Seligmann, *Alfred Stieglitz Talking*, New Haven: Yale University Library, 1966.

321 "I suppose . . . at"—Dorothy Seiberling, "Horizons of a Pioneer," *Life*, March 1, 1968.

324 "Go . . . better"—Ted Reid to author, June 10, 1977.
"Miss . . . contemplation"—Peter Plagens, "A Georgia O'Keeffe Retrospective in Texas," *Artforum*, May 1966.

327 "sorceress"—Mary Daniels, "The Magical Mistress of Ghost Ranch, New Mexico," *Chicago Tribune*, June 24, 1973.

329 "I'm Georgia . . . left"—The Reverend Robert Kirsch to author, September 1, 1977.

329–30 Kirsch quotations—Ibid.

330 "Well . . . funny"—The Reverend Jim Hall to author, August 23, 1977.

331 "It was . . . grand"—Michaela Williams, "Georgia O'Keeffe, 80, Revisits Chicago," *Chicago Daily News*, June 17, 1967.
"It would . . . chin"—Grace Glueck, " 'It's Just What's in My Head,'" *New York Times*, October 18, 1970.
"She had . . . life"—Flora Straus to author, April 4, 1977.

332 "I . . . one"—William Clew, "43 Paintings to Be Shown," *Worcester Evening Gazette*, October 3, 1960.

333 "Why of . . . out"—Agnes Murphy, "At Home with Georgia O'Keeffe," *New York Post*, May 12, 1963.
One works . . . life—Lee Nordness, *Art USA Now*, Lucerne, Switzerland: C. J. Bucher, 1962.

334 "You hang . . . eye"—Lloyd Goodrich to author, July 5, 1975.
"All I . . . again"—Letter from Lillian Stoll to author, March 7, 1978.
"It . . . best"—Blanche Matthias to author, November 22, 1978.

Chapter Fourteen

Other sources include Claudia O'Keeffe, Catherine Klenert, Meridel Rubenstein, Alan Pearson, and numerous friends and acquaintances who do not wish to be identified.

337 "What can . . . beginning"—Tom Zito, "Georgia O'Keeffe," *Washington Post*, November 9, 1977.
"He came . . . him"—Hope Aldrich, "O'Keeffe Center of Legal Battle," *Santa Fe Reporter*, January 25, 1979.
"a wilted leaf"—Kristin McMurran, "A $13 Million Lawsuit," *People*, February 12, 1979.

339 "The clay . . . speak"—Amei Wallach, "Georgia O'Keeffe," *Newsday*, October 30, 1977.

342 'She's in . . . him"—Jane Oseid to author, August 21, 1977.

343 "I think . . . all"—Archer Winsten, "Georgia O'Keeffe Trying to Begin Again in Bermuda," *New York Post*, March 19, 1934.

344 "how . . . happen"—Georgia O'Keeffe, *Georgia O'Keeffe*, New York: Viking Press, 1976.
"casual . . . naive"—Sanford Schwartz, "Georgia O'Keeffe Writes a Book," *The New Yorker*, August 28, 1978.

"O'Keeffe . . . celebration"—Benjamin Forgey, "O'Keeffe at Ninety," *Washington Star*, November 15, 1977.

345 "an extraordinary . . . memory"—Hilton Kramer, "Stieglitz's 'Portrait of O'Keeffe' at the Met," *New York Times*, November 24, 1978.

347 "Just . . . paint"—Deposition by Doris Bry, October 17, 1978, *O'Keeffe v. Bry*, U.S. Southern District Court, New York City.
"intolerable . . . for her"—Affidavit by Georgia O'Keeffe, June 10, 1977, *O'Keeffe v. Bry*, U.S. Southern District Court, New York City.

348 "Juan . . . together"—Aldrich, "O'Keeffe Center of Legal Battle."

350 "I've . . . know?"—Martha Edelheim, "Georgia O'Keeffe: A Reminiscence," *Women Artists Newsletter*, December 1977.
"It's . . . sleep"—Michaela Williams, "Georgia O'Keeffe, 80, Revisits Chicago," *Chicago Daily News*, June 17, 1967.

350–51 "She was . . . hill"—Letter from Lilli Horning to author, March 14, 1978.
"There is . . . cane"—Schwartz, "Georgia O'Keeffe Writes a Book."
"You are . . . fantastic"—Edith Evans Asbury, "Silent Desert Still Charms Georgia O'Keeffe, near 81," *New York Times*, November 2, 1968.

354 "She tried . . . O'Keeffe"—Blanche Matthias, "Stieglitz Showing "Seven Americans," *Chicago Evening Post, Magazine of the Art World*, March 2, 1926.
"You have . . . it"—Alexander Fried, "An Artist of Her Own School," *San Francisco Examinr*, March 16, 1971.
"Women . . . helped me"—Amei Wallach, "Georgia O'Keeffe," *Bergen County/Passaic County (N.J.) Sunday Record*, November 6, 1977.

355 "the great mother goddess"—Mary Beth Edelson to author, January 19, 1977.

356 "probably . . . women"—Letter from Meridel LeSueur to author, May 14, 1979.
"Paint what's . . . exciting"—Nessa Forman, "Georgia O'Keeffe and Her Art: 'Paint What's in Your Head,'" *Philadelphia Bulletin*, October 22, 1971.

356–57 Merrill quotations—Carol Merrill to author, August 10, 1977.

359 "I can . . . me"—Zito, "Georgia O'Keeffe."
"Families . . . devil"—Susan Young Wilson to author, May 31, 1977.

360 "I've always . . . don't"—Charlotte Willard, "Georgia O'Keeffe," *Art in America*, October 1963.

"taken . . . wanted"—WNET-TV documentary, *Georgia O'Keeffe.*

"to the relentless . . . experience"—Theodore Roszak at the American Academy of Arts and Letters.

362 "I store . . . ranch"—Leo Janis, "Georgia O'Keeffe at Eighty-Four," *Atlantic Monthly,* December 1971.

"Living . . . place"—Ibid.

"When I . . . gone"—Henry Seldis, "Georgia O'Keeffe at 78: Tough-Minded Romantic," *Los Angeles Times, West magazine,* January 22, 1967.

"I . . . fear"—Mary Lynn Kotz, "A Day with Georgia O'Keeffe," *Art News,* December 1977.

Selected Bibliography

Books

Alloway, Lawrence. *Topics in American Art Since 1945*. New York: W. W. Norton & Co., 1975.

Ariail, James M. *Columbia College 1912–1968*. Columbia, S.C.: Columbia College, 1968.

Bacon, Peggy. *Off with Their Heads*. New York: Robert M. McBride and Co., 1934.

Baur, John I. H. *Nature in Abstraction*. New York: The Macmillan Co., 1958.

Brett, Dorothy. *Lawrence and Brett: A Friendship*. Philadelphia: J. B. Lippincott Co., 1933.

Bry, Doris. *Alfred Stieglitz: Photographer*. Boston: Museum of Fine Arts, 1965.

Bulliet, C. J. *Apples and Madonnas*. Chicago: Covici, Friede, Inc., 1930.

Castro, Jan Gordon, *The Art and Life of Georgia O'Keeffe*. New York: Crown, 1985.

Chicago, Judy. *Through the Flower*. New York: Doubleday & Co., 1975.

——. *The Dinner Party*. New York: Doubleday & Co., 1979.

Coke, Van Deren. *Taos and Santa Fe*. Albuquerque: University of New Mexico Press, 1963.

Dell, Floyd. *Women as World Builders*. Chicago: Forbes & Co., 1913.

Dijkstra, Bram. *Hieroglyphics of a New Speech*. Princeton, N.J.: Princeton University Press, 1969.

——, ed. *A Recognizable Image: William Carlos Williams on Art and Artists*. New York: New Directions Publishing Corp., 1978.

Dow, Arthur Wesley. *Composition*. 20th ed. New York: Doubleday, Doran and Co., 1938.

Eliot, Alexander. *Three Hundred Years of American Painting*. New York: Time, Inc., 1957.

Fergusson, Erna. *Our Hawaii*. New York: Alfred A. Knopf, 1942.

Field, Hamilton E. *The Technique of Oil Paintings and Other Essays*. Brooklyn, N.Y.: Ardsley House, 1913.

Foster, Joseph. *D. H. Lawrence in Taos*. Albuquerque: University of New Mexico Press, 1972.

Frank, Waldo. *Time Exposures*. New York: Boni and Liveright, 1926.

————, and Lewis Mumford, Dorothy Norman, Paul Rosenfeld, Harold Rugg, eds. *America and Alfred Stieglitz: A Collective Portrait*. New York: Doubleday, Doran and Co., 1934.

Geldzahler, Henry. *American Painting in the Twentieth Century*. New York: Metropolitan Museum of Art, 1965.

Georgia O'Keeffe: A Portrait by Alfred Stieglitz. New York: Metropolitan Museum of Art, 1978.

Green, Jonathan, ed. *Camera Work: Critical Anthology*. New York: Aperture, 1973.

Greenough, Sarah and Juan Hamilton. *Alfred Stieglitz: Photographs and Writings*. Washington, DC: National Gallery of Art, 1983.

Hapgood, Hutchins. *Victorian in the Modern World*. New York: Harcourt, Brace and Co., 1939.

Harris, Ann Sutherland, and Linda Nochlin. *Women Artists: 1550–1950*. New York: Alfred A. Knopf, 1976.

Hartley, Marsden. *Adventures in the Arts*. New York: Boni and Liveright, 1921.

Haskell, Barbara. *Arthur Dove*. San Francisco: San Francisco Museum of Art, 1974.

Headley, Phineas C. *The Life of Louis Kossuth*. New York: Derby & Miller, 1852.

History of Dane County, Wisconsin. Chicago: Western Historical Assn., 1880 and 1906 editions.

Homer, William. *Alfred Stieglitz and the American Avant-Garde*. Boston: N.Y. Graphic Society, 1977.

Huxley, Aldous. *The Art of Seeing*. New York: Harper and Bros., 1942.

————, ed. *The Letters of D. H. Lawrence*. New York: Viking Press, 1932.

Jones, Howard Mumford, ed. *The Letters of Sherwood Anderson*. Boston: Little, Brown & Co., 1953.

Kellner, Bruce. *Carl Van Vechten and the Irreverent Decades*. Norman: University of Oklahoma Press, 1968.

Kootz, Samuel M. *Modern American Painters*. New York: Brewer and Warren, 1930.

Kossuth, Louis. *Memories of My Exile*. New York: D. Appleton & Co., 1880.

Krinsky, Carol H. *Rockefeller Center*. New York: Oxford University Press, 1978.

Kuh, Katharine, *The Artist's Voice: Talks with Seventeen Artists*. New York: Harper & Row, 1962.

LaFollette, Suzanne. *Concerning Women*. New York: Harper & Bros., 1926.

Lane, James W. *The Work of Georgia O'Keeffe: A Portfolio of Twelve Paintings*. New York: Knight Publishers, 1937.

Langren, Marchal E. *Years of Art: The Story of the Art Students League of New York*. New York: Robert M. McBride and Co., 1940.

Levy, Julien. *Memoir of an Art Gallery*. New York: G. P. Putman's Sons, 1977.

Lippard, Lucy. *From the Center: Feminist Essays on Women's Art*. New York: E. P. Dutton, 1976.

Lowe, Sue Davidson. *Stieglitz: A Memoir/Biography*. New York: Farrar, Straus, Giroux, 1983.

Luhan, Mabel Dodge. *Movers and Shakers*. Vol. 3, *Intimate Memories*. New York: Harcourt, Brace and Co., 1936.

———. *Taos and Its Artists*. New York: Duell, Sloan and Pearce, 1947.

Lyman, S. E. *The Story of New York*. New York: Crown, 1964.

McBride, Henry. *Florine Stettheimer*. New York: Museum of Modern Art, 1946.

McCausland, Elizabeth. *Marsden Hartley*. Minneapolis: Univeristy of Minnesota Press, 1952.

Mellquist, Jerome. *The Emergence of an American Art*. New York: Charles Scribner's Sons, 1942.

Morrill, Claire. *A Taos Mosaic*. Albuquerque: University of New Mexico Press, 1973.

Morris, Lloyd R. *Incredible New York: High Life and Low Life of the Last Hundred Years*. New York: Random House, 1951.

The Mortar Board. Chatham, Va.: Chatham Episcopal Institute, 1905.

Mumford, Lewis. *The Brown Decades*. New York: Dover Publications, 1931.

Munro, Eleanor. *Originals: American Women Artists*. New York: Simon and Schuster, 1979.

Naef, Weston J. *The Collection of Alfred Stieglitz*. New York: Metropolitan Museum of Art and The Viking Press, 1978.

Neilson, Winthrop, and Frances Neilson. *Seven Women: Great Painters*. Philadelphia: Chilton Book Co., 1969.

Nordness, Lee, ed. *Art USA Now*. Vol. I. Lucerne, Switzerland: C. J. Bucher, 1962.

Norman, Dorothy. *Alfred Stieglitz: An American Seer*. New York: Random House, 1973.

———, ed. *Selected Writings of John Marin*. New York: Pellegrini and Cudahy, 1949.

———. *Stieglitz Memorial Portfolio*. New York: Twice-a-Year Press, 1947.

Northrop, F.S.C. *The Meeting of East and West*. New York: The Macmillan Co., 1946.

O'Keeffe, Georgia. *Some Memories of Drawings*. New York: Atlantic Editions, 1974.

———. *Georgia O'Keeffe*. New York: A Studio Book of the Viking Press, 1976.

Pack, Arthur N. *We Called It Ghost Ranch*. Abiquiu, N.M.: Ghost Ranch Conference Center, 1966.

Phillips, Duncan. *A Collection in the Making*. New York: E. Weyhe, 1926.

Rich, Daniel Catton, ed. *The Flow of Art: Essays and Criticisms of Henry McBride*. New York: Atheneum, 1975.

Ringel, Fred, ed. *America as Americans See It*. New York: Harcourt, Brace and Co., 1932.

Rose, Barbara. *American Art Since 1900: A Critical History*. New York: Frederick A. Praeger, 1967.

Rosenfeld, Paul. *Port of New York: Essays on Fourteen American Moderns*. New York: Harcourt, Brace and Co., 1924.

Rouse, Parke. *Cows on the Campus*. Richmond, Va.: Dietz Press, 1973.

Seligmann, Herbert. *Alfred Stieglitz Talking*. New Haven: Yale University Library, 1966

———, ed. *Letters of John Marin*. New York: An American Place, 1931.

Sochen, June. *The New Woman: Feminism in Greenwich Village 1910–1920*. New York: Quadrangle Books, 1972.

Street, M. B. *The Wyckoff Family in America: A Genealogy*. Rutland, Vt.: The Tuttle Co., 1934.

Tedlock, E. W. Jr., ed. *Frieda Lawrence: The Memoirs and Correspondence*. New York: Alfred A. Knopf, 1964.

Trachtenberg, Alan, ed. *Memoirs of Waldo Frank*. Amherst: University of Massachusetts Press, 1973.

Young, Mahonri S. *Early American Moderns*. New York: Watson-Guptill, 1974.

Periodicals and Other Sources

Art Institute of Chicago Catalogue 1905–06. Chicago: AIC, 1905.

Asbury, Edith Evans. "Silent Desert Still Charms Georgia O'Keeffe, near 81." *New York Times*, Nov. 2, 1968.

Brook, Alexander. "February Exhibitions: Georgia O'Keeffe." *The Arts*, Feb. 1923.

Canaday, John. "Georgia O'Keeffe: The Patrician Stance as Esthetic Principle." *New York Times*, Oct. 11, 1970.

Chatham Episcopal Institute Catalogue 1904–1905. Chatham, Va.: CEI, 1904.

Coates, Robert M. "Propfiles: Abstraction—Flowers." *The New Yorker*, July 6, 1929.

Coffelt, Beth. "A Visit with Georgia O'Keeffe." *San Francisco Sunday Examiner & Chronicle*, Apr. 11, 1971.

Cohn, Susan F. "An Analysis of Selected Works by Georgia O'Keeffe . . ." Ph.D. dissertation, New York University, 1974.

Columbia College Catalogue 1914–1915. Columbia, S.C.: Columbia, 1914.

Davis, Douglas. "O'Keeffe Country." *Newsweek*, Nov. 22, 1976.

Eldredge, Charles C., III. "Georgia O'Keeffe: The Development of an American Modern." Ph.D. dissertation, University of Minnesota, 1971.

Flint, Ralph. "Lily Lady Goes West." *Town and Country*, Jan. 1943.

"Georgia O'Keeffe Turns Dead Bones to Live Art." *Life*, Feb. 14, 1938.

Glueck, Grace. " 'It's Just What's in My Head.'" *New York Times*, Oct. 18, 1970.

Goossen, E. C. "O'Keeffe." *Vogue*, Mar. 1, 1967.

Greenberg, Clement. "Art." *The Nation*, June 5, 1946.

Hoffman, Katherine A. "A Study of the Art of Georgia O'Keeffe from 1916–1974." Ph.D. dissertation, New York University, 1976.

Hunter, Vernon. "A Note on Georgia O'Keeffe." *Contemporary Arts of the South and Southwest*, Nov.-Dec. 1932.

Janis, Leo. "Georgia O'Keeffe at Eighty-Four." *Atlantic Monthly*, Dec. 1971.

Kalonyme, Louis. "Georgia O'Keeffe: A Woman in Painting." *Creative Art*, Jan. 1928.

Kotz, Mary Lynn. "A Day with Georgia O'Keeffe." *Art News.* Dec. 1977.

Kramer, Hilton. "Georgia O'Keeffe." *New York Times Book Review*, Dec. 12, 1976.

Lifson, Ben. "O'Keeffe's Stieglitz, Stieglitz's O'Keeffe." *Village Voice*, Dec. 11, 1978.

Looney, Ralph. "Georgia O'Keeffe." *Atlantic Monthly*, Apr. 1965.

Luhan, Mabel Dodge. "Georgia O'Keeffe in Taos." *Creative Art*, June 1931.

McBride, Henry. "Curious Responses to Work of Miss O'Keeffe on Others." *New York Herald*, Feb. 4, 1923.

———. " Georgia O'Keeffe's Exhibition." *New York Sun*, Jan. 14, 1933.

———. "O'Keeffe at the Museum." *New York Sun*, May 18, 1946.

McCoy, Gannett. "The Artist Speaks—Part IV: Reaction and Revolution," *Art in American*, Aug.-Sept. 1965.

Malcolm, Janet. "Photographs: Arts and Lovers." *The New Yorker*, Mar. 12, 1979.

Matthias, Blanche. "Stieglitz Showing Seven Americans." *Chicago Evening Post, Magazine of the Art World*, Mar. 2, 1926.

Milliken, William M. "White Flower by Georgia O'Keeffe." *Bulletin of the Cleveland Museum of Art*, Apr. 1937.

Mumford, Lewis. "O'Keeffe and Matisse." *New Republic*, Mar. 2, 1927.

———. "Autobiographies in Paint." *The New Yorker*, Jan. 18, 1936.

Oaks, Gladys. "Radical Writer and Woman Artist Clash on Propaganda and Its Uses," *New York World*, Mar. 16, 1930.

O'Brien, Frances. "Americans We Like: Georgia O'Keeffe." *The Nation*, Oct. 12, 1927.

O'Keeffe, Georgia. "Can a Photograph Have the Significance of Art?" *MSS*, Dec. 1922.

———. "Stieglitz: His Pictures Collected Him." New York Times Magazine, Dec. 11, 1949.

Plagens, Peter. "A Georgia O'Keeffe Retrospective in Texas," *Artforum*, May 1966.

Pollitzer, Anita. "That's Georgia." *Saturday Review*, Nov. 4, 1950.

Read, Helen Appleton. "Georgia O'Keeffe—Woman Artist Whose Art is Sincerely Feminine." *Brooklyn Eagle*, Mar. 2, 1924.

———. "The Feminine Viewpoint in Contemporary Art." *Vogue*, June 15, 1928.

Robinson, Vivian. "Famed Artist Remembers Amarillo as Brown Town." *Amarillo Globe-Times*, Aug. 26, 1965.

———. "Artist's Journey to the Top Began at West Texas." *Amarillo Globe-Times*, Aug. 27, 1965.

Rose, Barbara. "Georgia O'Keeffe: The Paintings of the Sixties." *Artforum*, Nov. 1970.

———. "Visiting Georgia O'Keeffe." *New York Magazine*, Nov. 9, 1970.

———. "O'Keeffe's Trail." *New York Review of Books*, Mar. 31, 1977.

Rosenfeld, Paul. "American Painting." *The Dial*, Dec. 1921.

———. "The Paintings of Georgia O'Keeffe." *Vanity Fair*, Oct. 1922.

Rubenstein, Meridel. "The Circles and The Symmetry: The Reciprocal Influence of Georgia O'Keeffe and Alfred Stieglitz." Master's thesis, University of New Mexico, 1977.

Schwartz, Sanford. "When New York Went to New Mexico." *Art in America*, July-Aug. 1976.

———. "Georgia O'Keeffe Writes a Book." *The New Yorker*, Aug. 28, 1978.

Seiberling, Dorothy. "Horizons of a Pioneer." *Life*, Mar. 1, 1968.

Seligmann, Herbert. "Georgia O'Keeffe, American." *MSS*, Mar. 1923.

Strand, Paul. "Georgia O'Keeffe." *Playboy*, July 1924.

Tomkins, Calvin. "The Rose in the Eye Looked Pretty Fine." *The New Yorker*, Mar. 4, 1974.

Tryk, Sheila. "O'Keeffe." *New Mexico*, Jan.-Feb. 1973.

University of Virginia Summer School Catalogue, 1912–1916 editions, Charlottesville: University of Virginia.

United States Census Reports, Dane County, Wisconsin, 1860, 1870, and 1880.

Wallach, Amei. "Under a Western Sky." *Horizon*, Dec. 1977.

Willard, Charlotte. "Georgia O'Keeffe." *Art in America*, Oct. 1963.
Wilson, Edmund. "Stieglitz Exhibition at the Anderson Galleries." *New Republic*, Mar. 18, 1925.

Exhibition Catalogs

Catalogue of the Alfred Stieglitz Collection for Fisk University. Nashville: Fisk University, 1949.
The Eye of Stieglitz. New York: Hirschl & Adler, 1978.
Goodrich, Lloyd, and Doris Bry. *Georgia O'Keeffe*. New York: Whitney Museum of American Art, 1970.
Hartley, Marsden. "A Second Outline in Portraiture." *Georgia O'Keeffe: Exhibition of Recent Paintings, 1935*. New York: An American Place, 1936.
Moore, Ethel, ed. *Letters from 31 Artists to the Albright-Knox Art Gallery*, Buffalo: The Buffalo Fine Arts Academy, 1970.
O'Keeffe, Georgia. *Alfred Stieglitz Presents One Hundred Pictures, Oils, Water-Colors, Pastels, Drawings by Georgia O'Keeffe, American*. New York: The Anderson Galleries, 1923. (O'Keeffe Statement.)
————. *Alfred Stieglitz Presents Fifty-one Recent Pictures, Oils, Water-Colors, Pastels, Drawings by Georgia O'Keeffe, American*. New York: The Anderson Galleries, 1924. (O'Keeffe Statement.)
————. "About Myself." *Georgia O'Keeffe: Exhibition of Oils and Pastels*. New York: An American Place, 1939.
————. *Georgia O'Keeffe: Catalogue of the Fourteenth Annual Exhibition of Paintings with Some Recent O'Keeffe Letters*. New York: An American Place, 1938.
————. "About Painting Desert Bones." *Georgia O'Keeffe: Paintings—1943*. New York: An American Place, 1944.
———— *Georgia O'Keeffe: Exhibition of Oils and Pastels*. New York: An American Place, 1940. (O'Keeffe Statement.)
Paintings by Nineteen Living Americans. New York: Museum of Modern Art, 1929.
Pisano, Ronald G. *The Students of William Merritt Chase*. Huntington, N.Y.: Heckscher Museum, 1973.
Rich, Daniel Catton. *Georgia O'Keeffe*. Chicago: Art Institute of Chicago, 1943.
————. *Georgia O'Keeffe: Forty Years of Her Art*. Worcester, Mass.: Worcester Art Museum, 1960.
Wilder, Mitchell A., ed. *Georgia O'Keeffe*. Fort Worth: Amon Carter Museum of Western Art, 1966.

Index